ORTHODOXY

ORTHODOXY

Paul Evdokimov

ORTHODOXY

Preface by Olivier Clément

New City Press
Hyde Park, New York

Published in the United States by New City Press
202 Comforter Blvd., Hyde Park, NY 12538
www.newcitypress.com
©2011 New City London (English Translation)

Translated by Jeremy Hummerstone and updated for this edition by
Callan Slipper from the 1979 French edition published by Desclée de Brouwer
©1979 Paul Evdokimov

Cover design by Leandro de Leon

Library of Congress Cataloging-in-Publication Data

Evdokimov, Paul, 1901-1970.
  [Orthodoxie. English]
  Orthodoxy / Paul Evdokimov ; preface by Olivier Clément.
     p. cm.
  Includes bibliographical references and index.
  ISBN 978-1-56548-369-9 (pbk. : alk. paper) 1. Orthodox Eastern Church—Doctrines.
  I. Title. BX320.3.E9413 2011
  230'.19—dc22   2011009674

Printed in the United States of America

Contents

Part Two: Ecclesiology

Part Five: The Eschaton or the Last Things

Preface to 1979 Edition

The appearance in 1965 of *Orthodoxy*, a masterpiece of synthesis, was a landmark in religious publishing and earned for its author a doctorate of theology from the Institut Saint-Serge in Paris. Paul Evdokimov here circumvents all scholastic theology on the one hand, and the traditional approach of the 'Dogmatic' theologians on the other, to develop an original synthesis of Orthodox theological thinking. Although he constantly quotes the Fathers, he does so creatively, so as not simply to repeat them, but to incarnate their spirit in our own time and for our future. In addition, he enriches Patristic thought by bringing to bear on it the two great movements that have occurred in Eastern Christianity: the theology of the divine energies in the 14th century which enlightened our understanding of the material world and human culture; and the Russian religious philosophy of the first half of the 20th century with its prophetic intuitions, its Pentecostal understanding of the modern world, and its vital eschatology. A theological approach in which the human intelligence progresses by an *ascesis* of repentance, of the great conversion of the heart, *metanoia*, is here set forth so as to show, or rather celebrate, the *theosis* or deification of the whole human person... An understanding we might call eucharistic, gathering together and clarifying the experience of life in the Church, an understanding inseparable from the golden chain of holiness, including the holiness of intelligence, which the Church venerates in those whom she calls the 'Fathers'.

The work opens with two chapters of 'Historical Introduction', which, however, contain scarcely anything strictly chronological but consist rather of a study of the essential elements of the Tradition, as it has been variously embodied in different times and places: it is history, but seen through the experience of the Resurrection, in the ever-present 'memory' of God. Here is a role for a 'Hellenism' rendered down in the crucible of biblical revelation, every self-contained theory broken open by negation and antinomy, that happy combination of the Semitic genius with the Indo-European. Doctrinal elaboration is constantly kept in check by the 'existentialism of ascesis'; the spirit of Orthodoxy is revealed as 'philo-kalic', seized by that divine-human beauty which according to Denys the Areopagite is the 'cause of all communion'. In the original ontology here formulated, 'being' means the infinite depth of personal existence and of the commun-

ion of persons, for 'love is higher than being', as an old man says at the end of
The Devils when he is torn from his selfish desires by the discovery of the Gospel.

Between the Historical Introduction and Part One, Paul Evdokimov inserts a
short chapter called *Pro Domo Sua*, in which he defends the Orthodox Church
against accusations that it is disorganized and ineffectual. This he does in the
name of communion and freedom, praising that 'charismatism' which sets the
greatest value on the irreducible person. 'We assert and shall assert with our dying
breath the Gospel message that the personal is more important than the general
and abstract, and the liberty of the children of God than the organization ... '

This moving work, indispensable today for appreciating the true nature of Orthodoxy, which in the West has been misunderstood for so long, was originally
provided with polemical notes collected in an appendix, but these now need re-
vising. *Orthodoxy* was written in the 1950s and published only after a long delay.
It bears the marks of an age when Catholicism, despite the remarkable liturgical
and Patristic renewal undertaken by a few isolated theologians, was cut off from
the ecumenical movement. Paul Evdokimov was closely concerned with the work
of CIMADE [*Comité Inter-Mouvements Auprès Des Evacués*, a youth organization founded in 1939 to resettle people displaced from Alsace-Lorraine] and his
ecumenical contacts were almost all with Reformed theologians: this is reflected
in his remarks in *Orthodoxy* about the western churches. The Second Vatican
Council is never mentioned, nor the acts of reconciliation undertaken by
Athenagoras I and Paul VI in 1964 and 1965. By the time the book was finished
Evdokimov had been invited to the Council, and from then onwards he was in
ever closer touch with the Catholic world, especially with the contemplatives.
The Catholic Church's rediscovery of the local eucharistic community, Paul VI's
talk of 'sister churches' in his meeting with the Patriarch of Constantinople, the
growing familiarity with icons, the Byzantine liturgy and the Jesus prayer: these
are a few of the developments that would now need special attention. We note in
passing, and not without irony, that the Catholic Church was by that time, at least
among its intelligentsia, preoccupied with every kind of 'human science' and 'alternative philosophy', and subject to a multitude of liturgical and charismatic
fashions, and so was experiencing freedom and disorder for itself – more perhaps
than the Orthodox Church, which maintains, albeit at the risk of petrification,
great dogmatic rigour combined with monumental liturgical expression, even
while becoming increasingly chaotic as an historical institution. This gap between
ecclesiology and spirituality on the one hand, and sociology and ethics on the
other, still awaits the lucid analysis that only another Evdokimov can undertake.

The essence of *Orthodoxy* is the constructive survey of its subject, which takes
up almost the whole work.

It is significant that Paul Evdokimov begins his account of Orthodox thought
not with a theology but with an 'Anthropology', which is the title of Part One,
one of the longest parts of the book. This is in effect a *Christology of humankind*,
explaining its 'deification' in Christ by the Holy Spirit. According to the Fathers,

'God became human so that humans might become God'; the existential approach to revelation offered in the second part of the formula is founded on the statement in the first. Evdokimov quotes Gregory of Nazianzus: 'There is no other way to know God than by living in him.' This 'personalist' approach is based – since humankind is made in the image of God – on the mystery of the Trinity, the unique means by which unfathomable transcendence attains substantiality, to be a centre of communion, existing not only among others, but in them. The Inaccessible awakens human beings and really communicates himself to them, unifying them and opening their 'hearts', where all their faculties, especially the intelligence and the *eros*, are joined together and transfigured. 'In the hierarchy of the make-up of the human being, primacy belongs to the heart': the intelligent heart, the 'heart-spirit', whose calling is to become consciously the place that belongs to God.

The free vocation of humankind is to manifest 'the striving of the icon [which humankind secretly is] towards the original, of the image towards its archetype.' Attracted by the beauty of Christ, quickened by his Breath, 'in transcending itself, the person is formed.' From this perspective, the relation of freedom and grace is seen not in terms of cause and effect (as if one and not the other must be the cause of salvation), but in terms of encounter, love, involvement. 'God can do anything,' Evdokimov liked to say, 'except compel human beings to love.' The true nature of human beings is the freedom to be open to grace, or to shut it out. The true nature of human beings is this drive to go beyond, to transcend the self, 'and be plunged into the infinite ocean of the divine' which radiates from the face of the Transfigured, 'and there to find their longings assuaged.' 'Being made in the image of God we also possess the grace of that image, so if we follow our true nature we shall be working in the direction of grace.' The resulting person is 'supernaturally natural, more natural than nature.' This uncreated grace, which is the outpouring of glory, life and light, abounds in the mystical Body of Christ and gives us more than salvation – the enlivening of our whole being; the 'deification' which is not the obliteration of humanity but its fulfilment, for the human being can be human only in God. By beginning his study with an 'anthropology' of deification, Evdokimov emphasizes that Christianity is the revelation of the divine-human.

The next three parts are devoted to the Church: her mystery (which surrounds, justifies and transcends her structures), her faith (for it is by the experience of faith that we learn to live in communion), and her prayer, by which she enters the life of the Trinity. The reader with little theological background would be well advised to begin this book at Part Four, 'The Prayer of the Church', which is a true phenomenology of life in the Mystery; here Evdokimov examines the sanctification of time and space ('the temple'), icons, the liturgy and the sacraments. Through the institutional life of the Church, but also beyond it, people find her to be the living body, divine and human, in which they can share in the life of God. The essence of the Church is prayer, by which humankind learns what it means 'to be in God, to live in his grace, to be reborn, regenerated.' Every local church, in its sacramental life of communion – Evdokimov here makes good use of the ideas of Fr Nicholas Afanasiev – shows forth the Mystery of the resurrection, which opens up the world to penetration by the divine energies. The Church is the beauty of creation, the world on its way to deification. All the beauty of the world is purified, freed and harmonized in that of the icons. All the beauty of the world is summed up in Her who 'personalizes human sanctity', whose human nature is penetrated by the fire of the Spirit: the *Theotokos*, the Mother of God. 'The *fiat* of the Creator evokes the *fiat* of the creature: Behold the handmaid of the Lord... So we can see the Church in her function of mystic womb, continuing in childbirth, the perpetuation of the *Theotokos*.' She is the 'woman clothed with the sun' of Revelation, bringing into the world the offspring of the universal resurrection, the universal transfiguration.

The fifth and final part deals with the *Eschaton* or 'last things', a major preoccupation of Russian religious philosophy in general and of Paul Evdokimov in particular. Perhaps because of the challenge of the Revolution and its aberrant Messianism, the great Russian Christian thinkers rejected a pietism of the individual 'good death' in favour of the vital cosmic eschatology of earlier Christianity. The Resurrection unleashed a vast metamorphosis in which all, even the dead, must share, for the Kingdom will *also* include the transfigured earth, into which the 'glory and honour' of the nations and civilizations of history will come, as Revelation says. The eschatological process is already at work, it lights up the present; the saint is one who brings to the surface of the world the hidden incandescence of the Body of Christ. The Parousia will not be the return of Christ into the world but the 'passing over' of the world into Christ, and will require active preparation on our part. By the strength of the life-giving Cross, Christians must overcome the power of darkness within themselves and make actual the victory of Christ over hell and death, so as to radiate the energies of the Resurrection into every realm of existence, down to the very foundations of culture. These energies impregnate history, guiding it towards its fulfilment, while piercing it with eternity, and multiplying in it, by the extension of the liturgy and the shining forth of Easter, a complete symbolization of the Kingdom. Inevitably their presence is both judgement – a merciless denunciation of idols, to the point of martyrdom if necessary – and inspiration. Monks are the prophets of the Kingdom which they anticipate here and now. Around them, monasticism is internalized and diffused, and moves from the desert into the city, bringing into being a creative spirituality. Evdokimov was deeply affected by reading *The Brothers Karamazov*, in particular the example of Alyosha sent by his *staretz* to the heart of the world to transform, as Fyodorov suggested, 'the common work of human beings into a vast effort of revival, of resurrection. 'Only Christ, holding the whole of human nature within his hypostatic unity, saves every creature from disappearance, and places it in the light and presence of God... Is Christ the king of history? Yes, but kenotically, as in his entry into Jerusalem – unnoticed by historians, but more than visible and utterly evident to faith.' Like Simone Weil, Evdokimov appeals to a saint-liness that is both kenotic and creative, humble but capable of radiating life into all the complexity of history. The thoughts of the great Russian religious philoso-phers, above all that of Berdyaev on spiritual meaning and Bulgakov on the cos-mic dimensions of the Church, are here brought together and held in balance.

In Evdokimov's *Orthodoxy*, the Russian diaspora in western Europe, espe-cially in France, bears fruit: it rediscovers the continuity of the Orthodox Tradition from the Fathers, and from the elaborations of Byzantium onwards; it demon-strates the creative power of that Tradition; it makes explicit, in the meeting with the Christian (but also atheist) West, a vision of Christianity that is resurrectional and transfiguring, secure from the strictures of René Girard's 'scapegoat' theory of religion. The work ends with the assertion that nothing in the history of Christ-ianity is alien to Orthodoxy, and that the time is coming for the Orthodox to share in a common approach that is both unified and diverse, and of an inexhaustible richness. Evdokimov appeals to the ecumenism of the contemplatives, of people of prayer, of all who desire not accommodations between churches, whether diplomatic or whatever people are willing to settle for, but 'the centre where the lines converge'. Today this appeal still shows us the way.[1]

Olivier Clément

---

[1] Clément wrote this preface when he included *l'Orthodoxie* in his Collection Théophanie, de-signed to increase the understanding of Orthodox and Oriental Christianity in the West. The full version of the last sentence of this preface, shortened in our translation since it is not rel-evant in the present context, was: 'Today this appeal still shows us the way and sets the tone for our series.'

Editor's Preface to the English Edition

This book is indeed a masterpiece as Olivier Clément says in his preface. Its value can hardly be exaggerated. It is both an introduction to the rich insights of Orthodoxy and a creative synthesis that, especially for Western thinkers, challenges and offers the possibility of new avenues of reflection.

Nonetheless, the book itself presents certain minor difficulties. While it still speaks as freshly as it did, and will do so into the future, it also bears the marks of the times in which it was written. Despite his penetrating scholarship, for instance, every now and then Paul Evdokimov espouses opinions with regard to Western forms of Christianity that appear ill-founded. At the same time he occasionally uses turns of phrase that are more disparaging of rabbinic Judaism or aspects of Islam than careful theologians of succeeding generations would allow themselves. These rare slips are blemishes uncharacteristic of the argument in general. The saying holds true for Evdokimov as it does for most people: he is more correct in what he affirms than in what he denies. Sadly, Evdokimov is no longer with us so we cannot ask him whether, in the light of the dialogues that have taken place between Christians and among religions, he would now like to amend his text. It is hard not to think he would.

This book is put before the public, therefore, because of its merits. Any difficult expressions or dubious opinions that infrequently may arise should not distract us from those.

Historical Introduction

1

Introduction

According to Amiel in his *Journal Intime* Christianity is 'the oriental aspect of our culture'. In typically western fashion, he tries to show that our spiritual roots are in the East, that we are all debtors to the Greeks and Jews. Similarly Théophile Gautier, on seeing St Sophia in Constantinople, was moved to exclaim, 'Byzantine architecture is assuredly the necessary form of Catholicism.'

Meeting Orthodoxy for the first time, someone trained in the school of the great masters – Descartes, Aquinas or Calvin – is apt to feel the shock of the unfamiliar, notwithstanding that it was once common to all.[1] Disciplined by the spirit of Roman law, used to clear thinking and formal logic, he will be strongly tempted to contrast this well organized world to the 'vague mysticism' of the Orthodox. But this would be to underestimate the subtle variety in the ways of approaching the Mystery and apprehending the truth. The contrast is not only between Athens and Jerusalem, Greeks and Jews, it is between ways of understanding history: on the one hand, Rome, Hippo, Augsburg, and Geneva; and on the other, Jerusalem, Antioch, Alexandria, and Byzantium.

'Where your treasure is, there will your heart be also,' says the Gospel. But what attracts the heart is by no means the same from person to person. It may be the pursuit of goodness – and its reward, the beatific vision of God; it may be God in his sovereign power justifying the elect by faith alone; or the new creature, deified and brimming over with divine love for mankind; or the infallibility of the Pope, or that of Scripture, or that of the Church, the Body of Christ.

In the presence of the same God, are we different people? Or, more important, does the God of Apostolic Christianity appear later as the Catholic God, the Protestant God or the Orthodox God, just as for the great artists Christ was by turns Byzantine, Flemish, Spanish or Russian? There is an irreducible root of original religious truth that goes deeper than any national character or culture, deeper than the image

---

[1] We know what difficulty Melanchthon had in translating the *Confessio Augustana* into Greek. Faced by the tradition of Athanasius, Basil, Gregory and Irenaeus (as he called it in his letter to Joasaph II, Patriarch of Constantinople, in 1559), he struggled to find a terminology that was sufficiently Lutheran for his purpose. See Ernst Benz, *Wittenberg und Byzanz*, Marburg 1949.

stamped on the heart of any particular people. This raises the huge problem of Apostolic tradition, and of faithfulness to its spirit, by which every tradition is judged.

There is no such thing as direct access to the Scriptures, circumventing the living interpretation of the Holy Spirit who speaks through the prophets and saints in every age. It is not possible to progress from the 'Kingdom of God' of the synoptics, St John's concept of 'eternal life', and St Paul's Christology, to the Patristic theology of the Trinity, without being taught and guided every step of the way. Above all it is necessary to be incorporated by the Spirit into the charismatic fullness of the Church, where heaven is in communion with earth. That is why the Church of the Apostles, when threatened by Judaeo-paganism, did not try to counter the speculative arguments of the gnostics in their own terms, but concentrated rather on proclaiming the reality of the incarnate Word in all its thrilling immediacy. The *patres apostolici* and the apologists guarded the living memory of the Lord. And in their turn Origen, Irenaeus and Athanasius possessed not mere texts, but the faith itself, and in the golden age of the Councils they handed down that chalice of Life, without spilling a single drop.

Today the points of divergence are obvious to everyone. The Orthodox, looking towards Rome, see the *Filioque*, the Immaculate Conception, and papal infallibility. The Protestants, the congregation of sinners saved by faith and grace alone, look at the Orthodox and see the hierarchical priesthood, the Apostolic succession, the synergy of divine grace and human will, and the holiness of the new creature. But this by no means gives a true picture of Orthodoxy, which is not simply a middle way between Catholicism and Protestantism but is spiritually complete in itself, homogeneous and indivisible. Its essential meaning is in its life, and cannot be captured by any definition. The inquirer should respond with a good will to Fr Sergei Bulgakov's invitation, 'Come and see'. For Orthodoxy is the least prescriptive form of Christianity, the least translatable into concepts. If on first acquaintance it seems old-fashioned, that comes of its being so close to its Palestinian and evangelical origins. In spirituality, worship, and prayer its very soul can be traced back to the 'forefathers of God', St Simeon, St Anne, St Joseph and St John the Baptist, to the Apostles, and the first generation of Christians. Whoever encounters the Orthodox world with an open mind soon discovers that this is Christianity in its original form, its very seed, immeasurably enriched by many generations of experience, but always nourished by the same single root deeply planted in the generous earth of Palestine. What may appear to be pious unworldliness is really an age-old attitude of expectancy, which, combined with the elements of this world, makes up the sacred letters of the word *maranatha*.[2] Eschatology, basic to its very nature, shielded it

---

[2] In the 19th century in the West metaphysical anxiety was confined to a few isolated thinkers, such as Carlisle, Ibsen, Kierkegaard, L. Bloy. In Russia the whole literary world was overwhelmed by forebodings of revolutions to come. When a pastor, visiting Russia, asked a priest what was the burning issue for the Russian Church, the priest replied without hesitation, 'The Parousia.'

from the pressure of the secularized world and kept it in ignorance of modernism, progressivism, wild sectarian enthusiasm or fundamentalist obscurantism.[3] The recent tendency in the West to return to eastern Patristic and liturgical sources is sufficient evidence that the accusations by scholars that Orthodoxy has become a museum or a mummified corpse are ill-founded or malicious.

The unprejudiced observer will see one consistent principle running right through every detail of Orthodox life: faithfulness to the primitive Tradition. The Council Fathers expressed their constant intention by sealing their acts with the hallowed formula, 'so believed the Apostles and the Fathers'. The daily reading from the Epistles in the liturgy is called, significantly, 'the Apostle', for in it the Apostle is effectively present and speaks. Elsewhere the witness is that of the Martyrs and Confessors, the 'wounded friends of the Bridegroom', upon whom love and devotion have been lavished, who point to the Church founded on their blood and utter faithfulness. Again, the voice of the Fathers is heard on the first Sunday in Great Lent, the celebration of the 'Triumph of Orthodoxy', which commemorates the extraordinary achievement of the Councils.

Providentially Orthodoxy has suffered no internal dissension, escaping both the Reformation and the Counter-Reformation. It has been untroubled by religious wars and controversies, or any competition for converts. It holds unaltered the faith handed down from the Apostles. Even today, in a time of astonishing developments in theological studies, the Church is recognizably the same in its organization, spirituality, prayer and teaching as it was at the time of the Seventh Ecumenical Council in 787, when the *Una Sancta* was as yet undivided, and looked back to the Apostles as to the recent past.[4]

The Lord has spoken and has withdrawn from this world. He has sent the Paraclete, and from now on until the end of the world he will return or be present only under the hidden form of the Spirit. Just as there is no way to the Father except by the Son, so there is no way to the Son except by the Holy Spirit. The *epiclesis*,[5] the invocation of the Spirit, is the beginning of all communion with Christ and the Father. Between the Word of God and our response, between God and

---

[3] The schism of the Old Believers had nothing to do with doctrinal heresy, but resulted from their tragic disappointment when the Kingdom failed to materialize. Seized by millenarian and theocratic Utopianism they revolted against history, even to the extent of purification by fire and eschatological suicide. As for the sects, they were never numerous and were always exotic implants, mingling with the Russian soil to produce strange and misshapen hybrids; they have no connection with Orthodoxy.

[4] Is this immobilism? 'The luxuriant tree firmly planted on a rock.' Professor Fedotov's image shows Orthodoxy attached to the rock of Tradition and at the same time confronted by the same pressing problems as exist in the West. Perhaps its cosmism and fundamentally eschatological character, and above all its theology of the Holy Spirit, align it today with the theology of the avant-garde.

[5] The special invocation of the Holy Spirit in the eastern Liturgy, and by extension, the action of the Spirit preceding any manifestation of Christ.

humanity, there is the Spirit who *Christifies* us by taking what is in the Son and making it known to us (John 16.15). And that word of Truth the Spirit of Truth utters unceasingly, and calls it the Church. Made up of sinners, 'those who are perishing', and being wholly incorporated in Christ, the Church *is* Christ – *totus Christus* – and therefore divine, holy, infallible.

St John's message is of the 'victory that overcomes the world' – for 'the Word was made flesh' and 'we have seen his glory'. The contemplation of that glory is the very essence of Orthodoxy, linking the Cross with the sealed Tomb that is burst open by the pressure of Life, and following the triumphal march of early Christianity, when the victory over death was carved on sarcophagi in cemeteries all over the world and proclaimed at every crossroads. St Seraphim conveyed the true spirit of Orthodoxy as he greeted everyone with 'Christ is risen, my joy'; that elation is the note of the approaching Kingdom.

The profound asceticism of the Cross, the overflowing source of life – 'Open to me the door of repentance ... give me tears of penitence' – driven by the force of its inner momentum, issues in this song of freedom: *Abyssus abyssum invocat*: 'Out of the depth of my iniquity, I call to the depth of your mercy ... for by virtue of the Cross, joy has come to the whole world!' Humility, self-effacing but fervent adoration, attains to that ultimate reality, Origen's 'touching of the soul', whereby the Word of Life is 'felt'[6] – 'what we have heard, what we have seen with our eyes, what we have looked at and touched with our hands' (1 John 1.1).

That spirit – 'the Apostle' – is by no means the exclusive possession of the eastern Church, which is itself Orthodox only to the extent that it faithfully safe-guards and transmits the common inheritance: 'For this life was revealed, and we have seen it and testify to it' (1 John 1.2).

1. HELLENISM

Western interest in Hellenism declined from the 6th century onwards, until it was revived by John the Scot Erigena in the 9th century, by the schools of Chartres, Laon and Paris in the 12th, and by the German mystics and the Italian Renaissance in the 14th. The eastern university of Constantinople, founded in 425 by the Emperor Theodosius II, while remaining Greek in culture, came to over-shadow the pagan schools of philosophy at Athens, which were eventually closed down by Justinian in 529.[7] Meanwhile Constantine's city expanded rapidly, and by the 7th century dominated Arab-occupied Syria and Egypt; for ten centuries this was the eastern spiritual capital, and here Orthodox Christianity took shape.

---

[6] Ἀφή, see Rahner, 'Le début d'une doctrine des cinq sens spirituels chez Origène', *R.A.M.* 1932, p. 113-145.
[7] Fr Fuchs, *Die höheren Schulen in Constantinopel*. In 475 the library at Constantinople contained 120,000 volumes.

Orthodox thought, supple, reasonable, concise, with its leaning towards mystical contemplation, developed continuously out of the finest traditions of the ancient world. Byzantium in its full maturity displays the unmistakable genius of Greece, but in Christian clothing, having emerged from the baptismal fonts, and being now securely grounded in the new biblical context. 'We have preserved of pagan culture whatever seeks or contemplates the truth,' says St Gregory the Theologian.[8] This baptism of the Greek heritage produced a new synthesis of the Tradition and settled the style of Byzantine Christianity, whose culture eventually outweighed the more oriental traditions – the Nestorianism of Antioch and the Monophysitism of Egypt. Later there was a similar struggle between the Egyptian and Greek monastic traditions, between a mysticism that was obscure and opaque and one that was balanced and reasonable. The latter, under the early influence of St Gregory of Nyssa and of Denys the Pseudo-Areopagite, was soon assimilating the best elements of neo-Platonist thought. Balance, where the tensions were strong in either direction, was difficult to achieve, but once attained, it imparted the restraint and moderation that are essential qualities of Byzantine contemplative study.

This innate dialectical tendency is perhaps seen to best effect in sacred art, by which we are enabled to rise above all theological statement to the rarefied air of the mountain tops. The inner rhythm of the iconographic tradition keeps closely in step with the liturgy, which is our living experience of the transcendent, and accompanies our soaring thoughts, then surpasses them, to reveal what is hidden and express what cannot be uttered. While the word is the logical form of truth, the icon is the material symbol that makes the mystery visible; through the transparent skin of this world it fashions the ultimate unchangeable reality, clothing it with fabric woven from the light of Tabor, and disclosing the heaven that lies behind the earthly phenomena. With the deftness and lightness of the Holy Spirit it penetrates the world and allows the divine reality to burst through. Humankind becomes accustomed to living in the realm of transcendence; the supernatural becomes familiar and intimate, and assumes its role as the arbiter of human existence.

2. SOCIAL CHARACTER

Because it has always been at home with metaphysics, Byzantine theology is thoroughly human and social in character. Fascination with the nicest distinctions of Christian belief is not the preserve of the learned few, but is enjoyed by the whole people. The human mind, once it is furnished with a perfectly refined apparatus of philosophical terms and categories, is capable of receiving the gifts of

---

[8] *P.G.* 36, 502. See Salaville, 'De l'hellenisme au byzantinisme', in EOR, vol. 30, 1931.

Revelation. This does not actually concern philosophy at all, which is concerned rather with itself. What we are seeing here is the glorious achievement of Byzantium, namely the miracle of *theognosis*. The theology of the Fathers has always been open to human wisdom in all its branches, especially the magnificent humanism of the Greeks, but it does not stop there; it is a practical and realistic *paidagogos* that gradually raises human thought to the experience of a direct relationship with God, initiates the person into the pure contemplation of the 'flame of things' and leads at last to the threshold of *hesychia*, the ultimate coming face to face with God, the pneumatization of the human being.

The first five centuries saw the Tradition develop to its full strength. And in order that the faith should be settled on firm foundations, reason could not be allowed to remain sufficient to itself, but was put to the service of truth, transcending itself so as to be situated at the heart of doctrine. Thought was no longer autonomous, but participated in and expressed what was greater than itself.

3. THE PLACE OF INTERPRETATION

St Paul, speaking to the Athenians in their own terms, draws out the implications of what they already believe. Seeing the monument 'to the unknown god', he interprets him as Christ. There is no further need for reason to discover either itself or anything else, still less to make anything up; Christian thought is in the first place an intuitive grasp, a creative understanding, of revealed truth – an *interpretation*. According to the well known Byzantine dyarchy or 'symphony' of the two powers, the Patriarch possesses the spiritual privilege of interpreting the truth. Even Jesus says 'nothing of himself', but conveys the truth given by the Father. The Church possesses the spiritual gift of interpreting the Holy Scriptures. The doctrines, the inspired writings of the Fathers, the devotional tradition, together make up a living commentary in which the Word himself is constantly present as the interpreter of his own words.

Every heresy has its root in some excess of interpretation, a breach of the rules laid down by Apostolic Tradition. It is clear from the history of doctrinal controversy that the *virtus traditionis* is governed not by pure intellect but grows out of the Church's experience of God, the simple attentiveness to Christ from within his Body, as it allows itself to be schooled by his own interpretation.

The armchair speculation of the great heretics is sterile and self-stifling. Doctrine distils the essence of Revelation, but the flow of its logical arguments is constrained on either side by the banks of unutterable unknowing; as St Basil says, 'Knowledge of the divine essence entails perception of his incomprehensibility.'[9] The Christological or Trinitarian doctrine clearly transcends the laws of

---

[9] *Epistola* 234, n. 2; *P.G.* 32, 868.

logic and number, but theology, without ever leading into unreason, raises thought
to the metalogical plane where our formal laws simply do not apply. Without de-
stroying or contradicting them, it accustoms us to wholesome distinctions: 'To
affirm something at one time, then something else at another time, when both are
true, is characteristic of every good theologian.'[10] Thus St Gregory Palamas
demonstrates the coexistence of different planes of being. Affirmations that apparently contradict each other (antinomies) can be simultaneously true, if each is
understood in its own terms without excluding the other. The Truth is not therefore irrational, because it must include all aspects, the rational among them, and
go yet further. It is never 'only this', but 'this and also that', unity through transcendence. The only thing excluded is error or heresy, which is the result always
of exalting a part of the truth into the whole, and this curtailment, the pernicious
denial of the *pleroma*, becomes in the end self-contradictory and meaningless.

4. THEANDRISM, THE PRINCIPLE OF BALANCE

Passing through the waters of Baptism the human spirit undergoes both death
and rebirth. Human intelligence shares in the intelligence of Christ. In preference
to the historical method of Antioch which dissected and elucidated the letter, the
Church chose that of Alexandria, which looked for the hidden meaning and drew
out the essence of it. Allegory is purged of the excesses such as we find in Origenism, and at the same time any tendency to conceptual anthropomorphism or
ethical immanentism is strictly avoided. The hidden depth of belief, its essential
heart is, like the very nature of God, always beyond human grasp; God's constant
and infinite remoteness renders humankind, his creature, open to salvation. Nevertheless the paradox of Christianity consists in the balance between the radical
transcendence of God in himself – *Deus absconditus* in his essence – and the immanence of God at work in creation – *Deus revelatus* in his energies; the grace
of the Incarnation is that God the lover of mankind transcends his own transcendence. The crowning achievement of the Councils was to reject Nestorian dualism
(the separation of the divine from the human), equally with Monophysitism (the
assertion of the divine to the exclusion of the human), and thus to establish *theandrism*, which is the immovable foundation for the synergism of the two energies, divine and human. Dyophysitism and Dyotheletism (the harmony of two
natures and two wills in Christ) forge the golden key for every theological problem. Indeed, according to the fundamental doctrine of Chalcedon[11] the divine

---

10 *P.G.* 150, 1205.
11 Mansi, *Coll concil.* VII, col. 116. 'The Only-begotten makes himself known in two natures
without mixture, without change, indivisibly, inseparably: ἀσυγχύτως, ἀτρέπτως, ἀδιαιρέτως,
ἀχωρίστως.'

and human are united without confusion and without separation, and the deeply mysterious 'exchange of idioms' between them[12] gives rise to *theosis*, the defining term of Orthodox spirituality.

5. THE AWARENESS OF GOD

The sophisticated art of persuasion, the science of rhetoric for which the Greeks were famous, largely accounts for the practical and realistic nature of Patristic thought.[13] St Basil, according to his friend St Gregory of Nazianzus, took as his golden rule the ancient adage: τὸ πᾶν μέτρον ἄριστον – perfection is moderation in all things. The sermons of the Fathers, the many confessions of faith and the first catechisms, while never losing sight of their object, envisage it always in relation to the hearer, the catechumen. Synesius said that the art of arts, for the Greeks, was 'to be able to converse with people.'[14] But at the same time there was a desire to Atticize, to return deliberately to an archaic form of the language consciously removed from 'profane use'[15] and so to create the 'sacred' language of the liturgy.[16] The ceaseless trembling before the mysteries of the faith, the instinctive need, and consequently the genuine devotional use, of ascetic catharsis and sacramental initiation, spring from the deeply ingrained tradition of *epignosis*, the 'awareness of God'.[17] All the manifestations of the sacred – the consecration of time in the liturgy, the ordered space of the Temple, the vision of the icon – perfectly convey this awareness. The result is the unmistakable Byzantine style, the outward expression of Orthodox spirituality, which so thoroughly saturated everyday life as to suppress 'the profane' and transform even the palace of the *Basileus* into a huge monastery where everything was ordered liturgically and the *Basileus* himself was known quite naturally as 'external bishop' and 'ecumenical deacon'.[18] Its pattern was the earthly Empire at the service of the Kingdom of Heaven. There was nothing museum-like about it – quite the contrary, it was alive, reaching out beyond the ephemeral. It was the passionate love, to the point of martyrdom, of that *kat'holon* (catholicity), of all that is summed up by

---

[12] 'The communication of idioms' is the exchange of properties between the two natures in Christ which are united in the life of the single Hypostasis of the Word.

[13] *Eulogy, P.G.* 36, 573 B.

[14] See Norden, *Die Antike Kunstprosa* II, 2, p. 463.

[15] *Cotidiana vilescunt.* Ancient proverb: everyday things become vile.

[16] See Dom O. Rousseau, 'Les langues liturgiques de l'Orient et de l'Occident', in *Irénikon,* vol. 29, 1956.

[17] The expression comes from Fr Gabriel Horn, 'Le miroir et la nuée', *R.A.M. 1927,* in Prov. 2.5, the Septuagint and the Vulgate translate the Hebrew *ath* by ἐπίγνωσις, Symmachus by γνῶσις. Origen (in *Contra Celsum* – 749) referring to this text speaks of the 'divine meaning' and translates it by αἴσθησις. St Gregory of Nyssa copies Origen.

[18] See Dvornik, *Le schisme de Photius*, Paris 1950, (*Unam Sanctam* 19).

the rule, *what has been believed* – lived – *everywhere, always and by all.* This unquenchable thirst for the transcendent moulded the Byzantine character, giving it the ineffaceable shape of Orthodox *traditionalism*, unswervingly faithful to its Apostolic origin.

In the golden age of the first five centuries the great Rulers, Fathers and Doctors of the Church settled the broad principles of the *Paradosis* that they then handed down to the generations that came after. Leontius of Byzantium in the 6th century and St John Damascene in the 8th century sought to systematize the doctrine of the Church. Then in the 7th century there were the lightning-flashes of the prodigious mystical writer, St Maximus the Confessor; in the 11th century the solitary blaze which lit up the Byzantine sky in the engaging person of St Simeon the New Theologian, the Studite mystic, that 'poor lover of his brothers'; and finally in the 14th century there was the dazzling legacy of St Gregory Palamas. The Synod of Constantinople in 1351 canonized the Palamite doctrine as the most authentic expression of the Orthodox faith. In the course of defending the hesychast contemplatives of Athos, St Gregory Palamas synthesized Patristic thought (especially that of St Athanasius, the Cappadocians and the Areopagite writings) in a theology of the glory of God founded on apophaticism, which especially from that time onwards was integral to Orthodox religious philosophy. Palamism is centred on the Light of Tabor; it affirms the traditional distinction[19] between the utterly transcendent and unknowable essence of God and the uncreated grace or 'energies', permeating and deifying creation, by which he is truly known.

6. MYSTICAL KNOWLEDGE

Harnack's ingenuous remarks about what the Church Fathers made of philosophy are now of historical interest only. In the *Fount of Wisdom* St John of Damascus demonstrates clearly that truth depends not on dialectic, but on the content that we assign to the terms and categories of reason. Revelation propounds irreducible truths, and in response logic is continually forced to modify its terms and their content (e.g., *ousia*, hypostasis) or to invent completely new categories (e.g., theandrism). Logic and the processes of intellect follow their allotted course and work to their proper conclusions, but the content of Patristic thought, because of its originality and the transcendent nature of its object, would burst any system apart. Humankind learns to interpret its experience as a profound spiritual parable. Following the divine Forerunner who enters into the sanctuary of the Trinity (Heb. 6.20), the human being penetrates 'within the veil'. Only afterwards, at the next stage, does the vision receive an intellectual framework. It is rational in form only because it was mystical at first; and this is the history of all doctrines. Every

---

[19] See e.g. the texts of St Basil and St Gregory of Nyssa, *P.G.* 29, 497-775; 45, 248-1122; 32, 684-694; 45, 115-136; 32, 325-340.

heresy, by contrast, begins with a rational affirmation, which then sucks strength from the faith and eventually distorts it.

The Byzantine approach to knowing God is Aristotelian in its formal logical process of proofs and definitions, but Platonic in respect of their metaphysical content. The underlying philosophical method is not *deductive* but *postulative*, the postulates being plain statements of doctrine. Denys rightly says that this kind of philosophy 'does not demonstrate the truth, but lays it bare to sight in symbolic form, and so causes it to enter without argument into the soul that is athirst for sanctity and light.'[20] The postulates do not come from 'philosophy ... according to human tradition, according to the elements of the world' (Col. 2.8), they are doctrines of revelation; they are given to us as 'symbols of faith', tested by the experience of witnesses. They are the essences of the Wisdom of God penetrating deep into the mortal flesh of beings to make the wholly 'new creature'. We are not speaking here of any philosophical *system* but solely of the philosophical *method* which is brought to bear on the truths about God, and is instructed by them. Dialectic is thus at the heart of belief and the Scriptures. Moreover the mystical experience of light turns theology into 'mystagogy' (St Maximus) and in this new dimension 'enlightened spirits' transcend all pure thought.

Christian neo-Platonism, already evident in St Gregory of Nyssa, was assimilated by Byzantine culture most fully in the Areopagite school.[21] St Maximus, St Simeon, and above all the monastic tradition, which was instinctively opposed to any purely speculative philosophy, found it to be the best means of expressing Orthodoxy. The Fathers re-evaluated philosophical contemplation as 'propaedeutic' to spirituality, saying that the Greek philosophers were 'disciples of Moses'. Others like Psellus saw in every true thought an early sign of Messianic hope. Plato is called the 'precursor of Christianity' because he alone sensed what lay beyond intelligence, and his reasoning came to a stop in the contemplation of the One.[22] Aristotle never escaped from the categories and 'demonstrations' of logic, and his theology is found wanting because it treats doctrine in too human a manner.

Neoplatonism preserved eastern thought from the downward slide into anything like mediaeval scholasticism,[23] and above all from the nominalism unknown in the East. At the end of the 11th century the West took a decisive turning which separated it from the East, when it passed from the world of likeness and participation, and wholeness of perception, to a universe of efficient causes, and training in scholastic analysis. The biblical and Patristic vigour faded and gave way to theological argument. For century after century

---

[20] *Epist.* IX, 1, *P.G.* 3, 1105 CD.
[21] Writings first mentioned at the Council of Constantinople of 553 and commented on by John, Bishop of Scythopolis.
[22] By contrast the simple-minded monks of Mount Olympus of Bithynia, at the very name of Plato uttered curses against the Greek Satan!
[23] See the very violent reaction of Simeon of Thessalonica, *Dialogue against Heresies, P.G.* 155, 140.

the mission of the Church was lacking in real evangelical spirit. To scholastic epistemology, with its analytical and rational approach to religious knowledge, the East preferred 'sapiential gnosis', in which belief, mystical contemplation, theology and philosophy converge. While the West constantly exhibited a need to define, the East felt not only no need to define, but the actual need not to define.[24] The Roman Mass is noticeable for its didactic, catechetical emphasis, compared with the predominantly mysterious Eastern liturgy;[25] and this is a difference not only in approach and method, but in how deification is understood. The West is preoccupied in its moralizing way with how a human being will render account to God.[26] The same tendency is seen in the western preference for a pedagogical form of the coenobitic life, more apt for the exercise of perfecting the virtues, and easier to control. In the East it is the eremitical life, a more direct way to the unity and simplicity which are prerequisites for the deified state, that is valued as God's gift to the elect.[27] The anchorite's apparently selfish pursuit of holiness remains the norm even for coenobites, and it is still the narrow way for those called to become burning lights and salt of the earth. Nevertheless there is no compartmentalization, and St John Chrysostom holds up exactly the same ideal to married people in the world, telling them that to live good lives they must be 'like monks in everything else.'[28] In the time of the Fathers there was only one spirituality, which applied to all, and that was monastic discipline: mastery of the senses, prayer, and the reading of holy Scripture. Tradition rates the ascetic life as one of the gifts of the Spirit.[29] The saints are wonder-workers, martyrs, healers and also ascetics.

7. EFFICIENT CAUSE AND FORMAL CAUSE

East and West diverge yet again in their understanding of grace and salvation. To scholastic theology, the action of God on the world is, in Aristotelian terms, the effect of an *efficient cause*. By means of powers superadded by grace, humankind aspires to the direct vision of the divine being. Their spiritual capabilities restored,

---

[24] Cf. Congar, 'Neufs cents ans après', in *L'Eglise et les Eglises*, Ed. Chevetogne, I, p. 46; M.D. Chenu, *La théologie au XII* s., Vrin, 1957.
[25] See Baumstark, *Grundgegensätze morgenländischen und abendländischen Christentums*, Rheine, 1932.
[26] See G. Bardy. *'Le sens de l'unité dans l'Eglise et les controverses du V* s.', in *L'Année théologique*, 9, 1948, p. 167.
[27] See Dom A. Stolz, *L'Ascèse chrétienne*, Ed, d'Amay, 1948, pp. 52-55.
[28] *Hom. in epist. ad. Haebr.*, 7. 41.
[29] St Cyril of Jerusalem, *Catech. myst.*, 16, 12.

the faithful are organized into one society – *ecclesia militans* – in order to conquer the world and attain the supreme Good; this is a fundamentally moral and judicial view of the fruits of the Redemption. For the East the divine is the interior *raison d'être* (the *formal cause*) touching and shaping the essential nature of beings. Each created being is a visible sharing in the divine being, a likeness designed to correspond with the divine idea of Man. It attains perfection to the degree that the image and likeness runs right through its whole structure. Humanity thus restored and deified is then open to grace, pneumatization by the life-giving energies. Humankind flourishes only according as it shares the attributes of the divine life – immortality, simplicity, integrity. The work of Redemption is thus an integral part of the fullness of the Incarnation: the *perichoresis* or communication of idioms sanctifying and transforming humanity. So on the one side we see a rather ethical and moralizing anthropology leading to supernatural merit, the conquest of the world and the beatific vision of God; and on the other an anthropology that is *ontological*, the illumination and transformation of humankind, and its deification by being 'participants in the divine nature' (2 Pet. 1.4). In the West the emphasis is on the capacity to *act* according to a divine mode, in the East it is on the new *creature* and its *existence* according to a divine mode. In the Latin tradition it is not enough to be made in the image of God, because even in Paradise, before the Fall, humankind needed to be endowed with supplementary grace. In the East the image is sufficient in itself to receive the divine light, which enables us to see in Christ, not the *satisfaction for sin* (the 'theology of atonement'), but *nature putting itself back to rights* (the theology of restoration): the likeness is restored and so is the original nature. Sin has wounded the unity of the human being, asceticism and the sacraments heal it; which is why monasticism is so important as a prophetic sign and standard.

In the West, the apostolicity of the Church is expressed in the priesthood (often to the point of identifying the Church with the priesthood) in its most active aspect: hierarchical power, specialist preachers, trained missionaries and religious orders formed for particular purposes.

In the East, the priesthood of the monks is never an essential part of their monasticism, which is in principle a spiritual gift conferred on those in the lay state for the sake of a special vocation. It is in the charismatics (priests or plain monks), the *startzy* with the gift of discernment, the exorcists and the contemplative anchorites that the 'apostolic heart' is most clearly displayed. 'The perfect human being becomes equal to the apostles,' says St Simeon.[30] It is in reading hearts, prophesying the Kingdom and revealing it to be present, and driving back the rule of demons, that they speak of God and exercise the apostolic ministry, making visible the 'wholly other' of eternity. It must be understood that monastic chastity, the 'angelic state', is never opposed to marriage but is a sign, valuable in itself, of the *Parousia* and the Kingdom. What mat-

---

[30] See Dom O. Rousseau, *Monachisme et Vie religieuse*, Chevetogne, 1957, p. 26.

ters is chastity of the soul, 'purification of the heart', something quite different from merely formal, physical chastity.[31]

The Code of Justinian (Novella 133) says, 'The monastic life, like the contemplation practised within it, is a holy thing.' Contemplation, hesychasm, illumination, makes the monastic state into a mystery of the new creature, which outweighs any work the monks may do[32] or any legalistic understanding of their vows. This explains the lack of variety in the eastern religious orders – all the monks are 'Basilian'. Within the monasteries, however, we see a variety of *spiritual ranks or conditions: rasophore, microschema, megaloschema.*[33] By contrast with the new western code, the monastic vow is considered to be indissoluble, and the rules never allow any lessening of observance for the sake of worldly occupations; the monastic condition is thus the standard for every soul, it is essentially the coming of the Kingdom in the depths of the heart, and the trembling of the soul – humility – before the gates of Paradise.

8. MONASTICISM

The best point of entry to Orthodox spirituality is monasticism, its formative influence from the very beginning. Monasticism reminds us at once of the famous St Anthony (250-350)[34] and St Pachomius (252-346), and the redoubtable Thebaid, the cradle of so many giants of the Spirit, whose light irradiated the surrounding arid and burning desert. These outstanding masters of experimental science taught the highly refined art of living in utter obedience to the Gospel.

The key to understanding the appeal of monasticism is its utter rejection of evil[35] and its categorical refusal to compromise or conform. Its vehemence sternly demanded the forthright renunciation of the confusion and formlessness of this world, and the establishment at its margins of a city of monks. Their heavenly-minded service and their longing for the Kingdom contradicted the all-too human element of the Empire, whose adoption of the name of Christian had been perhaps over-hasty.

In the time of the persecutions the Christian faith was manifested most fully by the martyrs, whom the Church cherishes as her own heart, calling them 'those

---

[31] Cf. Origen, *P.G.* 12, 728 C.
[32] In the West new orders were formed for special purposes which are not strictly monastic.
[33] Rasophores: those who wear the monastic habit; microschema: the little habit; megaloschema: the large habit.
[34] See *Studia ancelmiana*, No 38, Rome 1956.
[35] When St Anthony withdrew to the desert, the demons complained: 'Leave our country; there is nowhere left for us.' Cassian emphasized the desire of the ascetics to fight the demons face to face: *Coll.* 18, 6; 7. 23. See K. Holl. *Enthusiasmus un Bussgewalt beim griechischen Mönchtum*, Leipzig 1898.

wounded by the love of Christ'. When the martyr becomes a 'spectacle' he does
so before God and the angels, and so preaches Christ. Origen said that the time
of peace is favourable to Satan who robs the Church of her martyrs. Christ is
present in the heart of the martyr in a particular way. 'Are you able to drink the
cup that I am about to drink?' (Matt. 20.22). In this saying the martyr is the cup
of the Eucharist realized in a Christian life, a 'memorial' of the Passion presented
before the face of the Father, and thereby a celebration – an immediate one – of
the Marriage of the Lamb. According to earliest tradition the martyr enters immediately into the Kingdom.

After the edict that established the Church in history and gave it a legal status
and peaceful existence, witness to the last things, hitherto borne by the martyrs,
passed to monasticism and was there transformed into a service of *eschatological
maximalism*. The monastic state came to be seen as a second baptism; thus the
'baptism of ascesis' superseded the 'baptism of blood' of the martyrs. *The Life
of St Anthony*[36] has been called 'the earliest hagiographical essay about a person
who achieved sanctity without tasting martyrdom.'[37] 'The perfect human being
is equal to the apostles ... like St John such persons can turn to others and tell
them what they have seen in God. They can do it and they must. They cannot do
otherwise.'[38] Monasticism is a constant and extremely powerful reminder of 'the
one thing necessary', of the gaining of the fruits of salvation through the ascetic
endeavour of 'invisible combat', the unremitting struggle of 'a warrior who attacks the passions', in the memorable words of St Nilus. In the silence of the
hesychasts' cells, in the school of those 'taught by God', there took place the
slow and astonishing transformation of a human being into a new creature. Here
at least, in the caves of the hermits or in the monastic communities, we can say
that this metamorphosis, this evangelical *metanoia* was successful.[39]
     Was it Christian, this unwavering hostility of the desert towards the Empire?
Extremism always carries with it the danger of excess, of exclusivism, of the
forcing apart of different levels of being. As time passes, however, we see the
single evangelical truth which throws into relief both aspects of human existence,
showing them to be complementary, each justifying the other, so that the fullness
that was carried in the womb of the Incarnation may be expressed in all its breadth
and length and depth and height. Monasticism left the world, only to bless it from

---

[36] St Athanasius, *P.G.* 26, 867-908.
[37] *DAL* XL, coll. 1802, art. of D. Leclercq, 'Monachisme'.
[38] I. Hausherr, 'Simeon the New Theologian', in *Orientalia Christ.* XII, 1928, p. 30.
[39] St Basil directed monasticism towards communal life. Nevertheless, the eremitical ideal
never lost its appeal. As the example for hermits, Simeon of Thessalonica (d.1428) pointed to
the Lord himself, while for the coenobites he pointed only to the Apostles. *P.G.* 155, 913. For
the history of monasticism see F. Heller, *Urkirche und Ostkirche*, 1937. For Russian monasticism, I. Smolich, *Russisches Mönchtum*, Augustinus Verlag, Würzburg 1953.

the desert and bear it in its unceasing prayer. And in the maximalism of the monks the world found its measure, its scale of comparison, its rule of life. Struck with amazement at the Stylites, it discovered in the attitude of prayer, in the act of adoration, humankind's essential nature – to allow itself to be 'ground between the millstones of humility to become fine bread, agreeable to the Lord'[40] – and finally it discerned in the spirit of detachment the eschatological principle that governs history itself. By its truly evangelical aspiration to the 'impossible', monasticism saved the world from the most dangerous presumption ('autopisty' and 'autorhythm'[41]) and taught it the eternal depth of the Spirit. 'The Triumph of Orthodoxy', the feast originating in the 7th Ecumenical Council, is a summing up of the doctrines of all the Councils in the iconographic vision of the Transcendent. It was no accident that the iconoclasts attacked not only icons but also monasteries; the monastic ideal was precisely that living icon composed of earthly angels and the one thing needful; it was the maximalist corrective to the minimalism of Imperial society. In our own time the awakened interest of the Latin Church in the sacred art of icons, and that of Protestant churches in the monastic life, are examples of one part of Christianity in search of a lost Christian dimension. In the evolution of the typical Christian, the 'new human being', monastic asceticism has played a decisive and formative role. Its skill in discerning spirits, its cultivation of spiritual attentiveness, its strategy of invisible warfare, and its science of the mastery of the spiritual over the material – these, while always keeping close to a plan that was utterly concrete, rendered it transparent so that it became a means of experiencing the nearness of the Kingdom.

The way was strewn with precipices. There was the Monophysite contempt for human nature to overcome, the pride of the 'elect', the Catharism of the 'pure', and its immediate corollary, the mistaking of obscurantism for apophatic obscurity, of comfortable ignorance for *'docta ignorantia'*.[42] On the other hand, the culture of the ancient world in its final stage set the highest value on breaking every restriction or boundary. The antidote to masochistic mortification and punishment was supplied by a balanced asceticism, which corrected its excesses, restored matter – the flesh of the resurrection – and inscribed on the sarcophagi of the world in letters of joy the message of Easter and the Parousia.

St John Climacus (525-605)[43] Abbot of Sinai, famous for his *Ladder of Divine Ascent*, shows that the purified heart is characterized by unwearying love for

---

[40] The *Apothegmata* of the Fathers recount the advice given to Arsenius: 'Take flight, stay silent, and keep peace in your heart; these three things will free you from sin'. And Abba Andrew said, 'Three things are good for monks: leave your native land, live in poverty, and silently exercise patience'. But a special vocation is required for this eremitical form.

[41] Putting faith in your own strength, the spirit of self-sufficiency.

[42] The expression comes from Nicholas of Cusa; Denys calls it 'pious agnosticism', a knowing that is 'unknowing'.

[43] *P.G.* 88, 596-1209.

God, whom it must 'love like the betrothed'. His commemorative office on the
30 May describes him as 'inflamed with divine love, being all unceasing prayer,
all ineffable love for God'. The experience of God as Being banishes the illusory
being of evil (St Gregory of Nyssa) and makes a monk 'the being who truly is',
the existent in the image of the divine Existent. The end of true monasticism is
to be united to, and to express, the Holy Trinity.[44]

9. THE EXPERIENCE OF ASCESIS

While Plato in the *Phaedrus* describes philosophy as meditation on death, equating
it to the art of dying well, asceticism goes further, and initiates us into the art of resurrection (John 5.24); the ascetics even call the human spirit 'resurrection'. This
closely matches the Fathers' theory that the Christian heart is essentially the 'return
to Paradise'; in other words, our existence is determined by the original destiny of
Adam, which we gradually find our way back to through the healing of the sacraments and ascetic purification.[45] Asceticism is in no sense a 'philosophy', even less
is it a moral code; it is transformation by participation in the 'wholly other'. It is a
balanced discipline, centred on all the richness contained in the biblical notion of
the heart. If God the Philanthropist becomes a human being only for love of humankind, what is human becomes 'God according to grace' only by love for God.
Any ascesis or science without love will not come near to God.[46]

   Cognition is natural to humankind, to be 'existent' properly belongs only to God;
being existent is prior to knowledge. St Gregory of Nazianzus underlines, 'to speak
of God is a great thing, but to purify oneself for God is still better.'[47] Similarly St
Simeon the New Theologian: 'There is no other way to know God than to live in
him,' and then humankind is 'flooded with being.' St John of Damascus in expound-
ing the uniqueness of God, whose essence is to exist, sheds much light on the experience of dread and anxiety, as described by Heidegger. For St John dread is the
extreme degree of that fear inherent in a troubled conscience. Terror in the face of
death (*terror antiquus*) is a natural part of empirical existence. Humankind may
have lost the memory of the immortal life of Eden, but it is still reminded of its ori-

[44] St Maximus, *Amb., P.G.* 91, 1196 B.
[45] St Cyril of Jerusalem said to the newly baptized, 'If you break with the devil, burst the bonds
and tear up the ancient treaties made with hell, then the Paradise planted in the East will be
open to you.' *Catech. mystag.* I. 9.
[46] The Vatican Council refined the Decree on Faith of the Council of Trent, emphasizing its
intellectual nature. Faith is clearly distinct from charity and is an intellectual agreement or decision: 'The act of Faith in itself, even when not motivated by charity, is a gift of God, and
avails for salvation' Denziger, n. 1791). In the East, faith is an act of *metanoia* of the whole
human being and is situated in the heart, the metaphysical centre, and engages all the faculties
of the spirit; it is the conscious epiclesis, the *fiat* leading to the Christification of the person.
[47] *Oratio* XXXII, 12; *P.G.* 36, 188 C.

gins; lifted out of nothingness, human beings live under the constant threat of a return to nothingness, of annihilation – the death complex. By the law of nature the memory of nothingness tends to eclipse that of the creative act of God and the first outpouring of the divine life. But more important than that, behind the screen of the natural there is hidden either devilish torment – the unquenchable burning of the desire to be equal with God – or the longing of the image in search of its divine archetype – the *eros* for the archetypal life of Eden. God can never be found by reason, but reason can rediscover itself and recognize itself in God. There no longer exists, after the Fall, any immanent way. We come from God only to cast ourselves on him and sink into his depths. That is why the Christian understanding is never the product of an intellectual system, but evolves in a fully historical existence that is elevated to become the place of encounter with God, of his Theophany. The ultimate purpose of the sacraments is precisely to *prolong the visibility of the historical Christ*. Every mystic is above all an ascetic; never a dreamer detached from reality, but a being fully immersed in a world that is solid and real from top to bottom. In their heroic struggle against the Monophysites and the Monothelites,[48] the martyrs were defending the sheer concreteness of the Incarnation; in historic matter they could see the flesh of the Kingdom.

10. LITURGICAL THEOLOGY

While 'orthodoxy' comes from δόξα and means both right belief and right worship, the experience of ascesis proves that the two meanings belong together in *orthozoë* – right living – and that Orthodoxy is a matter much more of praying than of teaching. Evagrius[49] and St Gregory of Nyssa teach that, 'if you are a theologian you will pray truly, and if you pray truly you are a theologian.'[50] The emphasis of monastic spirituality is chiefly on an intimate relationship with God. Mysticism, speculative and contemplative, which reached its highest cultivation in the monasteries, has always been inseparably joined to its source in the liturgy, which, being the 'canon' of piety, is responsible for Orthodoxy's distinguishing characteristic, liturgical spirituality.

By the 8th century the tradition was becoming settled and its various strands were being brought together in works of synthesis. The 'summa' of St John of Damascus[51] marked the end of the Patristic age, the point where innovation gave

---

[48] The Christological heresies which ascribed only one nature and one will to Christ.
[49] *Traité de l'oraison.* 60. The state of theological receptivity necessitates a 'gift of prayer'; *Ibid.,* 87.
[50] Prayer is the audacity to converse directly with God – Θεοῦ ὁμιλία. *P.G.* 44. 1124 B.
[51] The chief work: *La source de la connaissance* (in the 3rd part: *De la foi orthodoxe*) sums up Greek theology; translated into Latin in the 12th century, it brought the tradition of the Fathers to the attention of the West.

way to encyclopaedic collections, quotations and appeals to the *consensus pa-trum*. It was at the same time, however, that the theological themes which are the very lifeblood of Patristic thought were absorbed into liturgical poetry.[52] During a certain pause in intellectual vitality, Byzantium was able to create the most profound theological synthesis in her liturgy. According to St Simeon the New Theologian the divine light burned at the heart of the Church as brilliantly as in the time of the Apostles, engendering a joyful optimism that could come only from experience and that cried, Death shall have no more dominion over us.

Step by step with liturgical life there evolved continuously in the monasteries the tradition of applied theology of the great mystics. In the 10th century it was St Simeon the New Theologian and his emphasis on participation in the divine light. Πτωχὸς φιλάνθρωπος, 'the poor, the friend of human beings', enriches them all with the richness of his poverty – the love of God. For him the resurrection begins here and now, before the passage to the next world. St Simeon continued the tradition of St Gregory of Nyssa and of the 'Spiritual Homilies',[53] that of the direct experience of the indwelling of God. With St Simeon mysticism reached one of its highest peaks, and while his influence was similar to that of less wide-ranging spiritual masters – St Macarius, St Isaac of Nineveh, or St John Climacus – his hymns to Love set his contemporaries on fire, and the enduring vitality of his presence, down to this day, comes from the impulse of his charity to impart his mystical joy, his radiant and infectious sanctity to everyone.

Mount Athos is where the first discussions on hesychasm took place, and they resulted in the Synods convened in the 14th century to discuss the doctrine of St Gregory Palamas. St Gregory marks the last and definitive flowering of Byzantine spirituality; he was raised up once and for all to reaffirm the heart of Orthodox spirituality, the sharing of God by himself through his divine energies, which is the meaning – and the limit – of the mystery of *theosis*.

11. HESYCHASM

Hesychasm is one of the features that clearly distinguishes the eastern Church[54] from that of Rome.[55] From St John Climacus through to Nicetas Stethatos and St Simeon the New Theologian, the teaching was elaborated that humankind is

---

[52] At this time the ecclesiastical calendar was ordered by Emperor Basil II, texts were being edited by Simeon Metaphrastes, etc.

[53] Attributed to St Macarius of Egypt.

[54] The Synod of Constantinople of 1351 definitively canonized the doctrine of St Gregory Palamas as the authentic expression of the Orthodox faith.

[55] 'This doctrine considered in its fundamental principle is not only a grave philosophical error; it is also truly heretical from the Catholic point of view.' This was the considered judgement of Jugie, in *Palamas*, *DTC*, coll. 1764, vol. XI.

destined to share the light of the Holy Spirit and his divine energies; with St Gregory Palamas it achieved its perfect form. Before coming to rest on Mount Athos, hesychasm had a continuous history from the very origins of the monastic movement.[56] Alongside the coenobitic ideal, which found expression in the Rules of St Basil and of St Theodore the Studite, great importance had always been attached to the ancient practice of the anchorites, pure contemplation and interior silence. The two traditions are not opposed but complementary, proceeding from the same monastic and spiritual source. However, in the great monasteries, with their increasingly complex social economy and activity, the lifeblood of mysticism eventually showed signs of drying up, and it was left to the hesychastic hermits to keep the tradition alive. This was the whole point of the contemplative revival that took place at Athos under the inspiration of St Gregory of Sinai.[57] His message was that all contemplation has but one end, wholeness of spirit.[58]

When the 14th century was fully under way, there came violent reaction from westernized Orthodox circles. In the succeeding conflict between Orthodox mysticism and western scholastic rationalism, the tone was set by the anti-Palamites, Gregoras, Barlaam, Manuel Calecas, and Demetrius Cydones and his brother Prochorus. Barlaam denied the central thesis of Palamism, the distinction between the divine essence and its operations. For him only the arguments of reason were valid, and any intuitive insight of a mystical nature was a source of error; he even said that interior illumination was tantamount to the materialization of God. In this he followed St Thomas, who rejected the Augustinian doctrine that knowledge could be gained through divine illumination and intuition, and asserted that God could be present in the mind only through the exercise of reason. Demetrios Cydones, although wholly Greek, did not hide his enthusiasm for St Thomas's *Summa Theologica*, writing to his friend Calopheros, 'With him our faith is provided with every possible proof;' and according to his brother Prochorus, 'To know the wisdom of God is to know his essence,'[59] which is as much as to say that deification results from purely intellectual activity! The conflict was not one of rival philosophies – Aristotle and Plato were appealed to on both sides – but a deeper one concerning doctrine. It was the difference between the 'high road' of an autonomous cataphatic theology, and an apophatic approach that attempts to affirm nothing beyond its own limits.

According to the former, the logical concept of God adequately expresses his Being. From the concept of the Being the attributes of God – his simplicity and

---

[56] See J. Bois, 'Les hesychastes avant le XIVe siècle', in *Echos d'Orient*, 1901, vol. V.
[57] See the account of Nicodemus the Hagiorite in *The Philocalia*, Athens, 1893, vol. II, p. 242.
[58] This is achievable even in the conditions of married life, according to G. Palamas, *P.G.* 150, 1056 A.
[59] *P.G.* 151, 693-716.

unity – can then be deduced analytically. So far as God is Being, ontological laws can be applied to him. Any antinomic notion is excluded because it would contradict the universal rule of logic, which is thus elevated to a means of communion with the divine.

According to the latter, the divine 'superessence' is utterly beyond the grasp of humankind, which is forced to make the antinomic affirmation (which is never a contradiction) that God is completely inaccessible in himself, but manifested immanently in the world. God 'issues forth' in his energies and is totally present in them. The energy is never only a part of God, it is God in his revelation, without the loss of any of the still-hidden intrinsic essence. The energies are common to all the persons of the Holy Trinity, they are uncreated and are accessible to the creature. They have no effect on the divine unity, indivisibility and simplicity, any more than the distinctions between the persons result in a composite God. Even St Augustine was obliged to call God *'simpliciter multiplex'*.[60] God is more than Being, especially under his logical form, because he is the creator of every form, and therefore above and beyond every concept. The simplicity of God is 'wholly other' than our idea of simplicity. It already follows from this that every doctrinal affirmation is antinomic and metalogical, but never contradictory.

This controversy has immediate repercussions in the highly complex problem of grace. In the West grace is a transcendent quality, but created, which makes it possible for justification to be juridically *imputed* to us. The Reformers were to press this notion to its limit, giving 'imputation' the meaning of 'declaration' (by 'forensic' grace): human beings would be declared *outwardly just* by the Tribunal, without really being so in their nature – *semper justus et peccator*. In the East, on the contrary, grace is the energy of God, deifying humankind ontologically and making it a genuinely new creature, just and holy in itself, but always according to grace.

This is the affirmation underlying all Eastern theology: the essence of God is radically transcendent; only his 'operations' (energies, grace) are immanent and shareable. This is not in the least an abstract matter, but one of *life or death* – because it concerns the very realness of communion between God and humankind. The human cannot commune and participate in the essence of God – that would mean that it was God – but any communion with a created element (supposing grace to be created even though supernatural) is not communion with God at all. But if human beings enter into the most real communion with the divine operations, the manifestations of God in the world, then they have received the whole nature of God, as in the mystery of the Eucharist. Communion is neither substantial (pantheism) nor hypostatic (which belongs only to Christ) but *energetic*, and in his energies God is totally present. For the Anti-Palamites, however, deification, or the beatific vision of the essence of God, is a form of 'logical' communion which goes hand in hand with causal determinism

---

[60] *De Civit. Dei* 12, 18.

and the rational proof of God's existence.[61] Rationalist intellectualism brings God down to the level of human intelligence. The Euclidian or Cartesian craving for rational clarity absolutizes this intelligence and exalts it into an attribute of God, making it *the site of divine communion*. Lacking the restraint of apophatic theology, cataphatism is pushed to its conclusion.

In its mystical teaching Palamism is entirely Orthodox: the mysticism is that of 'the divine obscurity' – the shadows of God, the fringe of his light. From knowing on the human level, the Spirit lifts us by way of participation to knowing on the level of God. It is the Johannine knowledge of God by the indwelling of the Word and by the light within, which latter is the sensible effect of uncreated divine light. Mystical experience reveals it under its interior, hidden aspect, and can also reveal it externally in the haloes of the saints, the light on Tabor or at the Resurrection, to the bodily eyes, once they have been transfigured and opened to the supernatural by the Spirit. Indeed, according to Palamas[62] the Transfiguration of the Lord was actually that of the Apostles, of their momentary capacity for contemplating the glory of the Lord that was hidden beneath his kenosis. That light or glory of God is the energy by which God becomes wholly present, the resulting vision being a real contemplation 'face to face' – the 'mystery of the eighth day', the perfect state of deification.

12. SYNTHESES

Nicholas Cabasilas [63] (d. 1371) generalizes from the example of the great mystics, so that all can learn from their monastic methods and see that their lives too can be suffused to the depths of their being by all the charismatic operations of the life of the Church. His treatise on the sacraments is called simply *Life in Jesus*. The title alone eloquently shows the extent to which the heart of Orthodox mysticism – life in God – is to be found in the mysterious, sacramental side of the Church. On the other hand the sacraments continue the visible historical existence of Christ, attested by 'epicletic'[64] acts of the Holy Spirit. By acts of memorial the sacraments 'reproduce' the life of Jesus, making it possible to follow Christ symbolically step by step along the path that leads to salvation. The life of every

---

[61] The Vatican Council decreed that natural reason alone can attain to the certain knowledge of God. *Acta*, col. 255, Denziger, n. 1653. The Thomists did not recognize any *distinct* faculty of the soul within the *one* intelligence. For the Greeks, on the contrary, the νοῦς, the repository of the triune image and the 'eye of the understanding' knows intuitively by the gift of the Spirit. While the *ratio* knows by reflected light, the μέγα νοῦς is directly inspired.

[62] *Homily on the Transfiguration*; *P.G.* 151, 433 B.

[63] His real name was Chamaetos. Not to be confused with Michael Cabasilas the Sacellarius. See P.S. Salaville, 'Cabasilas le Sacellaire et Nicolas Cabasilas' in *Echos d'Orient*, Oct. 1936.

[64] From 'epiclesis', the invocation of the Holy Spirit.

person in Jesus is the same thing as the life of Jesus in persons, the 'threefold indwelling' and the pneumatization of the human being by the divine energies.
Liturgical mysticism is *accessible to all*, engaging with every life on the historical
and spiritual levels, and bringing about the real and concrete *incorporation* of
the faithful in Christ, which is their Christification: 'until Christ be formed in
you' (Gal. 4.19).

In every place where Orthodoxy is practised the heritage of the Councils and
of the Fathers of the Church is conveyed in an easily recognized local form. Cyril
and Methodius, the Apostles of the Slavs, were Greeks from Thessalonica; they
brought not only the Bible but also the liturgy, that living interpretation of Scripture, redolent with the very life force of Patristic Byzantium, which the Slavonic
genius received and assimilated through its own vernacular style, as is strikingly
apparent in the Russian icons. It is hard to pin down exactly what distinguishes
the styles, but the supreme accomplishments of Greek and Russian iconography,
respectively the Vladimir Mother of God and Rublev's Holy Trinity, spring from
the same theological principles, the same vision of the one indivisible Tradition.

13. THE SAD PARTING OF THE WAYS

In the East the same synthetic method is applied to ecclesiology as to the doctrine
of the Trinity: the Persons are first distinguished so that their unity may be affirmed – which is the theology of the Cappadocians; similarly, it proceeds from
the fullness of each local Church to the communion of other entities that are
equivalent to it and consubstantial. So it is that organic unity is visible in conjunction with all the diversity of traditions, each with its own native character.
In the West, especially among the Thomists, the approach to theological problems
is analytical, beginning with the divine Whole, then proceeding to the Persons.
In the same way the Roman Whole precedes the local churches which are *parts
of this Whole*, so that uniformity of language and worship are presupposed. The
West prays 'for your holy catholic Church', and the East, 'for the prosperity of
the holy churches of God'.[65]

In the East from early times, the multiplicity of Apostolic seats was conducive
to their perfect equivalence. In the West, Rome because of its situation enjoyed
absolute power as the centre of the Church. That situation encouraged the Pope
of Rome to feel more and more that he was the sole successor of Peter. Orthodoxy, by contrast, followed the idea of St Cyprian: every bishop is seated on the
cathedra Petri, as the local symbol of the universality and unity of the faith. The
Apostle Peter was the first to preside over the eucharistic assembly and every
bishop is his successor, i.e., he is Peter in his sacramental authority. Thus the

---

[65] See Y. Congar: 'Neuf cents ans après', in *L'Eglise et les Eglises*, Ed. de Chevetogne, v. 1 p. 17.

Catholicos of Seleucia-Ctesiphon was 'Peter, head of our ecclesiastical assembly'. Every patriarch is an independent spiritual head, and the direct successor of Peter.[66]

While Orthodoxy sees itself as the *perpetuation of Pentecost*, wherein power is distributed on the collegial and conciliar principle, Rome considers itself to be the *perpetuation of Peter*, the only Prince and omnipotent Vicar of Christ. Despite canons (the 5th of Nicaea and the 8th of Ephesus) that set precise limits to his power, the Patriarch of Rome was never slow to impose his judgements on the local churches.

The Papal State, where the Pope held the two swords and crowned the kings, exalted him to the unique dignity of bearer of the universal power in all its forms, and that by divine right. Documents such as the Donation of Constantine or the False Decretals, although forgeries, were perfectly consistent with the ideology that was evolving. The Greeks for their part demonstrated a great lack of sophistication, behaving pragmatically and therefore irrationally, displaying an attitude which would erupt later in the greatest misunderstanding in the whole history of the Church. Plunged in doctrinal discussions, often locked in local conflicts without reaching any solution, they looked *pragmatically* and empirically towards a disinterested third party who would be able to cut through the knot. When they appealed to the West, to the Pope, the eastern Christians were simply seeking an impartial judge to solve a particular problem on a unique occasion – not a voice from above, but one from outside. Here we see clearly the birth of two irreconcilable ecclesiologies, irreducibly different as to their dogmatic principles and existing in mutual ignorance. The Christianization of Roman law legitimated the western theocracy of the Middle Ages, founded on the power embodied in the popes. In the East the *sacerdotium* and the *imperium* were the two gifts of God which complemented each other in one *sacred diarchy*. Eastern theocracy sought and created the spiritual conditions that were capable of safeguarding the doctrinal purity of the faith whose end is expressed by monasticism: the birth of the new creature. There is only one *Basileus* of *all* the Christians and the Empire is *the place* of the Church. This explains why the Church followed the Empire as it expanded, and why Constantinople, being the capital and *therefore* the seat of the chief Patriarch, took precedence over the ancient patriarchates. The independence of the Church came from the Empire and was guaranteed and professed by the Emperor, and this made it completely unaware of every other primacy, including that of Rome. Indeed, the 'symphony' of Church and Empire, of Patriarch and *Basileus*, left *no hierarchical place* for the power of the Pope of Rome, and the Greeks were by nature unable to understand the Latin *'tertium datur'*; they were completely unaware of the grandeur and magic that was steadily becoming

---

[66] See B. Chabot, *Synodicon Orientale*, Paris 1902, p. 294; W. de Vries, 'La conception de l'Eglise chez les syriens séparés de Rome', in *L'Orient syrien*, 1958.

attached to the Papacy in the West. The Greeks were falling from grace, under the harsh accusation of betraying the truth; the accusation was certainly true *technically* and the Greeks, unwittingly, did everything to lead western minds into error. In fact, having been consulted as an arbitrator, once the discussion was settled, Rome completely disappeared from the eastern view. The Roman historian Mgr Battifol says clearly, 'the East did not see Rome as it saw itself ... the perpetuation of Peter ... St Basil knew nothing of it, any more than St Gregory of Nazianzus or St John Chrysostom. The authority of the Bishop of Rome was an authority of the highest distinction, but it was never seen in the East as an authority of divine right'.[67] From the eastern point of view the Pope, like every bishop, was subject to the Council, without recourse to which no definition of doctrine is imaginable.

It was in the 11th century that the misunderstanding became more serious, when the Popes arrogated to themselves authority in the East. According to the decree of the Council of Florence (1439) – the last, tragic meeting of East and West – the Pope of Rome is the chief of all the local churches and therefore of the whole Church; he holds his power directly from Jesus Christ whose Vicar he is, and has more authority than any Council; he is not only father but also doctor of all Christians, who all owe him obedience. Here we have the classical western theory of the *plenitudo potestatis* of the Roman Pontiff; his superiority over the Council is a prerogative of the *cathedra Petri*. It is the *embodiment of absolute power*. Nilus Cabasilas, in the second half of the 14th century, showed the cause of the schism to lie in the unwavering opposition of the Councils to the notion that papal decrees were valid *ex sese*.[68] Since the 13th century, eastern theologians, alarmed to discover an irreconcilable disagreement, have emphasized the difference between the Apostolate and the Episcopate, thus immediately undermining the pretension of the popes to assume the authority of the Apostle Peter. The apostolic dignity is intransmissible and belongs to the whole Body of the Church.

From the 4th century to the 9th there had already been at least seven periods of schism between East and West, amounting to more than 200 years altogether. The rupture of 1054 has never been healed.

The centralized ecclesiology of Rome was imposed according to the monarchical pattern. Confident in their spiritual system which was utterly foreign to the East, Rome authoritatively rejected all those who differed from her. The last ties were violently broken by the Crusades: 'rather the Turkish turban than the Latin tiara' summed up the bitterness of the cruelly deceived Byzantines. They suffered profoundly in their encounter with a brutal and horrific heresy; the purity of the faith represented an unmistakable limit and explains their sudden revulsion;

---

[67] 'Cathedra Petri', in *Etudes d'histoire ancienne de l'Eglise* (Unam Sanctam) Paris 1938, p. 75.
[68] *De causis diss. in Ecclesia, P.G.* 146, 685. Cf. A. Palmieri, *Theol. dogm. orth.* II, p. 83.

there was no possibility of compromise with the Roman heresy by any appeal to 'economy'. The doctrinal question of the *Filioque*, which had itself been imposed on the Popes by political imperial power, occupied the foreground, but it could no longer be properly discussed in the spiritual climate engendered by the Roman primacy, which was already a fundamental heresy in the eyes of the Orthodox.

The evidence of history is overwhelming and cannot be too often stated: *in the Church of the Councils unity was the expression of the Truth.* Unity never arises out of human organization, but Truth brings into being and imposes its own structure of unity; only thus are people organized in ecclesial assembly, in eucharistic liturgy. Unity can never be attained by inclusivism, the separation of unity from the fullness of the faith in a compromise. The utter and irrevocable failure of the inclusivist attempts of the Councils of Lyons in 1274[69] and of Florence in 1439 demonstrated that, as a way to solve dogmatic controversies, submission is always a dead end.

For Orthodoxy the question never arises of submission to an historical institution, still less to any power except that of love. To aspire sincerely to the Truth – and here Orthodoxy is absolutely faithful to the original Apostolic tradition – it must be *embraced* and it is this participation in the dogmatic Truth in its fullness that leads *ipso facto* to the communion of the Church, Orthodoxy.

14. SLAVONIC BYZANTIUM

In the East the Fathers were never interested in formal ecclesiology. They knew what the Church was without feeling the need to define it. Similarly on the subject of relations between Church and State, the late 9th century code of Byzantine law, the 'Basilica',[70] is clear evidence that the famous 'symphony' of the two powers is not a juridical principle but a statement of faith, following directly from the doctrine of the Incarnation, from its fullness. The holy emperors and princes form a very distinct category alongside the holy martyrs, ascetics and Fathers of the Church. Their sanctity is essentially different from the monastic kind, and sprang from the religious mission of the Empire and its rulers: the defence and propagation of the faith. The Code of Justinian actually begins with the Nicene Creed; doctrine belongs at the very heart of what is falsely and casually called 'Byzantine caesaropapism'. It was precisely the concord between the patriarchs

---

[69] For accepting the decrees of this heretical council, Michael Paleologue was immediately excommunicated. Princes may have been too easily pardoned for their moral offences, but they were never pardoned for crimes against the faith.

[70] The manual of Byzantine law published between 879 and 886 under Basil 1st in preparation for the work of legislative revision – the 'Basilica'. Published by Zacharia von Linenthal: *Collectio librorum juris graeco-romani in editorum Leipzig*, 1852.

and princes that mitigated the sometimes excessive rigorism and maximalism of the monks; but any threat against the purity of the faith was shattered sooner or later on the unmovable rock of the Church.

The spiritual nature of the coronation rite of the emperor marked the entrance of the Empire into the sacred enclosure of the Church. The Church was the universal rule of life, so that, for example, the Byzantine army adopted the title of 'Christ-loving', and from the moment of this development in self-awareness, the *Basileus* is always shown in icons kneeling or prostrate before Christ. The necessary balance was difficult to maintain and was achieved by the edge of the sword; while never being conquered by the State, the Church was subjected by history to severe temptations.

In the 9th century, the brothers St Cyril and St Methodius of Thessalonica transplanted into the soil of the Slav countries not only Christianity, but also the theocratic ideal embodied in Byzantium, thus founding *Slavonic Byzantinism*. The speed with which Bulgaria and Serbia aspired to a theocratic dignity equal to that of Constantinople was symptomatic of their strong desire for autonomy.

In the 15th century, Byzantium was fading from sight. The fall of Constantinople followed the aborted treachery of Florence like a divine chastisement. The crown of the *Basileus* passed to the Prince of the Russias as if to confer a celestial blessing on the Tsar of all the Christians, the lawful heir to the Orthodox Kingdom. Ivan III married the niece of the last *Basileus* and endowed Moscow with the arms of Holy Russia: the two-headed eagle left the shores of the Bosporus and stretched his wings over the vastness of the Russian steppes. The Church became the guardian of the very heart of national life, impressing its newfound dignity on the people, who by a supreme effort shook off the pagan ascendancy and drove away the Tartar hordes for ever. In the popular consciousness, in the words of the monk Philotheus,[71] the spiritual centre of the world was removed to Moscow: two Romes (Rome and Constantinople) are fallen, the third, Moscow, stands, and the fourth will never be. This denial of the 'fourth' clearly demonstrates Philotheus's eschatological outlook: Moscow marked the arrival of the last times. At Constantinople the cross fell from the sanctuary of St Sophia, and the appellation 'catholic' passed to the cathedral of Moscow; from the same spiritual principle came the true meaning of the universal title of Tsar. Ivan the Terrible in 1557 was confirmed by the East in this dignity. In 1589, Jeremiah the Patriarch of Constantinople elevated the Metropolitan Job to the title of Patriarch of all the churches of Russia.

---

[71] The idea of the Orthodox Third Rome first appeared at Tver in 1453 in a letter from a distinguished scholar, Thomas, to Grand Prince Boris of Tver. In 1461 it was mentioned in the panegyric of Grand Prince Basil of Moscow. Philotheus, a monk of the Monastery of the Saviour near Pskov, derived from it the principle of absolute government, which he set out in a famous letter to Tsar John IV. See V. Malinine, *The Ancient Monastery of St Eleazar, Philotheus and his Epistles* (in Russian), Kiev 1901.

But the great Muscovite centralization, the rapid growth of the Empire and of its political power, outstripped the spiritual advance; people's consciousness of the Church fell behind and sought refuge in a simple fidelity to the past. Conservatism degenerated fatally into formal ritualism. The official face of Russian Orthodoxy reflected its separation from its interior tradition, which was spiritually Byzantine. In their struggle against the heretics the Bishops of Novgorod appealed to the state police, thus paying homage, implicit but none the less disquieting, to the western Inquisition. The 'Council of 100 Chapters' (Stoglav, 1551) preached faithfulness much more to the past than to the Truth and by its narrow ritualism prepared the ground for the schism of the Old Believers. The increasingly autocratic State laid great emphasis on its rights in regard to the Church, while passing over its duties in silence. Increasingly it neutralized the Church by neutralizing its social activity, the administration of charitable works. The tragedy of the Third Rome was its utopianism, the *national messianism* which took the place of the *ecumenical mission* of Byzantium, and thus imported the poison of secularism.

The 17th century marked a profound crisis. Stephan Javorsky and the theologians of Kiev introduced Latin theology, which Theophan Prokopovich counterbalanced with a tendency to Lutheranism. Peter the Great established western absolutism and set about secularizing the State, rejecting any notion of the Church as the *conscience* of the nation, and reducing it to ministering only to the faithful, in ways that he was careful to define. From that time onward, the State delegated to the Church certain functions according as it found them useful to itself. The ancient Patriarchate was replaced by a Synodical system on the Protestant model, called 'The Department of the Orthodox Confession'.

But side by side with *Great Russia* there was the growth of *Holy Russia* with its deepening mystical tradition, the institution of the *staretz*,[72] and its innumerable pilgrims seeking the celestial city. At the end of the 15th century St Nil Sorsky (1433-1508) introduced the hesychasm of Mount Athos and left a remarkable treatise on Orthodox ascesis and a Rule of the monastic life. At the end of the 18th century, St Paissy Velichkovsky (1722-1794) founded a whole monastic school based on the *Philokalia* and the Jesus Prayer. His disciples returned from Moldavia to Russia, revived the tradition of continuous prayer and established the *startzy*. The most famous centres were the monasteries of Optina and Sarov, the latter illuminated by St Seraphim, who died in 1833, a contemporary of Pushkin. That St Seraphim and Pushkin were contemporaries but ignorant of each other is evidence of the tragic segregation of spiritual and cultural life – the problem of how to relate them was to prove a great difficulty for Russian thinkers of the 20th century.

---

[72] I. Smolich, *Leben und Lehre der Starzen*, Vienna 1936.

Russia[73], faithful to the Byzantine mystical tradition, became associated with a particular kind of devotion, that to the kenotic, humiliated Christ, as shown by 'the fools for Christ'. At the same time we see the *startzy*, assisting the holy Princes in the service of the world, and representing their own charismatic ministry both in and *for* the world. The tragic conflict between Joseph of Volokolamsk (1439-1515) and Nil Sorsky is that between social organized Christianity and the charismatic tradition of poverty and mystical contemplation. The tradition of Nil and his disciples across the Volga, opposing external ritualism, put all the emphasis on the inner source of the spiritual life. While not in the least neglecting social and charitable work among the poor, the monks' task was essentially different; it was prophetic. The monk's first duty was to witness to the presence, here and now, of the Kingdom, of which 'the Third Rome' was but a faint and passing shadow. For their part, tragically isolated by their schism, the Old Believers fought violently against the Kingdom that had fallen from holiness, and introduced the theme of the Antichrist which would underlie and profoundly influence Russian thought in the ages to come.

Holiness, true Orthodox spirituality, would flourish unobtrusively in the shadow of political events, in the silence of the monasteries.

On the eve of the Revolution, there was the rediscovery of icons, and Russian literature and social theory were feverishly seeking an ultimate synthesis; more important, the uninterrupted tradition of the Jesus Prayer and the theology of the Holy Spirit ensured the continuity of Byzantine spirituality, of Orthodoxy.[74]

---

[73] J. Cologrivov, *Essai sur la sainteté en Russie*, Ed. Bayært, Bruges 1953; E. Behr-Sigel, *Prière et sainteté dans l'Eglise russe*, Paris; G. Fedotov, *Treasury of Russian Spirituality*, Sheed & Ward, London 1950.
[74] In Romania in our own time a disciple of the startzy of the famous monastery at Optina has revived the tradition of the Jesus Prayer which goes back in that region to Paissy Velichkovsky.

2

Byzantium after Byzantium

Basil Tatakis in his *Philosophie Byzantine*[1] entitles his last chapter 'Byzantium after Byzantium', by which he means Orthodoxy in Russia. The end of Byzantium was only the end of the Empire. Byzantium, the spiritual motherland of Orthodoxy, remains.

For six centuries Russia assimilated the remarkable Byzantine heritage, and in the 19th century a grand systematization of all its themes was embarked upon; it was summed up in the appeal by Fr Sergei Bulgakov, the greatest theologian of the age, to return to the central truth of Chalcedon, the theandrism on which Orthodoxy is founded.[2] The idea of God-Mankind, basic to the thinking of Vladimir Soloviev,[3] and thereafter to that of Russian theologians generally, is centred on the harmonious interchange of the divine and human elements in the Christological *perichoresis*, a dialectic of image and likeness, of the given and the potential, that rules out any monist hypothesis. Fr P. Florensky[4] skilfully demonstrated the logical principle of identity to be a dead end and explored the fundamental concept of consubstantiality and likeness.[5] The faculty of intuition is directed not towards the rational principle of contradiction or sufficient reason, but towards the spiritual antinomy of harmonious opposites, the dazzling obscurity of the Wisdom of God. This is no ontological dualism but the polarity of the modes of existence: the numinous and the phenomenal, the holy and the demonic, being and nothingness.

The Incarnation, since it is the inmost reality at the heart of every being, is thus multiplied and extended over the whole human race, so that all of history is Christified. According to Soloviev, Christ the God-Man is fulfilled in Christ who is God-Humankind, which is the Church of human beings, angels and the cosmos. Slavophiles, applying the theandric principle to gnoseology or epistemology, in-

---

[1] *Histoire de la Philosophie* by E. Brehier. 2nd supplement: *La philosophie byzantine*, Presses Universitaires de France, 1949.
[2] 'On the path of doctrine', in the review *The Way*, No 37, 1933 (in Russian).
[3] *Lectures sur la Théandricité*, 1881. English translation: *Lectures on God-manhood*, New York 1944.
[4] *The Pillar and Ground of Truth*, 1913 (in Russian); there is a German translation in *Östliches Christentum, Dokumente herausgegeben von N. v. Boubnoff un Hans Ehrenberg*, Munich 1925; *Signification de l'idéalisme*, 1915.
[5] Christian thought is concerned with the 'homoousial', the foundation of personal existence; its opposite is 'homoiousial' philosophy, dealing with immobility and lifeless objects.

sist that consciousness and knowledge go hand-in-hand. When human intelligence (the 'gnosis' of Clement of Alexandria) is directed towards religious matters, it changes. Intelligence, associated with the 'heart' in the biblical sense, goes beyond discursive reason, cerebral *dianoia* going towards intellect – *nous*, which is capable of illuminated knowledge and unitive love. Knowledge is the function of being alive, of the existent human person integrating all the faculties of the spirit. A similar 'living knowledge', according to the Slavophile notion, works towards the integration of a consciousness completely contained within the Holy Spirit, which unlocks hidden meaning by participating in the eternity of the Holy Spirit. Humanity 'situated in history' finds itself between nothingness and the One who exists, and in its act of knowing brings about a change in being by making itself its own subject, as *one who exists*. Soloviev[6] comes close to the thought of Palamas in distinguishing between being and existence; being is the ontological predicate of the existent subject. In all one-sided ontology the predicate is hypostasized and skirts abstraction. The thinker is first and foremost one who exists, through participation seeking to understand what belongs to being. This existential attitude learns to see being much more as light, fire or breath, than as anything static or fixed.

God is beyond any conception of the Absolute, so he cannot be approached by any rational argument from causality, as if he were a being; God *exists*, so arguments must start from the *apophatic evidence* of *Deus absconditus* (the apophatic aspect of the argument of St Anselm.[7]) Such reasoning sees every form of life as a liturgical 'memorial', i.e., *in relation* to God, pointing to him. In any intentionally directed thought, the idea of God is intrinsically, inevitably, present.[8] Because the truth is already present in the thought, reason is employed not logically, to deduce the truth, but *evidentially*, to reveal it .

There is a thoroughgoingness about Russian thought that cannot tolerate any compromise or middle way, and that gives it at times a historio-philosophical view focused on eschatology. In every systematic objectification, in every formal sacralization and elevation of the relative into the absolute, it sees a sign of the end of the world. Following St Simeon the New Theologian, Berdyaev[9] shows that the Fall was the exteriorization and objectification of existence. Eschatology, by contrast, is the returning towards the interior, the re-entry into the aeon of the Spirit. The conception of evil as a phantasmal, illusory state, after the teaching

[6] *La crise de la philosophie occidentale*, 1874; *Les principes philosophiques de la connaissance intégrale*, 1877; *Critique of Abstract Principles*, 1880 (in Russian).
[7] See P. Evdokimov, *L'aspect apophatique de l'argument de saint Anselme*, Journées anselmiennes de l'abbaye du Bec-Hellouin 1959. *Spicilegium Beccense*, p. 233.
[8] See S. Franc, *La connaissance de l'être*, Aubier 1937; *The Inconceivable*, Paris 1939 (in Russian).
[9] *L'Esprit et la liberté*, Ed. Je Sers, Paris 1933. *De la destination de l'homme*, Ed. Je Sers, 1935. *Cinq méditations sur l'existence*, Aubier 1936.

of St Gregory of Nyssa, is intensified when the world is seen in phenomenological terms. Tchaadaev[10] sets chronological history in its eschatological context and Soloviev[11] says that the completion of history is intrinsic to it. For Berdyaev this completion is inescapable, because every work of creation or inspiration is rooted, socialized and democratized in this world. History postulates its end, and therefore its meaning – which brings us back once again to the doctrine of Chalcedon. While Gogol[12] was inwardly torn between the two poles of the formula of Chalcedon, Boucharev[13] was already sketching out a transrational synthesis of the culture as situated in Christ. Dostoyevsky violently rejected any notion of Monophysitism, likewise the monism of the German idealists,[14] and wrote an imposing defence of Christian teaching about humanity and the universe. In the encounter with modern western acosmism, Soloviev, Florensky, Bulgakov, Trubetskoy and Zenovsky have applied their sophiology to solving the problem of the cosmos and of the metaphysical unity of all the dimensions of the created order.

It is a striking paradox that Byzantium, with its thoroughly spiritualized monastic view of the world, should have been inspired to generate such an immensely rich culture. The same spirit was at work in the Russian scholars as they sought to *ecclesiastify* life. Feodorov,[15] the extraordinarily learned scholar and solitary, fought to revive the memory of all the dead who had been so sinfully forgotten, so that their combined wisdom might be put to the service of the Resurrection.

Where the western Church distinguishes between orders of being, the eastern insists on unbroken continuity, seeing them as lesser and greater versions of the same thing. Thus, the 'supernatural' is the natural fully restored to the likeness of God. The truest form of knowing is faith, and the truest form of society is the Church. Accordingly Orthodoxy seeks in the structure of society, indeed in every social organization, the image of the 'absolute Society' of God the Three in One. The Byzantine *symphony* is not a contract or demarcation of rights, but the presentation of the faith, *the application of doctrine*, so as to reveal the catholic nature of all the ministries at the service of the one Kingdom; every office in the Church is charismatic, every believer is a priest, king and prophet of the royal priesthood. In the closed world of phenomena there exist only individual beings; but the divine bestowal of personhood on the human being raises it to the reality of spiritual existence.

In the *Ladder of Divine Ascent* St John Climacus speaks of a succession of incursions into the Spirit, which is also the transformation of the being into light, of which the saints leave traces in their wake. In the 19th century St Seraphim

10 'Lettres philosophiques', in *Téléscope*, 1829; in *Héritage littéraire*, 22-24.
11 *Trois entretiens.* 1900. Trans. Fr. ed. Plon-Nourrit, 1916.
12 *Confession d'un auteur; Correspondance avec des amis.*
13 *Orthodoxy and Reality* (in Russian).
14 His critique of Kant and Hegel aligns him with Kierkegaard.
15 *Philosophy and the Common Cause* (in Russian), Kharbine 1928 (new edition).

centred all his teaching on the spiritualization of human beings by the gifts of the Holy Spirit.

Fr Bulgakov[16] was inspired by the biblical theology of the Presence to study the heavenly origin and mysterious life of the word, the most basic element of thought. 'When Jesus makes himself present to us, we see the mysteries hidden in the Scriptures' (St Simeon). A passage considered in the abstract is dead, and reasoning from it will lead to heresy. The whole significance of the Tradition lies in discovering Christ, whose presence fills all the forms of the faith: 'The faith brings with it not only the arrow, but the Archer as well'.[17] 'Any other approach to the study and reading of the Scriptures,' says St Simeon, 'will simply plunge us into error.' The Presence makes us see works as *symptomatic* of the new Creature in Christ.

From this point of view, A. Kartachov speaks forcefully of an actual *theocracy* and even of a *Christocracy*,[18] combining the most Messianic and eschatological terms with the most concrete and historical. But progress never follows a straight line; evolution and decay take place side by side. Historical realizations are relative. Soloviev used to say that the State can do nothing towards bringing about Paradise except to prevent the world from turning into hell. Such an outlook goes beyond optimism and pessimism; it might even be called tragic optimism, for it depends on human freedom, on a free consent to the Parousia. Feodorov, writing of the conditional nature of the Apocalypse, made this arresting observation: the terrible judgement is possible only because we can conceive of its not happening.

One of the greatest gifts of the Spirit, freedom, presupposes in the Church a refusal to order its life according to any principle of power. This does not in the least rule out hierarchy, but it does rule out clericalism. The *organism* of grace cannot be confined to any organization, let alone be itself organized, and it excludes any principle of formal law. 'Canon law' is not at all like juridical law. It prescribes nothing in terms of Justice and its laws, but in every age draws attention to the forms in which *doctrinal truths* are most suitably incarnated, fleshed out in history; and then it is indicating not principles but life itself.

The only power known to the Church is the unique power of love, the pastoral 'gift of charity', 'fatherly tenderness' that every bishop receives: 'The kings of the Gentiles lord it over them; and those in authority over them are called benefactors. But not so with you' (Luke 22.25-26a). The bishops do not rule but lead, unite and guide. The spiritual attributes of the priesthood do not depend on personal qualities but are functional and objective, opening the way to Jacob's ladder, the sacraments. The authority of a saint, by contrast, is always personal, tran-

[16]*Philosophy of the Name* (in Russian), YMCA Press, 1953.
[17] St Gregory of Nyssa, *Commentary on the Song of Songs*, *P.G.* 44, 852 A-B.
[18] A. Kartachov, *The Rebuilding of Holy Russia* (in Russian), Paris 1956, p. 88.

scending any function, disclosing the coming of the Spirit in his spirit – and here the gift is *personal.*

Orthodoxy is attentive to the 'groanings which cannot be uttered' and does all its theology under the sign of the epiclesis. The Son asks the Father to send the Spirit and so to complete his own sending of the Word. Thus Christ is seen as the great Forerunner of the Paraclete. The strong inclination which every theologian has, to make his theology Christocentric, perfectly expresses the kenosis of the Holy Spirit, who never wishes to be the centre of attention. Fr Bulgakov, writing on the Trinity, has shown conclusively that only a perfectly balanced Trinitarian theology is proof against every deviation. The Fathers bear witness that theology is both prayer and liturgy, entailing the offering of the spiritual sacrifice: 'Be a holy priesthood, to offer spiritual sacrifices acceptable to God through Jesus Christ' (1 Pet. 2.5). In the mystery of the Parousia the Son and the Spirit play a similar part in the Trinitarian economy: they are one in the Father and their diunity mediates to the world the inaccessible face of the Father, expressing the *filiation* with perfect clarity: 'For all who are led by the Spirit of God are children of God' (Rom. 8.14). They are to be 'conformed to the image of his Son, in order that he might be the firstborn within a large family' (Rom. 8.29), so they are 'sons' in the Son, whom the Father adopts in Christ by the Holy Spirit. Filiation bestows on them the status of *heirs* to the Glory. In his exegesis Mgr Cassien[19] throws into relief the Pauline theology of the Church-household, οἰκία, 'the household of God' (Eph. 2.19). The mystical marriage – the family, the household, 'the domestic church', all these images are used with the utmost boldness to refer to the divine Church, the Holy Trinity. 'You have received a spirit of adoption. When we cry, "Abba! Father!" it is that very Spirit bearing witness with our spirit that we are children of God' (Rom. 8.15-16). When we say the Lord's Prayer we are permitted to take upon ourselves the very condition of Christ; during the Liturgy, just before Holy Communion, the priest introduces the prayer with these words: 'And make us worthy, O Master, with boldness and without condemnation to dare to call upon thee, our heavenly God and Father, and to say, *Our Father...*' The eternity of the Father's is opened up to show that humankind was created the child of God, so adoption is only a return to the dignity of that original birth.

---

[19] 'Le Fils et les fils, le Frère et les frères' in *Paulus-Hellas-Oikumene*, Athens 1951; 'Doxology of Divine Love' in *Russian Thought* (in Russian), Paris 1947; 'The Family of God' in *The Ecumenical Review*, vol. IX, 1957.

3

Pro Domo Sua

We have consciously adopted a descriptive, strictly objective approach. Our faith teaches us that the truth is self-evident; it has no need of justification, still less of proofs. Those simplistic apologists who fail to understand this, and rely, like Job's comforters, upon aggressive polemics to make up for their ignorance, cannot stand up to critical scrutiny. It was Job, after all, that confounder and underminer of the too well ordered, whom God in his mysterious wisdom chose for his messenger.

It is perfectly true that Orthodoxy seems disorganized, even at times anarchical; its discipline is often slack; there is a tendency for every theologian to found his own school. But Orthodox catholicity, springing up into our very hearts to sustain and nourish us, is in the world but not of the world, so it cannot be organized, objectified or reduced to a system. There is no formal criterion for determining the ecumenicity of the Councils, but they are none the less real for that, and they govern our whole life; the 'power of love', which is the spiritual essence of episcopacy, is subject to no legal formula. We affirm and shall affirm till our dying breath the evangelical message that the personal and the liberty of the children take precedence over the general, the abstract and the organized. So, for example, the 'disorder' of divorce is allowed, even at the cost of contradicting the 'letter', because the personal must never be sacrificed to the 'order' of the collective. The canons and discipline are there to *serve doctrine*. If everything in the Church were regimented we should no longer be at ease with ourselves or with God. Because our conception of the Church is eucharistic, it is present to us in its fullness wherever we find it, with a freedom that cannot be constrained, centralized or standardized. Federalism means the democratization of the Spirit, but universalism has a fatal tendency to spiritual totalitarianism. 'Organized truth' for the masses results in a uniformly instructed and docile herd. Aristocratic disorder makes us suffer, but being openly hieratic, it safeguards the uniqueness of every individual and his destiny. The Church is taught by the Church, its living Tradition incorporating as few doctrinal formulas and as many opinions as possible. But the very impossibility of dispassionately taking the Tradition apart and weighing the purity of each element reminds us that it is not a piece of machinery, but a living mystery. It is a tree, luxuriant and firmly planted on a rock; at the very sight of it we realize that any attempt at simplification would be hopeless.

A great Latin theologian, in his otherwise admirable book on Dostoyevsky, says something very Roman. He considers that in the Legend in *The Brothers Karama-*

zov, Christianity tends to side with the Inquisitor, while Christ represents the destructive anarchy of the Church. 'Miracle, mystery and power' make up the Church's structure, and without these three principles what will become of its theocratic authority? Now, for the eastern Church the miracle is in the sacraments, the mystery is in illumination by the Holy Spirit, and the power is only that of love. It is in the most intimate experience of God, which paradoxically hides much more that it reveals, in the very mystery of grace, that East and West draw apart.

Orthodox anarchy is highly relative, and only surface-deep. In doctrine and worship, in the one thing necessary which is the Eucharist, we are all members one of another. The mysterious voice of Christ speaks to us unceasingly throughout history, 'Do not quench the Spirit', do not enslave yourselves to the too well ordered at the cost of a violated conscience and the ultimate danger of 'organizing' the breathing of the Spirit.

We do not have spiritual directors, we have confessors and spiritual fathers and we are guided by the blood of the martyrs. Whoever cannot bear the 'yoke' of Orthodox freedom will go somewhere else, which in practice means becoming 'fundamentalist' – more papist than the Pope, or grotesquely Protestant: anabaptist, sectarian, fanatical: 'They went out from us, but they did not belong to us' (1 John 2.19).

In Orthodoxy freedom and order are not opposed to each other; freedom prospers in the kind of orderliness displayed in its clear doctrinal system and integrated liturgical structure, because it is essentially mysterious and hidden. However, it will resist power imposed from outside or the anarchy of priestly egalitarianism.

The spiritual authority of the *startzy*, the inner monasticism of every layman, the special gifts of every faithful believer, belong to the theology of the Holy Spirit, and not the theology of the Institution in the western sense. Of the latter it is better to speak in terms of bald descriptive fact, which is by its very nature unorganizable.

Today East and West are merely geographical terms; truth is freed from all territorial constraint and calls us to a true universalism. As the modern person in his or her nakedness confronts death, the divine choice offered is starker than ever: 'I have set before you life and death, blessings and curses. Choose life so that you and your descendants may live' (Deut. 30.19). The options crystallize into the divine and the demonic; there is nothing in between. The world is suffused with intense longing for the deepest truth, for time that opens on to eternity, for space that opens on to the Kingdom. It is the same longing with which the new creature yearns to be brought fully into the Presence.

Christianity is looking into the depths; by its response to the challenge – Fill them with love – it will stand or fall. 'Let anyone with ears to hear listen...' Under the scrutiny of the light from Tabor searching into every geographical place we must all accept the ultimate freedom: to follow the Virgin in her *fiat* at the Incarnation, by uttering on behalf of history the eschatological *fiat* to the Parousia. The Church, the liturgical place for all God's children, fulfilling its vocation on earth while turned towards the 'Dayspring from on high', is already the prefiguration of the Church of the Kingdom.

PART I
Anthropology

1

The Eastern Premises of Patristic Theology

Political events at the end of the fifth century separated East from West. As the Roman Empire disintegrated, the great cultural centres of the East – Alexandria, Antioch, Constantinople, Seleucia-Ctesiphon – grew in strength. From the fifth century onwards, Rome and Byzantium found themselves willy-nilly having to deal with different problems, so that their local traditions drew apart, and theological reflection proceeded in different social and intellectual climates. In the West the influence of Augustine (never well known in the East) took a strong hold, and despite Scot Erigena, familiarity with the Fathers declined. Not until the appearance in the twelfth century of the first translation of the works of St John of Damascus was this process to be reversed.

However, in referring to the 'tradition' of East or West we are aware that the word has now become altogether too broad to be applied in any geographical sense. There is no strict separation between the Byzantine, Syriac, modern Greek, Romanian or Slavonic traditions (the Nestorian, Coptic, Syrian, Armenian and Georgian writings are still little studied or known today).

Nevertheless, certain identifiable dominant characteristics have evolved through the centuries; it is possible to speak of a direction in eastern Orthodoxy, even of an instinct, notwithstanding the coexistence at the heart of the same communion of differences in style and emphasis.[1]

---

[1] In the 17th century there were westernizing Orthodox: e.g. the Romanizing Metropolitan Peter Moghila and the Calvinizing Patriarch Cyril Lucaris.

By 'eastern' or even 'Greek' we refer to the great Patristic line; St Irenaeus, Clement of Alexandria, the two Cyrils, St Athanasius, the Cappadocians, the Corpus Areopagiticum, Leontius of Byzantium, St Maximus, St John Damascene, St Simeon the New Theologian, Nicolas Cabasilas, St Gregory Palamas. And then the monastic tradition: St Macarius of Egypt, Evagrius, St Nil of Sinai, Mark the Hermit, Diodochus of Photice (Centuries of Spiritual Perfection), St John Climacus (The Ladder of Divine Ascent), the Letters of Barsanuphius and John, monks of the monastery of Seridos; John Moschus (The Spiritual Meadow), the Centuries of Thalassius, an Abbot in Libya; the Catecheses of Isaac of Nineveh, the hymns of St Ephrem the Syrian; Theodore the Studite, Nil Sorsky, Paissy Velichovsky, St Seraphim of Sarov. Finally there are the decisions of the Councils, and the liturgical and iconographical tradition.

1. PATRISTIC THEOLOGY

The soul reflecting on itself can at the most sense its origins, grasp its creaturely status. By natural reason it can become aware of the glory of God and even conceive of 'absolute Being'. But further than this it cannot go, because according to St Paul (1 Cor. 8.3 and Gal. 4.9), the awareness of God (as 'absolute Value' and Father) is a sheer gift of revelation. It is God's initiative, his mindfulness of humanity, that awakes the human response, the calling on the name of God: 'You that love my soul'.[2] This revelation springs from the divine philanthropy whose pre-eternal decision it was to take flesh and be conditioned by the *place* of incarnation: humankind in the image of God, freely endowed with faith and the innate grace of contemplative openness: 'The human being contains within a certain measure of the awareness of God'.[3]

Contemplation, *'theoria'*, comes from Θεωρεῖν, to look closely at something. What begins as simple perception can be raised to intellectual seeing, and thence to superintellectual seeing. Multiple points of view contemplate the many, the eye of the soul sees the one reality, the divine Monad.[4] This kind of vision – never abstract, because its end is love – is also 'theognosis', spiritual union, participation. Ascetic *catharsis*[5] certainly purifies the way in which we look at the outside world, but we still learn nothing of God by looking at his works except his power. Only by the inward experience of enstasy and the divine indwelling can the soul transcend all purely intellectual knowing (the 'theology of symbols') and attain to God, as he offers himself in his grace; this is the very concrete experience of direct, not conceptual, awareness, the 'spiritual feeling' of the divine nearness, the presence of God in the soul.

The East distinguishes between, on the one hand, 'intelligence'[5] concerned with the coexistence of opposites and their reconciliation in 'unity and identity by grace',[7] and on the other, 'reason', discursive thought based on the logic of contradiction and formal identity, directed towards the multiple, and hence tending to exclude God. Now 'intelligence resides in the heart, thought in the brain'.[8] This explains why the Orthodox faith is never defined in terms of intellectual as-

---

[2] St Gregory of Nyssa, in *Cant.* h. 2; *P.G.* 44, 801 A.
[3] St Gregory of Nyssa, *Beatit.*, or. 6; *P.G.* 44, 1269 BC. This knowledge is always charismatic. Origen is very categorical on the subject, the grace of *theoria* raises persons above themselves. See *Contra Celsum, P.G.* 11, 1481 C; 1484 C.
[4] St Gregory of Nyssa, *P.G.* 44, 952 A.
[5] *Catharsis*: an effort of purification.
[6] According to St Paul, those who are spiritual possess 'the mind of Christ' – the wisdom taught by the Spirit (1 Cor. 2.10-16).
[7] St Maximus, *De ambig., P.G.* 91, 1308 B.
[8] Evagrius, *Gnostic Centuries*; See K. Rahner, 'Die geistliche Lehre des Evagrius Pontikus', in *ZAM*, vol. 8, 1933.

sent, but is a matter of living proof, a 'sense of the transcendent': 'Lord, the woman who had fallen into a great number of sins, when she *perceived thy divinity...* '[9] An essential aspect of faith is the experience of love and knowledge inseparably united in the heart-spirit, working together to transcend the intellectual and sentimental, bringing about *metanoia*, the complete turning round of the whole human person.[10] St Simeon the New Theologian goes so far as to deny the presence of the Holy Spirit in anyone who is not himself aware of it and who thinks that to be reclothed in Christ it is enough to be baptized.[11] Diadochus speaks of 'feeling', αἴσθησις, and Macarius of 'spiritual feeling' – awareness of the presence is a spiritual gift. The term has nothing to do with sensuality or psychological emotion, but emphasizes all the concreteness of real-life experience of the spirit. It means the sensitivity of the *nous* whose intellectual character is formed by mystical experience. St Gregory of Nyssa[12] calls this grasping of the presence of God in the soul the 'consciousness of the Parousia', αἴσθησις παρουσία, and, also following Origen, he speaks of the 'consciousness of God' and of the 'sense of God' ('the soul possesses a certain power of touching, by which it touches the Word'[13]); St Maximus names it 'higher sensation'[14] and says, 'I call the experience true knowing in action, which goes beyond any concept ... participation in the object, which reveals itself beyond any thought';[15] similar participation is experienced through contemplation, and is called by St Gregory Θεολογία ου Θεογνωσία.[16]

Theology contains a doctrinal element, the objective *didascalia* or catechesis of the Church, but draws its essential nourishment from the spiritual riches of the teaching of the saints and their experience of the Word. One of the works of

---

9 Matins of Great Wednesday, 8th tone, hymn of Cassia.

10 Eastern theology is opposed to any dividing up of the mind into autonomous compartments: love, cognition, faith, hope. Love, if it is spiritual, is intelligent, and the intellect situated in the heart is ruled by charity; faith, according to the Epistle to the Hebrews, is 'the evidence of things not seen', and is therefore a pre-conceptual and supra-rational intuition of the heavenly mysteries. The Holy Spirit is called by the Fathers, 'intellective light', transforming multiplicity into unity by participation in the ineffable archetype of the Trinity. The Holy Spirit is the divine Theologian, for according to St Cyril of Alexandria: 'The Trinity is glorified by you' (*Hom. div.* 4; *P.G.* 77, 992). So the Spirit is certainly not hypostasized love but the 'Giver of love' out of the utter perfection of the Trinity. In the light of this fullness, faith without love is illusory (St Macarius, *Homil. spir.* XV, 1; *P.G.* 34, 761) and faith without knowledge is valueless (St Dorotheus, *Doctr.* XIV, 3; *P.G.* 88, 1776).

11 *Chapitres théologiques, gnostiques et pratiques*, 1-36, 3-47, 3-58.

12 *P.G.* 44, 1001, C.

13 *In Cant.*, *P.G.* 44, 780 C; 1001 B.

14 *Cent. gnost.* 2, 74; *P.G.* 90, 1160 A.

15 *Qu. a. T.* 60; *P.G.* 90, 1160 A.

16 *P.G.* 44, 376 A; 44, 372 D; similarly, for St Simeon the New Theologian, to theologize is to give an account of what one can see with the aid of the divine light.

Denys the Pseudo-Areopagite is called Περί μυστικῆς θεολογίας – *Mystical Theology*; this is the theology of the mystery that can be known only by revelation and participation. It takes hold of the utterances of God at the heart of the *phanies*, the manifestations of God. The divine transcendence teaches us that we can never approach God except by withdrawing from him, and in so doing, finding ourselves already in him.

The doctrinal controversies over the Truth at the time of the Councils were never concerned with purely theoretical knowledge; their aim was the highly practical one of identifying the only right path to salvation and union with God. Unlike the speculations of the Gnostics, they dealt with questions of life or death for mankind. What preserves the mystical experience of the Fathers from any sectarian excess or heretical distortion is its firm doctrinal structure, its ordering according to the pattern of the *Opus Dei*. Theology thus understands liturgy in very broad terms as 'to gather up all things' in Christ (Eph. 1.10), assembling for the Eucharist. In their writings the Fathers often move seamlessly from theorizing to prayer and dialogue with God. In these instances St Isaac the Syrian sees 'the flame of things' – perhaps the best definition of theology there is. Much more than systematic science, art uncovers the hidden truth of the things of heaven and earth and opens the way to participation-communion with the eternal world of God. While always incorporating the doctrinal element of catechesis, theology aspires at its highest to become living theognosis: the *way of experience to union with God.*

For the Fathers, theology is essentially the contemplation of the Trinity: Θεωρία τῆς ἁγίας Τριάδος.[17] Patristic tradition resolutely denies the possibility of any direct vision of the divine essence, which is radically unknowable; the light can be seen only in reflection, supremely in the mirror of the purified soul, which 'receives into itself the disc of the sun', and is plunged at last into the sense of the nearness of God.

This knowledge through the indwelling of the Word is mystical theology. Its central feature is the divine 'Parousia' in the soul, which cannot be apprehended except by the eyes of faith, 'the eyes of the Dove'. It is a question not of knowing something about God, but of 'having God in oneself'.[18] Where 'symbolic theology' leaves off, awareness of the Word's enlightening presence begins to take hold. Evagrius of Pontus,[19] whose influence pervades all eastern spirituality, asserts that 'one who has not seen God cannot speak of him,'[20] but he eschews any

---

[17] St Gregory of Nazianzus, *Or.* 15; Evagrius, *Cent.*, 7, 52; *Practicos* 1, 3; *P.G.* 40, 1221 D.
[18] St Gregory of Nyssa, *Sermon on the Sixth Beatitude.*
[19] Evagrius, Deacon of Pontus (d. about 399). The 5th Council condemned his Origenist doctrinal deviations, but his spirituality is perfectly orthodox. See Villier, 'Aux sources de la spiritualité de saint Maxime: les œuvres d'Evagre de Pontique', in *Revue d'Ascet. et de Myst.*, IX, 1930; I. Hausherr, in *Orientalia christiana*, XXII, 2, 1931; *Le traité de l'oraison d'Evagre le Pontique*, in *RAM*, vol. XV, 1934.
[20] *Cent.* 5, 26.

unorthodox interpretation by explaining, 'one who longs to see the face of the Father who is in heaven, does not expect for a moment to perceive any outline or a face while he is praying'.[21] Through proper contemplation, vision is internalized in the soul, which becomes 'the dwelling-place of God':[22] 'A person at prayer is reclothed with light without form, he is *the place where God is*'.[23] Theory and practice are here closely connected: 'hasten to transform your image to the likeness of the Archetype'.[24] Theology comes to meet eucharistic reality: 'the essential nature of the being that shares itself – μετεχόμενον – must transform the one that shares – τό μετέχον[25] – into itself', 'by union with the Immortal, humanity shares in immortality'.[26]

Theology in its higher form becomes the point where aesthetic *catharsis* converges with the contemplation of the light reflected on the soul through unitive prayer, so that St Gregory of Nyssa and Evagrius can define it in a way that explains the term 'mystical': 'if you are a theologian, you will pray truly; and if you pray truly, you are a theologian'.[27] The theologian is one who knows how to pray; the liturgical *opus* assimilates the human spirit to its own purpose: unceasing communion with God. Theology then becomes the describing in theological terms of the illuminating presence of the Word. It is in no way a speculation on the mystical texts but the mystical way itself, the *generator of unity*.[28] It entails a return to bareness of the spirit, a stripping-down to the pre-conceptual state of pure receptiveness enjoyed by Adam – 'contemplation was Adam's privilege in Paradise'[29] – and then necessitates above all the 'spiritual gift of prayer'.[30]

Theology is thus exalted into a spiritual ministry, for 'nobody can know God unless God himself teaches him' and 'there is no other way of knowing God than by living in him...'; 'to speak of God is a fine thing' says St Gregory of Nazianzus with tongue in cheek, 'but [justifying his title of the Theologian] it is better still to purify oneself for God.'[31]

Orthodoxy is not the religion of the Word in the Reformation sense; it does not express itself in terms of a dialectic which, even when it is 'paradoxical', remains none the less conceptual. The eastern Church, in reading the Scriptures, seeks to go beyond them to the one who uttered them: 'before every reading, pray and beseech God to reveal himself to you', teaches St Ephraim. It is a dialogue between the human spirit and the Spirit of God, but a dialogue which engenders a unity that 'deifies': as St Simeon says,

---

24 *Gnosticos*, 151.
25 St Gregory of Nyssa, *P.G.* 44, 740 A.
26 *Great Catech.*, 37, 12.
27 *Treatise on Prayer*, 60.
28 St Denys, *De div. nomin.*, 701 b.
29 Dorotheus, *Doctrina*, I, 1.
30 Evagrius, *Treatise on Prayer*, 87.
31 St Gregory of Nazianzus, *Oratio*, XXXII, 12; *P.G.* 36, 188.

'God unites himself only to gods.'[32] Origen urged his theological pupils to pray for 'kisses of the Word'. A theologian, for St Macarius, is one 'taught by God' – θεοδίδακτος – and it is the Spirit, according to St Simeon, who turns a scholar into a theologian, for the important thing is not to be instructed intellectually about God, but to be *filled with God*: 'so that having received him in us, we might become what he is.'[33]

The Fathers were perfectly familiar with the culture of their time; they made use of all the techniques of philosophy, but they always aspired to go beyond conceptual theology to 'the science that becomes love'.[34]

As opposed to any form of passive quietism, grace requires *praxis*, it is σύμπραξις, and while the virtues are God's gift, human beings are still called to contribute their part of 'sweat of each of the virtues'.[35] St Simeon said that no one should be given sacramental authority who believed in the sufficiency of outward form alone. For the Fathers the word 'virtue' meant predominantly 'strength' or 'health': 'by virtue the human being is made similar to God.'[36] According to St Basil, 'true theology frees us from the passions'[37] and Nicetas Stethatos teaches that knowledge needs to be energetic, expressed in acts. 'Theology without action is the theology of the devils,' says St Maximus.[38] The dynamism of faith evokes in response 'the divine gift of the Spirit which reveals the meaning of theology.'[39] *Theognosis*, being spirit-directed, presupposes that the divine light has already descended on the soul that has been purified by spiritual discipline. Ultimately the Spirit is just as much the true subject of theological knowledge, manifesting and interpreting the Word, as he is the object, for 'he will take what is mine and declare it to you' (John 16.15). The revelation is perfectly one: it originates in the Father, is at work in the Son, and is completed by the Spirit. Jesus speaks of his manifestation in terms of communion: 'we will come to them and make our home with them' (John 14.23), which is why 'God says that blessedness is not the knowledge of certain things concerning himself, but his dwelling in humankind.'[40] 'I thank you that you, the God reigning over all, have become one spirit with me, without confusion and without separation.'[41] The theandric principle teaches that the human being is not a true individual,

[32] *Philokalia*, English translation by Kadloubovsky, London 1951. p. 113.
[33] St Gregory of Nyssa, *Cant.* 44, 740 A.
[34] St Gregory of Nyssa, *P.G.* 44, 96 C.
[35] AB. Isaiah, *Logos*, 22, N. 8.
[36] St Gregory of Nyssa, *P.G.* 44, 1177 A.
[37] *P.G.* 31, 581 A.
[38] *Ep.* 20; 581 A.
[39] Evagrius, *Cent.* 4, 40.
[40] St Gregory of Nyssa, *VIth Homily on the Beatitudes*, *P.G.* 44. 1272 C.
[41] St Simeon, St Gregory of Nyssa, 'Hymns of Divine Love', in *Vie Spirituelle* 28, 1931, p. 202.

a person, except as a member of the Body; human consciousness is designed to work in communion with others and in cooperation with divine grace.

Theologians are not forced to strive for an impossibly high degree of sanctity, but ascetic *catharsis* is required of all. The approach to the charismatic ministry, to handling the holy things of God, must be with trembling, in order to resist any overweening claims of a purely encyclopaedic science that thinks it has all the answers: 'whoever turn their gaze towards theology keep their life and faith in perfect harmony.'[42] Orthodoxy is famous for its sparingness in bestowing the title 'theologian'. Only three people possess it as an attribute of their sanctity: St John the Theologian, the most mystical of the four Evangelists, St Gregory the Theologian, celebrant of the Holy Trinity, and St Simeon the New Theologian,[43] the author of hymns in praise of union. This choice shows clearly that theology is a matter not of reason but, as St Paul says, of 'the mind of Christ' (1 Cor. 2.16); at its highest, stripped of all unwarranted speculation, it aims at deifying union, *theosis*, and progresses by way of knowing-and-communion to participation; and 'the being that shares itself must transform into itself the one who shares.'[44] The Fathers insist that ascesis is the preparation for theology, and that prayer is a state – κατάστασις – of the mind.[45]

2. THE THEOLOGICAL METHOD OF THE FATHERS

Eastern theology, directed towards God, can be seen at once to be apophatic *theognosis*, the negation of every human or anthropomorphic definition, picking a way through the shadows, skirting the inaccessible divine light. The apophatic principle states, concerning God: we know only that he is – ὅτι ἐστίν[46] – not what he is – τί ἐστιν.[47] It was at the end of the 13th century, in the wake of the Augustinian tradition and its desire for direct vision, that there developed in the West a precise theology of the beatific vision and of knowing God face to face. In the East the emphasis was on the impenetrability of God's secret nature: 'no one has ever seen God.' The Son has rendered him knowable, but the only 'face to face' knowledge is that of the incarnate Son, who is the mysterious imprint of the Father. The radically transcendent essence of God is never seen, but there is utterly real participation in the uncreated energies; there is therefore no possibility of direct beatific vision. St John Chrysostom denied the vision of the divine

---

[42] St Gregory of Nyssa, *In Ps.* c. 14; *P.G.* 44, 577 D.
[43] 'One of the most vigorous poetic temperaments of eastern Christianity', according to P. Maas, *EOR*, 1928, p. 97.
[44] St Gregory of Nyssa, *P.G.* 44, 740 A.
[45] Evagrius, *Cent.*, suppl. 29.
[46] And again, existence here is certainly not that of creatures.
[47] St Maximus, *P.G.* 91, 1229 C; 91, 1224 BC.

essence even for the saints in heaven.[48] At the Council of Florence, Mark of Ephesus denied it even for the angels. According to St Isaac the Syrian, the vision of God can never suppress faith, but makes it 'second faith', faith of a higher order:[49] a vision of the invisible, which loses none of its invisibility. The essence of God is beyond any name, any utterance, which is why we have a multiplicity of names: Good, Righteous, Almighty. And even when we call him infinite and not begotten, by using the negative we are confessing our powerlessness and verging on apophaticism. God is absolutely incomparable. He is that in any case because there exists no possible scale of comparison. When we say God or Creator, we are referring only to that aspect of him turned towards the world, the God of 'economy', of his providence; never God in himself. Positive, cataphatic, 'symbolic' theology, applies only to his revealed attributes, the manifestations of God in the world. This recognition of God in his acts is possible only thanks to *revelation*; all discussion or logical deduction concerning him is immediately ruled out, because his Being cannot be described in words. Expressing him conceptually can only be an exercise in approximation, using language 'creatively'; the reality behind all such talk is absolutely original, irreducible to any system of thought. A 'logical' God, to whom we ascribed our own logical principle as a divine attribute, would be only an idol of our own making. Round the depth of God there is a circle of silence.

The cataphatic method proceeds by affirmation, but in defining and naming God it limits him and renders his own teaching *incomplete* – 'for now we see in a mirror, dimly ... now I know only in part' (1 Cor. 13.12). It has to be *completed* by the apophatic method which proceeds by negation, or opposition to all that belongs to this world. This is by no means to belittle positive theology but to be clear about its scope and limitations. Negative theology accustoms us to insurmountable distance, which is also our safeguard: 'conceptions make idols of God,' says St Gregory of Nyssa; 'nothing can be grasped except by wonder.'[50] Now wonder, if genuine, is precisely symptomatic of the attitude taken up at a point beyond all knowledge, 'beyond even unknowing, at the supreme height of the mystical writings, where the mysteries of theology, simple, unconditional, invariable, are laid bare in a darkness of silence beyond the light.'[51] By contrast, the sensory and the conceptual blunt the hidden meaning and lead to guessing and error. This is nothing to do with agnosticism, for 'by that very unknowing, he knows what passes understanding.'[52] Nor is it anything to do with human powerlessness; it concerns the unfathomable and unknowable depth of the divine being.

---

[48] See Tixeron, *Histoire des Dogmes*, vol. 2, p. 201; similarly St Maximus, *Commentary on the Celestial Hierarchies of Denys*, 4, *P.G.* 4, 56 BC.
[49] Ed. Bedjan, p. 320.
[50] *De vita Moys.*, *P.G.* 44, 377 B; *In Cant.*, *P.G.* 44, 1028 D.
[51] Denys, *Myst. Theol.*, *P.G.* 3, 1000.
[52] Denys, *Myst. Theol.*, *P.G.* 3. 1001.

The indistinctness inherent in faith safeguards the mysterious *nearness of God*. Mysterious, because paradoxically the more God is present, the more he remains hidden in shadow. The expression 'dazzling shadow'[53] is an attempt to convey his utterly real nearness and at the same time his utter elusiveness; the human being can hope to experience only 'the drops of the night.'[54] That is why faith, in its fullest sense, seems to St Gregory of Nyssa[55] the only way to union, because it presupposes the complete detachment and surrender of the soul. The mystical darkness becomes one with the mystical light, culminating in the highest self-renunciatory understanding and sacrificial love; unlike any philosophical mode of knowing, it is 'knowledge by similarity' or knowledge by analogy and participation. It is not reducible to a mere corrective principle, a precaution against overstepping the mark,[56] but constitutes a self-sufficient and distinct theological method.

This is not to say that mystical knowledge is unattainable, but that this knowledge is present only in the degree to which it transcends itself, and so saves its soul while losing it. Apophatic negation elevates the human spirit and prepares it to be the 'place of God'. Nothing can then open it except a sovereign initiative from God. The terms Super-good and Super-existent, for example, are negation-affirmations that enable us to *describe* the inconceivable with a degree of positiveness. But this happens only when the spirit is at the point where it is plunged into the creative experience of unity.

The liturgical prayer, 'come, O faithful ones, let us meet with uplifted hearts in the upper room', invites us to an elevation of spirit *nearer to God* by our participation in the higher order of being: 'upper room' both signifies that order, and refers to the mystery of union through the Eucharist. It is never a matter of adapting the dogmatic antinomies to our logic, but of changing our nature by adapting it to the order of the Holy Spirit, i.e., deification. In the course of seeking God, the human being is found by him; in the course of pursuing divine truth, the human being is seized by it and *lifted to the level of eternity in the Kingdom*. 'To find God you must seek him without ceasing ... truly to see God is never to have tired of desiring him.'[57] The apophatic method is itself a powerful instructor to every theologian in the proper attitude that his discipline requires: *humanity does not speculate, but is changed*.

In its own helplessness, in the act of renouncing its self-mastery, the soul finds God. By unconditional self-offering, humility in action, it is made receptive and

---

[53] St Gregory of Nyssa, *Vit. Moys.*, *P.G.* 44, 1001 B.
[54] St Gregory of Nyssa, *P.G.* 44, 1057 A.
[55] *P.G.* 45, 945 D.
[56] St Thomas, *Quaestiones disputatae*, qu, VII, a, 5.
[57] St Gregory of Nyssa, *P.G.* 46, 97 A; 44, 404 D.

prepared for contemplation. Stripped and purified, it keeps holy vigil, ready for
the coming, the Parousia, of God, and the experience of his closeness. True theology is to look with the eyes of the Dove, the Holy Spirit, and, beyond the multiplicity of points of view, to gaze on the divine Monad, who 'remains hidden
even in his epiphany.' [58]

[58] St Maximus, *Amb.*, *P.G.* 91, 1048 D, 1049 A.

2

Anthropology[1]

1. INTRODUCTION

The Fathers of the Church were never interested in constructing a complete anthropological system. It is true that, in the course of refining their theological language, they always spoke of humanity in terms of its correspondence to the 'image', but except for St Gregory of Nyssa, who wrote a treatise, *De opificio hominis*, they confined themselves to a few passages on the subject, and the occasional expression of interest.

Side by side with theology, there was the 'voice from the desert', the experience of the ascetics and their total awareness of the depths of depravity; this was practical, applied anthropology, telling us directly about the 'invisible struggle' for the truth about human nature. And finally St Maximus the Confessor, St Simeon the New Theologian, and others with the gift of seeing 'with the eye of the creator', have provided masterly systematic accounts of their mystical contemplation.

St Photius, Patriarch of Constantinople (d. 891), speaks from the heart of the Patristic tradition when he says that it is 'in its own makeup that humankind first encounters *the enigma of theology*'.[2] Because human beings are created after the image of God the Three in One,[3] their life is theological by virtue of their very humanity; they are the 'theological place' par excellence.

The 'image' as a means to knowledge offers two possible methods: ascending or descending. St Augustine[4] examines the human soul, and from the image in-

---

1 See P. Kern, *The Anthropology of St Gregory Palamas*, YMCA Press, 1950 (in Russian); G. Florovsky, *Les Pères de l'Eglise d'Orient des IVe-VIIIe siècles* (2 vol., 1937); L. Karsavine, *The Holy Fathers and Doctors of the Eastern Church*, Paris 1926 (in Russian); V. Lossky, *The Mystical Theology of the Eastern Church*, Cambridge: James Clark 1957; P. de Labriolle, *Histoire de la litterature latine chrétienne*, Paris 1944; A. Puech, *Histoire de la litterature grecque chrétienne*, Paris 1930; F. Cayré, *Précis de Patrologie et d'Histoire de la Théologie*, Paris 1930; B. Altaner, *Patrologie*, Herder, 1938.
2 *Amphilochia*, question CCLII.
3 For the Fathers 'theology' means above all Trinitarian theology. When it came to discipline, Trinitarian heresies were the most severely punished.
4 'Self-knowledge and knowledge of God are so intimately bound together that the heart at the same instant knows itself, and through itself knows God.' (E. von Ivanca, 'La connaissance immédiate de Dieu chez saint Augustin', *Scholastik*, 1938, p. 522).

scribed there, progresses to the idea of God, so making, in methodological terms, *an anthropology of God.*[5] St Gregory of Nyssa,[6] pursuing the theory of conformity, proceeds from God, the *prototype*,[7] to the human, the *type*, which is defined as essentially the image of Him who is. By means of the divine, he 'creates' the human. Thus the eastern Fathers compose *the theology of humankind*. The anthropology, moreover, will differ according to the moment when it is said to originate. If humankind is considered only within the bounds of its earthly history, from the Fall onwards, the reading of the Bible will begin at the third chapter of Genesis and stop at the account of the Last Judgement.

St Augustine, propounder of the doctrine of original sin and the pessimistic notion of the *massa damnata*, laid the strongest emphasis on the utter corruption of human nature. Such a vision issues logically and tragically in the doctrine of predestination. While the Bishop of Hippo stopped short of this fearsome consequence out of pastoral considerations, there were others, during the Reformation, who eagerly pursued his argument to its pitiless conclusion: double predestination.[8] According to this, Christ in *his mercy* shed his blood only for his elect, and God even in the act of creating the world intended a state of separation; from the very beginning there was to be a place for the damned, hell, and a category of human beings to fill it; and this is supposed to show *his justice*.

We can admire the wise prudence of the Orthodox for never having sought to formulate a doctrine of the final destiny of humankind; they are content to leave it as a mystery that cannot be put into words, all speculation about time and eternity, which is in any case precarious, being prevented by the scriptural expression, αἰῶνας τῶν αἰώνων – 'ages of ages', a term so imprecise as to mean no more than any elapse of time. On the other hand, the eternal coexistence of heaven and hell eternalizes the dualism of good and evil: it may not have been from everlasting, but it will last for ever.

Sin, being a perversion, will set limits of its own to any anthropology that takes as its starting point the *demoniacal element* of human nature: in the beginning the angel with a fiery sword, barring the way to Paradise, and at the end the dreadful assize and the lake of fire. The way to Paradise and the Kingdom of God, a realm of utter transcendence, will be through a breach torn in this earthly existence.[9] If the anthropology is not based on a sound doctrine of the image of

---

[5] This is the psychological theory of processions, the close inspection of the human heart to reveal the image of the Trinity within it. Cf. Augustine, *De Trinitate*, *P.L.* 42, 931-982.

[6] *De opificio hominis; Macrinaria; Ad imagem Dei.*

[7] Humankind cannot be defined except from above, from its divine Archetype, and that is why Orthodox theology does not accept the idea of 'pure nature'.

[8] To allow election to grace and reject election to death is 'puerile', 'a very great foolishness', according to Calvin.

[9] In the Office of Christmas the liturgical text based on John 1.51 says that the angel with the flaming sword goes away from the Tree of Life: the Eucharist.

God, the Incarnation will be an act of divine arbitrariness, something added and extraneous (*gratia forensis*), an incursion of the strange and transcendent, compelling the human by means of grace (*gratia irresistibilis*).

Eastern anthropology is founded explicitly on the *divine element* in human nature, the *imago Dei*, and so goes back to the state that existed before original sin. Indeed, for the Fathers, the human being is always defined by its earliest condition, that of Eden, which, even after the Fall, presses with all its weight on his earthly existence. Eschatology as a dimension of time is intrinsic to the experience of history; it allows us a mystical grasp of the first and last things, and therefore presupposes a certain immanence of Paradise and of the Kingdom of God. 'Paradise is become again accessible to humankind, says St Gregory of Nyssa.[10] We have an inborn longing for immortality and Paradise. These, although lost, always remain definitive of our true nature, and are therefore the origin of all longing, and this longing finds its answer in the entirely real presence of the Kingdom. And liturgical time is eternity *here and now*; liturgically oriented space is *the here and now* of the Kingdom.[11] Eternity is neither before nor after time, but operates within its own dimensions.

The Last Judgement still belongs to time; it is turned towards history, examining the past. Anthropology, then, leads eschatologically on to its true end: the *sacramentum futuri*, the integration of the whole earthly economy with the Kingdom of Heaven. The holiness of the new creature rises above the upheavals of history that announce the coming of the Kingdom, already in this earthly life. The titles accorded to the Virgin in the liturgy – 'Paradise', 'Door of the Kingdom', 'Heaven' – are not flights of poetic fancy, but expressions of the liturgical realism that gives to history a kind of axis: the utter reality of the new creature and its destiny in Christ. 'The Christian soul is returned from Paradise', say the Fathers; history is the 'quaking of the soul (of humanity) before the doors of the Kingdom.'[12]

Different understandings of God and of his relationship with humankind have given rise to endless subtle variations in theology. The Incarnation itself can be explained as an ordinance designed to regulate everything from alpha to omega. Christ will save because he is predestined to be the Saviour, as Judas is to be the traitor. The grace of salvation will act *on* humanity, despite and if necessary *against* it. This is salvation by grace alone, where the *felix culpa* is *felix* to such an extent that it releases the unstoppable flow of atonement and its medium, the 'organized grace' of the Church.

---

[10] *P.G.* 49, 401; also St Gregory of Nyssa, *Treatise on Virginity*, *P.G.* 46, 374 C D.
[11] *Annus est Christus* – liturgically the whole year and every day is the day of Salvation. *Templum est Christus* – every point in space is a particle of the *Templum mundi*, sacred in proportion as it participates in the universal presence of Christ.
[12] St Isaac, Wensinck, p. 310.

Humankind's role, its share in the work of its salvation will always keep its antinomic, paradoxical aspect. On the one hand, 'If God weighed our merits, then no
one would enter into the Kingdom,'[13] and on the other hand, 'God can do anything
except force humanity to love him.'[14] In the same way, when an ascetic abases
himself through acts of humility, he is subjectively, in his own eyes, worthless; but
objectively, for God, for the world and for the angels, he is the new creature of in-
estimable human worth; any attempt to explain or analyse this mystery destroys it
and immediately distorts everything. 'It is only mercenaries who calculate,' says
St John Chrysostom. The mystery is well expressed in the doctrine of the agreement
of the two wills in Christ. This affirms the completeness of Christ's human will,
which is 'changeless' precisely because, while having the potential to change, it
freely follows and conforms itself to the 'changeless' divine will. The apparent determinism of that 'changeless' at the heart of the operation of love, is the most paradoxical manifestation of freedom. For freedom also possesses its own spirit of
renunciation and sacrifice. But inspiration – *in-spirare* – that is accomplished only
by total self-giving to the other cannot be determinism; indeed, it spells destruction
to selfish or possessive restriction in all its forms, for self-offering is the very formula of freedom in which love finds its highest expression.

'You will know the truth, and the truth will make you free.' (John 8.32) When
we first meet it, we cannot know the truth otherwise than freely, for any good
thing, if forced, is turned into evil; but in return the truth brings a positive content
to every form of freedom, fills it (Eph. 4.21-24), directs it, and in so doing really
sets us free. Freedom that is negative or empty, 'being free from', becomes positive freedom, 'being free to'. Freedom is the form, the 'how', of truth, which is
in turn the content, the 'what', of freedom. If we say that the content of freedom
is indifference of choice, arbitrariness – *liberium arbitrium* – we shall find it has
no content at all, for in that case content and form coincide and are identical: free
freedom, pure arbitrariness. On the other hand the positive content, truth, can
only be a call, an invitation to its 'feast of values', an invitation that implies the
possibility of refusal. That is why *tsedaqa*, justice, and consequently justification,
has no juridical significance in the Bible; rather it shows the nature of our relation
to God, that it is one of reciprocal love. Faith is that profound and secret *yes* that
humankind utters at the source of its being; and then, 'a person is justified by
faith' (Rom. 3.28). In the act of faith the human being becomes intelligible to itself, is placed freely, resolutely and totally in the object of its faith: religious
truth, attested, *justified* by its very rightness. But as soon as the human being descends from the peaks of apophaticism, reason casts its net over the mystery, im-
prisoning and misshaping it to its own dimensions. The prefix *prae* in

---

[13] Mark the Hermit, 'Of justification by works', in *Philokalia*, vol. I.
[14] See A. Blum, 'Contemplation et ascèse', in *Études Carmélitaines*, 149, p. 51.

praescientia and *praedestinatio* already encapsulates the wisdom of God in the categories of time and reduces the Incarnation to a mere soteriology (doctrine of salvation). Causality also plays its part; too great a stress on the *felix culpa* as an instrumental cause explains why the Reformers were reluctant to acknowledge Adam as free, even before his Fall (supralapsarianism). But would not this make Adam the universal archetype of Judas, a mechanism by which acts of God are implacably set in motion and forced through? If so, it is better for freedom to fail than to succeed, because, in the *culpa*, there is no longer any Incarnation. The Incarnation is reduced to no more than a technical means of rescue.

Typical in the East are the thought and experience of the famous 7th century ascetic St Isaac the Syrian, whose words, while redolent of the aridity of the desert, nevertheless keep alive the traces of that 'flame of things' of which he was the eminent visionary. Contemplating the earthly mission of Christ, he is conscious above all of his infinite compassion towards humanity. For him the amazing generosity of the 'Philanthropist's'[15] love so far outweighs the soteriological aspect, that he can conceive of the Incarnation's taking place *even without the Fall.*[16]

The ultimate reason for the Incarnation is to be found not in humanity, but in God; it is rooted in his pre-eternal and unutterable desire to become human and make his humanity into a Theophany, his dwelling-place. According to Methodius of Olympus, 'the Word descended in Adam before the ages,'[17] and St Athanasius parts company with 'economic' Christology (Philo, the Apologists, Origen): the Word made flesh is conditioned not by the world, but by God alone.

The great syntheses of St Maximus the Confessor[18] underline this point and continue the tradition of St Irenaeus[19] and St Athanasius:[20] 'God created the world so that in it he might become human and that humans by grace might in it become god, and share the conditions of divine existence ... God's purpose in uniting himself with the human being was to deify it,' which is an entirely different matter from forgiveness and salvation only.

---

[15] Denys the Pseudo-Areopagite applied the name *philanthropia* [love of humanity] to the Incarnation – 'lover of mankind', which has become the liturgical term most commonly used.

[16] Mar Isaac of Nineveh, *De perfectione religiosa.* See Irenee Hausherr, 'Un précurseur de la théorie scotiste sur la fin de l'Incarnation' in *Revue des Sciences Religieuses*, 1932. We can imagine a similar influence of St Maximus on the theology of Duns Scotus. For the different emphases in the doctrine of the Incarnation, mystical among the Orthodox and moral in the Latin Church, see the article by F. Vernet in *Dictionnaire de Théologie Catholique*, vol. VII, coll. 2469. Cf. P. Beuzart, *Essai sur la théologie d'Irenée.*

[17] *Le Banquet des dix Vierges*, III, 4.

[18] See *Ad. Thalassium Scholiae*, Cap. theol.

[19] See *Advers. haereses* and the *Epideixis.*

[20] See *De Incarnatione contra Arianos.*

The creation can be understood only in the God-Man: the world was conceived and created within the awe-inspiring reality of the Incarnation. Not restricting himself to the outline laid down by the Fall, God was sculpting the human face while in his Wisdom looking at the celestial and eternal humanity of Christ.[21]

If the Incarnation was brought about by the Fall, it was Satan, the evil one, who would condition it. Fr Sergei Bulgakov[22] draws attention to the formulation in the Nicene Creed: Christ came down from heaven and was incarnate 'for us men *and* for our salvation.' The succinctness of the Creed rules out any possibility of vain repetition. 'For our salvation' refers to the *redemption* and 'for us men' to the *deification*, the two together amounting to a summary of the Incarnation. The theology of the Holy Spirit, of glory, of holiness impels us beyond the merely negative purification of 'existence in Satan' to concentrate on the positive and infinitely creative 'life in Christ'. Henceforth the 'royal priesthood' follows Christ our Forerunner[23] within the veil into the trinitarian sanctuary to share in the liturgical activity of the eternal Pontiff (Heb. 6.19-20). In the Eucharist the celestial reality of Christ becomes ours. 'Let the rest be worshipped by silence,' says St Gregory of Nazianzus[24] confronting us with evidence which forbids analysis, 'for the mentality of the crowd is not attuned to profound truths ... we must not reveal to the imprudent what we have understood of the depth of mercy.'[25] The Incarnation seeks 'to gather up all things in him, things in heaven and things on earth' (Eph. 1.10), with a view to accomplishing the 'wisdom, secret and hidden, which God decreed before the ages for our glory' (1 Cor. 2.7).

The economy of glory is above and beyond any exercise of choice by angel or human being, Lucifer or Adam. The Incarnation entails the highest degree of communion. The doctrine of deification presupposes the humanization of God, being at once its source and completion. The answer to the Fall is atonement and judgement. Nothing corresponds to the heart of the Incarnation but the Kingdom of God, which is its fulfilment. It is the advent of the Kingdom that enables us to see in the life of the Church not only the way of salvation and the sacramental means to attain it, but also, here and now, salvation itself. Anthropology, however, in its extreme reductionist versions, begins with original sin and leads to the judgement of double predestination, which in this case is not even judgement, for if everything is predestined there is nothing to judge. The divine Archetype is also cut off from part of the whole which he is called to recapitulate in himself.

---

[21] 'The firstborn of all creation' (Col. 1.15); 'The second man is from heaven' (1 Cor. 15.47); 'the one who descended from heaven, the Son of man' (Jn 3.13).
[22] *Agnus Dei*, Aubier, 1943.
[23] Heb. 6.19-20; see Mgr Cassien, 'Jésus le Précurseur', in *Théologie* v. 27, Athens 1956.
[24] *P.G.* vol. 36, col. 653.
[25] St Maximus, *Qu. a. T.* 43; *P.G.* 90, 413 A; *Cent. gnost* 2, 99, *P.G.* 90, 1172 D.

Anthropology, in its eternal spaciousness, springs up in Paradise and flows into the fullness of the Kingdom, into the mystery of the final apocatastasis,[26] the summing up of heaven and earth. This is the divine plan, the undoubted purpose of the Incarnation, excluding no one in its universal scope. Nevertheless, the end remains hidden and unpredictable; at the most we can be receptive and hopeful. But receptive hope can also signify that the apocatastasis depends not only on God, but on our charity, on his miracle.

2. THE BIBLICAL ACCOUNT OF HUMAN NATURE

The terms used in the Bible bear the mark of different ages and societies. As a result its 'technical' vocabulary lacks precision, and there are bound to be apparent inconsistencies from one book to another, or even between the Testaments.

To understand biblical anthropology we must avoid from the start any classical Greek dualism of soul and body, of two substances at war: 'the body is a tomb' for the soul, σῶμα – σῆμα. In the Bible the inner conflict that is part of the makeup of every human being is seen from a completely different point of view, that of the Creator. His desires are opposed to the desires of the creature; holiness is opposed to the state of sin; normal behaviour to perversion; freedom to necessity. The flesh, *bâsâr*, σάρξ, means the complex whole, living flesh. The human being leaves the hands of God a 'living soul', he or she has no soul, but *is* soul, *is* body, is ψυχή, *nephesh*. If the soul disappears, what remains is not a body but dust of the world, 'the dust returns to dust.'

All that is created is 'very good'; evil is not inherent in the creature, which was good in the beginning, but is admitted from outside; and it comes not from below, from the material, but from above, the spiritual. It originates in the angelic realm and comes to us by the exercise of human choice. Only then does it penetrate us, dwelling in the 'cracks' left in the creature when its integrity was shattered and its ordered structure perverted. This is the essence of the biblical teaching on personality. The disunity of human nature is not the result of a so-called fall of the spiritual into matter, which is the gnostic explanation, and salvation is not to be sought in the freedom of matter, or in the return to the 'One' of neo-Platonism. It is the law of nature that all aspects and elements of our humanity should be fully developed and integrated in the spirit. This integrity ensures that knowledge, in the biblical sense, is never the autonomous exercise of any single human faculty, but is an interaction of the whole being (the Jews thought with their heart). For that reason it is often compared to getting married; to marry somebody is above all to 'know' that person. The nuptial language also

---

[26] St Gregory of Nyssa, in *Christi resurr.*, or. 1; *P.G.* 46, 609 CD; St Gregory of Nazianzus, *Oratio*, 40, 36; *P.G.* 36, 412 AB.

underlines the original interdependence; it is by his knowledge of humankind, in 'marrying' it, that God awakens it to true knowledge, and it is in knowing God and only thus that humankind knows itself.

The *pneuma, ruach*, the spirit, 'the divine breath' is our means of communion with the transcendent, which is possible because of our 'communion in essence', the presence in us of that mysterious ingredient which enables us to say that 'we are his offspring' (Acts 17.28). 'If humankind is destined to enjoy divine benefits, it must have received in its very nature a *kinship* with what it is to share;'[27] the spirit can unfold only in the conditions that belong to it, the divine environment: 'The contemplation of God is the life of the soul.'[28]

The principal theme of Johannine thought, the indwelling of the Spirit of God, entails the presence of a corresponding faculty in humanity capable of receiving and being shaped by it – the human spirit, *pneuma*: 'That very Spirit bearing witness with our spirit that we are children of God' (Rom. 8.16). St Paul's notion of filiation (the divine aspect) corresponds to St Peter's emphasis on our participation (the human aspect of the same act): that you 'may become *participants* in the divine nature' (2 Pet. 1.4). So we can say that the *pneuma* marks humankind as being of heavenly origin and possessing the first-fruits of the Kingdom. Human beings 'confessed that they were strangers and foreigners on the earth'[29] (Heb. 11.13), seeking the heavenly city. *Homo viator* is in a 'state of transition' to the future Passover; more than that, he is that Passover (*pesach* means 'transition, crossing over').[30]

The spirit then is that most highly developed part of human nature which is in touch with the transcendent, participating in it in a manner consistent with its own structure, being itself made 'in the image'. St Gregory of Nyssa expresses this very forcibly, saying that, because it is made in the image of God, humankind has no autonomous existence apart from this participation. It is essentially 'in transition', and will come to resemble completely either the divine or the demonic, and this entails cosmic consequences; humankind shapes the whole material world to itself. Thus, the biblical conflict is not simply between soul and body, but is altogether deeper; it takes place in the metaphysical space between the earthly and the heavenly, between the *homo animalis* and the *homo spiritualis*, between their autonomies. It reveals an ontological abyss between the baptized person, the believer, and the unbeliever, marking out two realms of eternal reality.

---

[27] St Gregory of Nyssa, *Or. Cat.*, c. 5; *P.G.* 45, 21 CD.

[28] St Gregory of Nyssa, *De infant.*, *P.G.* 46, 176 A.

[29] For this reason a group of ascetics is called a *synodia*, a caravan on the return journey to the true homeland, Paradise.

[30] For the consideration of humanity, not as a purely human being, but in transition 'between two', see M. Scheler, *Vom Umsturz der Werte*, 1919, vol. I. p. 296.

For the purposes of preaching, the Fathers of the Church were compelled to bring the Hebrew genius face to face with that of the Greeks, and by creatively accommodating one to the other, to effect that *renewal* of the intellect and its categories of which St Paul speaks (Rom. 12.2; Eph. 4.23). The very language of Scripture, whether Hebrew or Greek, has a special character which requires a certain manner of interpretation.[31] In all their doctrinal elucidation the Councils and the Fathers were chiefly concerned to express biblical ideas in a fashion supple enough to leave the greatest possible room for the free operation of the Word. The meaning of the sacred texts would never be entirely revealed by philology alone, but required the intuitive Patristic penetration into the very lifeblood of the Bible, the appropriation and assimilation of the *epignosis*, or 'the sense of God' in Horn's felicitous translation.[32] This explains some fluctuations in terminology from biblical times onwards. St Paul often gives ontological terms an ethical meaning: the new Man and the old, inward and outward, mind and spirit; the *nous* stands variously for the spirit, the understanding and the conscience. The dichotomy of body and soul coexists with the trichotomy of body, soul and spirit. We can however say that in the Bible the soul vivifies the body, makes it a 'living soul', and the spirit 'pneumatizes' the whole human being. The spirit is a religious category, a qualifying principle, an influence, imparting to everything a transcendental hue, expressing itself through mind and body and colouring them by its presence. It is too broad in meaning to be applied to the hypostatic centre.[33] It is rather the spiritualization of the very manner of existing, a receptivity, the opening up to the divine indwelling. The body contains the mind, but each obeys its own laws; the spirit is not to be understood as the third realm, the third layer of the human structure, but the principle which runs through mind and body, making them spiritual; asceticism is precisely the permeation by the Spirit first of the spirit, and then of the whole person, so that body and soul are transparent to the spiritual. At the opposite extreme, human beings can 'quench' the Spirit (1 Thess. 5.19), be 'carnally minded', be reduced to mere flesh, the flesh of the Flood, destined for 'sarcophagi'.

---

[31] We can even say that the Greek text of the LXX is an *inspired translation*. E.g. Isaiah 7.14 – *almah*, in Hebrew 'young woman', is refined in the *inspired interpretation* of the Greek translation to *parthenos*, 'virgin', and was fixed as such in the text of the Gospel (Matt. 1.23).
[32] R.P. Horn, 'La Vie dans le Christ', in *Revue d'Ascétique et de Mystique*, 1928.
[33] See B. Zenkovsky, 'La structure hiérarchique de l'âme' in *Travaus scientifiques de l'Université Populaire de Prague*, II, 1929; *Das Bild des Menschen in der Ostkirche*.

3. THE BIBLICAL NOTION OF THE HEART

St John of Damascus calls the human being *microcosm*, the universe summed up, because it contains within itself the design of everything. The human being is not only a synthesis of the first five days of progressive creation, which were fulfilled in him on the sixth day, but also possesses a quality that makes him unique: he is made in the image of God, and therefore *microtheos*.[34] To enter the depth of this mystery we must introduce the biblical term *heart, leb*, καρδία.[35]

This has nothing to do with the centre of the emotions as described in manuals of psychology. For the Jews the heart is the organ of thought, where all the faculties of the human spirit are integrated; and psychologists know only too well that reason and intuition are never far removed from the pre-existing and irrational choices and sympathies of the heart.

The human being is a visited creature, indwelt and inspired from within at the very source of its being by the Spirit of truth. Its relation with the divine inhabitant of its heart constitutes its moral conscience, the place where truth speaks

The human being can make its heart 'slow ... to believe' (Luke 24.25), can shut or harden it; doubt can make the human being 'double minded' (Jas. 1.8), or bring about a demonic disintegration into 'many' (Mark 5.9). To cut the transcendent root (to borrow Plato's excellent terminology: 'the spirit depends on its root in the infinite') is, in the biblical sense, folly: 'Fools say in their hearts, "There is no God."' There is nothing left then but an agglomeration of 'little eternities of pleasure' (Kierkegaard). According to ascetic teaching, the love of self, φιλαυτία, usurps God's place in the heart and takes possession of the being which, bereft of God, now turns against him, leaving the spirit a prey to the senses, whose end is death. A prayer addressed to the Virgin, who is the personification of chastity and integrity, speaks for the heart in this diseased condition: 'By thy love, bind up my soul' – out of this mental confusion make my soul to spring forth. It is what St Paul means when he asks for 'singleness of heart' (Col. 3.22), and the Psalmist when he cries, 'Lord, unite my heart' (Ps. 86.11).

The heart is the centre radiating its influence throughout the whole human being, while remaining hidden from it in its mysterious depth. 'Know yourself' chiefly means this depth; we are told by the experts, 'Enter into yourself, and there find God, the angels and the Kingdom.' Its innermost being is inaccessible. I am indeed aware of myself, but although that consciousness is mine, it can nei-

34 St Gregory of Nyssa, *Hom. op. cap.* 16; *P.G.* 44, 180 AB.
35 See B. Vycheslavtsev, *Le cœur de l'homme dans la mystique hindoue et chrétienne*, YMCA Press, Paris 1929; Max Scheler, *Formalismus in der Ethik*; H. DE B., *La Prière du Cœur*, Paris 1953; *La Prière de Jésus*, par un moine de l'Eglise d'Orient, Ed. de Chevetogne (collection Irénikon); 'Le Cœur', *Etudes Carmélitaines*, 1950.

ther reach nor grasp the real me;[36] the self is manifested in its activities but is otherwise beyond knowing.[37] The consciousness is bound by its own limitations, which it will never exceed. My feelings, thoughts, acts, consciousness, belong to me, are 'mine', and all these things are objects of my awareness, but the real 'me', the self, is beyond 'mine'.

Only mystical intuition, originating in God and penetrating his 'image' in humanity, can reveal it; and its symbol is the heart. 'Who can understand the heart?' asks Jeremiah (17.9-10), and he answers at once, 'I the Lord test the mind and search the heart.' St Gregory of Nyssa neatly expresses the mystery: 'Since our spiritual nature is made in the likeness of the Creator, it resembles what is superior to it, and manifests *in its own unknowableness* the mark of the inaccessible Nature.'[38] St Peter speaks of *homo cordis absconditus* – ὁ κρυπτὸς τῆς καρδίας ἄνθρωπος – *the hidden man of the heart*, meaning that it is in the hidden depth of the heart that the human 'me' is found. *Deus absconditus* is mirrored in *homo absconditus*, apophatic theology in apophatic anthropology.[39]

'Where your treasure is, there will your heart be also.' The human being is defined by what is in its heart, by the object of its love. St Seraphim calls the heart 'the altar of God', the place of his presence and the means by which he may be approached. For St Maximus, the world is a cosmic Temple of which humankind is the priest, 'offering it to God in the heart and on the altar' and entering into the great divine silence.[40]

In opposition to Descartes, the poet Baratynsky said, *amo ergo sum*, which sums up the words of St Gregory of Nyssa: 'Our Creator has given us love as the expression of our human face.'[41] In the hierarchical structure of the human being the heart takes precedence;[42] it is there that life is lived; it has a built-in sense of direction, it is magnetized like a compass needle: 'You have formed us for yourself, and our hearts are restless *till they find rest in you.*' (St Augustine) 'God has placed in the human heart the desire for himself,'[43] hence St Gregory of Nyssa's excellent name for God, 'You that love my soul.'[44]

---

[36] The 'me' here is not the 'me' known by experience, but the spiritual self, transcending all intellectual enquiry, the *Selbst* of Jung: 'The self is like a cup ready to receive divine grace.'

[37] 'Those who are spiritual discern all things, and they are themselves subject to no one else's scrutiny' (1 Cor. 2.15).

[38] *De opificio hominis*, *P.G.* 44, 155.

[39] See B. Vychevslavtsev, ' The Image of God', in Review *Voie*, No 49 (in Russian).

[40] *Myst.*, *P.G.* 91, 672 C.

[41] *De opificio hominis* c. 5; *P.G.* 44, 137 C.

[42] L. da Vinci said, 'Love is the child of profound knowledge,' but that is exactly the opposite of the truth: knowledge is the child of profound love.

[43] St Maximus, *Amb.*, *P.G.*, 91, 1312 AB; St Augustine, *Conf.* I, 1.

[44] In *Cant.*, hom. 2; *P.G.* 44, 801 A.

4. THE HUMAN PERSON

The heart denotes the unutterable depth of *homo absconditus*, the centre of personal influence, the person. So great is this depth that even the most positive philosophical personalism cannot satisfactorily define the person.[45] This can come only from the doctrine of the Trinity, which reveals the nature of the human person. Each divine Person subsists in the giving between one and another of the Three, and their 'circumincession'. This is the *co-esse*, the Person being *for* and essentially *by* communion. Strictly speaking, it is only in God that the Person exists. The human being has a longing to become a 'person', which it realizes in communion with the divine Person.

Renouvier used to say, '*Faire et, en faisant, se faire*'; but Gabriel Marcel has the right point of view: the person comes into being *by going beyond the self*;[46] 'his motto is not *sum* but *sursum*.'[47] Metaphysics merges into mysticism and Marcel himself doubts whether it is possible to say exactly where the boundary lies.[48]

Greek philosophy is familiar with the notion of the individual, but knows nothing of the notion of the person, at least in the modern psychological sense.[49]The Fathers of the Church varied in their interest in the idea, defining it at first by analogy with the Trinity; only after the Council of Chalcedon did it find its way into Christology and anthropology. The Fathers speak of the divine Persons, but without using conventional philosophical terms. Their arguments are metaconceptual, and, like all formulations of doctrine, are coded indications of divine transcendence. Thus the three Substances are not three Gods, but three principles, three self-aware centres of the one existence and the one Trinitarian self-awareness, whose distinction and unity, irreducibility and consubstantiability, must equally be acknowledged.

After the Council of Nicaea the Cappadocians[50] defined the term 'hypostasis' or person by distinguishing it from the *ousia*, nature or essence. But this distinc-

---

[45] See the cosmological conception of Renouvier, *Le Personnalisme*; the moral and social conception of E. Mounier, *Manifeste au service du personnalisme*; R.T. Flewelling, *Creative Personality*; Berdyaev, *De la destination de l'homme*, Paris 1935.

[46] That is the whole meaning of *epectasy* in St Gregory of Nyssa – the infiniteness of the Beloved drawing the self to reach out beyond itself towards the always unattainable (*Vit. Moys.*; *P.G.* 44, 401 AB). God is always the same distance away; it is the desire that grows; and it will never be satiated because every beginning engenders a new beginning (in *Cant.*, homily 8; *P.G.* 44, 941 C)

[47] *Homo viator*, p. 32.

[48] *Du refus à l'invocation*, p.190.

[49] For the Stoics, the person signified the role that is played here on earth (*Manuel d'Epictète* 17; *Entretiens* I, 29), and this is the origin of the legal definition of the term in Latin. Cf. Trendelenberg, *Zur Geschichte des Wortes Person*, Kant Studien, 1908.

[50] St Basil, St Gregory of Nazianzus, St Gregory of Nyssa.

tion is quite different from that between the individual and the species, the particular and the general. The hypostasis is defined by its relations: Father, Son and Holy Spirit. It is also the unique manner whereby each appropriates the one nature and so shares the one divine life. But it is also everything in itself that surpasses these relations: *the One in himself.*

This notion of the irreducible and incomparable *oneness* that makes each individual a unique being, a person, comes to us from religious belief. It eludes all rational definition[51] and can be grasped only by intuition or mystical revelation. God in his wisdom 'has confined each being within the bounds he has assigned to it, allotting it its own rhythm within the harmonious composition of the universe;' if it exceeds these, 'it is lost.'[52]

The person is a mode of existing that suffuses and renders personal the whole being; it is the unique entity that thinks of itself, reflects on itself and decides for itself.[53] It is the subject and the bearer which possesses and embodies the particular being. Every being that exists must be *enhypostasized*[54] in a person (thus the human nature of Christ is enhypostasized in the hypostasis of the Word). The person is the integrating principle that brings all aspects of the being into a unity, with its communication of idioms, a 'circumincession' or perichoresis (thus the spirit takes flesh, the body is spiritualized and the soul lives through the body and animates it).

The Chalcedonian Definition,[55] εἰς ἓν πρόσωπον καὶ μίαν ὑπόστασιν, uses two Greek terms, *prosopon* and *hypostasis*, and this distinction is of the greatest importance. Both signify the person, but with different emphases. The *prosopon* is the being in its psychological aspect, contemplating its own interior world, aware of itself, following an evolutionary course through ages of progressive self-knowledge, and appropriating by degrees the nature of which it is the bearer. The *hypostasis* is the being in its aspect of openness and transcendence towards God. This second aspect is crucial for grasping the theandric nature of the person, while never forgetting that the Person, in the absolute sense, exists only in God, and that every human person exists only in his image.

The person cannot be reduced to the individual; equally, it is not something added to the ensemble of body-mind-spirit; it is rather the subject, the bearer, the

[51] The constant admission that philosophy can never distinguish clearly between individuality and personality is fully exemplified in the corresponding articles in *Vocabulaire de la philosophie* by A. Lalande.
[52] St Gregory of Nyssa, *C. Eunom.*; *P.G. 45,* 365 B.
[53] St Gregory sees it in the 'power of discernment and contemplation': *De an. et res; P.G.* 46, 57 B.
[54] The term comes from Leontius of Byzantium. Every nature is realized only in its hypostatic centre, is enhypostasized in it (*Contra Nestorium et Eutychium*).
[55] The Christological definition of the 4th Ecumenical Council in 451.

principle of life on which the ensemble is centred, and here we see how fundamental the 'hypostasis', with all that the term connotes, is for the destiny of a
human being. The hypostasis is the surpassing of the self, of the merely human,
i.e., it is in the surpassing of the self that the person comes to be. The mystery of
the person as hypostasis lies in its own active transcendence towards God: 'For
in him we live and move and have our being' (Acts 17.28). Humankind is already
discovering itself unaided and creating the person through interaction with other
human beings, but he attains the full truth only when he encounters the awareness
that God has of him, and finds himself enfolded in the personal relationship with
the divine Thou. At this depth, the merely human is surpassed and we receive
our innermost, hypostatic self, which is not ours by right, but is given and completed by grace (the 'identity by grace', or hypostasis by grace, of St Maximus
the Confessor).

Every human being possesses a rudiment of personhood, a psychological centre of integration and self-consciousness, a metaphysical self around which the
whole being gravitates; this is the *prosopon*, a universal attribute of the substance.
Deeper than this, however, although all are called, few are chosen to be fulfilled
as *hypostases*. The hypostasis realizes and consciously assumes the higher status
of *imago Dei*; it is the instrument and place of communion with God, revealed
by him as theandric, fashioned after the image of Christ: in the age to come, as
St John says, 'we will be like him' (1 John 3.2).

This theandrism is powerfully present to start with in the *imago Dei*. To the
extent that it is actualized the *prosopon* and the *hypostasis* will germinate and
flourish, and the natural being will be converted into the Christlike being. As it
follows the course of sacramental initiation the human being is completely re-
fashioned according to its Archetype, Christ, just as a statue is modelled to resemble the original. In Christ, however, God is actually united to the human, in
total and *unique* communion, for the place of communion is the Word, and the
whole of human nature, with its 'prosoponian' personal human consciousness,
is taken into his divine hypostasis, or 'enhypostasized'. In every human being
conformed to Christ the human person is the place of communion and receives
en Christo its theandric structure and, by virtue of that communion, becomes a
hypostasis. The divine awareness is placed within human self-awareness, estab-
lishing a theandric state: 'We will come to him and make our home with him
(John 14.23), 'it is no longer I who live, but it is Christ who lives in me' (Gal.
2.20); as a pastor St Paul's longing was 'until Christ is formed in you' (Gal. 4.19).

'The human being,' says St Basil, 'is a creature that has been commanded to
become God'[56], to become deified hypostasis. This notion is defined with great
clarity by St Maximus the Confessor:[57] in order to become *hypostasis* the person

---

[56] Quoted by St Gregory of Nazianzus in his funeral oration for St Basil, *P.G.* 36, 560 A.
[57] *De ambiguis*, *P.G.* 91, 1308 B.

(*prosopon*) is called 'to reunite through love the created nature with the uncreated nature ... by the acquisition of grace.' So we see that God, because of his philanthropy, takes on human being; the human being, *by grace*, unites in its created hypostasis the divine and the human after the image of Christ, and indeed becomes a created god, a god according to grace. The hypostasis, it becomes clear, is thus: the person of a deified being. In Christ deified human nature is enhypostasized in a divine person. In the deified human being the created person, by its very deification, is united to the deifying divine energy, which is then enhypostasized in that person. The hypostasis is the personal presence, unique and incomparable, of the theandric life of each Christian. The radical, mystical, 'transessential' difference between the former human being and the new creature is unmistakable. But here, all phenomenological analysis gives way to 'transphenomenology', reaching beyond what is immediately present, to holiness. The category of the individual belongs to the entirely natural realm of sociology and biology. By nature it is a part of a larger whole, from which it is distinguished by opposition, delimitation, or isolation. On the natural level the *prosopon* can be confused with the individual, being only potentially a person; once actualized the person seeks to become the hypostasis. The hypostasis is a spiritual category, not a part of a larger whole but containing the whole within itself, which explains its capacity for enhypostatization.

Someone we consider to be a strong personality is merely a particular mixture of the elements of nature, but with certain pronounced traits, which nevertheless do not prevent our assigning him to a recognizable type. The mystic, however, strikes us by his sheer uniqueness, and an outlook on the world that is utterly personal in an absolute sense. He has never been seen before.

5. FREEDOM

Theandrism has other implications too, especially in the matter of the will and freedom. According to Christological doctrine the will is a function of nature. Since the aim of asceticism is detachment from all the demands of the world and nature, it seeks above all the renunciation of the natural will. But it is in this very renunciation of the natural will that true freedom is achieved, because by it the person is elevated and freed from every individual and natural limitation, and made 'catholic', infinitely enlarged, 'omnicontinent'. Ultimately the truly free person is extended to contain the whole of human nature, after the example of the divine Person who contains the whole life of the Trinity; for Christianity, according to St Gregory of Nyssa, is an 'imitation of the nature of God',[58] and the

---

[58] *De professione christiana*, *P.G.* 46, 244 C.

chief vocation of the saints is to be 'not only united to the Holy Trinity, but to express it and imitate it in themselves.'[59]

'God honoured humankind in conferring freedom on it,' says St Gregory of Nazianzus, 'so that goodness should belong by right to the one who chooses it, no less than to Him who placed the beginnings of goodness in its nature.'[60] Humanity is free, for it is the image of divine freedom and that is why it has the power to choose.

However, for St Maximus the very need to choose is evidence of imperfection;[61] free will is a limitation of true freedom, being the inevitable consequence of the Fall; a perfect nature has no need to choose, since it knows instinctively what is good and pursues it. It is interesting to see that the modern philosopher Louis Lavelle has the same idea. For him 'existence consists above all in the exercise of an act of freedom; where that is lacking, our being is reduced in status to that of a thing.'[62] Our spirit of discernment chooses between several possibilities in order to find what is right. But 'freedom is nearly always defined in terms of choice,' whereas in its highest form it is 'an activity that produces its own reasons, instead of being governed by them.'[63] Thus freedom is elevated to the level where 'the freest acts, which are also the most perfect, are those in which there is no choice.'[64]

It is in freedom that the person is realized, being freely opened to the grace that presses on every soul in secret, without ever constraining it. 'The Spirit begets no will that resists him. He transforms by divinization only the one who desires it.'[65] The person is afflicted with anxiety by his own arbitrariness, which lies in wait for him, apt at any moment to reject life and say no to existence. Humanity is constantly torn between 'emptying out' and 'filling up': this is the great and noble risk of every existence, the supreme test of hope. 'The divine power discovers a hope for the hopeless, and a way through the impenetrable.'[66] The impenetrable is the conflict between what ought to be and fallen reality.

Values are not created by freedom, but are given life and flesh by our personal *discovery* of them. Each person experiences this discovery as the creation of something new, but what is being created is the person's relationship with the values, which is unique and has never existed before; in this sense it can be said that human beings are what they do.

---

[59] St Maximus, *Amb.*, *P.G.* 91, 1196 B.
[60] *P.G.* 36, 632 C.
[61] *Opuscula Theologica et Polemica*, *P.G.* 91, 16 B; *Amb.* 91, 1156 CD.
[62] *Treatise on Values*, I /325.
[63] *Id.* I /428.
[64] *The Powers of the Self*, 155-156.
[65] St Maximus, *Qu. a. T.* 6; *P.G.* 90, 281 B. The grace of the Holy Spirit bestows a spiritual gift only according to the capacity of each person to receive it. *Amb.*; *P.G.* 91 1121 C.
[66] St Gregory of Nyssa, *De hom. op.*; *P.G.* 44, 128 B.

Every human being bears a 'conductive image' of the pre-existent wisdom of God, a personal *sophia*. Of the divine existence he is a living plan, which he must interpret in his own way, mastering his own meaning and constructing his own destiny. Thus existence is the effort of discovering and living the truth that is in him; as Kierkegaard said, 'I know the truth only when it becomes life in me.' Life never arrives at a final state of completion, and never repeats itself; there never is a final state of completion, nor, strictly speaking, any repetition; every act, being personal, is unprecedented and unique, in an eternal series of beginnings. Every morning of the human life is like the dawn of creation – pure divine intention – and according as we are faithful to it, we are borne moment by moment towards a new springtime, towards the absolutely desirable and the absolutely unspoilt.

Our relationship with the transcendent cannot be expressed in terms of a Kantian 'heteronomy', because *hetero* is exactly what the 'theonomy' is not. To depend on God means to receive the revelation of his inwardness, to comprehend the Word's indwelling: 'I do not call you servants any longer, ... but I have called you friends' (John 15.15). Autonomy, however, 'encapsulates' the human being, shuts it in on itself. St Anthony[67] distinguishes three opposing wills in humanity. There is the will of God, saving and working from within, which is theonomy, whereby the human being freely cooperates with God's will, making it his own. There is the human will that, while not irredeemable, is unstable and untrustworthy, which is autonomy. Finally there is the demonic will, external to humanity, which is heteronomy.

If freedom is simply rigid subjection to divine activity, so that there is no choice but to repeat or imitate it, then to be free after the divine image means nothing. As St Maximus says, 'humankind, begotten in freedom by the Spirit, was able to move of its own accord,' i.e., spontaneously.[68] The Gospel puts the ethics of the friends of God above those of slaves and mercenaries.[69]

The Christological doctrine of the unity of the two natures in Christ is refined in the doctrine of the two wills, which in turn implies a unity of two freedoms. The psychological notion of the will should not be confused with the metaphysical one of freedom. Freedom is the metaphysical basis for the will. The will is still bound to nature, subject to immediate necessities and ends. Freedom originates in the spirit, the person. In its perfect form it seeks only truth and goodness. In the future consummation, whatever freedom desires, according to the image of the divine freedom, will be identical with goodness and truth; it is the final resolution of Kierkegaard's paradox, that subjective belief and the truth are the same thing, so that truth turns out to be freedom in action.[70]

---

[67] *Philokalia*, vol. I.
[68] *Amb.. P.G.* 91, 1345 D.
[69] Cf. Berdyaev, *De la destination de l'homme*, Paris 1935.
[70] See Kierkegaard, *Repetition, The Concept of Anxiety, Journals, Postcript.*

As long as our freedom is exercised within the *opus Dei* it will never cease to be true freedom. The Virgin's *'fiat'* was an expression not of mere submission but of a truly free personality. This was the act that all her previous life – in the temple, according to tradition – had been leading up to; she had been watched over by the Spirit, and protected also by her own intense recollectedness – so clearly depicted in the icons of the Annunciation, where she appears not surprised and astonished by the unexpected, but awestruck at the mystery of this long-awaited moment; the angel bringing the tidings and the Virgin listening to him together form a perfect harmony. Here is the history of the world in a nutshell, theology in a single word; the fate of the world, even of God, waits in suspense for that free outpouring. The Virgin's freedom is expressed in her constant desire for nothing but what will be released by her *fiat* – the childbearing of God; and in this we see that she is utterly consecrated, holy and pure. Even God does not invent the truth, but has it eternally in mind until, 'he spoke, and it was done'. The freedom of humanity made in the image of God is to reproduce that very springing up of the truth which pre-exists humanity.

In taking flesh Christ has allowed us not to imitate, but to re-live his life, to be conformed to his essence, and this is exactly what the sacraments and the litur-gical cycle teach us. 'God is not an idea to be proved, but a being in relation to whom we live ... seeking for proofs is a blasphemy, and making Christianity be-lievable ... is the destruction of Christianity' (Kierkegaard). We must choose be-tween living and – in the strongest sense of the word – existing, and we must understand our fate as bound up with the 'second person', the divine Thou. Faith is never mere intellectual assent, nor is it submission pure and simple, but faith-fulness of the person to the Person. This is the relationship of marriage, of the epithalamion, to which the Bible returns whenever it speaks of the relationship between God and humankind.

In uttering the *fiat*, I acknowledge that I am a beloved creature. The divine will springs out of my own will, becomes mine: 'it is no longer I who live, but it is Christ who lives in me' (Gal. 2.20). God asks humankind to carry out the Fa-ther's will as if it were its own. That is what it means to be 'perfect, as your heav-enly Father is perfect' (Matt. 5.48).

As the Son was born, and is born eternally, so the one who has chosen the truth is brought to birth by it and chooses it eternally, each time living it anew. The only thing that freedom can truly seek and desire is to contain the uncon-tainable, which is utterly 'foolish' by the standards of this world, and therefore utterly wise. You might even say that it was for absolutely no reason that 'God first loved us', and thus has already allowed us to experience something of his divine freedom. In his love God loves us freely for no merit of ours; his love has already been given, and imparts freedom to our own response.

The dizzy imaginings of the divine Wisdom, as she disports herself (Prov. 8.31) with the human race, can embrace only beings like herself, gods; 'God unites himself only to gods', says St Simeon. These receive everything from God, and even more; in the reality of their persons, they have received as a gift something of their own, something that comes only from the free activity of their hearts, that freedom which alone clothes a person with the marriage-garment for the heavenly banquet. St Gregory of Nazianzus exclaims in astonishment, 'Humankind is a game of God.'[71]

Freedom produces her own reasons instead of being subject to them. She proclaims, 'Thy will be done.'[72] It is because we could just as easily say, 'Your will be not done,' that we can say yes. The two freedoms agree with each other; according to St Paul, 'in him it is always "Yes"' (2 Cor. 1.19), which admirably explains the text of Matthew 18.19, 'if two of you agree ...;' and true unity is impossible except in the will of God, where every limitation is transcended and the whole new eucharistic reality of the Body springs up whose immediate expression is prayer. But this Yes has to be brought forth in the secret source of our being, which is why the one who utters it on behalf of us all is a Virgin, Mother of the living and life-giving Source.

We can now understand why God does not give orders, but issues invitations, appeals: 'Hear, O Israel!' The decrees of tyrants evoke sullen resistance; the invitation of the Master of the banquet the joyful acceptance of 'anyone with ears'. The elect is the one who accepts the invitation, who takes the gift into his hand. 'They shall come and sing aloud on the height of Zion, and they shall be radiant over the goodness of the Lord, over the grain, the wine, and the oil ... their life shall become like a watered garden'(Jer. 31.12).

God has entrusted his freedom, the image of himself as Creator, to 'earthen vessels' and comes to look at himself there. The human race lives in time, and time was created *with* it, for humankind is essentially an unfinished being; it was created in such a way as to leave a gap in which it is called to make itself, to create itself, to invent itself after the image of the Existent. 'We are συνεργοί with God' (1 Cor. 3.9), workers together with him in the same service, in the same divine activity. And if it is possible to fail, if God's creative act can be undone, that is because the freedom of 'gods', their free love, is the essential human quality: 'And I will take you for my wife for ever ... and you shall know the Lord' (Hos. 2.19-20); 'I have loved you with an everlasting love ... O virgin Israel' (Jer. 31.3-4); 'Be fruitful and multiply.' We must understand this injunction in the fullest sense: the bursting forth of the new creature, of wellsprings of holiness.

The human person, in its horizontal dimension, is capable of containing everything human; and it is this accessibility that makes it truly personal, a *prosopon*. But its *hypostatic* foundation is in its vertical dimension, its theandric structure

---

[71] *P.G.* 37, 776.
[72] For St Maximus this is freedom in its purest form, being simple and entire.

– 'That Christ may be formed in you' – and thus recreated humanity 'grows to the stature of Christ'. The subject of freedom, and of every form of knowledge, is therefore never just the human being in itself, but the human being as a member of the Body knit together in Christ, so the human conscience is by nature never cut off from others, but collegial,[73] and 'theandric', as Pseudo-Denys expresses it; 'the theandric energy' in Christ[74] being the unity of two wills and two freedoms in a single act, μοναδικῶς,[75] where the emphasis is on the unity, but without in the least weakening the autonomy of either.

The original meaning of the Latin word *persona*, like the Greek *prosopon*, was 'mask', a term that contains a profound understanding of the human person. It tells us that there is no such thing as an autonomous human order, for to exist is to participate in being or non-being. In the participation the human being realizes the icon of God or the demonic grimace of a monkey of God. There is no such thing as a simply human face. Since the Incarnation, God has been no longer only God: he is God-Man. But this works both ways: Man is also no longer only Man, but either a theandric or a demonic being. St Gregory of Nyssa puts it succinctly: 'Humankind is composed of people with the face of an angel and people wearing the mask of the beast'.[76] A spiritual person 'continually adds fire to fire till the end of his life;'[77] humankind can rekindle the flame of love or the flame of Gehenna; it can convert its Yes into infinite union or by its No undergo a hellish disintegration.

The theological enigma embedded in the heart, the relation between the person and nature, the freedom of the *hypostasis* – in short, all that is meant by 'humanity', brings us to the central notion of anthropology: 'in the image and likeness of God.'

6. THE IMAGE OF GOD

Since the 15th century the idea of the image of God has played no part in philosophy. It lingered as a faint echo in the moral conscience till Kant excluded it from the realm of the transcendent with his 'pure will'. Many a theological dictionary speaks today not of the image, but of its loss, and then only in articles about original sin. The Kingdom that governs the course of history has been supplanted in our minds by Paradise Lost. Preaching, neutralized by an underlying pessimism, which is the wearing down by history, loses its vehemence. On the other hand

---

[73] The expression is Fr Congar's translation of the Russian word *sobornost*.
[74] The expression is also adopted by St Maximus, *Amb.; P.G.* 91, 1056 BC.
[75] *Ibid.* 91, 1044 D.
[76] *P.G.* 44, 192 CD.
[77] St John Climacus, *Scala paradisi; P.G.* 88, 644 A.

the crucial difficulty for modern personalism is how to reconcile the unity of consciousness – which is a metaphysical unity, being the same for all – with the plurality of its personal centres, i.e., people. Does the single universal consciousness pass through people, each of whom has his own consciousness? Without a model that integrates the two they are mutually exclusive. However, all anthropologists happily agree on the definition of the human as 'a being who longs to surpass itself,' who strives for what is greater than itself, for what is 'wholly other'; the human being is the child of both riches and poverty, and the 'poor' in it reaches out towards the 'rich'. We need another St Paul to speak to the anthropologists and identify a new 'altar to the unknown god', to give a *name* to this profound longing which is the expression of humanity's deepest nature, the *imago Dei*. The anthropological *kerygma* of the Fathers of the Church proclaims that the image has nothing to do with regulating or managing people, but defines the essence of what it is to be human.[78]

The Church has always been chiefly concerned to maintain the purity of the faith handed down from the Apostles. Doctrine, the anchor of salvation, the crystallized Word of God, is above all soteriological;[79] it is a matter of life and death. To take one example, a single word, ὁμοούσιος – 'consubstantial' – is enough to correct any heretical tendency to stray: the Son's consubstantiality with the Father is the sole foundation of Christ's divinity, and hence, through our consubstantiality with Christ's humanity, of our salvation. St Athanasius[80] develops St Irenaeus's statement:[81] 'God becomes human so that humans may become god'. This is the golden rule that determines all Patristic anthropology. According to St John's pithy definition (1 John 3.4-6), sin is lawlessness – ἀνομία – 'transgression' of the proper limits of human nature. Sin is revealed by 'the law', whose function is to mark the precise frontier between what is κατὰ τάξιν, orderly, and what is disorderly and chaotic, confusing the ontological strata of the human being. Pathology offers a diagnosis and instigates the healing process that will penetrate to the root of the perversion and effect a cure by restoring the nature to its adamic state. The *ethical catharsis*,[82] the cleansing of the passions and desires, is completed in the *ontological catharsis: metanoia*,[83] by which the whole economy of the human being is rebalanced. The essential thing is to restore the archetypal image, the *imago Dei*, which is most purely revealed in Christ, whom the Fathers call the Archetype. At the mo-

---

[78] See P.C. Kern, *The Anthropology of St Gregory Palamas*, YMCA Press, Paris 1950 (in Russian).
[79] Soteriology: the doctrine of salvation.
[80] *De Incarnatione Verbi, P.G.* 25, 192.
[81] *Adversus haereses*, *P.G.* 7, 873.
[82] An ascetic term meaning the effort to purify oneself.
[83] A Gospel expression: radical change, conversion, repentance.

ment of incarnation, Christ, 'the image of the invisible God' (Col. 1.15), seeks
no angelic or astral form, nor does he need any adaptation in order to appear
human; for, according to the Fathers, God, even while creating humankind, already had the 'Christ-prototype' firmly in mind,[84] so that in Christ 'the imprint
of the Father' and Christ 'ecce homo', the image of God and the image of humankind are united. 'Humanity is like God', is justified by the corresponding
completely 'out of this world' statement, 'God is like humanity.'[85] Thus God is
incarnate in his living icon; God is not here as an exile; humanity is the human
face of God.[86]

The *imago* is that third term of resemblance, of conformity, of correspondence,
which allows us to see humankind in God, 'the face of God expressed through
human features,'[87] and the divine in humankind, humankind deified – even to the
point that we can reverse the usual formula, that the Incarnation is conditioned by
the Fall, and say instead that 'in the beginning,' in very principle, the human race
was created 'in the image' with a view to incarnation-deification, and its creation
was therefore essentially *theandric*[88] in 'inspiration' (*in-spirare*).

The *imago*, from the human point of view, is more than just the only link between the original and the copy. In the time of the Old Covenant we can see it as
the means by which humankind was prepared for the fulfilment that was to be
revealed in it; like the Forerunner the image awaited and announced the Incarnation. It announced what had brought it into being and the destiny for which it
was intended, and so in a sense brought about the event. On the divine side, it
reveals God's desire to take on humanity. 'The divine *Eros*,' says St Macarius,
'made God come down to earth,'[89] forced him to 'leave the silent peak.' Divine
and human desires converge in the historical Christ in whom God and the human
race see and recognize each other as in a mirror, 'for the love of God and the
love of humankind are two aspects of a single whole.'[90]

The Fathers of the Church are not entirely consistent on the subject of the
image, a concept so rich that we can see in it in various aspects of our nature

---

[84] Cf. B. Brinkmann, *Geschaffen nach dem Bilde Gottes;* P. Bratsiotis, 'Genesis 1.26 in der
Orthodoxen Theologie', in *Evangelische Theologie*, 2nd year, papers 7/8, Munich 1952; Paul
Zacharias, 'Signification de la Psychologie de Jung pour la Théologie chrétienne', in *Synthèses*,
No. 115.

[85] St Clement of Alexandria, *P.G.* 9, 293 B; he says also that the Jews receive the Law, pagans
philosophy, and Christians the Truth in its fullness, *Strom.* VI, 9.

[86] The basis of iconography according to the canons of the 7th Ecumenical Council of Nicaea
in 787.

[87] St Gregory of Nyssa, *In Ps.* c. 4; *P.G.* 44, 446 BC.

[88] Theandric: divine-human.

[89] *Homilia*, XXVI, 1.

[90] St Maximus, *Ep.* 3; *P.G. 91,* 409 B.

without thereby exhausting it. St Athanasius states firmly that our participation in the divine is ontological, so much so that 'creation' itself comes to mean 'participation'. Κατ'εἰκόνα – 'in the image' – is not simply moral duplication but the cause of the enlightenment of the human *nous*,[91] the bestowing of the capacity for theognosis. Of this enlightenment St Basil says, 'You will see in yourself, as in a microcosm, the imprint of the divine wisdom.'[92] This is not intellectualism, however, because intelligence is viewed not as self-sufficient but as it was originally intended to be, oriented towards God. This is the classical eastern understanding of theology as experiential knowledge-and-communion. The desire for communion is innate: 'By our very nature, we possess a burning desire for the good ... everything longs for God.'[93]

St Gregory of Nazianzus enlarges on another aspect: 'As a creature of earth I am attached to earthly life, but being also a particle of the divine, I bear in my heart the desire for the life to come.'[94] Being 'in the image' connotes the spiritual gift bestowed in the beginning; the image comes furnished with the indestructible presence of the grace inherent in human nature, conveyed in the very act of creation. 'The jet of invisible divinity' blown into the soul, predisposes it to participate in the divine Being. Human beings are not only morally structured, ordered by decree after the divine pattern, but they belong to the γένος, the divine race; as St Paul says, 'we are God's offspring' (Acts 17.29), and St Gregory of Nyssa, 'humankind is related to God;'[95] *as the image, humanity is predestined to theosis.*

According to St Gregory of Nyssa humankind's creation 'in the image' raises it to the dignity of God's friend, sharing some of the conditions of the divine life. Human intelligence, wisdom, speech, love, are the image of the same powers in God. But the image goes still more deeply in replicating the ineffable mystery of the Trinity, to that depth where the human being is a riddle to itself: 'It is easier to know heaven than oneself.'[96] In the very act of indicating what is unknowable in their created nature, human beings finds themselves to be *absconditus*. St Gregory fastens on the dizzying power of free self-determination,[97] the autonomy of every choice and decision – αὐτεξουσίας. But the self-determination is precisely that of one whose very constitution is in the image. Exercising the human being's axiological faculty of evaluation and judgement, it is master of its own nature and of every other creature; indeed, the human being is revealed in its dig-

---

91 The principle of intelligibility, reason, intelligence, the mind. See Regis Bernard, *L'image de Dieu d'après saint Athanase*, Paris 1952.
92 *P.G.* 31, 213 D.
93 *P.G.* 31, 909 BC; 912 A.
94 *Poemata dogmatica*, VIII; *P.G.* 37, 252.
95 *Orat. cat.* 5; *P.G.* 45; 21 CD.
96 *De opificio hominis; P.G.* 44, 257 C.
97 Cf. St Macarius, *Homilia* XXIII, *P.G.* 34, 591.

nity as a cosmic word. The difference between God and the deified human being of the Kingdom is that 'the divine is uncreated, but humanity exists by creation.'[98] Christianity is defined in terms of the *imago* as 'the imitation of the nature of God:'[99] the Trinity poured out, reflected in the multitude of human hypostases united in the same single human nature.

St Theophilus of Antioch, speaking of the transcendent nature of this dignity, says, 'Show me your human being and I will show you my God.'[100] It is of the essence of the divine Person to be free, that is, ultimately mysterious. Being in his image, the human being also is a person and a freedom. God 'dwells in unapproachable light' (1 Tim. 6.16); the *imago* covers humanity with the same thick cloud. Following St John Damascene, and later St Gregory Palamas, we can define humanity by its awareness that it exists in the image of 'Him who is', the Existent, and is thus in contact with his ineffable mysteriousness.

The art of spiritual contemplation, at its most highly developed, is precisely that of seeing every human being as the image of God. 'A perfect monk,' says St Nilus of Sinai, 'will after God esteem all human beings as God himself.'[101] This explains the apparent paradox that, in opposition to any anthropological minimalism, the tradition of the ascetic masters is marked by joy and a *maximal* estimation of humanity.[102] Indeed, monastic maximalism is both eschatological – with the last monk on earth comes the end of earthly life and the beginning of the Kingdom – and visionary – the dignity conferred by the image is threefold: prophetic, royal and priestly.[103]

From the great tradition of St Macarius of Egypt,[104] St Isaac the Syrian, and others, we have inherited not a doctrine but an experiential science. Therapists who have seen the innermost depth of the heart have nothing to learn about human wickedness – St Andrew of Crete defines it in his famous Canon: humankind makes an idol of itself – but this plumbing of the depths also yields a wholly different kind of knowledge, the revelation of the new creature entirely reclothed with the divine form. 'I bear the stigmata of my iniquities, but I am in the image of thine inexpressible glory.'[105] 'Between God and humankind there

---

[98] *De opificio hominis; P.G.* 44, 184 AC.

[99] St Gregory of Nyssa, *P.G.* 46, 244 C.

[100] *Epist. ad Autolicum, P.G.* 6, 1025 B.

[101] *P.G.* 79, 1193 C.

[102] 'Our nature is essentially good,' says St Anthony (in the *Life* by St Athanasius); nature created after the image of God can only be good. By Redemption our nature does not become supernature, but is restored to its first state, to its 'natural' truth. See V. Resch, *La nature ascétique des premiers maîtres égyptiens*, p. 9.

[103] The three dignities of the royal priesthood of the faithful.

[104] There are doubts about the authenticity and origin of the sermons attributed to St Macarius of Egypt, but they were a strong influence on the development of eastern mysticism.

[105] Troparion of the funeral Office.

is the closest relationship.'[106] So the anthropological laboratory of the desert saw an astonishing advance into our knowledge of the human vocation; like the unjust steward in the parable, humanity helps itself generously from the riches of the divine love in order to 'lay up treasure' and 'build the Kingdom'. Artists work with the material of the world around them; ascetics sculpt their own faces and model their whole being with divine light.

Humankind has a unique position in the world, mid-way between the spiritual realm of the angels and the material realm of nature, being itself the embodiment of both – a point of particular interest to St Gregory Palamas. What distinguishes humanity from the angels is that it is in the image of the Incarnation; in it pure spirit is incarnate and penetrates the whole of nature by its life-giving energies. An angel is 'second light', pure reflection; it is the messenger and minister of the things of the spirit. But in the human being, the image of the Creator, the material of the world acquires spiritual value; it is called to create holiness and be the fount of it. Human beings do not reflect light, but become it,[107] become spiritual, so that angels minister to them. The initial command to cultivate Eden foreshadows the development of 'culture' in the grand sense, which in turn anagogically[108] typifies the worship, the cosmic liturgy, the unceasing song of 'everything that has breath': 'I will sing to the Lord as long as I live' (Ps. 104.33); the song that comes from a fulfilled humanity, the prelude, here on earth, to the liturgy of heaven. In the apt words of St Gregory, humankind is 'a musical organism, a wonderfully composed hymn to the power of the Almighty.'[109] Above the lineaments of sin, the original destiny of humankind presses down on his historical destiny, and shapes him according to the definition of St Basil: 'The human being is a creature that has been commanded to become God.'[110]

Traversing the immense field of Patristic thought, infinitely rich and subtle, we sense that it avoids all systematization in order to safeguard its astonishing suppleness. We may however draw certain basic conclusions. First we must banish any idea of the image as substance: it was not inserted in us as a component of our being; rather the *whole* human being has been created, sculpted 'in the image'. The primary expression of the image is the hierarchical ordering of the human being with the spiritual life at its centre. This centrality and primacy of the life of the spirit explains our fundamental longing for the spiritual, the absolute. It is the impetus of our whole being towards its divine Archetype (Origen),

---

106 St Macarius, *Homilia*, XLV.
107 God – the archetypal light – enters into humanity. St Gregory of Nazianzus, *In Sanctum baptisma, or.* XV. St Gregory of Nyssa and St Gregory Palamas emphasize the transformation of human beings into light.
108 In ascending order.
109 *P.G.* 44, 441 B.
110 St Gregory of Nazianzus, *In laudem Basilii*, or. 43, 48; *P.G.* 36, 560 A.

the irresistible longing of our spirit for God (St Basil), the human *eros*, reaching for the divine *Eros* (St Gregory Palamas). In short, it is the inextinguishable thirst, the intense desire for God; in the memorable words of St Gregory of Nazianzus, 'It is for you that I live, speak and sing.'[111]

To sum up, each faculty of the human spirit reflects the image, but the image is essentially the whole spirit-centred human being, called to self-transcendence before being plunged into the infinite ocean of the divine, there to have its longing assuaged.[112] It is the reaching of the icon towards its original, of the image towards its *arche*. 'At the heart of the image,' says St Macarius of Egypt, 'Truth launches human beings in pursuit of itself.'[113] In our desire for God we find him already present, for 'the divine life is a love that is continually at work'[114] and 'finding God consists in seeking him unceasingly.'[115]

7. THE DIFFERENCE BETWEEN IMAGE AND LIKENESS

Humankind is created *betsalmenu kidemoutenu*, 'in the image and likeness.' For the Hebrew understanding, which is always very concrete, *Tselem*, image, has the strongest meaning. The making of graven images is forbidden by the Law because the image is something real, what it represents is really present in it. While *demouth*, likeness, resemblance, suggests something distinct from the original, the image is entire, all of a piece, and cannot be modified or altered. It can however be reduced to silence, driven back and rendered useless by changes in ontological conditions.

We come back to the Hebrew term *tsemach*, seed or grain. Creation, energy and the springing up of life, as well as the positiveness of biblical times, are *tsemach*, seed that evolves, develops, undergoes fertilization and transforms the time of wearing down and ageing into the time of building up and bringing to birth. The repetitions of cosmic, cyclic time, become progression, growth, the wholesome pressure towards completion. In this driving forward, there is no re-creation; all is controlled by the seed, by what it was in the beginning, by the original destiny; the Fathers insist that Christ *resumed* what had been thrown off course and interrupted by the Fall. The Kingdom is the flourishing of the seed whose growth was halted by the sickness of the Fall that Christ came to cure.

---

111 *P.G.* 37, 1327.
112 Every limit contains in its essence a beyond, its own transcendence, and that is why the heart finds rest only in the infinite (St Gregory of Nyssa, *Vita Moys.*, *P.G.* 46, 96 C.)
113 *Spiritual Homilies.*
114 St Gregory of Nyssa, *An. et res.* 13, *P.G.* 46, 96 C.
115 *P.G.* 46, 97 A.

The image of healing is the most common in the Gospel; it is even normative: the Resurrection is the healing of death.

Creation in the biblical sense is like the grain that yields a hundredfold, and always continues to increase: 'My Father is still working, and I also am working.' It is the alpha that is directed towards the omega and already contains it, that renders each moment of time precisely eschatological, opens it on to its final completion and so judges it. The Messiah is called *tsemach* and the very notion of *messiah* is derived from fullness; creation entails the Incarnation, which is completed in the Parousia of the Kingdom. The world was created *together with* time, which means that it is unfinished, embryonic, thus furthering and guiding the synergy of divine and human activity until the Day of the Lord, when the seed shall come to final maturity.

'The end would be attained only if there finally existed what must theoretically have been there in the beginning, a divine humanity.'[116] Thus Bergson, in agreement with the Bible, rightly denies any rupture in ontological continuity: 'Behold, I make the last like the first.'[117] It is an axiom of the biblical revelation that the ἐν ἀρχῇ, *in principio*, of the first design is all of a piece with the *telos*, its completion. The 'children of the Most High' of the beginning are to be told in the end, 'You are gods' (Ps. 82.6). From 'the tree of life' in Eden, we are directed by way of the Eucharist 'towards the table without veil' of the Kingdom (Rev. 22.1-2). From the first unconscious perfection, we progress towards conscious perfection, in the image of the perfection of the heavenly Father. Being formed 'in the image' created members of the divine race, we are called to realize our ontological nature by becoming actually holy, perfect, gods by grace, sharing the conditions of the divine life: immortality, integrity and purity. The *image*, which is basically *objective*, leads by its intrinsic dynamism to the *likeness*, which is *subjective* and personal. The seed – 'created in the image' – opens out into 'existing in the image'.

All the Fathers make a clear distinction that is summed up by St John Damascene: *in the likeness* means 'likeness in virtue',[118] likeness in action. The Patristic tradition is both explicit and firm: after the Fall the essential nature of the image remains unchanged, but in its activity it is reduced to ontological silence. With the destruction of any capacity for 'likeness', the image is rendered useless, inaccessible to natural human powers.[119] The image, while fundamentally objec-

---

116 Bergson, *Deux Sources*, p. 23.
117 *Epistle of Barnabas*, VI, 13.
118 *De fide orth.* II, 12.
119 In losing the likeness humankind has disfigured the image (St John Damascene, *P.G.* 96, 576-7).

tive, can manifest itself and act only in the subjective likeness. St Gregory Palamas explains: 'Being in the image, the human being is superior to the angels, but
in the likeness it is inferior, because it is unstable ... after the Fall, we rejected
the likeness, but we did not cease to be in the image.'[120]

Christ gives human beings the power to act;[121] divine illumination restores
the likeness, at once setting the image free, whose effects become noticeable in
saints and children. St Gregory of Nyssa has left us his anthropological *kerygma*:
a being becomes human only when transformed by the Holy Spirit into an 'image
that resembles', an image-likeness. The image, being formative and definitive,
can never be either lost or destroyed; according to St Irenaeus, what is left is not
truly a human being.[122] In its function of conformity, of deiformity, it makes real
the saying, 'Be perfect as your heavenly Father is perfect.' When 'God shall be
all in all' his human temples will be conformed to the presence which fills and
enlivens them. Biblical 'filiation' excludes any notion of legal adoption; Christological teaching is clear that in Christ 'the sons in the Son' really are like God.
While God is incomparable, the human heart that God alone can plumb contains
something unique and *comparable*, 'a certain affinity to God,' as St Gregory of
Nyssa says; 'for to be akin to God the human must have in its nature something
corresponding to what is akin to it.'[123] 'God is Love' corresponds to the *Amo,
ergo sum* of the human being. The strongest link between God and the human
heart is loving and being loved.[124]

---

120 *P.G.* 150, 1148 B.
121Unction with Chrism is essentially the restoration of the likeness, while Baptism restores
the image.
122 *Adv. Haereses*, 5, 6,; *P.G.* 7, 1138 B.
123 *P.G.* 45, 21 C.
124 Kallistos, *P.G.* 147, 860 AB

3

Beginnings and Ends

1. THE CREATION

The origin of created being is beyond all human knowledge; only God can reveal to us why and how he created the world. By creation *ex nihilo*, God makes room for a being that is absolutely other, apart from himself, entirely removed from him 'not by place but by nature'.[1] 'God creates by his thought which immediately becomes a work';[2] 'he spoke, and it came to be' (Ps. 33.9).

'God contemplated all things before their existence, formulating them in his mind, and each creature received its existence at a particular moment determined according to his eternal thought and will, which is a predestination, an image and a model.'[3] These normative models cannot be found in the things themselves; only contemplation can reveal them, and always in the form of a calling that every creature, being free, can accept or refuse. The creature, defined purely by divine active intention, is therefore free from any static determinism. The 'thoughts' are not fixed in the essence of God, as Augustine taught, but are in his creative energies, in which living creatures can share, freely joining in a creative synergy to realize a world of real analogies.

First of all God created the ideal sphere of the world, 'the created aeonic eternity',[4] the unity of ideal principles that we can call created *Sophia*,[5] which influences and organizes every concrete unity in the world. Beneath the world of shifting and changeable phenomena is the ideal foundation, *Sophia*, which binds together the many in a living whole under its various aspects: cosmic, logical, ethical, aesthetic and anthropological. All true knowledge proceeds from the experience of things to their ideal structure; penetrating the outward appearance it gazes on the icon of the Wisdom of God. Such a 'sophiological' vision affirms

---

[1] St John Damascene, *De fide orth.*, I, 13.
[2] *De fide orth.*, II /2; *P.G.* 94, 865 a.
[3] St John Damascene, *De fide orth.*, I, 9.
[4] *Amb.*, *P.G.* 91, 13377 D; 1164 BC.
[5] Created *Sophia* corresponds to the *natura naturans* that governs the *natura naturata*, terms that appear in the 12th century in the Latin translations of Averroes; made famous by Spinoza (*Ethics* I / 29). The *natura naturans* is the living principle of every act; the *natura naturata* is the totality of beings and laws. See also St Thomas Aquinas, *Summa Theologica* I-II, 85; *De divin. nom.* IV, 21.

the organic bond between the ideal and empirical aspects of the world, while taking into account the perversities that result from the freedom of the creature to
deviate from its proper nature. The radical disordering of this relationship results
in what the sophiologists call the obscured face[6] of created *Sophia*.[7]

Created or earthly *Sophia* is made 'in the image' of heavenly *Sophia*, the Wisdom of God that contains his ideas of the world. Earthly *Sophia*, the created ideal
which is the root of the world, must attain its likeness to the heavenly *Sophia*,
but the freedom of the human spirit has upset its hierarchy and perverted the relationship of the creature with the 'sophianic' principles. Faults in the being allow
the infiltration of evil, which is the broth of parasitic and diseased growths that
make up a parody of *Sophia*, 'the nocturnal aspect of creatures,'[8] its demonic
mask.

Sophiology,[9] the glory of current Orthodox theology, is alone in raising the
great question about the cosmos. It is opposed equally to agnostic acosmism, and
to closed evolutionist naturalism, but sees the cosmos in liturgical terms. The
cosmology inherent in the liturgy interprets God's creation, revealing the original
conformity between the elements of the world and their ideal principle, the divine
thought; and this is the beauty of the world that human beings recognize according as they grow in communion with the Holy Spirit. St Gregory of Nyssa speaks
of 'the innate movement of the soul that impels it towards spiritual beauty'[10] and
St Basil of the 'burning, innate desire for goodness.'[11] A saint is intuitively aware
of this and sees the world, even in its present state, as spirit-bearing – 'heaven
and earth are full of your glory.' Viewed inwardly, nature reveals its capacity to
contain the infinite and to gather into one those separated elements that are, according to St Basil, already bound in 'sympathy'; similarly St Maximus in his
Centuries poetically depicts the divine *Eros* making the cosmos to spring out of
chaos.[12]

The world moves towards God in a cosmic liturgy, and God moves towards
the world. But the royal freedom of this meeting implies a precariousness in the
perfection of our original state.

_____

[6] The Sophiologists' distinction between the clear and the clouded face, the diurnal and nocturnal face, corresponds to the 'evening knowledge' and 'morning knowledge' of St Augustine.
Cf. Meister Eckhart, *The Nobleman*.
[7] See Fr Basil Zenkovsky, *The problem of the cosmos in Christianity; the basic principles of
Christian cosmology; questions of education in the light of Christian anthropology* (in Russian).
[8] E. Trubetskoy, *The Meaning of Life*, ch. 3, Moscow 1981 (in Russian).
[9] Among the various approaches to sophiology, we should mention those of V. Soloviev, Fr P.
Florensky, Fr Sergei Bulgakov, Prince E. Trubetskoy and Fr B. Zenkovsky.
[10] *P.G.* 44, 161 C.
[11] *P.G.* 31, 909 BC.
[12] *De ambiguis, P.G.* 91, 1260 C.

2. NATURE BEFORE THE FALL

In Orthodox theology grace is involved in nature from the very beginning, in the act of creation itself. The absence of grace would be a perversion annihilating nature, equivalent to the second death of the Apocalypse, something quite unthinkable. Nature is truly 'supernature', deiform and god-bearing in its very origins. In his essence humankind is struck in God's image, and that ontological deiformity explains how grace is 'co-natural' with nature, just as nature is conformed to grace. They are complementary and penetrate each other, thus sharing their very existence, 'the one in the other in the perfect Dove.'[13] However, the blessedness of Paradise was only the germ whose end is the deified state. When communion is freely broken, grace dries up; but the Incarnation restores order, and shows that the divine and the human belong together 'without either separation or confusion.' Hence St Maximus can define the purpose of life as 'reuniting the created nature with the uncreated nature through love, causing them to appear in unity and identity through the acquisition of grace.'[14]

Humankind is created to share in the nature of God (the *spiraculum vitae*) and God, through the Incarnation, shares in human nature. The deiformity of humankind corresponds to the humanity of God. The image of God in humankind and the image of humankind in God is that third term which really conditions the Incarnation, which makes ontologically possible the communion of two worlds. Christ is *perfectus homo* only because his nature is 'naturally' in communion with the divine nature, with the *perfectus Deus*. It goes without saying that 'naturally' does not in the least imply 'naturalism'; the divine is not at all natural to the human; there is between the two a *hiatus*, a great gulf, bridgeable only by participation in the divine, which is a spiritual gift, but of a spirituality that is inherent in human nature: 'If you are pure, heaven is in you; within yourself you shall see the angels and the Lord of the angels.'[15] In its innermost depth human being perceives God's presence and image, closer to it than it is to itself; the divine is paradoxically more human than humanity itself, which is a mere abstraction. Humanity, being deiform, cannot work out its destiny on its own. The soul is the place of presences and meetings, preordained by its conjugal nature to communion with its counterpart, whether in betrothal or adultery. The choice is not between the angelic and the animal, but between God and the demonic.

'Always and in everybody, God wishes to work the mystery of his Incarnation,'[16] for the Incarnation is God's response to his already established presence

---

[13] St Gregory of Nyssa, *In Cant.*, h. 15.
[14] *De ambiguis*, *P.G.* 91, 1308 B.
[15] St Isaac the Syrian. Russian translation edited by the Theological Academy of Moscow, 1854.
[16] St Maximus, *Amb.*, *P.G.* 91, 1308 C.

in humanity, to his image in humankind. So atonement is a matter not so much of human nature *making amends* as of its *being mended*. The Word leaves 'the peaceful silence' to establish the deifying communion, 'the synthesis premeditated and pre-existent before all ages.'[17] He is incarnate in the first, original nature (through his miraculous birth), he assumes our unfinished condition and perfects it; in him Paradise is already fulfilled as the Kingdom ('the Kingdom of God is near'). Following him, every creature recapitulated in Christ is *restored* and directed towards the *status naturae integrae*. That is why in the East atonement is usually discussed in physical and ontological rather than ethical and juridical terms; and the end is not 'redemption', or even 'salvation' (in the 'salvationist' or individual sense), but *apocatastasis*, universal restoration and healing.[18] Incarnation and *theosis* are complementary, so that we can see original justice not as a gift of grace but as the very *root* of the being, which corresponds to God's desire to re-establish himself in humankind. To this divine end humankind is in its essence cast in the divine likeness.

3. THE FALL AND THE ECONOMY OF SALVATION

The Fall severely inhibits the image of God but does not corrupt it. It is the likeness, the possibility of resemblance, that is chiefly affected. The Greeks teach that *homo animalis*, although deprived of grace after the Fall, still keeps its essential human qualities; but while the image might not be tarnished, the original relationship of humankind to grace is so disordered that only the miracle of atonement can restore it to its 'natural' truth. In its fall humankind feels deprived, not of anything additional, but of its true nature, which is why the Fathers say that the essence of the Christian soul is the 'return to Paradise', its longing for its true nature.

In the West, human nature is taken to comprise intellectual and animal life, spiritual (supernatural) life being added to and even superimposed on the purely human

---

[17] St Maximus, *Qu. a. T.* 60; *P.G.* 90, 612 AB.
[18] Fr de Bachelet (*Dictionnaire de Théologie Catholique*, vol. 2, col. 688) observes that the thinking of the Fathers 'scarcely ever stays on individuals, but is directed at humanity and its purpose in the earthly economy'. Origen in his *Homily on Leviticus* portrays Christ as unable to enjoy perfect bliss as long as a single member remains sunk in evil (*In Levit. hom.* 7, n. 2) – 'for we make up a single body waiting for redemption'. Similarly, St Hippolytus: 'Desiring the salvation of all, God calls us all to form a single perfect Man' (*On Christ and the Antichrist*, ch. 3 & 4). Clement of Alexandria: 'The *totus Christus* is not divided... He is the new Man, entirely transformed by the Spirit' (*Protreptic*, ch. 11); St Maximus: 'To put on the entirely new Man, who is created by the Spirit in the image of God' (*Capit. theolog. et oeconom.*, cent. 2. ch. 27).

economy. Chiefly in the reaction to Baianism (the teaching that grace was an integral part of nature) and in Tridentine theology, grace was understood in the West[19] as extrinsic to the creature; if the supernatural order had to be superimposed, then nature must be essentially foreign to it. The Reformers perpetuated this belief, developing the supernatural grace of the scholastics into an anti-natural principle. In eastern spirituality, to follow nature always leads to an encounter with grace. In the East, the phrase 'in the image of God' exactly describes what humankind naturally is. To be created in the image of God brings with it the grace of that image, so in eastern spirituality to follow one's true nature is to work in the direction of grace. Grace is co-natural, supernaturally natural to nature. Nature possesses an innate need for grace, a gift that spiritualizes it from the start. The term 'supernatural' in eastern mysticism is reserved for the highest degree of deification. The natural order is thus conformed to the order of grace, is completed in it and finds its highest expression in the grace that deifies. St John of Damascus defines ascesis as 'the reverting of what is contrary to nature to what is proper to it.'[20] At Baptism nature is reclothed in the white garments that properly belong to it. The image embraces intellectual and spiritual life, uniting the νοῦς and the πνεῦμα; it is animal life that is added on.[21] Before the Fall this animal life was external to humankind but open and turned towards it, waiting to be spiritualized and humanized, but events were overtaken by the fall of the senses so that animal life was added on to human nature. 'The passions are not the essence of the soul but something extra.'[22] The forbidden fruits of the two trees in the biblical narrative have a clearly eucharistic meaning: the whole point is the eating. Eating the forbidden fruit amounts to a 'demonic eucharist' in which the worldly element (fruit) and the demonic (disobedience of the command) are introduced into human nature; this is clearly expressed in the rite of exorcism in the sacrament of Baptism.

'When we discard our ugly dead garment of animal skins (for I take the "garment of skins" to mean the form of animal nature with which we were clothed in consequence of our dealings with the sensory world) we shall cast off along with

---

[19] Cf. H. de Lubac, *Surnaturel*, Paris 1946. See also *Introduction aux 'Centuries sur la Charité' de saint Maxime*, by Fr Pegon.

[20] *De fide orth.*, I, 30; *P.G.* 94, 976 A. The supernatural was indeed the true nature of humankind in Paradise. His task, according to St Irenaeus, was 'the absorption of the flesh by the spirit,' aided by his communion with the divine. The principle still holds good. As St Augustine finely puts it, 'Whoever is not spiritual in carnal things, becomes carnal in spiritual things'.

[21] Jean Danielou says, 'Here [in western theology] we are presented with a 'natural' humanity, to which grace is added... According to St Gregory [of Nyssa] the opposite is true: the image of God was there to begin with, and it is the 'natural' humanity that was added' (*Platonisme et théologie mystique*, Paris 1944, p. 63). See also the article by Y. Congar, 'La doctrine de la déification', in *Vie Spirituelle*, 1938. H. de Lubac, *Surnaturel*, Paris 1946.

[22] St Isaac the Syrian, *Hom.* 3.

it all that has been added to us as a result of that animal skin.'[23] The white garment received in Baptism marks the return to the 'spiritual body'. The biological and animal nature signified by the garment of skins appears alien to the true nature of humankind because it was added before it could be spiritualized, before humankind, appointed as steward of creation, could subordinate the material to the spiritual. Assimilation came too soon and caused a fault in the order of being.[24] As a result of this disorder animal nature, although good in itself, is a debasement of humanity.[25] 'It is not desire that is bad, only a certain sort of desire, concupiscence.'[26] It is the axiological faculty, the discernment of value, which is affected:[27] 'Away from God, reason becomes like the beast or demons, and distanced from its nature, desires what is foreign to it.'[28]

Ascesis reaches its full glory in its longing for true nature; its struggle is never against the flesh but against deformations of it, above all against their underlying spirit. Thereafter it is concerned not so much with forgiveness and the restitution of grace, as with transformation and complete healing. The ascetic state of 'impassible passion' anticipates the age to come, of which the submission of wild beasts to the saints is an eloquent sign.[29]

The spring is poisoned, for the spirit is at odds with the structure of being. St Gregory Palamas regards the passions that come from nature as the least grave; they only express the weight of matter that results from its failure to be spiritualized. The true source of evil is the divided heart, 'the dispensary of justice and of iniquity'[30] where evil and good are found strangely side by side. As 'image', humankind always seeks the absolute, but away from Christ the 'likeness' cannot function, and sin leads astray the instincts of the heart, which then seeks the absolute in idols and quenches its thirst in mirages, lacking the strength to climb back to God. Grace reduced to a state of potentiality[31] can no longer reach humankind except by the supernatural path – supernatural, not in relation to nature,

---

23 *P.G.* 46, 148 D.

24 Clement of Alexandria sees the original sin in the fact that 'our ancestors embarked on procreation too soon' (*Strom.* III, 18).

25 'There is nothing wrong with things, provided they are not abused so as to inflict disorder on the spirit' (St Maximus, *Cent. Car.* 3, 4; *P.G.* 90, 1017 CD).

26 Didymus the Blind, *Fragmentia in Proverbia* XI, 7, *P.G.* 39, 1633 B.

27 St Basil, *In Psalm.*, 61, *P.G.*, 29, 480 A.

28 *Homil.* 51. Quoted by Fr C. Kern, *The Anthropology of St Gregory Palamas*, p. 408 (in Russian).

29 The animal world instinctively knows the 'odour of sanctity', the royal dignity that a saint possesses as a cosmic word. On the odour of sanctity, see E. Lohmeyer, *Vom göttlichen Wolhgeruch*, Heidelberg.

30 *Hom. Spirit.* XV, 32.

31 'Humankind has stopped in itself the effusion of divine grace' (Philaret of Moscow, *Addresses and Sermons*, I, 5).

but to its sinful condition. The truth of humankind is pre-existent to its double-heartedness, and resumes its dominance from the moment that humankind is in Christ. The vision from below must be complemented by the vision from above, which reveals that sin, like all negation, is secondary. No evil will ever be able to efface the original mystery of humankind, for there exists nothing that can annihilate in it the indelible stamp of God.

According to St Paul sin derives its strength from the law, which at the same time points to the true standard that is in Christ, which is sanctity. Similarly 'you will be like God' is not a pure illusion, for temptation takes truth for its springboard: 'You are all gods'. And original justice, lost but not destroyed, is a preparation for remorse and an invitation to penitence. The rite of burial expresses this clearly; we truly understand the impoverished state of the human being reduced to a corpse only when we are being raised to the glory of our first destiny. A caricature is demonic only in contrast with its ontological opposite, the icon.

Now we can see why the first destiny is so important in Greek Patristic theology: 'By Christ the integrity of our nature is restored', because he 'represents in a figure or archetype what we are',[32] and conversely, in Christ we become like him. The sacraments remake the first nature of humankind; the Holy Spirit, given to the first human being in the 'breath of life', is given to us in Holy Baptism and the Chrism of Unction. Penitence is essentially a therapeutic treatment; and in the Eucharist we have the leaven of incorruptibility, φάρμακον ἀδανασίας. Sanctity and miracles are signs of the return of the human to its original power; they are as much a special gift of the Spirit as they are the normal rule. Christ the Archetype remodels humankind, like a statue, after his image. The *opus Dei* centred on the paschal mystery not only anticipates the *status naturae integrae* but brings us to share it here and now.

---

[32] St Gregory of Nazianzus, *P.G.* 37, 2.

4

The Anthropology of Deification

In western theology the essence of God is identical with his existence. From this absolutely simple principle it follows logically that God *is what he has*, and no distinction can be made between his essence and his energies; the desired end of Christian life can only be the *visio Dei per essentiam*. Since there can be no interpenetration of the divine and human essences, deification is impossible – *tertium non datur*. Human beings are created for beatitude, and everything in them is directed towards the grace of the *visio beata*. Western anthropology is essentially *moral*, focused on the supreme Good, which is to be attained through good works undertaken in the Church Militant as it conquers the world.[1]

In the East, while positive theology refracts the unutterable mystery through the prism of thought, God's essence remains transcendent. It is beyond the reach even of the angels who are bathed in the 'trisolar' light. The hand of YHWH hides the face that 'none shall see and live'; every attempt to 'define' God is therefore punished by death. St Gregory of Nyssa says that the vision of God is granted even while it is being refused.[2] To see 'the back' of God (Exod. 33.23) means to contemplate his operations, his energies, but never his essence. The distinction in God between essence and energy, fundamental for St Basil[3] and afterwards for St Denys,[4] St John of Damascus,[5] and St Gregory Palamas,[6] does not affect the divine simplicity, which in the East is not even subject to the laws of logic. God in himself exceeds every concept of being, and the attributes that logically belong to him do not necessarily express, and can never define him. This distinction is the foundation of *theosis*, the deified state of the human being,

---

[1] After St Augustine, St Ambrose, Latin theology from the 12th century replaces the theology of *theosis* by the theology of filiation and of grace. See Lot-Borodine, 'La doctrine de la 'déification' dans l'Eglise grecque jusqu'au XIᵉ siècle', in *Revue des Sciences philosophiques et théologiques*, 1933, 1935; W. Lossky, 'La notion des Analogies chez Denys', in *Arch. d'hist. doct. du M.A.*, 1930. J. Gross, *La divinisation du chrétien d'après les Pères grecs*. Paris 1938; M. Cappuyns, *Jean Scot Erigène*, Louvain-Paris 1933. Y. Congar, 'La déification', in *Vie Spirituelle*, May 1935; J. Danielou, *Platonisme et Théologie mystique*, Paris 1944.

[2] *De Vita Moysis. P.G.* 44, 404 A.

[3] *P.G.* 32, 869 AB.

[4] *P.G.* 3, 640.

[5] *P.G.* 94, 800 BC.

[6] *P.G.* 150, 1176 BC.

its spiritualization by the divine energies. The energies are destined to be manifested in a place suitably prepared for them, and human beings are destined to be transformed in their light.

Orthodox anthropology is therefore not moral but *ontological*; it is the *ontology of deification*. It is founded not on the conquest of this world but on 'capturing the Kingdom of God', which works on this world from within, transforming it into the Kingdom, progressively enlightening it by the divine energies.

The Church then can be seen as the place where worship and the sacraments have the power to transform; it is revealed as essentially a Eucharist, the divine life in the human, the epiphany and the icon of heavenly reality. Under this aspect of *Ecclesia orans* the Church consecrates and sanctifies more than it teaches.

The Fathers enrich their understanding of the Pauline 'filiation' by Johannine interpretation: the Son is the one in whom God makes his abode, the place of divine 'indwelling'. The Holy Spirit leads us to the Father in Jesus Christ, making us members 'of the same body' (Eph. 3.6), an image obviously related to the Eucharist. St Cyril of Jerusalem strongly emphasizes the fact that the partakers of the Meal, the 'leaven and bread of eternal life', become one flesh, one blood with Christ, a point reinforced by the prayer of St Simeon Metaphrastes, read after Holy Communion:

O thou who, of thine own good will, givest me thy Body for food,
Thou who art a fire consuming the unworthy;
Consume me not, O my Creator,
But rather enter into my limbs, my joints, my heart,
And burn the tares of my transgressions.
Cleanse thou my soul, and sanctify my thoughts.
Strengthen my limbs, together with my bones.
Enlighten my five senses. Stablish me wholly in thy fear.

The human is 'Christified', 'the clay receives royal dignity ... is transformed into the substance of the king'.[7]

There is a close parallel between the way of the sacraments and the life of the soul in Christ.[8] Initiation through Baptism and Chrismation, culminating in the Eucharist, corresponds to the mystical ascent to the pinnacle of *theosis*. They are two representations of the same event, each clarifying the other, mystically identical. Here we see realized the golden rule of all Patristic thought, 'God became human so that humans might become god', and we touch the very heart of Orthodox spirituality: 'The human becomes by grace what God is by nature'.[9]

---

[7] Nicholas Cabasilas, *The Life in Christ*, translated by de Catanzaro, New York 1982.

[8] N. Cabasilas calls his treatise on the sacraments, *The Life in Christ*.

[9] The Fathers find a threefold foundation in Scripture for their teaching on deification: 1) the

The ascetic life is a gradual ascent to *theosis*, climbing the steps of the 'heavenly ladder'. The sacramental life, by contrast, offers grace instantly. A sermon of St John Chrysostom, read during matins at Easter, exactly catches this note of prolific generosity: 'Enter ye all into the joy of your Lord and receive your reward, the first and second alike; rich and poor, rejoice together; sober and lazy, honour this day; you who have fasted and you who have not fasted, rejoice today ... the feast is ready; all share in it.' According to the same author,[10] in the Eucharist Christ 'dissolves in us the heavenly reality of his flesh', instils it into us; and all the spiritual authorities emphasize the 'fire' that we devour in the Holy Communion. 'I came to bring fire to the earth' refers precisely to this eucharistic flame.

Like the bread and wine, the human being becomes a particle of the deified nature of Christ. The leaven of immortality, the very power of the Resurrection, is united to our nature and pervaded by the divine energies.[11] We could say that the mystical and spiritual life is the progressive conscious realization of the sacramental life. Both are described as a mystical marriage; they are essentially the same.

---

creation of humankind in God's image; 2) the filial adoption; 3) the imitation of God and of Christ. Moreover, the existence of superhuman, theandric beings is conditioned by their destiny to become 'paticipants' in the divine nature (2 Peter 1.4) and their origin as the 'offspring' of God (Acts 17.28). Clement of Alexandria cites (Psalm 82.6), 'you are gods, children of the Most High, all of you' (*P.G.* 8, 281 A). St Irenaeus prepares the way for the theology of St Athanasius. St Cyril speaks of the Spirit who deifies us – Θεοποιῦν – (*P.G.* 75, 1089 CD) and Denys the Areopagite substitutes the term Θέωσις for Θεοποίησις. God is humanized and the human is deified; this idea recurs with St Maximus (*P.G.* 91, 1113 BC). For him, incarnation and divinization are the two faces of the same mystery. St Gregory of Nazianzus puts it thus: 'God in the right place' – Θεὸς Θετός μεν – (*P.G.* 37, 690). St Gregory of Nyssa, in line with tradition, strongly emphasizes the irreducible distance – διάστημα – between the image and the divine Archetype, and the consequent impossibility of confusion.

[10] *Homily on 1 Cor.* St Gregory of Nyssa, and above all St Cyril of Alexandria, insist that divinization is effected by the deified flesh of the Word (*P.G.* 73, 577-580). On the ontological character of *theosis* in the Eucharist: St Simeon, *P.G.* 120, 321-327. According to St Gregory Palamas, the light on Tabor is a manifestation of the grace of the deifying energies (*P.G.* 154, 860-861).

[11] For St Macarius the 'spirit' in humankind is first and foremost its receptivity to the penetration of the whole being by the deifying energies (*P.G.* 154, 860-861).

ANTHROPOLOGY, LITURGICAL OR DOXOLOGICAL[12]

Discontinuity is foreign to the Orthodox mind; all ages and all planes of being are mysteriously and closely related. From this point of view even general history reveals religious truth – paganism being referred to in the Liturgy as 'an infertile, sterile church', but a church nonetheless. The Fathers often say that at the Fall integrity was 'smashed into little pieces by sin.'[13] God with infinite patience 're-assembles' the scattered particles to recreate the original unity. Hence the Fathers' notion, rich in consequences for the history of religions and for missionary work, of 'visits' of the Word, before the Incarnation, and among religious groups ignorant of the revelation; the Word has thus been manifested in a still more kenotic and hidden way, in the extra-biblical 'invisible church' of the pagans.

Since the planes of being are continuous, the angelic world is very close to the human; the nearness of the heavenly powers eases the passage from outline to completion, from emptiness to charismatic fullness – *gratia plena* – and gives 'hagiophanic' anthropology[14] its liturgical and doxological character.

The Little and Great Entrances during the Divine Liturgy are also the entrances of the ranks of angels. Humankind joins in their song, especially the *Trisagion*, 'Holy God, Holy and Strong, Holy and Immortal': the Father, the source of holiness, is the Holy; the Son, who triumphs over death, is the Strong; the Holy Spirit, the breath of life, is the Life-giver. And the second chant, the *Sanctus*, returns to the theme of the anaphora, the worship of the Trinity in the Eucharist; the service of human beings is united afresh with the service of angels in one surge of adoration: 'Holy, Holy, Holy, Lord God of Hosts, heaven and earth are full of thy glory'. 'Be holy' and 'be perfect' connote the same fullness, the glory of the future age that has already begun here below. A saint is not a superman, but one who finds out the truth about humanity – that the human is a liturgical being – and lives accordingly. The human is defined most precisely and completely in liturgical worship; it is the subject of the *Trisagion* and the *Sanctus*: 'I will sing to the Lord as long as I live'. 'Abba Anthony, who lived in solitude, learned one day in a vision that a man as holy as himself was practising in the world as a doctor; he had given the surplus of his goods to the poor and all day long sang the *Trisagion*, joining with the choir of angels'.[15] This is the activity for which humankind is 'set apart', made holy. Singing to God is the unique

---

[12] Doxology: the liturgical formula of glorification.

[13] St Maximus, *Quaest. ad Thalass.*, *P.G.* 90, 25 B. St Augustine understands this to be the image of Adam; at his fall he is smashed into pieces, which then fill the whole universe. God gathers up the fragments, melts them in the fire of his charity and restores them to unity (*In Psalm.* 95, N. 15).

[14] 'Hagiophany' comes from ἅγιος – holy, and refers to any manifestation of sanctity.

[15] *P.G.* 65, 84. See Dom Stolz, *L'Ascèse chrétienne*, Ed. Chevetogne, 1948, p. 71.

human vocation, humanity's unique 'work'. 'And all the angels stood around the throne and around the elders and the four living creatures, and they fell on their faces before the throne and worshipped God ... saying, "Amen. Hallelujah!" And from the throne came a voice saying, "Praise our God, all you his servants."' (Rev. 7.11 and 19.4-5) In the catacombs the most common image is that of a woman at prayer, *orans*; she represents the only true attitude of the human soul. It is not enough to engage in prayer; we must *become* and *be* prayer, be constructed in the form of prayer, transform the world into a temple of worship, into a cosmic liturgy.[16]We must offer not what we have, but what we are. This is a favourite subject in iconography, condensing the message of the Gospel into one word: χαῖρε, 'rejoice and adore ... let everything that has breath praise the Lord'. The whole world is marvellously relieved of its burden, humankind's own weight is lifted from it. 'The King of Kings, Christ draws near,' and this is the one thing needful. 'Let us who in a mystery represent the cherubim and sing the thrice-holy hymn to the life-giving Trinity now lay aside all earthly cares that we may bear aloft the King of all who is invisibly borne in triumph by the ranks of angels. Alleluia, Alleluia, Alleluia.' Like the 'amen, amen, amen' of the epiclesis,[17] this is the seal of the Trinity, and we find it again in the doxology of the Lord's prayer, 'the kingdom, the power and the glory'. This kingdom not only comes (the Liturgy is the *memorial* of the one who comes), liturgical time is already the coming, the Parousia; and it is in response to their vocation as a liturgical being that human beings are charismatic, spirit-bearing: '[You] were marked with the seal of the promised Holy Spirit, this is the pledge of our inheritance towards redemption as God's own people, to the praise of his glory.' (Eph. 1.13-14) There could be no more exact description of humankind's liturgical calling.

Patristic meditation is focused always on the *opus Dei*, the eternal doxology. 'I go forward singing to you,' says St John Climacus, demonstrating the same joy as we see in the sublime words of St Gregory of Nyssa: 'Your glory, O Christ, is humanity, which you have appointed as an angel and *singer* of your radiance ... For you I live, speak and sing ... which out of all my possessions is the only thing I have left to offer.'[18] Similarly St Gregory Palamas: 'Once enlightened, humanity reaches the eternal summits ... Even while still here below it is miraculously transformed, and joins in the unending song of heaven; standing on the earth like an angel, it leads every creature to God.'[19] The Church is deeply mystagogical, 'gracefully' bringing us into time and space under their liturgical as-

---

[16] *Cosmic Liturgy* is the title of the book by von Balthasar; he applies it to the theology of St Maximus the Confessor.
[17] The prayer for the consecration of the eucharistic gifts, the invocation of the Holy Spirit.
[18] *P.G.* 37, 1327.
[19] *P.G.* 150, 1081 AB.

pect, which combine to make the setting for the Church's worship. Here the life of the Lord is recapitulated moment by moment and miraculously offered as an experience for all the faithful to share; as the Church sings, 'Met together in thy temple, we see one another in thy heavenly glory.'

5

Asceticism

In the flight to the desert we see monastic asceticism in its extreme and eschato-logical form, people burning with the desire for the Kingdom going out to meet the Parousia. The irresistible attraction of the desert was threefold: freedom from all worldly preoccupations, the opportunity to fight face to face with the demonic powers, and the quest for the native country which was ours before the Fall.

The Gospel tells us that the desert is where the devils are particularly at home (Luke 2.24 and 8.23). When St Anthony[1] withdrew to the solitude of the desert places, the devils were enraged at this trespass on their preserves: 'Get out of our territory!' and at the sight of his disciples they trembled: 'There is nowhere left for us ... even the desert is full of monks.'[2] Cassian reveals the Desert Fathers' hidden intention: 'Wishing to fight openly and directly against the devils they brave the vast lonely spaces of the desert.'[3] The 'athletes' of asceticism[4] were a match for the devils; they alone could look them in the face and endure their ter-rifying presence. (And they speak of the devils' intolerable stink, of the 'nausea of the spirit' that they caused.[5])

Despite the authority of the rules of St Basil recommending that monks should live in communities, the eremitical life has in Orthodoxy always taken precedence over the coenobitic life.[6] Because monasticism is of the essence of the Church, monastic spirituality, as an inward state of the soul, is normative *for all*, express-ing in its various forms the profound longing for the 'one thing needful' of the Gospel. According to the 133rd *Novella* of Justinian, 'The monastic life is *a holy thing*'. Therefore, according to St Cyril of Jerusalem, asceticism is a gift of the Holy Spirit;[7] and St Basil,[8] in his *Rules*, compares the monks to 'the violent' of the Gospel who 'take the kingdom by force'. The megaloschema (the final de-gree, that of the 'large habit') is a state of grace in which the monk learns silence

---

[1] See L. Bouyer, *La vie de saint Antoine. Essai sur la spiritualité du monachisme primitif,* 1950.
[2] A. Stolz, L'Ascèse chrétienne, Ed. de Chevetogne, 1948, p. 35.
[3] Coll. 18, 6; also 7, 23.
[4] ἄσκησις means exercising, effort, struggle (1 Cor. 9.24-27; Matt. 11.12).
[5] See K. Holl, *Enthusiasmus und Bussgewalt beim griechischen Mönchtum*, Leipzig 1898, p. 145.
[6] See F. Heiler, *Urkirche und Ostkirche*, 1937, p. 367.
[7] *Mystagogic Catacheses*, 16, 12.
[8] *P.G.* 31, 632.

and the supreme contemplation of hesychasm. St Athanasius's description of St Anthony, the Father of monasticism, as one who achieved perfection *without tasting martyrdom*,[9] marks an important turning-point in the history of Christianity. The 'baptism of blood' of the martyrs is transformed into an 'eschatological baptism' of asceticism. The true monk attains not simply a state of the soul, but the integrity of 'an angel on the earth', he is '*isangelos*' – equal to the angels – with the face of 'crucified love;'[10] witnessing to the last things, he already experiences the 'little resurrection'. In the command, 'if you wish to be perfect, sell what you *have*,' he hears, 'sell what you *are*.' This is total offering; ethical renunciation leads to ontological renunciation, the giving up of self. Having given away all that you have, and become poor, you offer all that you are, and become rich in God. That is why the old canons permit suicide in only one case, that of a virgin threatened with violation. The free offering of virginity reveals the inner meaning of martyrdom: 'Thy lamb, O Jesus, crieth aloud unto thee; I long for thee, my Bridegroom, and, seeking for thee, I endure sufferings, I am crucified with thee, and in Baptism I am buried with thee. I suffer for thy sake that I may reign with thee, and I die with thee that I may live with thee.'[11] St Paul's greatest wish is fulfilled: 'I promised you in marriage to one husband, to present you as a chaste virgin to Christ' (2 Cor. 11.2). In addition, the Desert Fathers consider chastity of soul and purity of heart to be the expression of apostolicity; 'the apostolic person' is one who through the grace of the Spirit realizes the final promises of St Mark's Gospel (16.17-18).[12] The apostolic heart, enlarged by the breath of the Spirit, becomes a striking testimony to the love of God. Humanity having sunk beneath its nature, now rises above it by means of asceticism and recovers its human dignity, displaying the new creature.

The classical image of the transformation of human nature, which is the goal of all asceticism, is seen in the miracle at the Marriage of Cana, the changing of the water into wine. It is *metanoia*, the rebalancing of the whole economy of the human being or its rebirth in the realm of the Spirit. The rite of exorcism in Baptism cuts us off from the power of the prince of this world, and the rite of the tonsure demonstrates that we have become different, even in our very nature. So it is the most radical breach with the past, the utterly real death and the equally real coming of the new creature: 'Now all is new.' As Nicholas Cabasilas says, speaking of the rite of unclothing, 'We go towards the true light, bringing nothing with us ... we leave the garments of skin and retrace our steps towards the royal mantle ... the baptismal water destroys one life and out of it brings another.'[13]

---

9 See D. Leclerq, article 'Monachisme' in DAL, XI, col. 1802.
10 An Athonite icon depicts the monastic state in the form of a crucified monk; according to Cassian every monk suffers 'torment on the Cross'. (*P.L.* 49, 160)
11 Troparion of virgin martyrs.
12 See I. Hausherr, 'Simeon the New Theologian', in *Orientalia Christiana*, XII, 1928, p. 30.
13 *The Life in Christ*, trans. de Catanzaro.

Asceticism closely follows the course of the sacraments, in which to halt at any point is to go backwards. 'No one who looks back is fit for the kingdom', for this new life is totalitarian in its quest for the extreme, the impossible – 'folly' according to worldly common sense. Unlike all kinds of quietism, asceticism never loses sight of its goal of perfection and the age to come, and therefore calls for infinite progress.

Asceticism and moralism are essentially different. Moralism governs ethical behaviour by submitting it to moral imperatives. But any morality that rests on natural strength is brittle. Its appearance may well conceal pharisaism, 'the pride of the meek.' 'Virtue,' however, according to the ascetics, is human energy activated by the presence of God.

1. SYNERGY

The invincible optimism of Orthodox spirituality, its underlying character, comes from its idea of the image of God in Man, of its faith in Man, the child of God. It is opposed to Gnostic fatalism, or the unhealthy anxiety of predestination, or the gloomy vision of the *massa damnata*. The East has never been touched by the Pelagian heresy.[14] Fallen nature, profoundly vulnerable, can rise above itself only if lifted up by divine action. On the subject of the lost coin, Nicholas Cabasilas observes, 'It is the Master who has leaned towards the earth and found his image again'.[15] The Fall had weakened the potential creativeness of human behaviour, it had destroyed the likeness, but it had not reached the image, and that is why the Master can find it again. Thanks to the image, humankind keeps its original freedom to choose, some of the independence of judgement that it had in the beginning. Even in the time of the Old Testament, there existed the desire for good, which is evidence in itself of some integrity of the free will, even though the human race was unable at the time to actualize the desire in its own life. In their theology of grace the Fathers, following Origen, warn of the danger of confusing the free will of intention with free will of acts. As against the *non posse non peccare* of St Augustine, the eastern Church affirms that the first movement of the will, its capacity for formulating the *fiat*, the desire for salvation and healing, is entirely free from any constraint or causality. To some extent that desire is already *effective*, for it meets the answering desire of God, and thus prepares for and brings about the coming of grace. Nevertheless, even this capacity is never purely human; by anticipation, even before Christ, it is theandric, because the grace of adoption is innate, incorporate in humanity from its creation, and underlies every truly human action.

---

[14] Perhaps the school of Antioch in the person of Theodore of Mopsuestia shows some traces of this.
[15] *The Life in Christ*, trans. de Catanzaro.

Once the image has been 'quickened' in Baptism, and after the assent of the will (the rite of exorcism, of the renunciation of Satan and the profession of faith), grace restores the participation in the likeness in order to actualize the potential deiformity. The psychological body is fulfilled in the spiritual body, the self-centred and demonic individuality in the theocentric personality. Within the order of grace, the human being can no longer not be free, for, inasmuch as it bears the divine image, its freedom is conformed to divine freedom. The eastern Church could not follow St Augustine without recanting and betraying itself.[16]

According to the Greeks, God laid aside his unique power when he deposited the gift of freedom in the substance of humanity. St Maximus and Nicholas Cabasilas bring out the essential point: the human race is not a 'second activity',[17] for grace never takes the place of human freedom. The human being's will is its own and free from the beginning, which is quite different from the mere freedom of response – contrition or the refusal of grace ('the merit *de congruo*' of the scholastics).

The dialectic of the elect, and the salvation of these elect alone, has never found a place in the thought of the Fathers; Christ died *for all*, so salvation is *potentially* universal. The problem of predestination is deliberately ignored; as a problem it is insoluble and remains apophatic. The eastern Church follows the Spirit which 'brings up the rear in order to announce in advance', so the Parousia means much more the advent of Glory and the cosmic transfiguration than the Judgement.

'I believe; help my unbelief!' (Mark 9.24) is formulated by St Maximus thus: 'Humankind has two wings to reach heaven – one is freedom, and the other grace'. For every effort of the will there is a supporting response from grace. It

---

[16] The theology of the image, almost unknown in the West, is replaced by the theology of created grace. Pantheism is avoided by a created intermediary or 'medium' that regulates communion between God and humankind (Albert the Great, *Sentences* II, 26). *Habitus infus* ensures the supernaturalizing of the heart and directs human beings towards God, disposing them to acts of goodness. According to St Thomas, created grace assimilates us to the very nature of God (*In Ioannem* 17, lect. 5, 9. See J. Backes, *Die Christologie des heiligen Thomas und die griechischen Kirchenvöter*, Paderborn, 1931). For Eckhart the human being during its divinization is entirely passive; the new being is infused and does not belong to the creature; it is in a sense uncreated. There is a danger here of a certain automatism even in holiness. The being is not really transfigured, but divinization is added, just like grace, almost as a matter of justice... However the doctrine of *theosis* is not entirely absent (cf. St Augustine, *Sermo* 166, 4, *P.L.* 38, 909; 36, 565; Tertullian, *P.L.* 2, 316, 317; Ambrose, *P.L.* 16, 401-403).

[17] The Council of Trent took note of the difference when it distinguished between the Augustino-Thomist doctrine and the 'synergism' of the Greeks; however, in the late 18th century Professor Johann Pfeffinger at Leipzig was correctly teaching synergism, but not a trace of this was left in Protestant thinking.

is 'interaction', dialogue, exchange of idioms – never two causes working in parallel, or a simple relationship of the creature to God. Grace, of its very nature, is the birthplace of two initiatives, but it is granted only to our total self-offering.

'The toil and sweat'[18] of ascetic effort is ours by right and in no way diminishes the prevenient gratuitousness of grace. 'Works' in eastern spirituality signify not moral actions (in the sense of the Protestant opposition of faith and works), but theandric energy, human action within divine action. St Maximus the Confessor expresses it with admirable conciseness: 'God does everything in us: virtue and knowing, and victory and wisdom and goodness and truth, while we contribute absolutely nothing other than the good disposition of the will'.[19]

2. THE ASCETICAL LIFE

Negatively and seen from below, asceticism is 'unseen warfare',[20] unceasing, without respite; positively and seen from above, it is illumination, the acquisition of gifts, living by grace. St Seraphim of Sarov[21] aptly says of the foolish virgins in the gospel parable (Matt. 25.1-13), that they were full of virtues – though 'foolish', they were 'virgins' – but they were empty of the gifts of the Holy Spirit. That is why the prayer addressed to the Holy Spirit asks, 'purify us from every stain', and 'come and abide in us.'

An ascetic begins by looking at his or her own human reality. 'Know yourself,' for 'nobody can know God without first having self-knowledge.'[22] 'Those who have seen their sin are greater than one who raises the dead,' and, 'those who have seen themselves are greater than one who has seen the angels.'[23] The importance of this understanding appears when we remember that the great paradox of evil, according to St Gregory of Nyssa, is that it has plunged being into non-being. The essentially illusory, insubstantial character of evil is much emphasized in the thought of St Gregory; in addition he speaks of its *parasitic* character: the passions grow like 'warts' – μυρμηκίαι, monstrous excrescences on the being that is created good.[24] Atheist existentialism develops this into a phi-

---

[18] *Life in Christ*, trans. Broussalaeux, p.89; Abba Isaiah, *Logos* 22, N. 8, ed. Augustinus, p. 141.
[19] *Ad Thal.* q. 54; *P.G.* 90, 512 B. On the subject of the 'toil and sweat', we might say paradoxically that it is God who 'works' and the human being who 'sweats'.
[20] See *Unseen Warfare*, trans. by Kadloubovsky and Palmer, Faber & Faber, London. Cf. *Combatimento Spirituale* by Lorenzo Scupoli, published in Venice in 1589.
[21] 'The aim of the Christian life', conversation with St Seraphim recorded by Nicholas Motovilov in 1831.
[22] *Philokalia* (in Russian), V. 1: *Teachings on the life in Christ.*
[23] See A.J. Wensinck, *Isaac of Nineveh, Mystic Treatises*, Amsterdam 1923.
[24] *De an. et res.*, *P.G.* 46, 56 C; *De mortuis*, *P.G.* 46, 529 A.

losophy of the absurd: 'Being is without reason, without cause, without necessity;'[25] 'Every living thing is born without reason, is prolonged through weakness, and dies by chance.'[26]

We recognize here the three barriers of sin, noted by Nicholas Cabasilas,[27] that Christ has removed: natural weakness, the perverted will, and finally death. Without Christ, there is only a futile rebellion (Camus, Bataille) against absurdity, that must end in nothingness. Anxiety turns into the delirium of a 'tormenting joy', manifested in a 'savage and inhuman laugh.'[28] The last stage of the Fall leaves us in the solitude of the conscious refusal of grace, which is the conciliar definition of mortal sin.

The Canon of St Andrew of Crete (read during Great Lent)[29] and the Canon of St John Damascene (the funeral rite) introduce us to the perfect science of the human heart and represent a sort of ascetic diving suit in which to descend to explore the depths peopled by monsters.

After seeing the 'snapshot' of its own abyss, the heart really yearns for the divine pity: 'From the depth of my iniquities, I call to the depth of your grace.' The elevation is *gradual*, an anagogical movement up the steps of 'the Ladder of Paradise' of St John Climacus, of which only the last symbolizes charity. Thus ascetic wisdom warns us of the danger of casualness in any enterprise of love. True love comes as a fruit of spiritual maturity, and crowns it, perfects it.

The atmosphere of ever deeper and refined humility envelops the ascetical life from beginning to end. St Anthony, at the moment of his death, and already radiant with light, said, 'I have not even begun to repent.'[30] Humility alone has the power[31] to root out every spirit of resentment, rebellion and self-centredness, for it shifts the axis of life from the human person into God; the human being no longer makes the universe turn about its *ego*,[32] but is itself within God and therefore in exactly the right place.[33]

---

25 J.-P. Sartre, *L'être et le néant*, p. 713.

26 J.-P. Sartre, *La nausée*, p. 170.

27 *The Life in Christ*, trans. de Catanzaro.

28 G. Bataille, *L'expérience interieure*, p. 59. It is exactly Kirilov's experience in *The Devils* by Dostoyevsky: whoever sets himself up as God finishes by committing suicide and, at the climactic moment, bursts into laughter.

29 A remarkable poem of 250 stanzas, *P.G.* 97, 1306-1444.

30 *Metanoia*, transformation and regeneration, is not an act but a state of the heart and therefore has no limits.

31 Anthony said, groaning, 'Who then shall escape?' and a voice replied, 'The humble' (*P.G.* 65, 77 B). Humility, far from being the glorification of human worthlessness, is the very proper sense of the *distance* between God and humankind, so that humankind knows exactly where it stands.

32 The attitude symptomatic of every form of hysteria.

33 St John Damascene, *P.G.* 94, 1553 AB.

In the 'unseen warfare' of ascesis attention is concentrated on the spiritual source of evil. This marks a great difference from the Latin approach, as conveyed in the expression, *infirmitas carnis,* or in its even more extreme Protestant form, *creatura ex sese deficit.* Sin does not come from below, from nature; it is conceived in the spirit[34] and only then is given mental and bodily expression. Ascesis charts the hierarchical structure of nature and aims at the mastery of the spiritual over the material. This entails an ascetical restoration of matter, which, like the passions, is good in the hands of the masters of the spiritual life. According to St Maximus the Confessor, even ἐπιθυμία, concupiscence, once purified, can become a burning desire for the divine.[35]

3. THE PASSIONS

Before anything else purification attacks the dominance of the emotions – πάθος, the immoderate giving way to feelings. By means of the highly developed science of the 'custody of the spirit,' or spiritual attentiveness, ascetic *metanoia* penetrates to the very root of the passions. Clement of Alexandria sees in the passions 'a movement of the heart against nature.'[36] This Alexandrian conception of the perversion of order, distorted by desires for the sensible (passions), is shared by all the Byzantine spiritual masters. The Fall immerses the being in the senses, attaches the heart – the seat of the emotions – to matter, and so disrupts the divine communion. God becomes external in proportion as the passions become internal to a person, identifying themselves with the 'shadowy spirits lodged close to the heart.' That is why the chief object of ascesis is to externalize any propensity to flee from God; to free the human being from the world (meaning the passions), so that it is really *extra mundum factus.* The 'error of judgement,'[37] a defective sense of values, finds an object 'against nature,' is pleased with it and introduces disorder into the realm of reason, the spirit.[38] The memory becomes blurred, the watchful interior dialogue – the *syndyasmos* – is relaxed, and impure suggestions are welcomed. Desire becomes tinged with lust and anger and inclines towards the consent to sin.[39] From potential capability the will proceeds to the act and evil takes root, resulting in the terrible αἰχμαλωσία – captivity of the heart. That is why a perfect understanding of evil encourages us to persevere in developing

---

[34] Φιλαυτία – pride is the cause of the Fall and of all sin (St John Climacus, *P.G.* 88, 1626).
[35] *Qu. ad T.* ; *P.G.* 90, 269 B.
[36] *Strom.* II, 13.
[37] St Basil, *In Psalm.* 61, *P.G.* 29, 480 A.
[38] So for St Gregory of Nyssa the appearances of ghosts in cemeteries is evidence of the materialization of souls because of an excessive love of earthly things (*De an. et res.*, *P.G.* 46, 88 BC).
[39] Mark the Hermit, *P.G.* 66.

ascetic attentiveness, vigilance – *nepsis*, and is utterly opposed to the sectarian teaching of the Quietists (Molinos and La Combe), to whom everything is permitted because they are 'pure', having risen above good and evil. The denial or ignorance of ascesis seriously fails to acknowledge the laws of the spiritual life, and simplistic fideism inevitably confuses the psychological and the spiritual. 'Nobody unaided can know what he needs,'[40] but obedience to the ascetic rule leads to the perfect balance which preserves us from Quietist insufficiency and Pelagian excess.

Indeed, '*apatheia*, impassibility, means not that we never experience passions, but that we never welcome them;'[41] thus we shall see and recognize the evil before being actually tempted to commit it. The bad use of desires *against nature* is a diversion from the only desire *according to nature* which is desire for God, 'the ultimate desirable.' Ascetic progress never destroys the passions, but converts them into 'impassible passion'[42] and brings them together in silent expectation of the moment when God will reclothe the soul with the divine form. This is the basic pre-hesychasm of eastern spirituality which was later refined into hesychasm.[43] Through ascetic purification it becomes that passion for the faith whereby we experience the nearness of God only by his hiddenness and remoteness. *Eros* is purged of any spirit of self-centredness and possessiveness and becomes the strongest kind of love, concentrated charity; such an intense thirst for God can actually serve as a criterion for the recognition of holiness.[44] 'Really seeing God means never finding the satisfaction to that desire.'[45] The heart's ceaseless and infinite yearning for God, the continual transcending of desire itself, its 'inexhaustible transformation', results in the antinomic experience of the nearness of God. The more intense this experience is, the more radically transcendent it is seen to be. When the heart is surrendered in total self-sacrifice and humility, 'knowing is transformed into love and union.'[46]

4. THE ASCETIC WAY

The ascetical recollection of death is opposed to *accidie* – life-robbing dreariness and sadness – and becomes a powerful reminder of and joyful longing for eternity.[47] Penitence, for its part, deepens the image of Baptism, its descent to hell

---

[40] St Basil, *Monastic Constitutions.*
[41] *Philokalia, Centuries of Callistus and Ignatius.*
[42] St Gregory of Nyssa, *P.G.* 44, 772 A.
[43] See *The Life of St Anthony* by St Athanasius (*P.G.* 26, 835-976).
[44] St Gregory of Nyssa, *P.G.* 44, 1048 C.
[45] St Gregory of Nyssa, *P.G.* 44, 404 AD.
[46] St Gregory of Nyssa, *P.G.* 46, 96 C.
[47] According to the remarkable expression in a homily of Narsai, 'The death of Jesus has made our death into a sleep.'

and its victory over death. It provokes remorse for having offended the holiness of God, of having refused his crucified love to the point of adding to his wounds. The *donum lacrymarum*, the gift of tears, is evidence of the spiritualization of the senses.[48] The tears of penitence do not spring from any sentimental tenderness but are mingled with tears of joy as the continuation of the purifying waters of Baptism.[49] Being essentially practical and concrete, ascesis exorcizes evil by living a good life. The energies of the spirit are redirected: 'In the perfect heart the strength of the passions themselves – παθητική δύναμις – is turned towards God',[50] bringing rest, peace, *hesychia*.

Perpetual prayer becomes a constant state; the human being feels light, detached from earthly weight, stripped of its *ego*. The world in which the ascetic dwells is the world of God, astonishingly alive, for it is the world of those who have been crucified and raised to life. By the light of the flame burning in the depth of a 'poor' person's heart, we can see what the Gospel calls 'richness in God.' From 'having' and all it entails, the person proceeds to being. The person becomes prayer incarnate.

God is simple, and the heart of the Father is unity. Evil is complicated and therefore dispersed. Asceticism reunites and integrates the creature 'after the image' of the divine simplicity. An ascetic, in the unity of the interior world, contemplates 'the truths of things,' the thoughts of God, and by the power of his or her own unity tilts the material plane towards its ultimate destiny: the praise of God – liturgy.

In its mystical nature Orthodoxy is highly resistant to all imagination, to all figurative representation, whether visual or auditory, but at the same time it has invented devotion to icons, surrounding itself with images using them to construct the visible Church. The icon 'sanctifies the eyes of the beholders, and lifts their minds to the mystical knowledge of God.'[51] By the theology of symbols, it raises us towards a presence without form and without image. The icon comes from the Incarnation and takes us back to the immaterial God. Nature is portrayed in keeping with iconological teaching, dematerialized, detached from the earth, but entirely real.

Eastern mysticism is anti-visionary, holding all imaginative contemplation (meditation by using the will and the imagination) to be 'a snare of the devil', deceiving the mind with the illusion that we can 'capture divinity in pictures and

---

[48] St John Climacus teaches that 'The tears of penitence are a continuation of the waters of Baptism' ; see Lot-Borodine, 'Le mystère du don des larmes dans l'Orient chrétien', in *La Vie Spirituelle*, 1936. Also I. Haussherr, *Penthos, the Doctrine of Compunction in the Christian East*, Rome 1944.

[49] See I. Haussherr, *The Life of Simeon*.

[50] St Maximus, *De charit.*, III, 93.

[51] Synodicon of the Sunday of Orthodoxy.

forms.' Correct contemplation is intelligible and super-intelligible. Beyond speech and sight, there is enlightenment *divino modo*, invisible, inaudible and inexpressible. Knowing by unknowing plunges into the light of nearness without form. 'Circular contemplation' brings the soul back to the heart, enstasy coincides with ecstasy. Seeing the world as the icon of the heavenly leads us to the apophatic knowledge of the Trinity, to theology as the Fathers of the Church understand it.

6

Mystical Experience

The spiritual masters all agree in distinguishing three elements that make up the spiritual life: the divine, the demonic and the human.[1] The divine element is freely given: 'Flesh and blood has not revealed this to you, but my Father in heaven.' (Matt. 16.17) The divine presence is pure grace and utterly transcendent: 'this is not your own doing; it is the gift of God,' as St Paul says (Eph. 2.8). Secondly there is the demonic element, the 'murderer from the beginning, the father of lies,' who obstructs the path and makes every moment a relentless struggle: 'Discipline yourselves; keep alert. Like a roaring lion your adversary the devil prowls around, looking for someone to devour.' (1 Pet. 5.8) Here the human being is active on its own behalf, waging the 'unseen warfare' of ascesis. The final, mystical element is human receptiveness: 'Listen! I am standing at the door, knocking; if you hear my voice and open the door, I will come in to you and eat with you, and you with me.' (Rev. 3.20) This clear reference to the Eucharist can well be applied to what we can call the 'interior Liturgy', or even 'interior Eucharist', of the mystical life. Nicholas Cabasilas wrote a treatise on the sacraments entitled *Life in Christ*; Father John of Kronstadt called his book describing his eucharistic experience *My Life in Christ*. Progressive enlightenment by way of communion and participation is the very heart of mysticism. The term 'mysticism', incidentally, is western; Orthodoxy speaks of participation, pneumatization or *theosis*. But while every mystic is an ascetic, it does not follow that every ascetic is a mystic. *Theosis* is never a reward. 'God is our Creator and Saviour, not the one who measures and weighs our works.'[2] The human being offers his or her heart and every ascetical effort.[3] What comes from God is pure gift. 'If God weighed our merits, then no one would enter the King-

---

[1] St Seraphim says there are three wills at work in human beings: divine, human and demonic (Cf. A. D'Ales, 'La doctrine de la récapitulation en saint Irenée'. *Revue des Sciences religieuses*, 1916); St John Climacus in *Scala Paradisi* (26th step) identifies the triple origin of our acts: God, the devil and our own nature.

[2] On justification by works, Philokalia (in Russian) v. I; *P.G.* 65, 929-965.

[3] In his *Explicatio Div. Lit.* N. Cabasilas says, 'We give up one life in exchange for another. Now, to surrender our life is indeed to die. While making us sharers in his Resurrection the Lord requires that something of this great gift is reserved for him. But what? The imitation of his death: and that is by disappearing three times into the waters of Baptism as into a tomb.' Mme Lot-Borodine adds: 'This imitation is therefore an *offering*, which makes Baptism like the sacrament of the altar, where the sacred elements are always gifts' ('The deifying grace of the sacraments', in *Revue des Sciences philosophiques et théologiques*, 1936, p. 322, N. 1).

dom of God.' 'God does everything in us,' says St Maximus,[4] but this truth is dialectical and contradictory; the work of God is accompanied by human 'sweat'. The soul is concentrated not so much on salvation (in the sense of the individual salvation of the Salvationists) as on making the response that God is waiting for. At the centre of the immense biblical drama of God lies the interaction, not of grace and sin, but of the two *'fiats'*, the meeting of the love descending from God – κατάβασις – and the love ascending from humankind – ἀνάβασις, the Incarnation. If one thing in this world had to be saved, it would be not humankind, but the love of God, which came first. The liturgy strongly teaches theocentrism, the divine activity, and it makes humankind no longer self-centred; its gaze is directed not at the human, but at the divine. When celebrating the Nativity the liturgical emphasis is not on the human containing the uncontainable, but on the uncontainable who makes his dwelling in the human. However, mysticism is not necessarily identical with contemplation; that is only one of its forms. Mystical life is essentially life in the divine, and the divine, in the East, chiefly means not power, but the source that gives rise to the new creature and the new life.[5]

Classical doctrine distinguishes three ages of the spiritual life: 'God first revealed himself to Moses in the light (διὰ φωτός); afterwards he spoke with him in the cloud (διὰ νεφέλης); finally, having become more perfect, Moses contemplates God in the darkness (ἐν γνόφῳ τὸν Θεὸν βλέπει).'[6]

The first degree is πρᾶξις or *catharsis* – purification – of which the ultimate aim is ascetical ἀπάθεια. The second degree is called the cloud, the contemplation of God in his works and in his attributes or names (wisdom, power, goodness); contemplation that transcends the sensible and rises to the knowledge of intelligible things and of the divine power (the γνῶσις τῆς δυνάμεως). The third degree, the 'darkness', represents pure mystical experience, the sensing of the presence of God in the heart, when to go back into oneself is to turn towards God and gaze on his reflection in the mirror of the soul. The intelligible me is *reduced* to the self, which, as the *image of God*, can be seen as 'the place of God.'[7] The vision is indirect, reflected in the soul. Θεωρία when purified is unitive, unutterable and 'transdiscursive'; at its highest point it *creates unity* (ἐνωτική).[8]

The science of icons perfectly illustrates the principle of contemplation. The icon 'raises the intelligence to theognosis.' Having conducted us into the 'presence' of which it is a revelatory sign, it is totally effaced by it, and symbolic theology gives place to theognosis. The icon is a representation which paradoxically

---

[4] *Ad. Thalass.* q. 54; *P.G.* 90, 512 B.
[5] See Prince E. Trubetskoy, *The Philosophy of V. Soloviev* (in Russian), 1912; *The Meaning of Life* (in Russian), 1918.
[6] St Gregory of Nyssa, *The Life of Moses*, 11th hom. *Cant.*, *P.G.* 44, 1000 CD.
[7] Evagrius, *Practicos*, I, 70-71.
[8] Denys the Areopagite, *De divinis nominibus*, 701 B.

denies all representation, banishing all images by means of the beauty seen in it. It leads us from the invisible-in-the-visible towards the purely invisible.

Contemplation advances gradually through all the levels of awareness and the depths of reality that correspond to them in the world. Mystical experience closely follows the principle of phenomenological reduction: the first resurrection – detachment from the senses – leads to pure intelligibility, the stripping bare of the *nous*. Increased receptivity makes possible the restoration of the likeness to God that Adam had in the beginning. Made 'capable of God,' the spirit is directed towards *theosis* that culminates in perfect union. This spiritualization precludes any φαντασία or apparition, all phenomena of sight or hearing. The anagogical ascent is accompanied by successive purifications and strippings. The principle 'like is attracted to like' succeeds to 'like participates in like' – the progressive assimilation to God; 'the soul becomes wholly light.'[9] There is a movement from ignorance to gnosis, from φιλαυτία to ἀγάπη, from image to likeness. 'The Word of God was made human,' says Clement of Alexandria, 'so that you should learn from a human being how human beings might become god' according to grace.[10]

The end being the Θεωρία τῆς ἁγίας Τριάδος, the mysticism of light is fulfilled in the mysticism of darkness, gnosis in hypergnosis. But the highest mystical states entirely exclude any direct vision of God. 'Whoever imagines he has seen God, has seen only himself and his own imaginings,' says St Ephraem drily.[11] According to St Isaac the Syrian,[12] the 'vision of God' never supplants faith; the vision is 'second faith', never direct knowledge.

Both types of mysticism proceed apophatically. The mysticism of light coincides with the beginning of apophasis, which then continues into the mysticism of darkness, and *apophasis becomes an approach to knowing by way of unknowing*. So although St Gregory of Nazianzus speaks of very real knowing, and relates it to the incarnate Word and perfect communion with his humanity, nevertheless, according to St Maximus, St Gregory generally 'preferred negations on the subject of God [to the extent] that he would tolerate absolutely no [positive] argument or affirmation.'[13] Since human intelligence shares in God's nature, it also shares in his *unthinkableness*. This is the 'great evidence' revealed by the Holy Spirit, the '*Great Charism*', who pushes the *nous* beyond its proper limits'[14] into the darkness – γνόφος – and towards the ἔσχατον ὀρεκτόν, the supremely desirable. And this is possible not because the creature is feeble but because God is unfathomably deep. The darkness brings the goal of contemplation, maximum

[9] St Macarius, *Hom.* 1. N. 2, *P.G.* 34, 452 A.
[10] *Protreptic*, 1, 8.
[11] *Adv. Scrutatores*, 26, ed. rom., vol. 3, p. 47.
[12] Ed. Bedjan, p. 320.
[13] *Amb.*, *P.G.* 91, 1224 BC.
[14] St Andrew of Crete, *P.G.* 97, 1208 A.

vision, within reach, and is therefore 'luminous'. *Raised* to a state of humility and obedience, the soul loses all control. This condition of utter powerlessness it acknowledges and welcomes, then freely and joyfully offers up, and in this receptive state it recognizes God. So the darkness symbolizes the obscurity of faith and the experience of the nearness of God.

As God draws nearer, the more obscure he becomes. The intensity of his presence holds our spirit enthralled, showing that the initiative is always his. The *eros*, according to St Gregory of Nyssa, no longer contains anything egocentric or possessive; it is 'the intensity of *agape*,' ἡ ἐπιτεταμένη ἀγάπη.[15] The soul is irresistibly attracted to God as by a magnet; it attains him through desire rather than possession, through darkness rather than light, through learned ignorance rather than knowledge. Gripped by God's absolute transcendence the soul experiences his presence in its innermost depths. Mystical contemplation is beyond words; it is pure immaterial vision in which the senses and conceptual intelligence play no part. Ecstasy, in an 'exit into oneself,' becomes a kind of 'enstasy'; it detaches the mystic from himself and surrenders him to God. The cessation of all cognitive activity culminates in total hesychia, 'peace beyond all peace.' Mystical knowledge is thus of the 'transintellectual' kind, and is reached only at the end of a long process of negative theology. The *nous*, giving up intellectual activity, transcends itself and draws near to super-knowledge, ὑπὲρ νοῦς.[16]

The transcendence of God obscures all natural light, but his immanence renders the darkness more than luminous, more than clear because it gives birth to perfect union, ἕνωσις or deification, *theosis*.

1. THEOSIS AND THE HOLY SPIRIT

The creation of the world is the final stage in the descent of divine activity – from the Father, through the Son, in the Holy Spirit. By contrast, the ascent of humankind, the course of salvation, goes in the opposite direction – from the Holy Spirit (who the Fathers say is closer to us, more interior, than we are to ourselves) through the Son, to the Father; from the inner realm of the Spirit, through the members of the visible theandric Body, to the depth of the Father. In this ascent the Holy Spirit is revealed as the Spirit of Life, whose very breath is *agape*. St Basil[17] clearly defines the work of the Holy Spirit as intermediary: 'The creature possesses no gift which does not come from the Spirit, the Sanctifier who *unites*

---

15 *P.G.* 44, 1048 C.
16 According to Kallistos, *hesychia* is the 'highest state of intellectual activity,' because when the unity of the intelligence is realized, only silence can express it (*P.G.* 147, 888 A).
17 *P.G.* 32, 133 C.

us to God.' The highly refined pneumatology of the eastern Church identifies the
Spirit, the 'giver of life and treasure of grace,' as the active principle in every divine operation. This is not to imply any 'mystical monophysitism' or 'pneumati-
cism' that would dissolve the humanity of Christ in the uncreated light of the
Holy Spirit. The economy of the Son and that of the Spirit converge on the Father,
the source of Trinitarian unity and of the spiritual life of humanity. The saints are
fully in the reality of the Incarnation and their hearts are 'on fire with love for
the whole creation'. The Jesus Prayer expressly invokes the Saviour in his humanity and thus refers indirectly to the eucharistic mystery; but this entails the
epiclesis as a preliminary condition. The eastern Church does not distinguish precisely between spiritual gifts, moral and theological virtues, or between habitual
and actual grace, but emphasizes from the outset the transformation of nature,
and the working of grace in all forms of participation to bring about *theosis*. The
soul, enabled by grace to contain the Spirit, is *Christified* in the mystical γάμος,
the deifying adoption[18] by the Father.

The Creed refers to Christ as 'Light of Light,' and Baptism is also called 'illumination'. St Simeon says, 'When your soul receives grace, it will shine as brilliantly as
God himself.'[19] This is the heart of the teaching of St Gregory of Nyssa; the sun enters
into the soul and dwells there, perceptible to the eyes of faith. The eye, being of the
same nature as the sun, sees what is akin to it; light is its element. The eye not only
captures light, but emits it, but in order to do that, it must coincide with the eye of the
Dove, the Holy Spirit.[20] 'The glory of the eyes is to be the eyes of the Dove,'[21] the
human being sees by the Holy Spirit. Thus the hesychasts contemplate the light of
Tabor which displays the uncreated divine glory. The two ways, illuminative and unitive, converge in God and delight the spirit in a 'little resurrection', 'entrance into
formless light.' 'The more closely the spirit approaches the vision of God, the more it
sees the invisibility of the divine nature.'[22] This is the Life that is Truth, that can never
be transformed into knowledge.[23] However, the two most important aspects of mystical union are the utterly real proximity of God in the deified soul and the utter transcendence of the same God who remains *in se* for ever unapproachable and infinitely
remote. God freely brings a world into being and by means of his grace binds himself
to it; without absorbing the human person, he spiritualizes it through his energies.
More important still, 'those who want to save their life will lose it' (Mark 8.35). The
soul becomes fully real only as it ceaselessly goes beyond itself towards the Other; it

[18] St Macarius, *hom.* 1, 2, 3.
[19] In *La Vie Spirituelle*, May 1931, p. 209.
[20] St Gregory of Nyssa, *De infant.*, *P.G.* 46, 173 D.
[21] *In Cant.*; *P.G.* 44, 835 CD.
[22] This is *docta ignorantia*; St Gregory of Nyssa, *Vit. Moys.*; *P.G.* 44, 376 D.
[23] *Ibid.* 404 B.

no longer belongs to itself. All the irreducible contradiction of the synthesis is preserved.

The Holy Spirit brings the human spirit back to its ontological centre, showing it to be the image of God, open on the one hand to divine transcendence, and on the other to the subjective and inner life of all fellow members of the divine community. Cosmic charity reveals the essences or *logoi* of beings, the thoughts of God about the world, so that 'the heart burns with love for every creature.' By humble obedience, says St Basil, 'we are conformed to the crucified and obedient Christ,' and renounce any desire to possess the grace of the Spirit for our own.

The anti-contemplative tendency[24] sets *eros* in opposition to *agape* and confuses the inner life with self-centredness. But according to St Gregory of Nyssa, *eros* is spread abroad through *agape* and love of neighbour. 'God is the author of *agape* and *eros*,' says St Maximus.[25] The two are complementary; *eros*, impelled by the Spirit, goes out in search of divine *agape*. Epiclesis is fundamental to mystical union: it is because human beings have once more become spirit-bearing that they also become Christ-bearing. The Kingdom of God of the Gospels is the 'giving of the Holy Spirit.' According to western mystics such as Tauler or Eckhardt nothing comes between the soul and Christ. In eastern tradition, God can be made known only by God himself; it is by the Holy Spirit that we are united to the Son and through him to the Father.[26]

The inward nature of the spiritual life resolves the question: active or contemplative? St Maximus[27] accords equal value to the monastic and lay states: contemplatives experience the vision, those engaged in active life experience the presence. St Seraphim of Sarov answers it thus: 'If you acquire inner peace a multitude will find their salvation through you.'[28] Everything depends on the presence of God and on one's progress in deifying communion. But God in his sovereign freedom distributes his abundant gifts as he wills, so there are no technical rules for the mystical life; these are the province of ascesis. God mysteriously chooses the vessels he wishes to fill with his light, as he chose Peter, James and John to be witnesses of the Transfiguration.

Mystical love cannot be planned; the heart is open and receptive to its full extent, but at the same time its very receptivity is formed by doctrine. Outside the Church, no mysticism. While reaching the height of freedom, the mystical life is inwardly framed by doctrine lived in the sacraments, and is thus protected from

---

[24] Anders Nygren, *Eros und Agape*, Güteraloh 1937.

[25] *Div. Nom.* 4; *P.G.* 4, 265 C.

[26] That is why St Cyril of Alexandria insists on the part played by the Holy Spirit which deifies us – Θεοποιοῦν – (*P.G.* 75, 1089 CD); similarly St Gregory of Nazianzus (*Or.* 31, *P.G.* 36, 159 BC).

[27] *Cent. Car.* 6; *P.G.* 90, 985 AB; also 90, 1041 D.

[28] Behr-Sigel, *Prière et Sainteté dans l'Eglise Russe*, p. 139.

any confused sectarian thinking. The goal of mystical love, 'that two should be one,'[29] is above all an authoritative statement of Christological doctrine. After the Incarnation, every analogy of the faith is Christology. The formation of Christ in a person, his Christification, is neither unachievable imitation nor the application to a human being of the merits of the Incarnation, but the extension into the person of the Incarnation itself, operated and perpetuated by the eucharistic mystery. St Simeon the New Theologian shows the summit of the mystical life to be the personal meeting with Christ who speaks in our hearts by the Holy Spirit.[30]

2. PERPETUAL PRAYER

The classic form of spoken prayer is the recitation of the Psalms, 'the psalmody of the heart.' 'The word of Scripture fortifies the heart and drives away the devils.'[31] Any tendency to lyricism is restrained, all that is not essential is stripped away; Christ and disciple are laid bare. Separated from each and united to all, the soul ascends towards union with God. Spoken prayer merges into mental prayer, the spirit enters a Pauline rapture; to pray like this is to be already in the Kingdom.[32]

Having concentrated the heart by the exercise of attentiveness and temperance, the mystic then centres life on ejaculatory prayer, the constant silent repetition of the 'Jesus Prayer';[33] 'strike your enemy with the name of Jesus, there is no weapon more powerful on earth or in heaven.'[34] The Sinaitic and Athonite tradition of hesychastic mysticism is founded on veneration of the Name: 'Lord Jesus Christ, Son of God, have mercy on me a sinner.'[35] This prayer contains the whole message of the Bible in its simplest and essential form: confessing the lordship of Christ, then his divine sonship, then the Trinity; there follows the abyss of the Fall and the invocation of the abyss of the divine mercy. The beginning and the end are gathered

[29] This union is never fusion of the essence. The hypostatic union in Christ – κατὰ οὐσιάν – is unique to him. Our union with Christ is κατὰ φύσιν.
[30] See Fr Basil Krivoshein, 'The poor, loving humankind', in *Le Messager* of the Exarchate of the Russian Patriarchate in Western Europe, No 16, 1953.
[31] St Nil of Sinai, *De Oratione*.
[32] St Simeon, *Log.* 48.
[33] The best and most penetrating introduction to this tradition is to be found in *La prière de Jésus*, by a monk of the eastern Church, Ed. de Chevetogne, 1951. See also *Récit d'un pèlerin russe*, E. de la Baconnière, Neuchâtel, 1948; *La prière du cœur*, H. de B., Ed orthodoxes, Paris 1953.
[34] St John Climacus, *Scala*, c. 27.
[35] The word 'mercy' does not fully convey the meaning intended in the prayer. Two texts need to be taken together: Matthew 9.13 and Luke 18.13 which we find in the priest's prayer at the prothesis: Θεός, ἱλάσθητι μοι τῷ ἁμαρτωλῷ καὶ ἐλέησον με – 'God, be gracious unto me, a sinner, and have mercy on me.'

in a single word, the Name charged with the quasi-sacramental power of the presence of Christ. This prayer resonates unceasingly in the depths of the heart, keeping to the rhythm of breathing; the name of Jesus is in some way 'fixed' to the breath. The name is imprinted in a person, and in the name of God he is transformed into Christ, being directly initiated into the experience of St Paul: 'It is no longer I who live, but it is Christ who lives in me' (Gal. 2.20). To struggle with temptations face to face is only for those who are 'like St Michael, strong in God; we who are weak can only seek refuge in the name of Jesus.'[36]

The frequent invocation of the name of Jesus is an interior liturgy that brings us into the presence of God. The constant cry of every believer is, 'make my prayer a sacrament'[37] and to achieve that aim the perfect prayer must banish discursive elements, the λογισμοί, and reduce itself to a single word, μονολογία, the name of Jesus.[38] God is present to all, but through prayer of the heart, the human being becomes present again to the divine presence (St Denys).

In this tradition the name is regarded as a place of theophany; calling on the name of Jesus prolongs the Incarnation, and the heart receives the majestic presence of the Lord: 'I am going to send an angel in front of you ... Be attentive to him ... for my name is in him' (Exod. 23.20f.). The name is placed in the angel, whereupon he becomes the formidable bearer of the presence of God. We see clearly in the Bible the uttering of the divine name over a country or a person sets up a close relationship with God. The name of God could be pronounced only in fear and trembling by the High Priest on the Day of Atonement in the Holy of Holies in the Temple at Jerusalem.

Jesus Yeshuah means Saviour. *Nomen est Omen*, the name encodes and portends the power of the unique person and his destiny. Hermas[39] says: 'The name of the Son of God ... sustains the whole world,' for he is present in it and we adore him in his name.

3. RESTRAINT AND THE MYSTICAL STATE

The life of the mystic, nourished from the liturgical source and directed by doctrine, is striking in its perfect balance. There is nothing romantic or sensational about it, no hint of 'inner music', no fulfilling of psychological needs; it is characterized by restraint, spareness and lack of emotion. Its 'impassible passion' ruthlessly abjures any excitement of the eyes or senses, any tendency to curiosity.

---

[36] Correspondence of Barsanuphius and John edited at Vienna by Nicodemus the Hagiorite in 1816 (passage quoted in *La Prière de Jésus*, by a monk of the eastern Church, p. 26-27).
[37] N. Gorodetsky, 'The prayer of Jesus', in *Blackfriars*, 1942, p. 74-78.
[38] St John Climacus, *Scala Paradisi*, P.G. 88, 596-1209.
[39] *Shepherd*, III, XIV.

Even ecstasy, now considered a sign of the mystical state, 'denotes not the expert but the novice,'[40] as St Simeon says. 'If you see a young man climb up to heaven by his own will-power, seize him by the foot and throw him back to earth, because it will avail him nothing.'[41] According to John of Lycopolis, wonder-working, *fama miraculorum*, is the product not of the spirit but of the mind.[42] The common advice of the initiated to the novice is, 'If you have a vision of an angel, reject it, saying humbly, I am not worthy to see.' And the monk, accosted by Satan in the form of Christ, says, 'It is not here that I desire to see Christ, but elsewhere, in the age to come.' 'While you are praying,' says St Nilus of Sinai, 'do not force yourself to see some image or face; be immaterial in the presence of the Immaterial.'[43]

Rare indeed is the apparition from God that overcomes the instinctive resistance of the mystic: a vision, it may be, of uncreated light, an experience of luminousness and lightening of the body, even to the point of levitation, but no bleeding wounds, no devotional appeal to the senses. The icon, restrained, even dry, in style, deliberately suppressing sensuality by its convention of elongated bodies and darkened faces, banishes every trace of mystical eroticism.

It is a symptomatic fact that Orthodox piety knows nothing of stigmata.[44] Any imitation of the Passion, any dramatization of Christ's suffering humanity, any cult of redemption-through-suffering is utterly foreign to eastern spirituality. In the humanity of Christ we gaze on our archetype, and mystically speaking we seek not to imitate Christ, but to become *bearers of Christ*, to manifest his glory: 'Your face shines forth in your saints.' Similarly, the eastern Church venerates the Cross not as the wood of torment but as the Tree of Life in Eden, green once again in the midst of this world. The Cross is both sign and bearer of victory, enfolding the whole world in its arms, breaking the iron doors in pieces. Far exceeding all hope or expectation, it directly communicates the thrilling Paschal joy that springs from the Transfigured and Risen Lord.

The confessions and autobiographies so dear to western Christians are unknown in the East. The difference in tone is clear-cut. Contemplation never stops at the suffering humanity of Christ but penetrates beyond the kenotic veil. The mysticism of the Cross and the cult of the Sacred Heart in the West have their eastern counterpart in the mysticism of the sealed tomb, whence springs eternal life. That is why the tragic aspect of the mystical darkness, the night of the senses, is very little

---

[40] *P.G.* 143, 401 B.
[41] *Vitae Patrum*, V, 10, 111; *P.L.* 73, 932 BC.
[42] *Orientalia Christiana*, 120, 1939, p. 35.
[43] *P.G.* 79, 1193.
[44] See Lot-Borodine, 'De l'absence de stigmates dans la chrétienté antique' in *Dieu Vivant*, No 3.

cultivated in the East, where the concentration is all on the systematic stripping away of what is purely human, which is the beginning of ascetic science; it is the ascetical, not the mystical night; it is stripped of any emotional reference to wounds. In the union with God there is very little sweetness and melancholy.[45]

Theognosis takes priority over *eros*, but this cannot be expressed in words because love is itself cognitive; knowing is one with loving, spirit and heart come to mean the same thing. But the language of the mystics, in the few writings they have left us, is different from that of the theologians. The mystics talk of experience and of communion in terms that cannot be translated into any logical system. Thus on the one hand, 'God is the creator and the soul is the creature and they have nothing in common;'[46] and on the other, 'Whoever shares in the divine energy himself becomes in a sense light.'[47] So St Gregory Palamas can state as a principle, 'We must affirm both things at the same time, while preserving the contradiction as a measure of piety.'[48]

It is clear that the mystical state is the transcending of the very condition of creatureliness. God is more intimate to humankind than humankind is to itself and life in the divine is more supernaturally natural to humankind than life in the merely human. The baptized person, in whom Christ is an integral fact, experiences nothingness and also its contradiction, absolute being. Without abolishing the ontological gap between the two, Being fills the abyss with its presence. 'I am human by nature, and god by grace;' a being comes from nothing and lives the conditions of the divine life. God transcends his own transcendence: 'He comes suddenly and, without confusion, merges himself with me ... My hands are those of a poor wretch, I move my hand and my hand is all Christ.'[49] It is a Parousia; Christ comes down into the heart and forms it in his image: 'If you are pure, heaven is within you; it is within you that you will see the light, the angels and the Lord himself.'[50] St John of Damascus describes this as 'the return of what is contrary to nature towards what is proper to it.'[51]

---

[45] The only exception is St Simeon the New Theologian, whose approach in certain respects resembles that of St John of the Cross.
[46] *Hom.* 49, 4; 44, 8.
[47] *Homily on the Presentation of the Blessed Virgin in the Temple.*
[48] *P.G.* 150, 932 D.
[49] *Hymns of Divine Love.*
[50] St Macarius, *Hom. Spirit.*, 43, 7.
[51] *De fide orth.*, I, 30.

4. THE MYSTIC MOUNTAIN

Seen from above, a saint is already all woven out of light. With no thought of imitation, the saint follows Christ, inwardly reproducing his image: 'Purity of heart is love for the weak who fall.'[52] The saint's heart is enlarged and opens out in charity towards the world; it lives through universal evil, endures the agony of Gethsemane, and is raised to another kind of seeing that strips it of any tendency to judge: 'When you are purified you see the soul of your neighbour;' like sees like: 'When you see all people as good, and nobody seems impure, then you are genuinely pure in heart ... If you see your brother or sister in the act of sinning, throw over their shoulders the cloak of your love.'[53] Love like this really works; it 'changes the very substance of things.'[54]

The movement from the passions to continence, from sin to grace, is taken up into the movement from fear to love: 'The perfect person rejects fear, disdains rewards and loves with all his or her heart ... what is a charitable heart? A heart inflamed with charity for the whole creation, for others, for birds, for beasts, for devils, for all creatures ... that prays even for reptiles, moved by the infinite pity which is awakened in the heart of those who have become like God.'[55] 'The sure sign of perfection is this: you allow yourself to be delivered to the flames six times a day out of charity towards your neighbour, and it does not seem enough.'[56]

The soul is lifted up above every specific sign, beyond every representation and every image. The manifold gives place to the one, the simple. The life of the soul, image and mirror of God, becomes the life of the soul, dwelling of God. Mystically lifted up, the soul is orientated towards the Kingdom: 'If wisdom consists in the knowledge of reality, none will be called wise, unless they also embrace the things to come.'[57] 'In the last times,' says St Isaac, 'a spiritual person receives the grace that those times require.' The icons of the divine liturgy depict the lost sheep, the human race, taking their place with the celestial choir of angels before the mystic Lamb of the Revelation, who is encircled by the three spheres. Against the brightness of the heavenly world the royal crimson of the Passion stands out like the blaze of endless noonday, the iconographic colour of divine

---

[52] Nietzsche advises the contrary: 'If you see somebody losing his balance, give him a push'; and the rabbinic Wisdom says, 'Do not touch a drunkard; he will fall of his own accord.'
[53] St Isaac, *Sentences* XXXV, CXV.
[54] St John Chrysostom, *Hom.* 32, 1 Cor.; *P.G.* 61, 273.
[55] V. Soloviev in *The Justification of the Good* (Fr. trans. 1939, p. 72) observes that 'it is hard to condemn this description as over-dramatic or sentimental'; we should in effect be accusing ourselves of hardheartedness.
[56] St Isaac the Syrian, Wensinck, p. 341-342.
[57] St Gregory of Nyssa, *P.G.* 45, 580 C.

love reclothed with humanity. Humankind returns to its celestial dignity. Already at the Ascension of Christ the angels have cried out, 'Who is the King of glory?' and now they are thrown into astonishment before the ultimate mystery as the sheep become one with the Shepherd. The Song of Songs hymns the marriage of the Word and the Dove. The soul attracted ever more violently is cast into the luminous darkness of God. Words have lost their power; luminous darkness, sober intoxication, the well of living water, motionless movement.

'As you come into my light, you become beautiful; you begin to share my beauty ... The soul, as it approaches my light, itself becomes light.'[58] At this point there is no need to be taught by God, only to receive and be converted to him. Knowledge turns into love, as in the Eucharist: 'The wine that gladdens the human heart has, ever since the Passion, been called the blood of the vine'[59] and 'from the mystic vine flows sober intoxication.'

The soul is transformed into a dove of light, mounting continually; each successive ascent becomes a new point of departure, and grace is added to grace.

'Eros is God, who shoots the arrow of his only-begotten Son, after first moistening the three tips of the arrowhead with the life-giving Spirit; the arrowhead is the faith that creates an entrance not only for the arrow, but also for the Archer.'[60]

'Having once put your foot on the ladder on which God is leaning, do not cease to climb ... each step leads to one beyond.'[61] This is Jacob's ladder on which descend 'not only the angels, but the Lord of the angels' ... 'But how can I describe the unutterable, what no eye has seen, nor ear heard, nor the human heart conceived, how can this be expressed in words?'[62]

All movement ceases, prayer itself changes its nature. 'The soul prays outside prayer.'[63] This is hesychia, silence of the spirit, rest that is above all prayer, peace that surpasses all peace. It is the meeting face to face prolonged into eternity, when 'God comes into the soul and the soul flies into God.'[64]

---

[58] St Gregory of Nyssa, *P.G.* 44, 869 A.
[59] St Gregory of Nyssa, *P.G.* 44, 828 BC.
[60] St Gregory of Nyssa, *P.G.* 44, 852 AB.
[61] St Gregory of Nyssa, *P.G.* 44, 401 AB.
[62] St Simeon, *Homily*, XC, quoted by Lossky, *Théologie Mystique*, p. 230.
[63] Wensinck, p. 118.
[64] St Gregory of Nyssa employs the Pauline term *epectasy* (Phil. 3.11) in the strongest sense, meaning the upward surge, the extreme and ceaseless stretching out in which are combined the two aspects of a single act: ecstasy, going out, and enstasy, entering in. The soul launches itself beyond itself towards the Other and the Other comes to dwell in the soul, and is more intimate to the soul than the person to itself. This explains the paradoxical expressions: 'to have found God is to search for him unceasingly,' and 'we know that someone is progressing by the very fact that he or she has come to a stop'; that person is 'the well of living water' (see J. Danielou, *Platonisme et théologie mystique*; H. von Balthasar, *Présence et Pensée*).

PART II
Ecclesiology

1. REFINING THE QUESTION

Many theologians believe that ecclesiologically we are still at the 'pre-theological' stage. The Fathers have not left us any systematic treatises, or complete ecclesiology. In their time the vitality of the Church was so plain to see that the question of its nature scarcely arose. On the other hand, the very mysteriousness of the Church lends itself very little to any formal definition. In the words of Fr Sergei Bulgakov, 'Come and see: the Church can be understood only through experience, by grace, by sharing in its life.'[1] The need to define that life is a sure sign that awareness of the Church is swaning, that its life is not being experienced at first hand.

The definitions given in manuals of theology and catechisms are the product of particular circumstances.[2] They are not expressions of the Church's self-understanding or doctrine but arise out of theological arguments about ideas. The golden thread that guides every exploration into ecclesiology is the return to Patristic sources, and it leads not to definitions, but to a description of the life of the Church, starting with its faith. 'The Church exists not at all as an idea, but in itself; and for each member sharing the Church's life, that life is the most clearly defined thing in all his or her experience.'[3]

The outward, social aspect of the institutions masks their essential inner life, which only faith, 'seeing the invisible' (Heb. 11.1) can discern. Faith, while not betraying the Church's unutterable nature, teaches that it is the Body of Christ, the earthly continuation of Pentecost; it is the face of the Trinity, of the absolute Church of the three divine Persons.

2. THE VISIBLE AND THE INVISIBLE

In the Nicene Creed we say, 'I *believe* in One, Holy, Catholic and Apostolic Church'. While I know the Church as *visible and institutional*, the congregation of the faithful living according to precise rules, I believe in the *invisible*: the absent, the angels, the real and unceasing presence of God, the signs of grace. The life of God among humankind, the true unity of divine and human life, *theandrism*, rules out any separation between the visible terrestrial Church and the invisible celestial Church, but distinguishes the visible and the invisible, without confusion and without separation, in one and the same living organism, where 'heaven and earth have kissed each other.'

---

1 *L'Orthodoxie*, Alcan 1932, p.4.
2 See Fr G. Florovsky, 'Le Corps du Christ Vivant', in *La Sainte Eglise Universelle*, Ed. Cahiers théologiques.
3 Fr P. Florensky, *Colonne et Affirmation de la Verité*, p. 7.

3. THE CHURCH: ITS ORIGINS AND META-HISTORICAL NATURE

In speaking of the 'Notes' of the Church (One, Holy, Catholic and Apostolic) the catechisms tend to assume, simplistically, that the Church itself is known. However, before any mention of Notes, we need to distinguish the mystery of the Church in itself.[4]

Revelation (13.8) and St Peter (1 Pet. 1.19) speak of 'the Lamb slain from the foundation of the world,' i.e., the act of the creation of the world already contained within it the *Communio Sanctorum* of the Church, as the alpha and omega of the whole creative economy of God.

The world was created with a view to the Incarnation; in its very foundation, the world is virtually and potentially the Church. St Clement of Rome (2 Clement 14.2) says, 'God created man and woman; man is Christ and woman is the Church.' Similarly in the second vision of the *Shepherd* of Hermas the Church is described as an old woman: 'She is old because she was created first, before anything else, and it is for her that the world was made.' In Aristotelian terms we can say the Church is the 'entelechy'[5] of history; it is its subject-matter and its end, *telos*, and therefore the point at which history is fulfilled. The Confession of the Orthodox Faith places the beginning of the Church in Paradise.[6] When God comes 'in the cool of the day' (Gen. 3.8 AV) to talk with the man we see the *essential nature of the Church*, which is *communion between God and humankind*; it is prefigured in Eden, anticipated prophetically in the Old Covenant, accomplished in the Incarnation, and fully revealed in the Heavenly City (Rev. 21.22), the living temple of the marriage of the Lamb. The conjugal nature of the relationship, implied in the Old Covenant, is made explicit in the Song of Songs. From beginning to end, such a vision of the Church shows it aspiring to perfect communion, *theosis*. It is by its light, the most precious element in the Bible, that the Fathers constructed their theology of the Church, throwing into relief the most amazing fact of divine philanthropy: God becomes human, and in his very substance marries the created to the uncreated in Christ Jesus, God and Man, who by extension and through consubstantiality widens into Christ the Church: God and humankind, the fullness of divine-humanity.

Behind the face of the world that is passing, faith discerns the abiding fact: it is in the Church, the pre-ordained centre of the universe, that the destinies of the world and of each person are bound together. What the descent of the Holy Spirit does in Christ is done in every human being and in the human race by the deifying

---

[4] See Fr S. Bulgakov, 'The Church' (in Russian), in the review *Voie*, No 1, 1925; No 2, 1926; N0 15, 1929; No 16, 1929.

[5] The principle that determines the actualization of a power.

[6] *The Great Catechism* of Metropolitan Philaret, trans. into English by R.W. Blackmore, Aberdeen 1845, p. 82.

energies, 'uniting created nature to uncreated nature through love, revealing them as one and the same through grace' (St Maximus)[7]. It is in the Church that human beings 'work out their salvation,' which means, according to St Peter, that they are 'participants in the divine nature' (2 Pet. 1.4). Deified humanity is called to become the living imitation of the Trinity, *the unity of human nature in a multiplicity of hypostases*. The theology of the Church transcends any partial view; it sees the Church essentially as universal participation in the conditions of the divine nature: integrity and immortality.[8]

4. THE CHURCH IN GOD

There is an abundance of texts that say the mystery of the Church goes back beyond history: 'He chose us in Christ before the foundation of the world to be holy ... the mystery *hidden for ages in God* who created all things' (Eph. 1.4; 3.9). Its pre-existence in the wisdom of God emphasizes the *meta-historical nature* of the Church. While all forms of social life are contingent – existing or ceasing to exist as history determines – the Church, on the contrary, does not arise out of history but breaks into the world, precisely because *its genesis is elsewhere*. Just as 'the Lamb slain before the foundation of the world,' outside time, *enters* history and is sacrificed 'under Pontius Pilate' and 'at Jerusalem', being exactly situated in time and space; even so the Church, 'hidden for ages' in God, whose existence was prepared in Paradise and prefigured in Israel, comes down from heaven in tongues of fire and enters history at Jerusalem on the day of Pentecost. It comes down from heaven and springs from the pre-existent depths of creation. The hidden is gradually revealed as we draw nearer to 'the fullness of him who fills all in all' (Eph. 1.23). Things in heaven, and things in earth, and things under the earth, bow the knee and come together in the fullness of *totus Christus*.[9]

---

[7] *De ambiguis, P.G.* 91, 1308 B.
[8] Given already by anticipation in the sacramental economy.
[9] The Church condemned the gnostic delusions of the Valentinians about the final pair of the divine Ogdoad. The Church did not historically pre-exist the work of Christ. But neither is it a self-contained society created after the event by the community of believers. The idea of the Church is continuous with the Hebraic idea of the Qahal, the whole people of God, now united in Christ and always vastly larger than its manifestations, going back in its origins to the Wisdom of God and the Lamb slain before the foundation of the world. It is not yet the Kingdom (as Augustine mistakenly thought), nevertheless, 'to see the Church is truly to see Christ,' as St Gregory of Nyssa says (*P.G.* 44, 1048) – for we see it by the Holy Spirit. We must avoid the ecclesiological monophysitism of one invisible Church consisting of the elect, or one visible Church consisting of sinners. A balanced view is possible only with the aid of Christological theandrism.

5. THE THEANDRIC CONNECTION

The fundamental difference between orthodoxy and heterodoxy depends on the relationship by which an historical body is established as the Church. For Karl Barth, for example, the relationship is with God alone, who continually 'appears', his presence having the character of an 'event' (*ereignishaft*) as opposed to an 'institution'.[10] The emphasis is vertical; the divine act, like a tangent, *touches* the circle but does not *penetrate* it. For the Orthodox, the link is cross-shaped, the Church being at the intersection of the horizontal and vertical. The connection here is *theandric*. Theandrism constitutes the Church, places it at the centre of the world, transforms its human content into theandric substance by filling it with its reality, and thus supplies horizontal continuity: the Apostolic succession, the sacraments (the extension of the visible Christ), the incorporation of the faithful in the historical body. According to the Reformers the Church is on earth, visible but undiscernible; it is, so to speak, the Church 'itinerant'. It is certainly somewhere, but we cannot say exactly where: the sacraments may be correctly administered and the Word correctly preached, but the elect, marked with an invisible sign, are scattered everywhere and unidentifiable. For the Orthodox, the Church is objectively present where the Apostolic ministry of incorporation is exercised; where the Bishop, by his apostolic power, celebrates the Eucharist, demonstrates his authority and unites in himself the people gathered for the Liturgy, the Body of Christ.

6. INSTITUTION AND EVENT

'The Spirit blows where he chooses,' but above all he rests on the humanity of the Son – the Church; which shows that the events – the blowings – are operated and happen within the instituted Body. The Church originates historically in the *acta et passa Christi in carne*, in the Lord's Supper, and is kept in being by the Spirit of Pentecost. Like a lake, it is fed continuously by the spring of the Holy Eucharist, and by the rain of grace of the everlasting Pentecost. The Epiclesis shows that the two are systematically related: the Son sends the Spirit and the Spirit manifests the Son. 1 Corinthians 12 speaks of spiritual gifts that are not regulated: sanctity, the prophesyings of the *staretz*, the mystical life, cannot be confined by the definitions of the institution. The deifying energies can never be organized or institutionalized. Alongside the institutional forms there are events: 'Do not quench the Spirit. Do not despise the words of prophets.' (1 Thess. 5.19-20) Thus the Church transcends its own institutional reality. The essential thing

---

10. Cf. J.-L. Leuba, *L'institution et l'Evénement*, Neuchâtel-Paris, 1950; Fr Congar, 'Marie, l'Eglise et le Christ', in *La Vie intellectuelle*, Oct. 1951.

is never to oppose or separate these two aspects of the same grace: they are complementary. The institution is rooted in the overflowing source of the Spirit, and the event only happens within the framework of the ecclesial institution; the Spirit speaks to 'his own', the 'Christified'.

The visible Church is not only the visible society of Christians; it is also 'the Spirit of God and the grace of the living sacraments in that society'[11] i.e., its visibility is the place of the invisible, of its constant radiance. This organic unity characterizes both the Church militant and the Church triumphant and is equally true of all rules of salvation, earthly as well as heavenly. Consequently, seen from outside, the Orthodox economy can sometimes display an astonishing capacity for formal relaxation, even giving an impression of neglecting the earthly. This can be understood only from within: 'The Church is one because it represents one only spiritual Body, enlivened by one and the same divine Spirit and having one only head who is Christ.'[12] 'Even the earthly Church is a heavenly thing,'[13] 'the divine society.' The unique principle, Christ, rules heaven and earth: the Church sings, 'Met together in thy Temple, we see one another already in the light of thy heavenly glory'. The heavenly overflows the earthly.

7. THE CHURCH, A SACRAMENTAL COMMUNITY

The Church, situated at the boundary of two realms and inhabiting both simultaneously, is evidently, in relation to the world, transcendent. It is neither an organization, nor organized human life, nor even – and this perhaps least of all – 'organized grace', but the *theandric organism, the life of God in human nature*, which directly entails its structure as a *sacramental community*. Entering by way of Baptism, the neophyte is enlightened, experiences the Parousia of Christ and is remodelled after the image of his archetype; at his Anointing with Chrism he is sealed with the gifts of the Spirit and becomes a new creature; this new life unfolds and flourishes in the Eucharist. And the sacraments of initiation, according to the Fathers, are not signs but the *sources* of regeneration – *anagenesis*, part of the *esse*, the very essence of the Church. The social aspects of the sacraments are of no importance whatever compared with the fact that a *new creature* is born. The Church catechises and preaches, it proclaims and bears witness, but its first task is the *conversion of people*, in the strongest sense of a transformation that goes far beyond any mere intellectual assent or belief. The *ministry of the Word*, kerygmatic preaching, happens in the course of the *ministry of the sacraments* and is completed in the *ministry of incorporation*: the living members of

---

[11] Khomiakov, *L'Eglise est une*, § 1.
[12] *Catéchisme* du Metropolitan Philaret.
[13] Khomiakov, *op. cit.*, § 9.

Christ find themselves born in the Spirit – Πνεῦμα Ζωοποιόν[14] – the creator
and giver of a wholly new existence. 'The Holy Spirit brings souls to life, making
them mysteriously resplendent with the one nature of the Trinity.'[15]

8. EUCHARISTIC ECCLESIOGY

The early Church grouped together the three so-called major sacraments – Baptism, Chrismation and the Eucharist – under the name *initiation*. The neophyte
passes through three stages, being made a member of the people of God recapitulated in Christ, then consecrated priest, prophet and king; the process is completed in the Eucharist. The Eucharist is not simply one sacrament among others,
but is the completion of them all; it is truly the *Sacrament of sacraments*,[16] containing within itself the fullest expression of the Church. The Church is the continuation and perpetuation of the eucharistic *koinonia*.

The daily and weekly cycles of offices together are a preparation for the celebration of the Lord's Day, the sharing in the messianic Lord's Supper. Of its
very nature, the Liturgy knows nothing of 'spectators', who are by definition
'outsiders'; their presence is a disastrous departure from what had been the ancient practice, probably up till the 4th century.

The severity of the canons of the early Church towards those who wilfully
deprive themselves of the eucharistic Communion is *normative*, for their attitude
implies non-membership of the Church.[17] Being a member of the Church means
above all taking part in the Liturgy, and excommunication simply takes away
that sharing in the Meal. 'Outside the Church there is no salvation' is above all a
eucharistic statement: *solus christianus – nullus christianus. Solus* means outside
the eucharistic *koinonia*, outside the Church.

The Fathers call the Eucharist the 'immortal cure', in the strongest sense: before Communion the priest prays, 'May the partaking of thy holy mysteries, O
Lord, be to me neither judgement nor condemnation, but *healing* of soul and
body', and at the moment of Communion the priest says, 'unto the remission of
sins and unto life everlasting.' When St Paul speaks of 'unworthy' Communion
(1 Cor. 11.29) he is referring not to the moral state of the communicant, which is

---

[14] Nicene Creed.
[15] Anthem of the 4th tone, Office of Sunday.
[16] St Denys, *Ecclesiastical Hierarchy*, Chap. III, col. 424 C.
[17] The 11th Canon of Sardica, the 80th of the Council in Trullo, and the 21st of the Council of
Elvira prescribe excommunication for people who do not receive communion for three Sundays. According to the 2nd canon of the Council of Antioch any who come to hear the Scriptures but do not receive communion are in breach of order and must be excommunicated.

always questionable, but to shallowness of faith and a casual approach to the mystery.[18]

Fr Nicholas Afanasiev[19] discussing the question with admirable clarity, shows that returning to the order of the Church has nothing to do with personal eucharistic piety; it is the participation in the Meal by the whole Body every 'Lord's Day'.

'Day by day the Lord added *to the Church* those who were being saved' (Acts 2.47). Fr Afanasiev draws attention to the Greek text, ἐπὶ τὸ αὐτο; its translation by 'church'[20] is at once an excellent interpretation and an exact and sufficient definition of the Church: the Lord daily added the saved to the faithful who were gathered *in one place and for one purpose* – the Eucharist-Church. After Pentecost, wherever the eucharistic *koinonia* is to be found, there is the Church; where all are joined together in Christ as members, of the same flesh and blood, and therefore in no danger of atomization. The Fathers say the world is filled with fragments of the broken Adam; God brings them together in Christ and makes them his Body. The evil one, the devil, the divider, dislocates, breaks in pieces: the unclean spirit confesses, 'my name is Legion; for we are many' (Mark 5.9), and immediately in the light of Christ he reveals his nature: the singular, *'my* name', becomes the vicious multitude, 'Legion', and is scattered abroad in the plural, *many*. St Paul uses the same expression: 'we who are many,' disunited by the evil one, 'are *one body,* for we are all partake of the *one bread*' (1 Cor. 10.17). This is the essential eucharistic action of the Church. The demonic Evil One decomposes, reduces to a corpse; the Good One – the Christ-Church – reintegrates and restores to life.

9. ONE, HOLY

Fr Afanasiev also brings out the essential difference between a 'eucharistic' ecclesiology and one based on the idea of the universal Church.[21] According to the latter there is one universal body, the members of which – the local churches –

---

[18] St Gregory of Nyssa, St Cyprian and other Fathers insist on daily communion. St Basil recommends communion at least four times a week. St Ambrose says, 'Receive each day what is needful for that day. Live in such a way as to be worthy of it. Whoever is unworthy to receive the Eucharist every day, will also be unworthy once a year.' See Lot-Borodine, 'De l'eucharistie', in *Le Messager*, No 41 (in Russian); B. Sove, 'The Eucharist', in *Tradition vivante*, (in Russian).

[19] *Le Repas du Seigneur*, Ed. Orthodoxie et Actualité, Paris 1952.

[20] Cf. Acts 1.15; 2.1; the same use occurs in St Ignatius, Eph.13.1; Magn.7.1.

[21] 'The Apostle Peter and the Bishop of Rome', in *Pensée orthodoxe*, X, 1955 (in Russian).

are only parts.[22] Universalism is by nature centralist; it requires a centre of unity and of authority embodied in a form of monarchy, such as the Pope in Rome.

In eucharistic ecclesiology the word *ecclesia* means the people of God, called together no longer in the Temple of the Old Covenant, a particular place, but in the *Body of Christ*. The fullness of the Body is found in the Eucharist, which means that *every* proper local eucharistic assembly, i.e., with the bishop at its head, possesses all the fullness of the Church of God in Christ. 'The Church of God at Corinth', or in any geographical place, is the Church with its whole *the-andric* content. Universality belongs to the mystical Body, which, not being restricted in space, can be fully manifested in any given place. The multiplicity of Lord's Suppers has no effect at all on the uniqueness of the one and only Lord's Supper; the multiplicity of places has no effect at all on the unity of the one Catholic Church fully present *hic et nunc*. In the teaching of St Basil, 'The Spirit is present in each person who receives it, as if it were communicated to him alone'.[23] In his famous letter about pilgrimages to shrines, St Gregory says, 'The Spirit dispersed the Apostles throughout the world: now no place, however "holy", can claim pre-eminence.'[24] There are multiple manifestations of the unique *Una Sancta* that is always equal and identical to itself. The number of places and their attributes vary; the spiritual reality manifested in them is constant – the fullness of Christ on whom the Spirit rests. So St Ignatius was already teaching that every local church united with its bishop – the living sign of Christ – is the Catholic Church, *Una Sancta*. From this point of view, one profoundly different from the 'universalist', the Church cannot exist anywhere *in part*; it is indivisible, never a sum: 'Where Christ is, there is the Church'[25] – 'Where the Spirit is, there is the Church.'[26] Every local church possesses the vertical ecclesial dimension in its fullness, for 'our teaching is in accordance with the Eucharist, and the Eucharist in turn establishes our teaching' (St Irenaeus).[27] The divine presence can never be parcelled out. Now, if the local communities are only parts, we are forced to say that the divine presence is greater or less, according as the local church succeeds or fails in representing the whole Church. We have here a version of the familiar 'branch theory': the branches are supposed to be joined

---

[22] This fatally crypto-Roman conception is held even by certain Protestant theologians. On another level, the unilateral doctrine of the universal priesthood turns every lay person into an imperfect priest. The recent controversies about the ordination of women have revealed a radical clericalism, a sort of crypto-papalism... The Catholic-Protestant conflict will be a dead end so long as it is confined within the categories of mediaeval scholastic thought.
[23] *P.G.* 32, 108-109.
[24] *Epist.* 2, *P.G.* 46, 1012-1013.
[25] St Ignatius, Smyrn., 8.2.
[26] St Irenaeus, *Adv. haereses*, III, XXIV, 1.
[27] *Adv. haereses*, IV, 18, 5. For St Irenaeus's doctrine see Renz, *Die Geschichte des Messopfer Begriffes*, 1901.

eventually either in the invisible Church of one of the Protestant theologies, or in the visible 'vicar' of Christ, the embodiment of unity in Roman theology. Now, if the churches are in communion, that is not in order to make a more complete Church by joining them together, which is strictly nonsense ('between the body and the head, there is no gap to be filled,' says St John Chrysostom,[28] speaking of the Eucharist, and Nicholas Cabasilas:[29] 'One cannot go beyond, or add anything ... there is nothing more that one could hope to gain'), but to respond, on the one hand, to the overflowing charity of the Body, and on the other, to the force that drives missionary expansion, a sign not of the *catholicity* of the Church, but of the *ecumenical* spreading abroad of Christianity.

Every local church is 'vertically' the Church of Christ, and a bishop is never bishop of a part, still less of a national church; he is a bishop of the Church of Christ. 'Horizontally', however, the extent of his juridical and administrative power is always restricted to an area. The unity of the Church consists in the communion of equal members, who are *consubstantial*, in the image of the Trinity. Identicalness makes communion impossible, subordination destroys consubstantiality. The *Una Sancta* is the unity of distinct but equal manifestations of the one reality in different places. A Council is the place where mutual love is exercised. God addresses his revelations to the Council not because it is representative body but because it is charitable, which makes it the right setting for the definition of doctrine.

Tradition sets a high value on communion with the five patriarchates.[30] This association is the mark of full and equal membership of the Orthodox Communion. Catholicity leads to ecumenicity. The 34th Apostolic Rule says, 'The bishops must recognize the "primus" among them and do nothing without him ... nor may the "primus" do anything without the others. By this unity God will be glorified in the Holy Spirit.' The Trinitarian principle always works by agreement rather than by power. The preferred structure of the Church is *a single bishop at the head of a single Church in a single territory*. The bishops differ only in honour, or precedence. For 1000 years the role of *'primus inter pares'* belonged to Rome, and when Rome was separated from the Orthodox Communion the honour passed to Constantinople. 'First' means simply first in order, without implying any distinction in quality. 'The bishop of the first see must never call himself the exarch of the priests, or supreme priest' (48th Canon of the Council of Carthage). Since they have all received an equal grace from the Holy Spirit, the bishops are wholly equal in dignity: 'the relationship between patriarchs, including the Pope, must be one of co-ordination and not of subordination' (Nil Cabasilas). The 'Con-

---

28 *In Ephes.*, hom. 3; *P.G.* 62, 26.
29 *The Life in Christ*, trans. de Catanzaro.
30 Before the separation: Rome, Constantinople, Antioch, Alexandria and Jerusalem.

fession of Faith' of the Patriarch of Alexandria Metrophanes Kritopoulos (18th century) says, 'none is exalted above the others, and none is considered to be head of the whole Catholic Church.' The episcopate reflects the college of the Twelve. The place of Peter, historically, was assumed by the Bishop of Rome, but that implies no doctrinal infallibility, nor any jurisdiction over the churches. No Council made any such assertion until the Vatican Council, when the Roman Church separated itself explicitly from the Tradition.

God the Father has given all power to Christ the King, who is to exercise it till the end of the world; so he founded the Apostolic community on the model of the House and Family, Apostolic power being expressed paradoxically in service: 'their great ones are tyrants over them. It will not be so among you' (Matt. 20.20-28; 18.1-9). Every bishop is 'the living image of Christ', the man of sorrows and the servant of the Lord; he has only one power, that of charity, of pastoral tenderness, substituting himself for him who suffers; and only one means of persuasion, his martyrdom.[31]

10. 'ROCK OF OFFENCE' (Matt. 16.17-19)

For the Orthodox the problem of power is solved by eucharistic ecclesiology;[32] in the light of this the text of Matthew 16.18 does not mean that St Peter was ordained as primate of the universal Church with jurisdiction over the whole Body – Bishop of the bishops. The most we can say – and it must be said – is that as well as giving him the honour of apostolic witness, the Lord appointed St Peter as the first bishop, so fulfilling the inbreathing described in John 20.22. 'Apostle' cannot be confused with 'bishop'. The Apostle is by nature itinerant, 'sent out'. The bishop's jurisdiction is limited to his see or seat. The Apostles are unique in combining the personal calling to be witnesses of the Resurrection – their apostolicity – with the bishop's sacramental and pastoral power. Only the latter could be handed down to the bishops, which is why their title is limited to 'bishop, successor of the Apostle'. A bishop is always the bishop of a particular community. According to Ephesians 1.22-23 Christ is the only 'head over all things for the Church, which is his body, the fullness of him who fills all in all;' the same idea of the single head is expressed in Colossians 1.18 (and 1 Cor. 3.11) – so any notion of a vicariate is ruled out: 'I am with you always, to the end of the age' (Matt. 28.20). Tradition knows nothing of any universal jurisdiction. Matthew 16.17-19 records the promise by Christ to build the Church which as yet did not exist outside himself; the Church came into being at the Last Supper in anticipation

---

[31] See Metropolitan Anthony, *Collected Addresses on Pastoral Theology* (in Russian), Moscow 1909, p. 18.
[32] See op. cit., Fr Afanasiev, 'The Apostle Peter and the Bishop of Rome'.

(before the Cross and the Resurrection); it was fully present on the day of Pentecost, *at the precise moment of the Apostles' first Eucharist.* The local church at Jerusalem is therefore the *first* territorial institutional place; it closes the time of the Incarnation and opens the *time of the Church.* The same thing happened later in other places. For the moment, St Peter was the first bishop celebrating the *first* Lord's Supper; in that sense he was Petros, 'the rock', the eucharistic foundation that will last till the Parousia. Without the Supper and without the power to celebrate it, without this perpetuated 'Peter', the Church does not exist.

Apostolicity, so far as it means being an eyewitness of the Resurrection, was a personal distinction that could not be transferred. But even during the time when the Apostles were active – the 'Acts of the Apostles' – the post-Pentecostal Church needed a succession of bishops to 'take the place of God' when they presided at the eucharistic assemblies,[33] and here the Orthodox principle is clear: succession does not go according to a person or his personal power, but belongs to the *Church.* In the Catacomb of St Calixtus (2nd century) there is a fresco depicting the eucharistic tripos; a man stretches his hand over the bread while a woman stands with her hands uplifted in prayer. This is the exact image of the Church, the royal priesthood of adoration that belongs to all, from which the bishop is withdrawn and set apart by consecration in order to offer the sacrifice, to make known the presence of God before his people and preside over and direct the exercise of the general priesthood. These are the two ways of sharing in the one priesthood of Christ, the only Priest, and they are interdependent. The fact that a bishop cannot celebrate the liturgy on his own without the people shows that the Church consists of bishop and people, and it is from the whole theandric body that the episcopal power is derived: it is not personal but functional, at the service of the Church – *totus Christus.* There is nothing 'collective' about this power; it comes from God, but from God working in his Body; his nature is theandric. A bishop who is bishop only in name, without pastoral charge or a real see, cannot ordain and thus exercise full episcopal power. A bishop suspended from the priesthood can no longer exercise the priestly power; sacraments administered by him are invalid and deprived of sanctifying grace, because he is cut off from the source of his power, of which he is only the spiritual instrument. Only the theandric power of the Church has any force; outside the Church no sacrament.

Christ founded the Church on St Peter, the first bishop-president of the Lord's Supper, so inaugurating the universal Apostolic episcopate. Because of this, every Bishop of Jerusalem, Alexandria, Antioch or Constantinople, and of every diocese, is the direct successor of St Peter, with Apostolic power to celebrate the Eucharist. So St Cyprian at Carthage saw himself as succeeding directly to the

---

[33] St Ignatius, *Magn.,* 8.1.

cathedra Petri,[34] and therefore as the bishop whose defining power was that of celebrating the Eucharist.

The Apostolic Church is overflowing with gifts, but these all converge to open the way to brotherly communion. That is the 'one thing necessary', the Kingdom, which must bear the authentic stamp of the Church in its fullness. Nothing in it must be unclear or confused; the invisible must be fitly clothed, and guaranteed by the institution in which the liturgical action takes place. We see as a matter of historical fact that the Eucharist passed immediately into the hands of the bishops. The duly ordained bishop was appointed as a visible sign, the *witness who attests* the truth of the sacrament: 'Only the Eucharist celebrated by the bishop is valid; without him there can be neither Baptism nor Communion'.[35] Every sacrament is effective only in relation to the Eucharist celebrated in the Church by its bishop. The vital necessity to be fed with the Bread of Life entails the priesthood; *the priesthood is included* in the Lord's institution of the Eucharist: '*Do* this in remembrance of me'. The inbreathing of the Spirit and the partaking of the Lord's Supper convey the episcopal power of Peter and all the Apostles, and of their successors – the bishops. It is given for the sake of the Eucharist and to authenticate it on the Day of Pentecost and every 'Lord's Day'. In his great Catechism Metropolitan Philaret emphasizes the sacramental nature of episcopal power: 'What does governing mean? To instruct people in the faith. What distinguishes the degrees of the hierarchy? The deacon serves at the celebration of the sacraments; the priest completes them; the bishop has in addition the power to transmit to others the gift of ministering the sacraments and officiating, by the laying on of hands.'

According to St Irenaeus, 'our teaching is in accordance with the Eucharist, and the Eucharist in turn establishes our teaching'; in the same way every priestly power is directly related to the Eucharist. St Ignatius already has an explicitly eucharistic conception of the episcopate: 'one cup, one altar and one bishop.'[36]

The Apostles ensure the transmission of doctrine and its continuity, but most important of all they ensure the continuity of the life of grace. That is why communion in the Apostles' doctrine and *participation in the Apostolic breaking of bread* was held to be the distinctive sign, the 'Note' of the Church of God at Jerusalem (Acts 2.42).

---

[34] *De catholicae ecclesiae unitate*, IV, *Ep.* 43, 5. Nil Cabasilas says, 'Peter is the universal Teacher; as for the Pope, he is Bishop of Rome' (*P.G.* 149, 704 CD).
[35] St Ignatius, *Smyrn.*, 8.
[36] *Philadelph.* 3 & 4.

11. THE TRINITARIAN ASPECT OF ECCLESIOLOGY

The constant principle of Orthodoxy is that of likeness and participation. Not only its ecclesiology but its whole ethical and social philosophy is founded *on the doctrine* of the heavenly image, so that doctrinal truth has a direct bearing on people's daily life.[37] The question that vexes every age – the one or the many, the personal or the social – can never be solved except by transcending the merely human, in the realm of grace; natural strength is powerless and we can look only to the image of God, simultaneously one and threefold. The Christian world is called to reproduce in its existence the divine reality: 'The human being is commanded to become god according to grace' (St Basil),[38] and Christianity is an 'imitation of the divine nature' (St Gregory of Nyssa).[39] Similarly the *Apostolic Canons* (Canon 34) say that the Church must glorify the Father, the Son and the Holy Spirit in its very structure, expressing the unity of the multiplicity of human hypostases in the one human nature recapitulated in Christ. The absolute Church of the divine Trinity is the pattern of the Church of humankind, 'the community of mutual love':[40] unity in multiplicity.

12. THE DOCTRINE OF THE TRINITY

The Trinity is the sole ground of all reality; between that and nothingness, says Fr Florensky, there is no other choice;[41] to receive this revelation human thought must be crucified and reborn in the trisolar light of the truth, which far transcends every philosophical concept. God 'identically monad and triad' is beyond mathematical number: the divine Persons cannot be counted. The divine Triad is 'inquantitive'.[42] It is highly significant that the heresies most severely punished by the Church are those concerning the Trinity, because they undermine the very foundation of all truth. Human reason tends always to reduce the mystery of the Trinity either to the unity of a single essence manifested in three ways (the modalism of Sabellius), or to a polytheist doctrine of three gods. St Gregory the Theologian refuses 'to Judaize by means of the divine monarchy, or to Hellenize by means of the divine plurality.'[43] The Trinity presents itself at the outset and from

---

37 See Mgr Anthony, *L'idée morale des dogmes*, Paris 1910, pub. H. Welter.
38 St Gregory of Nazianzus, *In laudem Basilii Magni*; or. 43, § 48; *P.G.* 36, 560 A.
39 *De professione christiana, P.G.* 46, 244 C.
40 Khomiakov, *Quelques mots par un chrétien orthodoxe sur les communions occidentales.* Paris 1853.
41 *Colonne et Affirmation de la Verité.*
42 Evagrius, *Cent.* 6, 10-13.
43 *P.G.* 36, 628 C. The Plotinian, emanantist triad allows the *counting* of the One, then the Word, and thirdly the Soul.

all eternity as self-existent, simultaneously one and threefold; it 'dazzles the eyes
... and sheds on everything its ineffable radiance',[44] any notion of theogony, of
God's being born, or evolving into the Trinity, is ruled out.

13. THE FILIOQUE

Latin theologians approach the Trinity by *considering first the one nature* and
then progressing to the three Persons – *amans, amatus, amor* – [45] these being,
according to a particular metaphysic of the essence,[46] modes of existence of the
one nature. St Augustine emphasizes the Trinity in God rather than one triune
God.[47] The Father and the Son together display the unity from which the Holy
Spirit proceeds, resulting in the *Filioque* that divides West and East. Eastern theologians *consider first the three Persons*, and then work back to the unity of the
nature; they start with the distinct Hypostases and the manner proper to each of
appropriating the one nature. The Nicene Creed and the baptismal formula begin
explicitly with the three Persons. As Fr de Régnon so well expresses it, 'Latin
philosophy considers first the nature in itself and works down to the mediator;
Greek philosophy considers first the mediator and then works back to find the
nature. The Latin considers the personality as a mode of the nature, the Greek
considers the nature as the content of the person.'[48] In eastern theology the Hypostases ensure at the same time the unity and the diversity of the divine life, for
the unity is derived not from the nature but *from the Father* – μόναρχος and πηγή
– source and principle of the eternal circumincession: '*one only Father; therefore
one only God*' is the basic affirmation of the eastern Church.[49]

   St Gregory the Theologian devotes all his energy to showing that the monarchy of the Father is the source of the perfect equality of all: 'The three considered
together are God; each is God by consubstantiality[50] [with the Father]; the three
are [one only] God because of the monarchy [of the Father].'[51]

---

[44] *P.G.* 37, 984-985.
[45] St Augustine, *De Trinitate*, VIII, 10.
[46] Dom Stolz understands it as the absorption of the Persons into the divine essence, so that
the relationship between human beings and any one of them does not arise (*Théologie de la
Mystique*, Chevetogne 1947, p. 246).
[47] See M. Schmaus, *Die psychologische Trinitätslehre des heiligen Augustinus*, 1927.
[48] *Etudes de théologie positive sur la Sainte Trinité*, I, 433.
[49] Denys speaks of the πηγαία Θεότις, Father – source of divinity, *P.G.* 3, 645 B.
[50] This term is the imperishable glory of the 1st Council. It was introduced by St Athanasius
and called by St Gregory 'the eye of the universe', because with the aid of this eye – i.e. the
word ὁμοούσιος, consubstantial – we see the Truth.
[51] *P.G.* 36, 417 B.

St John Damascene sums up the Patristic teaching: 'The Persons are united not so that they may be confused together, but so that they may contain one another' – 'the Hypostases have their being in one another and there exists among them a circumincession – without any mixture or confusion – in virtue of which they are neither separated nor divided in substance ... the divinity is undivided ... just as if three suns were contained within one another, by their interpenetration giving off a single light.'[52] 'The Father, the Son and the Holy Spirit are One in all things except unbegottenness, filiation and procession.'[53]

What differentiates the Hypostases in Cappadocian theology is their relation to the origin, and the whole art of Patristic theology consisted in not giving any supremacy to the one essence over the three Hypostases, so as to preserve perfect balance.

In making the Holy Spirit proceed from the Father and the Son (*Filioque*), we emphasize the unity of the nature, because the Spirit, in that case, is breathed by the one nature of the Father and the Son; whereas for the Greeks the Son is begotten and the Spirit is breathed by the *hypostasis* of the Father. Since Latin theology begins with the principle of unity and moves to the common nature, the differences between the Persons are reduced to those between simple relationships within the one essence; they diversify it, but ensure its superiority over the Persons. There is too great an identification between the relationships of opposition, or rather between the 'oppositions of relationship', and the Hypostases; although the relationships designate and characterize the Persons, they are far from exhausting the mystery of each.

The *Filioque* thus shifts the principle of unity away from the hypostasis of the Father and towards the nature; it lessens the monarchy of the Father and destroys the Trinitarian balance, the perfect equality of the three Persons. It actually splits the threefold Monad into two dyads, 'Father-Son' and 'Father-Spirit', and diminishes the Spirit to the advantage of the Son. If the Spirit proceeds from the Father-Son, considered as a single principle, those two Persons are transformed into one impersonal deity, the original substance. The reduction of the Persons to oppositional relationships makes the Son appear as the *Deitas*, but without the faculty of engendering (which only the Father possesses), and the Spirit to appear as what is left of the *Deitas*, but deprived also of the power of spiration (which only the Father-Son together possesses). We can understand why Duns Scotus wondered how the Spirit of Life could be 'a *sterile* Person'. It is the result of substituting the negative relationship of opposition for the positive relationship of communion.

The Latin formula of the *Filioque* appeared in Spain (at the Synod of Toledo in 589) first as an argument to use against the Arians who disputed the divinity

---

[52] *P.G.* 94, 829.
[53] *P.G.* 94, 828 D.

of Christ, and then to give greater emphasis to the consubstantiality of the Father and the Son. Then, as always happens in polemics, the argument was pressed too far, resulting in an over-correction and a distortion of the original doctrine. The great promoter of the *Filioque*, which took root in Spain, was Charlemagne. For political reasons he summoned a council in 807 to excommunicate what then constituted the Greek empire. According to a modern Catholic historian, 'the conferring of the imperial title on Charlemagne marks ... the intention to break with the Empire of the East.'[54] Pope Leo III, to demonstrate his intention to uphold the orthodox faith, caused two silver escutcheons bearing the text of the Creed in Greek and Latin, without any addition, to be engraved and fixed publicly on the bronze door of the cathedral of Rome.[55] But the usage became general in the West, and Rome bowed to the prevailing fashion. In 1014 Emperor Henry II had himself crowned at Rome and imposed the German rite of the Mass, and the Creed was sung for the first time with the interpolation in the cathedral of St Peter in Rome. Byzantium, faced with the Patriarchate of the West professing heresy, symbolically announced the rupture by striking the name of the Pope from its liturgical prayers. What the eastern Church objects to above all is not so much the change in doctrine as the schismatic and sectarian act of altering the sacred text, in defiance of formal prohibition by the Councils, without consulting the eastern part of the *Una Sancta*. This is the great sin against love, against the charitable nature of the Body; Khomiakov called it 'moral fratricide'.

The Trinitarian mystery cannot be explained by reason, but must be 'honoured in silence', the silence of apophaticism. And we must distinguish clearly between the life *within the Divinity*, where the Father is eternally the unique and hypostatic source of the Son and of the Spirit, from the *manifestation of the divine economy in creation*, where the Son communicates the Spirit: 'I will send to you ... the Spirit of truth who comes from the Father' (John 15.26). 'The Spirit is thus the eternal Joy of the Father and of the Son, where they delight in each other. This Joy is sent by the two to those who are worthy of it ... but he proceeds to existence from the Father alone'.[56]

In Trinitarian theology, the names of the Father, the Son and the Spirit denote their originative relationships, but do not exhaust the unique reality of each Person. So when we say that the Holy Spirit is the joy between the Father and the Son, that is nowhere near a complete account of the mystery of the Holy Spirit.

---

[54] J. de Pange, *Le Roi très chrétien*, Paris 1949, p. 167; Y. Congar, *Neuf cents ans après, l'Eglise des Eglises*, Ed. de Chevetogne, p. 26.

[55] The legate Humbert, in the document he placed on the altar table of St Sophia at Constantinople, reproached the Greeks for mutilating the Creed 'by cutting out the *Filioque*'! (See Dvornik, *Le Schisme de Photius*, Col. *Unam Sanctam*, No 19).

[56] St Gregory Palamas, *P.G.* 150, 1144. Cited by J. Meyendorff, 'La Procession du Saint-Esprit chez les Pères Orientaux', in *Russie et Chrétienté* 1950, No 3-4.

A simple revelation of God as one, with one sole hypostasis, would be impersonal; if love is to be communion, there must be relationship between hypostases – the Holy Trinity. Thus the Father begets the Son and manifests his essence in the hypostasis of the Son; similarly, he breathes the Holy Spirit and manifests his life in the hypostasis of the Spirit. Since the term ἀρχή is expressly reserved to the Father, the Latin *filioque* is absolutely unthinkable in the Greek tradition. Orthodox theology distinguishes clearly between the inward aspect of divinity, concerned with cause and origin, and its outward manifestations in life, revelation and creation. Only the Father is the causal principle, *monarchos*. He is Father, source, principle of existence and of divine unity (as St Gregory of Nazianzus calls it, *enosis*).[57] He is absolute beginning, and also the principle of circumincession,[58] of that 'eternal movement of love,'[59] the circular movement of the divine life that comes out from the Father, manifests itself and speaks in the Son by the power of the Holy Spirit, in order to be plunged anew into the Father: the eternal act of generation and spiration, going out from the source and returning to it.

If the Holy Spirit proceeds eternally from the Father by the *procession of origin*, he proceeds also by the Son, but only by *the procession of manifestation*. The Holy Spirit receives all that belongs to the Son ('he will take what is mine and declare it to you' – John 16.14). But the Holy Spirit also reveals the Son, giving him – but only in the sense of manifestation – existence, life; which is why 'no one can say "Jesus is Lord" except by the Holy Spirit' (1 Cor. 12.3). The Son loves the Father; his love becomes 'the breath of life,' the Spirit who upholds him and offers him to the Father; and in return, the Spirit rests upon the Son as the seal of the Father's love.

The language of the Creed is precise: the Christ-God-Man is 'incarnate by the Holy Spirit of the Virgin Mary.' The Holy Spirit conveys the presence of the Father who alone begets, but allows us at the same time to say that the Son is born διά, by means of, by and for the Holy Spirit. Similarly, at the time of the Epiphany, The Holy Spirit descends in bodily shape of a dove upon the Son at the very moment when the divine Fatherhood is revealed: 'You are my Son, the Beloved; with you I am well pleased' (Luke 3.22), (and, 'today I have begotten you.'[60]) Here the Holy Spirit is indeed the dove, the spirit of eternal birth, of fatherhood; he displays the movement of the Father towards the Son.[61]

---

[57] *P.G.* 36, 476 B.
[58] St John Damascene, *De fide orth.*, *P.G.* 94, 829.
[59] *Divin. nomin.*, *P.G.* 4, 221 A.
[60] Variant, cf. Psalm 2.7.
[61] To render the western conception of the *filioque* as acceptable as possible to the Orthodox, we can say that the Father gives to the Son the energy of spiration, not of origin but of manifestation. But in this case, the perfect balance of the Trinity requires that the Father gives to the Holy Spirit the energy of paternity, which equally is not of origin but of manifestation. The

14. THE CHRISTOLOGICAL ASPECT

In answer to the question *Cur Deus homo*? St Irenaeus set out his famous doctrine of recapitulation, the summing up of the whole world-order in Christ, the second Adam. St Athanasius took up the doctrine and made it the very heart of eastern Patristic thought: Christ, true God and true Man – consubstantial with the Father in his divinity, consubstantial with human beings in his humanity – became what we are so that we might become what he is.[62]

The emphasis was not on reconciliation, the remission of sins, or the propitiation of divine justice, but on the restoration of the image, the *rebirth* of the new creature in Christ. 'Through him the integrity of our nature is reconstituted' (St Gregory of Nazianzus). Christ resumes what the Fall interrupted – deifying communion – and brilliantly illuminates true human nature: 'Jesus is the archetype, representing what we are.'[63] 'We make our way back,' says Nicholas Cabasilas, 'to the place we originally started from' – 'we take off the garments of skins, and revert to the royal robe that was once ours' (that is the meaning of the rite of stripping at Baptism), 'we give up one existence in order to recover another.'[64]

Powerless of itself, but upheld by the powerful hand of Christ, nature rediscovers what it had lost and finds its way back towards the *status naturae integrae*: 'The human being is a creature that has been commanded to become god.'[65] St Maximus clearly points to that East towards which everything tends: 'Whoever knows the mystery of the Cross and the Tomb ... whoever penetrates still further and is initiated into the mystery of the resurrection discovers the end for which God originally created everything.'[66] The παθῶν Θεός, the 'suffering God' (St Gregory of Nazianzus), the sacrificed Lamb plumbs for us the dizzying depth of the Fall – as St John Chrysostom says, 'We need the life and death of a God in order to live.'[67] According to St Nicholas Cabasilas,[68] this mystery of divine charity – which we can honour only in silence – destroys the triple barrier that the perverted

---

Holy Spirit is breathed by the Father (origin) for, in, with, through, and by the Son (manifestation); and this dyad entails another, corresponding one: the Son is begotten by the Father (origin) for, in, with, through, and by the Holy Ghost (manifestation). Ἐκ τοῦ Πατρὸς διὰ τοῦ Υἱοῦ corresponds to ἐκ τοῦ Πατρὸς διὰ τοῦ Πνεύματος. The *filioque*, purely manifestation, is balanced by the *spirituque*, equally purely manifestation. This balance would improve the Nicene Creed, in which the divinity of the Holy Ghost is not sufficiently explicit.

[62] St Irenaeus, *Adv. haereses*; St Athanasius, *De incarn. Verbi*, cap. 54; St Gregory of Nazianzus, *Poem. dogm.* X; St Gregory of Nyssa, *Oratio catech.* XXV.

[63] *Orat.* 1, 7, XXXVI, 2.

[64] *The Life in Christ.*

[65] Saying of St Basil reported by St Gregory of Nazianzus (*P.G.* 36, 560 A).

[66] *P.G.* 90, 1108 AB.

[67] Similarly St Gregory of Nazianzus, *Or.* 45, § 28; *P.G.* 36, 653.

[68] *The Life in Christ.*

will erects between God and humankind: death, sin and self-sufficiency. The dazzling irruption of the Saviour 'is not a work of nature, but a mode of economic condescension' (St John Damascene),[69] the divine philanthropy that turns everything upside down (Denys);[70] his instrument, the cross – 'the unutterable sign of the Trinity' (the Office of the Cross) – leads to the sealed tomb, where the mystery of salvation is achieved. Enthroned on the right hand of the Father, Christ holds our human nature, without confusion and without separation, in the presence of the divine glory. In the sacrament of the Eucharist our 'consanguinity' with Christ demonstrates the perfect communion of the new 'Christified' race of Adam. The Patristic saying, 'what is not assumed is not saved,' unmistakably asserts the supreme reality of Christ – *wholly God and human*. Towards this union of the two natures – the divine and the human – all the economy of salvation tends, according to the eternal purpose of God; it was for the incarnation that the world was created. The Lamb of the Revelation is the alpha and omega of the world and of the divine creation (similarly Eph. 1.10). 'The unlimited is limited and the limited is stretched to the measure of the unlimited' (St Maximus).[71] The answer to every question about theodicy is found in what God has done: 'The Word was made flesh,' and, 'the Lamb slain from the foundation of the world.'

The definition of the Council of Chalcedon affirms, 'one and the same Son, our Lord Jesus Christ, at once complete in Godhead and complete in humanity, truly God and truly human ... recognized in two natures without confusion, without change, without division, without separation ... coming together to form one person and subsistence.'[72] The mystery is heightened by the use of the four apophatic, negative terms – ἀσυγχύτως, ἀτρέπτως, ἀδιαιρέτως, ἀχωρίστως – which forbid any explicit or positive consideration of the 'how' of this union, but affirm from the outset the unity of the divine-human life – the synergy of '*theandric energy*' (the expression of Denys the Areopagite in his 4th Epistle to Gaius). The emphasis is on the basic unity of the wills in Christ, without denying that they are two.

However, the unity can be understood only in virtue of the mysterious correlation to which St Paul alludes in his teaching about the two Adams, the one earthly and the other heavenly (1 Cor. 15.47-49), and of the Lord's own words about the Son of Man come down from heaven (John 3.3), a theme already well known from Daniel. Human nature can be enhypostasized in the divine hypostasis because it is already deiform, it corresponds to the divine image. It is this conformity of the celestial and terrestrial that governs the positive content of the negative formula of Chalcedon: the reality of *theosis*, the ontological capacity of

---

[69] *P.G.* 94, 1464 A.
[70] *P.G.* 3, 640 C.
[71] *P.G.* 91, 604 BC.
[72] Mansi, *Coll. concil.*, VII, col. 116.

attaining the deified state in which the human being lives by divine life, in divine conditions, in which it is god, but without any possible confusion because it is always and uniquely *according to grace*. The Christological 'without confusion and without division' extended into the human reveals the union of created nature *with grace*, with uncreated divine energy.

God is always identical to himself; however, 'the Word, all the while remaining what he was, becomes what he was not.'[73] The Creature makes himself his own creature and allows the *Theotokos*, in her human nature, to bring forth her God. 'The Church is as it were with child and in travail until Christ is formed in us, in order that each of the saints, by participation in Christ, might become Christ.'[74] Thus the formula of Chalcedon implies the mystery of *divine kenosis* that must be kept whole and uncontaminated by any desire to analyse the inexpressible. 'The mystery of economy consists entirely in the self-emptying and abasement of the Son of God' (St Cyril of Alexandria).[75] The divine deifies and the human humanizes. He who was in the form of God took upon him the form of a servant (Phil. 2.6-8) and 'for the joy that was set before him endured the cross' (Heb. 12.2). The expression 'theandric energy' exists simply to teach us that nothing in Christ can be only divine or only human; the one exists in the other; it is one way of conveying the Christological perichoresis, the interpenetration of the two natures in Christ, which is completely mysterious, except in the partial unveilings of the Epiphany, the cross and the Transfiguration of the Lord. Christ the Pioneer leads us to our glorious destiny hidden from all eternity in God and, overstepping the material Temple, constitutes us as his Body, *the Church*.

15. THE CHURCH, THE BODY OF CHRIST

The presence of Christ in every suffering creature will be revealed at the moment of Judgement (Matt. 25.40-44), but it already makes every one of us a member of Christ. The inscription on a vase containing relics of the martyrs, *In isto vaso sancto congregabuntur membra Christi*, illustrates very well the *realism* of the scriptural notion of the Body.[76]

St Paul depicts the Church as 'the *fullness* of him who *fills all in all*' (Eph. 1.23), meaning that the Body exists only in the unity of its members, such that every member bears within himself the whole Body. In counterbalance to this, Christ is not one member among others, but the *Head*, and indeed the principle that *binds them all together*. The very term ἐν σῶμα, 'body', was originally ap-

---

[73] St Theophilus of Bulgaria, *P.G.* 123, 1156 C.
[74] Methodius of Olympia, *The Banquet of the Ten Virgins*, *P.G.* 18, 150.
[75] *P.G.* 75, 1308.
[76] Yves Congar, *Esquisses du Mystère de l'Eglise*, Paris 1953, p. 115.

plied to the *Eucharist* (1 Cor. 10.17). The members are incorporated in one organism in which the life of God flows through human beings. There is another image, that of the 'mystical marriage' between the Lamb and souls, the faithful together making up one flesh, a single body.

The Church is the fullness (Eph. 1.23) when she attains her vocation as 'the complement of Christ'; according to St John Chrysostom, 'the head will be content only when the body has been perfected, when we are all conjoined and bound together;'[77] in the extension of the Incarnation, Christ=God-Man becomes Christ=God-Humankind, the Church.

'The entire Christ in the head and in the body;'[78] *totus Christus* is he and we, says St Augustine, and it is in the Eucharist that the Church is experienced here and now, manifestly one and manifestly Christ: 'between the body and the head, there is no gap to be filled,' says St John Chrysostom. At this point 'all are one in Christ,' (St Simeon) and the kiss of peace in the liturgy makes it explicit: 'greet one another with the kiss of peace;' and all the people do so, saying, 'The Church is become a single body and our kiss is the pledge of that union, enmity has been banished and charity is spread abroad.' Nicholas Cabasilas observes, 'One cannot go beyond, or add anything ... there is nothing more that one could hope to gain.'[79] Christians, in the yet unrevealed mystery of the faith, are not only united with one another, but they are one in Christ. Thus, the unity of the brethren described in Acts represents a true *Christophany*: Christ visible. And conversely, 'it is only in the community of the faithful that the Son of God can be found, because he dwells only in the midst of those who are united.'[80]

The Word of God is never addressed to isolated individuals, but to the chosen people leading a common life; the Judaeo-Christian society is opened to the Gentiles and forms a new race, *tertium genus*, spiritually transcending any biological limitations in the notion of 'race'. From the beginning Christianity was the Eucharist, the assembling for worship, the community, the Body, the Church. Becoming a Christian meant joining oneself there and then to the fellowship of the brethren. Personal conviction was less important than the need to be incorporated in the Apostolic family, in communion with the Twelve (Acts 2.42) – Apostolic *koinonia* was established as a 'Note of the Church' at Jerusalem.

Being the locus of Christ's real presence, and held together by the unifying power of the Holy Spirit, the Church is in the world but not of the world. It is a *divine society*, the life from henceforth of 'the age to come'. So life in the Church belongs to an entirely new realm of existence, where *values are reinterpreted* and transcended in an axiological *metanoia*.

---

[77] *In Ephes., hom.* 8, *P.G.* 62, 29.
[78] St Augustine, *Sermon on St John's Gospel, P.L.* 35, 1622.
[79] *The Life in Christ*, tr. de Catanzaro, New York 1982.
[80] Origen, *Comm. in Mat., P.G.* 13, 1188.

Mysteriously the Church is at the same time 'the Church of penitents, those who are perishing' (St Ephraem),[81] and the *communio sanctorum*, the 'communion of sinners' in 'holy things', deified by their participation in the 'one Holy'. This theandric unity of the body – Christology – postulates pneumatology: human hypostases have within them uncreated grace and created nature, held together by the Holy Spirit, so that possessing 'two natures' they may in their Christological integrity glorify the one and threefold God.

16. THE PNEUMATOLOGICAL ASPECT

'The splendour of the Trinity shone forth gradually'[82] (St Gregory of Nazianzus), and in that way revealed that 'no one can say "Jesus is Lord" except by the Holy Spirit' (1 Corinthians 12.3 and St Gregory of Nyssa[83]). The Son comes in the name of the Father to make him known, and to reveal and accomplish his will. The Spirit comes in the name of the Son to bear witness of him, to perfect and confirm with his gifts the work of Christ. Each divine hypostasis participates in the economy of salvation in his own way. While human nature recapitulated in Christ is one, and 'Christ is the centre where the lines converge' (St Maximus),[84] and 'makes them all into a single Body' (St John Chrysostom), [85] the hypostases, the human persons, are on the contrary manifold. The analogy with the body needs to be qualified. The personal must never be dissolved in the corporate impersonal; the unity of the Body requires, for the sake of its fullness, catholicity, the harmonious variety of the human hypostases. While Christ recapitulates and integrates human nature in the unity of his Body, the Holy Spirit enters into relationship with the persons, diversifying them with the charismatic fullness of *his gifts* and treating each one uniquely. The account of Pentecost clearly describes the descent of grace on each of those present, personally: 'a tongue rested on *each of them*' (Acts 2.3).

In the unity of the Body, each member retains his or her individual character: 'We are as if moulded into a single body but divided into personalities' (St Cyril of Alexandria).[86] At the heart of the unity in Christ, the Spirit branches out, and every member of the Body is named in the prayer of the Church. But the two are inseparable: Christ is manifested by the Holy Spirit and the Spirit is communi-

---

81 Quoted by Fr Florovsky, *Eastern Fathers of the 14th Century* (in Russian).
82 *Or.* 31, §§ 26-27; *P.G.* 36, 161-164.
83 *Contra Macedonium*, § 12, *P.G.* 44, 1316.
84 *Mystagogy*, *P.G.* 91, 668.
85 *Hom.* 61, § 1; *P.G.* 59, 361-362.
86 *In Ioannem*, XI; *P.G.* 74, 560.

cated by Christ; 'Watered by the Spirit, we drink Christ.'[87] According to St Irenaeus the process involves the whole Trinity: The Father is the *Unctor*, the Son is the *Unctus* and the Spirit the holy *Unctio*.

St Cyril reminds us that the 'Holy Spirit was given to the first man together with life.' As a result of the Fall, the Spirit's activity became *external* to nature, but at the holy Baptism in the Jordan it descended on the humanity of Christ and on the day of Pentecost became active *within* nature. Christ is filled with the Spirit, similarly the Virgin is *gratia plena*, and St Stephen, the first martyr, is filled with the Spirit. For St Ignatius, Christians are not only 'bearers of God', but 'filled with God.'[88] This comes about when the Lord breathes the Paraclete on the Apostles – *fills* them with the Spirit (John 20.22), the Church is manifested as the temple of the Spirit and the glory of God of Sabaoth *fills* heaven and earth.[89]

The sanctifying action of the Holy Spirit – called for in the Epiclesis – precedes every act in which the spiritual becomes embodied – i.e., every 'Christological' event. Indeed, at the moment of Creation, the Spirit moved on the waters, 'brooded' over the abyss whence sprung the world that would become the Church-Body of Christ. The whole of the Old Testament, in which 'the Spirit speaks by the prophets,' can be understood as the preliminary Pentecost in preparation for the arrival of the Virgin and the Nativity. The Spirit descends on the Virgin Mary and sanctifies her with a threefold holiness, and there follows the birth of Jesus, the Incarnation. On the day of the Epiphany, he descends on Jesus and makes him the Christ, the Anointed. On the day of Pentecost, it is from the tongues of fire of the Spirit that the Church, the Body of Christ is born. And in every sacramental act the Holy Spirit is at work, making a baptized person into a member of Christ, and bread and wine into Christ's flesh and blood. The immense importance of the epiclesis appears in the prayer to the Father for the sending of the Spirit at the consecration of Holy Chrism, and equally in the invocation at Baptism which confers on the water the character of blood. When the sanctifying act of epiclesis, the prelude to the coming of the Spirit, is finished, a form of the Body of Christ is revealed, then, thirdly, the Spirit acts to ratify these 'formalities' and displays the glory. At last the prophecy of Joel, cited by the Apostle Peter on the day of Pentecost, shows the Holy Spirit at work in history, sanctifying its flesh, suffusing it with his presence so that it becomes the glorious Body of the Kingdom, the Lamb of the new Jerusalem. 'I will ask the Father, and he will give you another Advocate ... the Spirit of truth ... [and] he will guide you into all the truth; for he will not speak on his own, but will speak whatever he hears, and he will declare to you the things that are to come.' (John 14.16; 16.13)

---

[87] St Athanasius, *Epist. I ad Serapionem*, *P.G.* 26, 576 A.

[88] *Eph.* 9.2, *Magn.* 14.1.

[89] The texts can be multiplied: Luke 1.15; Acts 2.4, 4.8, 9.17, 13.9, 13.52; Eph. 3.19; Phil. 1.11.

This is Christ speaking as the great Forerunner[90] of the Holy Spirit who perfects the work of Christ. 'He will declare to you the things that are to come': he moves freely beyond history and into another age. There is a variant of 'thy Kingdom come' – 'thy Spirit come'; the Fathers invoke the Spirit, the Kingdom and the Resurrection. With their *'maranatha'* the first Christians were already uttering the parousial epiclesis, inaugurating the Parousia. 'I came to bring fire to the earth' (Luke 12.49);[91] for St Simeon this fire that will purify the world at the end of time signifies the Holy Spirit, and according to St Seraphim[92] it works also in the soul of every baptized person, bringing into it the Kingdom of God.

This new life that flows within us comes from the 'Giver of life'; it is mysteriously united to us and becomes our own, just as Christ unites our nature to his hypostasis and makes it his. The Holy Spirit becomes interior to us, more familiar to us than we ourselves. The prologue of St John's Gospel says of the Word that 'in him was life.' The Spirit was interior to the Word. Our life also is entwined with the Spirit, and in that interpenetration attains its deifying reality. It is the heart of the St Seraphim's teaching on the goal of the Christian life, the acquisition of the Holy Spirit; for 'the Spirit causes the one nature of the Trinity to shine forth mysteriously in souls.'[93]

St John of Damascus teaches that 'the Son is the image of the Father, and the Spirit is the image of the Son.'[94] But the most complete kenosis is that of the Spirit, whose hypostasis is manifested only in his gifts – he is not incarnate like the Son: 'Your name, so desired and constantly proclaimed, nobody can say what it is,'[95] exclaims St Simeon. There is no one 'opposite' the Spirit who can be his image except the glorified Church, the *Communio Sanctorum* crowned with the *Theotokos*, and that is the ultimate mystery of the Kingdom.

The Spirit consecrates the universe and *inspires* the human spirit; like accepts like when for the first time 'humanity receives the Spirit at the moment of creation;' he is restored to humankind on the day of Pentecost, and the sacrament of Unction reproduces that event in everyone who is baptized.

It is the Spirit who calls within us, 'Abba, Father,' and it is by him that we can say 'Lord Jesus'; it is he 'who enables us to apprehend supernatural reality by making it usual and natural for us,'[96] and thus restores the nature we had in

[90] St Athanasius said, 'The Word took flesh so that we might receive the Holy Spirit'(*De incarn.* § 8; *P.G.* 26, 996).
[91] *Hom.* 45, 9.
[92] 'Entretien avec Motovilov', in *Semeur*, 1927.
[93] Anthem of the 4th tone, Office of Sunday.
[94] *P.G.* 94, 856.
[95] 'Hymne à l'amour divine', in *La Vie Spirituelle*, 27, 1931, p. 201.
[96] *Centuries* of Callistus and Ignatius in *Philokalia*.

Adam, but Christified by his presence. The Spirit guides us till death in obedience to the Son. The only adequate response from the creature to the Creator, from the person to the Person, from one who is poor and naked, is *humility*, the self-offering of utter obedience. In this act of interior liturgy the sacrificial matter is our Luciferian *ipseity* and following the epiclesis we are inspired to utter the *fiat*. In dying to self the person is brought to birth in the 'identification by grace' described by St Paul: 'It is no longer I who live, but it is Christ who lives in me' (Gal. 2.20). The human being never realizes its own person; the very thing that is most intimate to it is not 'its own', but eternally received. According to St Maximus, it is an 'identity by grace'[97] – ἡ κατὰ χάριν αὐτότης – which exists only so far as it is continually transcended and, in that transcendence, is no longer its own master. In the Christological encounter, the divine yes of the Incarnation meets the human *fiat* in a free and unconstrained exchange. Individual self-absorption is replaced by the person open to and centred on God. The renunciation of self brings freedom to go out towards the other; the infinite littleness of our humility releases the immense deifying energies of God.

The mystery of salvation is Christological but not pan-Christic. The epiclesis remains the indispensable and universal preliminary. St Basil, in his book on the Holy Spirit, gives this masterly definition of the Spirit's ministerial role: 'The creature possesses no gift that does not come from the Spirit; it is the Sanctifier who unites us to God.'[98]

Pneumatology is entirely an eastern study. Orthodoxy has never tried to reduce the Trinity to the unity of its nature in action, but is concerned rather to understand the economy of the hypostases by which in a single *action*, each hypostasis works in its own manner. The Spirit is the finger of God, the seal of the Son, the anointing of the Father and the Son, bearing witness to the Son, manifesting him, in a sense bringing him to birth ('incarnate from the Holy Spirit and the Virgin Mary'), and leading all to Christ. He is the active principle – 'Giver of life' and 'Treasure of grace'; the Greeks, without going into the scholastic classifications and distinctions of the different graces, see the grace of the Holy Spirit as governing our participation in the deifying energies.

The Spirit-bearing and Christified soul becomes a Christophany, enters into a personal relation with Christ. This is by no means an escape into interiority. The ascetic puts his steps in the steps of Christ – comes to resemble him, and is crucified (an icon of Mount Athos shows every monk crucified).[99] We must not forget the strong personal emphasis put by the great spiritual teachers on the mys-

---

[97] *Ad. Thal.* q. 25; *P.G.* 90, 333 A.
[98] *P.G.* 32, 133 C. See also the secret prayer in the Liturgy of St Basil. Similarly, St John Damascene, *P.G.* 94, 821 BC; St Gregory of Nazianzus, *P.G.* 36, 159 BC.
[99] It is reproduced in A. de Meibohm, *Démons, Derviches et Saints*, Paris 1956, p. 240.

tical marriage of the Lamb. The Holy Spirit is in us so that we can be in Christ, the little fishes in the Fish, sons in the Son, pleasing to the Father because the Church and every soul has become the bride of the Lamb.

17. THE MARIOLOGICAL ASPECT OF THE CHURCH

For the Fathers the maternal role of the Church naturally inclines it to Mariology. The Word, looked at objectively, is no doubt perfectly sufficient in himself; the insufficiency is in us; we need the maternal protection of the Church so that as children we can learn to read the Word at our mother's knee.

'The mere name *Theotokos*, Mother of God, contains all the mystery of Economy,' says St John Damascene.[100] The analogy has been made between Eve, Mary and the Church ever since St Irenaeus;[101] the Fathers see Mary as the Woman who is the enemy of the Serpent, the Woman clothed with the sun, the seat of the wisdom of God in its very principle, the integrity and chastity of being. 'There is only one Virgin Mother and I delight in calling her the Church,' says St Clement of Alexandria:[102] 'Mary, ever-virgin, τὴν ἁγίαν ἐκκλησίαν'.[103] While the Holy Spirit – πανάγιον – personalizes the very character of divine sanctity (St Cyril),[104] the Virgin, hagiophany, personalizes human sanctity. It is this archetypal integrity – σωφροσύνη – that makes her the heart of the Church. The essential virginity of her nature, apart from any act, is already triumphant over evil and holds unutterable power; the sheer presence of the 'most pure' is intolerable for the demonic forces. Bound in her essence to the Holy Spirit, Mary offers life and consolation; she is Eve-Life, keeping every creature safe and thus symbolizing the Church as mother and protector.[105]

'Wisdom has built her house, she has hewn her seven pillars. She has ... mixed her wine' (Prov. 9.1-2). This text brings together Wisdom and Mary; it speaks of the Church's ministry of prayer. The consecration of the Virgin to life in the Temple, according to the tradition, and her love for God, attain such a depth and such an intensity that the conception in her of the Son comes as a divine response condescending to the deepening of her life of prayer, to her openness to the energies of the Spirit.

She is 'Crown of doctrines', casting light on the Trinitarian mystery reflected in humanity: 'Thou hast given birth to the Son *without father*, that Son who was

---

[100] *De fide orth.* III, 12; *P.G.* 94, 1029 C.

[101] *Adv. haeres.*, I, III, c. 22. n. 4.

[102] *Pédagogue*, I, c. 6; *P.G.* 8, 300.

[103] *Hom.* IV; *P.G.* 77, 996.

[104] *De Trinitate.* See V. Mahe, 'La sanctification d'après saint C. d'Alexandrie', in *Rev. d'Hist. ecclés.*, 1909.

[105] In the icon of the Virgin holding the infant Jesus, the subject is certainly not the Virgin, but the Incarnation or the Church: the communion of the divine with the human.

born of the Father *without mother*.[106] The paternity of the Father in the divine
is answered by the maternity of the *Theotokos* in the human, representing the *maternal virginity* of the Church; which for Cyprian means: 'He cannot have God
for father, who has not the Church for mother.'[107]

Although she is of Adam's race, the Virgin is guarded from any personal impurity,
all evil being rendered powerless to affect her by the successive purifications of her
ancestors, by the special operation of the Spirit and by her outstanding act of free
will. The importance of the human response – that humanity could not be saved
without its own free agreement – is thrown into relief by Nicholas Cabasilas in a
neat synthesis of Patristic thought: 'The Incarnation was not only the work of the
Father, of the divine Nature and of his Spirit, but also the work of the faith of the
Virgin. Without the consent of the Most Pure, without the agreement of her faith,
this plan would have been as unrealizable as without the intervention of the three
divine Persons. Only after having instructed and convinced her does God take her
for Mother, and borrow the flesh that she is so willing to lend. Just as he wished to
be incarnate, he wished his Mother to bear him freely, of her own accord.'[108]

In acknowledging her perpetual virginity,[109] Orthodoxy does not accept the
idea of exemption entailed by the Roman dogma of the Immaculate Conception.[110] This dogma sets the Virgin apart, removes her from the common destiny
of mankind; it presents the possibility of being freed from original sin earlier than
the Cross, by means of grace alone. In that case, in order for the Redemption to
take place, it was necessary that it should already have happened, that the Virgin
should enjoy its effects before it was accomplished. If God was already justifying
the race of Adam by grace alone, such an intervention by God would, for the
eastern Church, render the Fall itself incomprehensible. Original justice for the

---

[106] *Dogmatic Theotokion* of the 3rd tone.
[107] *De cath. eccles. unitate*, c. 6.
[108] *Homily on the Annunciation*.
[109] Θεοτόκος – Deipara, is Ἀειπαρθένος: 'In the Nativity you have kept your virginity'. In
the icons the Virgin's head and shoulders are adorned with three stars, symbolizing her virginity
before, during and after the Nativity, and expressing her absolutely chaste integrity. The doctrine of the perpetual virginity emphasizes the realized state of the 'new creature' and the fulfilled mystery of the Church, which is 'the boundary between the created and the uncreated'
(St Gregory Palamas), *P.G.* 151, 472 B.
[110] The Orthodox rite of the Crowning (the sacrament of marriage) is very explicit: 'Bless
them, O Lord our God, as thou didst bless Jacob and all the patriarchs – as thou didst bless
Joachim and Anna – as thou didst bless Zacharias and Elizabeth.' This prayer places the birth
of the Virgin to her parents in the series of human births subject to the common law of nature.
It is significant that when the Council of Moscow in 1666-1667 approved the work of Simeon
of Polotsk, *The Sceptre of the Government*, it accepted it purely as a text that would be useful
in refuting schismatical argument; the Council said nothing about the Latinizing tendency in
Simeon's teaching on the Conception of the Virgin. There was some Roman infiltration into
the theology of southern Russia in the 17th and 18th centuries (Dmitri of Rostov), which ex-

Greeks was not a free privilege but the 'root of the being'. God does not act *on* human beings, but *in* them; he does not act on the Virgin with the gift *superadditum*, but he works entirely *within* by the synergy between the Spirit and the sanctity of the 'righteous ancestors of God.' Every imposed Good is converted into evil. Only the free submission of sanctity supplies the *objective human condition for Incarnation* which allows the Word to come 'to his own.' Grace does not violate or in any way force the order of nature, but perfects it. Jesus can take human flesh because humanity in Mary gives it to him, so it is not in the Redemption that the Virgin participates, but in the Incarnation; in the Virgin all say, 'Yes, come, Lord'. That is why the Fathers apply the statement in the Creed, 'incarnate from the Holy Spirit and the Virgin Mary', also to the mystery of the second birth of every believer born *ex fide et Spiritu sancto*; the faith of each one of the faithful is rooted in the Virgin's act of universal significance, in her *'fiat'*. The Annunciation, called the 'Feast of the Root' (St John Chrysostom), inaugurates the new age; the economy of salvation originates in the 'Mariological root' and Mariology is seen to be an organic part of Christology.

The *fiat* of the Creator is answered by the *fiat* of the creature: 'Behold the handmaid of the Lord.' The angel Gabriel is like a question that God addresses to the freedom of his generous-hearted child: does she really wish to contain the Uncontainable within her womb? In the Virgin's response bursts out the pure flame of the one who gives herself, and is consequently ready to receive. The Spirit works through the line of 'ancestors' and the purity of the receptacle *gratia plena* to their culminating point, where evil is disarmed; sin still exists but is no longer operative. Humanity brings its offering of bread and wine to the Temple, and God, in a royal gesture, transforms them into his flesh and blood, food of the gods. Humankind brings the purest offering, the Virgin, and God makes her his birthplace and the Mother of all living, the perfect Eve. As the Church sings on Christmas Eve: 'What shall we offer thee, O Christ? ... Every creature thou hast made offers thee thanks. The angels offer thee a song, the heavens their star, the wise men their gifts, the shepherds their wonder, the earth its cave, the wilderness the manger; but we offer thee a Virgin-Mother.' Clearly, Mary is not merely 'a woman among women,' but *the advent of Woman* restored in her maternal virginity. By her humanity the Virgin brings God to birth God, and Mary is the new Eve-Life; the motherly protection with which she covered the infant Jesus covers

---

plains why the devotion of that period shows some traces of heterodoxy. When the Virgin appeared at Lourdes she was reported to have said, 'I am the Immaculate Conception', but since the event took place on the day of the Annunciation – 25 March 1858 – the Orthodox Church understands this announcement to refer to the immaculate conception of the *Word* by his Mother. For the Orthodox, the Roman dogma *diminishes* the Virgin by turning her into a predestined 'instrument of grace'; it diminishes her humanity and deprives her of the dignity of being the one who freely, and in the strength of her humility and purity, and on behalf of all, pronounced the *fiat*.

the universe and all mankind. 'Jesus ... said to his mother, "Woman, here is your son." Then he said to the disciple, "Here is your mother."' – bestowing on him by this word from the cross the dignity of maternal intercession.

The Mother's humanity, her flesh becomes that of Christ, she becomes 'consanguineous' to him,[111] and is the first to realize the end for which the world has been created: 'the limit of the created and of the uncreated' (St Gregory Palamas),[112] and by her 'the Trinity is glorified' (St Cyril of Alexandria).[113] As the universal Eve, in bearing the Christ she gives birth to *all*, and thus gives birth to him in every soul, so the whole Church 'rejoices in the Blessed Virgin' (St Ephraem).[114] The Church, thus, is shown in its role of mystical womb, of extended childbirth, of *perpetuated Theotokos*.

St Maximus the Confessor defines the mystic as 'the one in whom the birth of the Lord is best manifested,' contemplation renders 'the fertile soul both virgin and mother,'[115] and St Ambrose adds, 'Every soul that believes conceives and gives birth to the Word of God; according to faith, Christ is the fruit of all of us, we are *mothers* of Christ.'[116] These words shed much light on the Gospel incident (Luke 8.19-21) and demolish the classical Protestant exegesis according to which Christ sounds disapproving; the emphasis is not on the Virgin, but on everybody: '*Whosoever* shall do the will of my Father which is in heaven, the same is my ... mother' – everyone is given the grace to bear Christ in his soul, to be identified with the *Theotokos*.

Christ is 'the way' and 'the door', the *unique* God-Man. The Virgin is *the first*, she anticipates humankind and the rest follow her; she is the 'right way', 'guide' and 'pillar of fire', leading them all towards the new Jerusalem. She is the first to undergo death as rendered powerless by her Son, and accordingly the canon that is read at the hour of death of every believer invokes her protection: 'In thine Assumption, O *Theotokos*, thou didst not forsake the world'. In her this world has already become the fully realized 'new creature' and the Church praises her in words of divine truth: 'Rejoice, thou Pinnacle of his commandments'. The Assumption closed the doors of death, the seal of the *Theotokos* is placed on nothingness; it is sealed above by the God-Man, and below by the first risen creature.

---

[111] We must understand the importance of this organic bond with which the Theotokos was given in the grace of her childbearing, and which is given to us all in the grace of the Eucharist, by which we too are made 'consanguineous' with Christ. We might add that western devotion to the humanity of Christ finds its Orthodox equivalent in devotion to the Theotokos.

[112] *P.G.* 151, 472 B.

[113] *P.G.* 77, 992.

[114] Hymn translated by E. Ammann, in *Le Dogme catholique dans les Pères de l'Eglise*, quoted in H. de Lubac, *The Splendor of the Church*, tr. Michael Mason, Ignatius Press 1999, p. 373.

[115] *Expos. or. dom., P.G.* 90, 889 C.

[116] *In Evang. s. Lucas*, II, 26.

The Roman dogma of the Assumption (1950) corresponds to the Orthodox feast of the Dormition[117] (κοίμησις), but is based on an entirely different theological understanding of nature and grace.[118] In effect, the 'Immaculate Conception' denies that the Virgin was subject to the universal law of the taint of original sin; she was consequently free from death, which explains the silence of the Roman dogma on the death and resurrection of Mary. The Orthodox liturgical feast of the Dormition, on the contrary, includes the death and burial of the *Theotokos* and her subsequent resurrection and ascent into heaven. In the Office of the feast, the Church sings, 'Arise, O Lord, into thy resting-place: thou and the *Ark* of thy holiness' (Ps. 131.8); – 'Following thy Son, thou didst submit thyself to the laws of nature, and after thy death, thou arisest to live eternally with thy Son' (1st Ode of Matins); – 'O Pure One, on this day thou art borne from heaven to earth' (Sticheron 1st tone of Vespers).

There is a correspondence between the feasts of the Virgin and those of St John the Baptist that suggests the 'relationship' of these supreme exemplars of humankind, but it breaks down at the feast of the Virgin's Robe (2 July and 31 August) and the three commemorations of 'the Invention of the relics of St John.' While the Virgin leaves her robe on earth 'instead of her body,' the relics of St John remain here below awaiting the 'eternal Spring'. The ascent of the Virgin is always called a *gift* of the Son to his Mother, and St John Damascene calls the Lord the 'debtor' of the *Theotokos*, thus calling attention to their mysterious intimacy. However, the Virgin is not thus spared the fate common to all; hers is simply reduced in time and anticipates the Parousia. While the death of her Son was freely chosen, the Virgin passed through death's door as subject to the universal law of fallen nature (the Canon of the feast composed by Cosmas of Maiouma is quite explicit on this point); she is raised by the power of her Son.

This event has a mysterious, hidden character, being venerated liturgically and in icons, but not mentioned in the preaching of the Apostles or in Scripture, which explains why it is outside the scope of doctrinal formulation by the Councils.[119] The reading, at the Office of the Dormition, of the text of Philippians 2.5-11, emphasizes the

---

[117] The feast originated at Jerusalem. Baumstark (*Liturgie comparée*, 1939) finds it in the dedication of a mid-5th century church at Kathisma, between Jerusalem and Bethlehem. Emperor Maurice extended it to the whole Byzantine Empire between 588 and 602, and Theodore 1st (642-649) introduced it at Rome. St John Damascene combined elements from local traditions (*P.G.* 96, 700-761).

[118] The Latin notion of 'pure nature', 'animal nature' to which grace and supernatural life are added, offers no doctrinal basis for devotion to the Virgin; only a reason to exalt her for her grace alone. Hence the internal, logical and 'inventive' necessity to formulate the dogma of the Immaculate Conception so that this 'miracle' (of which the eastern Church knows nothing) should be the dogmatic grounds for Roman Mariological veneration...

[119] In the 5th century St Juvenal, Patriarch of Jerusalem, said to the Byzantine Empress Pulcheria, 'There is nothing in Holy Scripture about the death of the Holy Mother of God and Ever-Virgin Mary; all that knowledge comes to us from a very ancient and trustworthy tradition.'

kenosis that the Virgin shares with the Son and particularly with the Holy Spirit, whose divinity is proclaimed simultaneously with the dignity of the *Theotokos*. But this veneration belongs to the inner life of the Church, a secret that is inaccessible except from within the experienced Tradition.[120] The Church celebrates this feast as a mystical second Easter and rejoices before the end of time in the glory of the first deified creature.

The Virgin is at the summit of the Church's holiness, and her virginity displays the *esse* of the Kingdom, holiness *in aeternum*; the *Sanctus* is her epithalamium. The lesson from Proverbs (8.22-30) at the feast of the Conception describes the Virgin as the seat of God's wisdom and celebrates the final attainment in her of the goal of divine creation.[121]

'Purification of the world' and 'burning bush' – 'Orans', the Virgin symbolizes the ministry of prayer, the spiritual gift of intercession. As the Bride, with the Spirit, she says, 'Come, Lord.' At the Judgement, the Word, the Truth judges and discloses the wounds, while the Holy Spirit 'vivifies' and heals. This aspect of the Wisdom conveyed by the Spirit is expressed in the ministry of the Virgin together with that of St John the Baptist. The icon of the *Deesis* shows them surrounding Christ the Judge and offering the prayer of the Church, interceding for mercy; this very icon thus deepens our understanding of the marriage of the Lamb with the Church and every Christian soul.

18. THE COSMIC ASPECT

The icon of Pentecost represents the cosmos in the form of an old man crowned, and stretching his arms towards the tongues of fire of the Spirit. Christ has walked on this earth, he has admired its flowers; in his parables he spoke of earthly things as figures of the heavenly; he was baptized in the waters of Jordan, he passed the *triduum* in the bowels of the earth; nothing in this world is foreign to his humanity or incapable of receiving the Holy Spirit. So the Church in its turn blesses the whole creation: at Pentecost the churches are filled with green branches and flowers; on the Feast of the Transfiguration offerings of fruit are blessed; the Feast of the Epiphany is the time of 'the great blessing of the waters'; during the evening office the Church blesses corn, oil, bread and wine; on the day of the Exaltation of the Cross, she blesses the four corners of the earth, thus bringing the whole realm of nature to bow before the saving sign of the invincible Cross. In an Orthodox church we see the company of the saints portrayed in the icons, but also plants surrounding the columns and reminding us of the teeming wildlife looking hopefully up at re-

---

[120] The episode of Athonius, shown on most of the icons of the Dormition and commented on liturgically in the Troparion of the 3rd Tone, explains that the glory of the Dormition can be appreciated only from within the liturgical life.
[121] '*Termino fisso d'aeterna consilio*', Dante.

deemed mankind. Biblical images take on a greater clarity: 'The heavens are telling the glory of God ... Let the floods clap their hands; let the hills sing together for joy at the presence of the Lord' (Ps. 19.1; 98.8-9); this deep intimacy, the essential communion between the cosmos and humanity, enables cosmic matter to become the conductor of grace, the vehicle of the divine energies. Creation is united in expectation of the 'cosmic liturgy'; only in the holy can all creatures meet together and sing the magnificent hymn to their Creator; the Virgin herself bears the cosmic and sacramental names, 'Ear of wheat and life-giving Cluster.'

19. THE NOTES OF THE CHURCH

'I believe One Holy Catholic and Apostolic Church'. The Council of Constantinople (381) thus defined the four attributes of the Church, the 'Notes' that express the fullness of its being and guarantee the continuity of the Lord's work until the Parousia. The distortion or belittling of any of these Notes deforms the very reality of the Church. In the presence of its mystery, reason is invited to 'take off the shoes' of juridical and formal logic so as to receive enlightenment from its teaching. It is significant that modern theology, while keeping the word 'ecclesiastical' to mean all that concerns the Church at large, has introduced the term 'ecclesial' to cover the more private matters of community and communion. This neologism subordinates the juridical and social aspect to the communal and mystical. Moehler, one of the Roman theologians most sympathetic to the East, said, 'The whole constitution of the Church is nothing other than embodied love,'[122] and the Russian theologian Khomiakov, 'The Church is the universal life of love and unity.'[123] How can we 'define' or 'formulate' the Church, if the Church is God himself revealed as mutual love?

20. THE UNITY OF THE CHURCH

'The Church is one', is the affirmation that most adequately expresses its nature. St Cyprian writing against the dissidents quite naturally entitles his work *Of the Unity of the Church*. This unity embraces time and space, the earthly and heavenly, the Church of human beings and angels. 'Has Christ been divided?' asks St Paul (1 Cor. 1.13) – for it is not in the nature of the Body to be fragmented. In its hymn at Pentecost the Church rejoices in its revealed character: 'When the Most High came down to confound the tongues he separated the peoples; when he sent

---

[122] *L'Unité de l'Eglise*, Coll. Unam Sanctam, Paris 1938, § 56.
[123] *Les confessions occidentales*, p. 54.

the tongues of fire, *he called the whole human race to unity*; with one voice we glorify the Holy Spirit.' There is one only Lord, one only Spirit, because there is one only God and Father of all. This call to unity stems from the monarchical principle of *the Father*, source of the Trinitarian unity, source of the ecclesial unity in which every act, anaphora, anamnesis-memorial is *for the Father* and *in the presence of the Father*: 'By the Holy Spirit every soul is quickened and raised while being purified; it is enlightened by the Trinity in its holy mystery.'

The plurality of autocephalous churches leaves intact the historical diversity of languages and cultures, but, like a symphony of many parts, the Church is essentially one in doctrine, in sacraments and in *koinonia*. Always and everywhere it professes the same faith, as if 'dispersed through the world, it inhabited a single house.'[124]

In Apostolic times *the churches* were the places where the one constant Body of Christ was manifest. Today the plural refers also to the fact that Christendom is divided, and therefore deprived of eucharistic intercommunion. From the Orthodox point of view it is the doctrine of the unity of the Church that marks it as Orthodox. Any extra-canonical Christian group belongs to Orthodoxy to the degree that it shares in divine truth. A heresy or schism is a phenomenon of the life of the Church; it may be nearer to the fullness at the centre or further away, and that is the measure of its orthodoxy. So any scheme of 'union' implies a progression to essential ecclesial 'unity' that is revealed according to its 'unique' nature: *the Church is one and it is unique*.

21. THE SANCTITY OF THE CHURCH

'Be perfect, as your heavenly Father is perfect.' The response to this impossible command lies in the Holy of holies of the Church, its superabundance of spiritual gifts by which, through the sacraments, we are made 'participants in the divine nature' (2 Pet. 1.4) and 'share his holiness' (Heb. 12.10). 'By the Holy Spirit, all creation is restored to its first condition.'[125] The Church ceaselessly calls for quickening grace to sprinkle the arid and desert soil of humanity: 'Send thy most Holy Spirit to sanctify and enlighten our souls.'[126]

'Christ also loved the Church, and gave himself for it, that he might sanctify it and cleanse it' (Eph. 5.25), making it a hagiophany, a manifestation of 'Him who is' and who is *the Holy*. The Revelation of St John anticipates the world to come: human beings and angels bow down before the Lamb singing the *Trisagion* and the *Sanctus*, holiness expressed in song; the Church is now the eternal divine liturgy, the communion of saints.

---

[124] St Irenaeus, *Adv. haeres.*, I, 3.
[125] Matins of Sunday, 1st tone.
[126] Prayer from the Office of the Ascension.

22. THE CATHOLICITY OF THE CHURCH
(ἐκκλησία καθολική)

Καθολική derived from καθ' ὅλου, *secundum totum*, according to the whole, *quia per totum est*, conveys an entirety which is not geographical, horizontal or quantitative, but vertical and qualitative, resistant to any fragmentation of *doctrine*. 'Where Christ Jesus is, there is the Catholic Church,'[127] expresses a unity and wholeness which is quite independent of historical and geographical conditions or numerical size.

The horizontal extent of the Church is its 'ecumenical' dimension. The οἰκουμένη was the 'inhabited earth', the ecumenical empire that was geographically coterminous with the Church. The title of the Patriarchs and the Councils – Ecumenical – signifies territorial universality, the whole Christian empire around its capital, as opposed to the local or provincial. The Patriarchs beyond the borders of the Empire (such as those of Georgia and Armenia) were styled *catholicos*.

Ecumenicity is only a secondary characteristic, a function, depending on historical circumstances, of vertical unity and depth of faith, worship, doctrine and dogma.[128] The Councils are 'ecumenical' because they are consciously 'catholic'. While the ecumenical grandeur of the Empire is transitory, the catholicity of the Church *abides*.

'If any city or country separates itself from the universal Church, the Church nevertheless will remain whole and incorruptible,' says Metropolitan Philaret.[129] A leading Russian theologian, Khomiakov, has drawn out the rich meaning of *catholicity* in his teaching on *sobornost*. *Sobornost* comes from *sobor*, assembly, council, synod, signifying that the *conciliar* principle stems from the inner catholicity of the Body. He has not said anything new, but has found an apt formula that synthesizes Patristic teaching; for him, the single word *sobornost* 'contains within itself a full confession of the faith.'[130] It is this utter commitment in faith, the thorough identification with the truth, that gives life to any local Church, causing it to be the *whole*, identical (everywhere and always) with the catholic essence. *Pars pro toto*: '*the Churches*' is plural in the same way as '*the Eucharists*'. The Epistle to the Smyrnaeans explains it thus: just as in the Eucharist Christ is entirely present, so each ecclesiastical community is the whole Body of Christ; where Jesus Christ is, there is the Catholic Church. The Prologue to the *Martyrdom of St Polycarp* says, 'The Church of God which sojourns at Smyrna, to the Church of God sojourning in Philomelium, and to all the congregations of

---

[127] St Ignatius, *Smyrn*. 8.2.
[128] See St Cyril of Jerusalem, *Cathecheses, P.G.* 33, 1044.
[129] *Responses and Opinions of Philaret, Metropolitan of Moscow* (in Russian), St Petersburg 1886, p. 53.
[130] 'Lettre au rédacteur de l'Union Chrétienne'. Fr Congar translates this term as 'collegial'.

the Holy and Catholic Church in every place.' Catholicity, by nature, belongs to every local church, which is the place of its manifestation.

Since the Church is the repository of divine Truth, that is where we must go, according to the Lord himself, if we wish to understand him clearly. The members do not come together to bring the Body to birth; the Church brings to birth her own children in Christ. She speaks to every human being but depends neither on numbers nor on her members, nor on the apparent success of her missions. Always one and the same, even when reduced to a 'little remnant', she loses none of the integrity of her Catholic truth. St Maximus the Confessor said to the Monothelites, 'If even the whole universe (the *oikoumene*) were in communion with you, I still should not be in communion.' At the first Council, St Athanasius stated the Catholic truth and led all the Fathers of the Council into the truth of the Church.

23. THE CONCILIAR STRUCTURE OF THE CHURCH

Khomiakov neatly defines the Church as 'the life of God in human beings.' Now, 'No one comes to the Father except through me'(John 14.6). This is said not in any narrow or exclusive sense, but to explain that God cannot be known except as the Communion of the three Persons – the self-existent Church of the Holy Trinity. We cannot 'come to the Father' as to one person on his own, while making an abstraction of the other two, but we come to the Father in the Son and by the Holy Spirit. And inversely, God, in relation to the world, reveals himself and speaks only to his image: the Church-community bound together by mutual love.

Just as the soul can never be localized, but permeates the entire being, so God is present in his entire people, from the patriarch to the humblest member of the congregation. His presence is in *the Body in its charitable aspect*, the agapeic bond which transforms a multitude into *one* in Christ; and on this miracle of divine philanthropy the conciliar structure of Orthodoxy is founded. It is radically opposed on the one hand to any anti-hierarchical egalitarianism and, on the other, to any monarchical principle – and therefore to any idea of a Vicariate of Christ. It is always Christ who rules the Church and every doctrinal decision is directly inspired by the Holy Spirit; the announcement, 'It seemed good to the Holy Spirit and to us,' used at the beginning by the Apostolic Council of Jerusalem, was to become the hallowed formula at all the councils. All the bishops share equally in episcopal grace so there can be no thought of any super-bishop. St Cyprian is clear: 'The episcopal charge is *one*; the various bishops share in it in such a way that each possesses it completely'.[131] Every episcopal power is exercised *in* the Church and *with* the Church and never *over* it, for that would transform the organism of love

---

[131] *De unitate Ecclesiae*. cap. IV.

into a juridical and clerical society, and create a division between the Church that teaches and the Church that is taught. The Encyclical of the Eastern Patriarchs of 1848 states, 'The guardian of piety and faith is the whole people of the Church.'[132] There is only one Church taught by Christ himself. The people are not opposed to hierarchy, for that is how they exercise their rightful role in the life of the Church – above all else they are members of the 'people of God', so the Orthodox magisterium is exercised only by agreement, with the *consensus* of the whole Body, which, by thus obeying the spiritual law of unity, is assured of being *conformed to the truth*. The decisions of the Councils are never imposed by monarchical power, or arrived at by democratic vote, but are always *ex consensu ecclesiae*, in accordance with the whole faith of the Church. Being 'Catholic' does not depend on formal membership of a juridical unity; but it is truth that brings about unity and transmits this quality to its members, makeing them Catholics.

24. THE COUNCILS

History shows that it is not enough for a constitution to be legally correct. Living mystery cannot be constrained within formal boundaries. Thus the Council of Sardis in 344 considered itself to be Ecumenical, but the Church kept it local. The Council of Constantinople in 381, the Eastern Council, has gone down in history as the Second Ecumenical Council. The Council called 'the Robber Synod of Ephesus' in 439 was repudiated by the Council of 451. The Council of Constantinople in 553 was acknowledged as Ecumenical only in 700. The Council of 754 was considered heretical, and that of 869 was annulled ten years later in 879. The Council of Florence in 1439 was rejected by the people despite its perfectly correct constitution. Local Councils have often been accorded Catholic doctrinal status, such as those of 1341 and 1351 on the Divine Energies. The doctrinal definitions of the Council of Jerusalem in 1672 enjoyed a great authority.

When a Council satisfies the legal conditions for full authority, and aspires to be 'Ecumenical', that is only the beginning. Every doctrinal or canonical decision must be 'received' into the Body by the people of the Church; only when it is incorporated to the flesh and blood of the Church, and become part of its essential life, is it regarded as Catholic, and acknowledged as springing from the Apostolic root. The Roman dogma of the infallibility of the Pope does not abolish the fact of the preliminary *consensus* of the Church, but it does remove its strict necessity, thereby negating the sole basis for the authority of papal definitions. The Pope 'consults' the episcopal college *before* making his own pronouncement, but it is not till the moment of the papal definition *ex sese* that it becomes dogma. In Orthodoxy, the *consensus* of the people of God is sought *after* the definition

[132] Mansi, vol. XL (1909), c. 407-8.

in order to confirm, if such should be the case, the divine character of the dogma formulated *ex consensu ecclesiae*.

The prototype of the Councils, that of Jerusalem, clearly demonstrates the unanimity of the life of the Apostolic community: 'All who believed were *together* and had all things common' (Acts 2.44). When they took a decision, 'the apostles and elders met together to consider this matter' (Acts 15.6). 'Then the apostles and elders, *with the consent of the whole Church...*' (15.22), 'it seemed good to the Holy Spirit and to us...' (15.28) The whole Church acts together, neither dividing the priesthood from the laity, nor confusing them, all the members of the Body being of one heart and mind.

During a period of rapid growth the bishops were under pressure to take on an increasingly representative role and to act on behalf of their churches. But St Cyprian, in exile, wrote to his clergy, 'I have decided to undertake nothing without your advice and the agreement of the people. On my return, we shall decide everything *together*.'[133] The monks took a very active part in the work of the Councils (as early as the Third Council); there were about 130 of them at the Seventh Council with the right to vote.

The bishops govern their communities according to circumstances, and ensure that the voice of the Church is heard. In times of disturbance, when the ties may be weakened between the bishop and his church, councils may be organized in different ways, giving a greater role to the laity. The Council of Moscow in 1917 included a large number of laity; these, however, constituted a lower, consultative chamber, decision-making being reserved to the bishops. The episcopal college is not a formal juridical authority but a spiritual organism, and only thus can it be *charisma veritatis certum*.[134] Submission to the episcopate is not a formal *condition*, but the irrepressible *expression* of the love of unity.

The Seven Councils were an institution not only of the Church but also of the *State*. The chief power belonging to the imperial prerogative was the power to summon a council. But the representatives of the State participated *externally*; they kept order and protected the free expression of opinion, but did not take part in voting. The decrees were signed by all the Fathers, and their acceptance by the Emperor, as the first member of the Church, gave them the force of law for all citizens. Agreement by the Council Fathers was on the basis of truth revealed by the Holy Spirit, so that the sessions did not result in the formation of minorities and majorities, or with opinions held in reserve. The decrees were accepted immediately as rules of discipline, but 'conditionally' till the moment when the whole Church should receive them 'unconditionally' as coming from a truly Ecumenical and Catholic Council and expressing infallible doctrines and truths. This character of finality explains the tradition whereby the Councils solemnly

[133] *Epist.* XIV, 4.
[134] St Irenaeus, *Adv. haeres.* IV, 21, 2.

declared their faithfulness to the doctrines that had been previously defined: 'Thus believed the Apostles and the Fathers.' A Council is 'Ecumenical' not because it is formally constituted by accredited representatives of all the local churches, but because it has borne witness to the faith and revealed the truth. It is the Holy Spirit that makes a Council truly Catholic, and this is confirmed by the Body at such a time as God wishes.

The conditions in which Councils meet today are very different, both in their own organization and in their relation to the secular powers, but the mystical reality of the Church remains exactly the same, as does the vital principle by which the faith is communicated. The Church possesses infallibility only in its theandric wholeness, in the depths of its being which is the *Sacrament of the Truth*. The *consensus* is not democratic, or the will of all, but it expresses the common desire to be conformed to the Truth, the permanent miracle of the Church: the perpetuated *totus Christus*.[135]

25. THE APOSTOLICITY OF THE CHURCH

According to the principle of *Apostolic succession*, the Church is rooted in history and at the same time freely transcends it. 'Apostolic' does not refer only to the historical origin of the Church in the Apostolic college – that would allow for changes in the initial doctrines during the subsequent evolution of the Church. It means rather that what has come down to us here and now is *identical* with what was entrusted to the Apostles in the first place. *Apostolic succession* is the principle by which we know for certain that the Church in the upper room on the day of Pentecost, or at any moment in history or today, is one and the same. 'Succession' means continued existence in time, the continuous passing on of the Tradition down the centuries until the end of history; and 'Apostolic' means that, while the events of history are necessarily consonant with the truth, the truth itself can be deeply apprehended only through the witness of the Apostles, i.e., the Church, enabling us to see behind the events. The principle remains constant while historical forms evolve around it. It is as though the Apostle – the constant principle – stands in midstream while the waves of history flow past him. As they reach him he picks out some as being of the same nature as himself and rejects others as alien or heterodox: 'Thus taught the holy Apostles and Fathers of the Church.' The Apostolic Succession, witnessing to identity of faith, doctrine and worship, the *same Eucharist*, reveals the Church as the *permanent Sacrament of the Truth*.

The Wisdom of God comes to us and speaks 'by the Church' (Eph. 3.10). The Spirit spoke *before* the Councils and speaks *afterwards*, for his true home is the

---

[135] Mgr Battifol observes that in the West and Rome the Bishop of Rome was seen not merely as the successor of Peter on his *cathedra*, but as the *perpetuated Peter* invested with his authority and power (See *Cathedra Petri*, coll. *Unam Sanctam*, 4, Paris 1938, p. 75-76).

Body gathered in the Eucharist: 'Our doctrine is in agreement with the Eucharist.' (St Irenaeus)[136] The Spirit is called down in order to transform the holy offering, but also to sanctify the faithful and make the Church holy and infallible. The task of formulating its truth cannot be confined to one agency, still less to a single person. Anything *'ex sese non autem ex consensu Ecclesiae' does not require the epiclesis*, which in the Church is the condition of the Truth. Even the Holy Spirit is not the Vicar of Christ, but the Witness attesting and revealing the presence of Christ in himself; and the two speak *by the Church*, in its wholeness, and communicate the truth from the heavenly Father.

The Church, the Sacrament of the Truth, being essentially identified with its source, the Eucharist, is also the *Sacrament of sacraments* (according to Denys the Areopagite).[137] It follows that since any sacrament is effective by the grace that belongs to it, grace itself can be manifested and bear fruit only at the heart of the Church, i.e., only if the sacrament is that of the Church. Thus the 'Apostolic succession', does not simply mean historical continuity; it cannot function outside the Church, being cut off from its source and proper surroundings.

The acts of a bishop cut off from the eucharistic communion of the Church are not acts of the Church and are void of spiritual power. Such power is not conveyed automatically along with a particular function, but springs from its source, the Church. The Apostolic succession, as the sign of Apostolicity and authentic spiritual gifts, rests on the Church, and is active in its operations; as soon as a functioning member of the hierarchy is detached from the Church, from the source, it dries up. Thus it is not the degree of Apostolic succession that validates a church's priesthood – and at the same time settles the ecclesial problem of the Reformation – but the validity of the priesthood that puts it within the Apostolic succession. The conflict between Orthodoxy and Reform lies not in the Apostolic succession itself, but in what it stands for, i.e., the Church in its sacramental reality as Sacrament of the Truth, and the hierarchical and spiritual organism which assures its continuity and attests its authenticity, the priesthood.

Not every local church can demonstrate a continuous historical succession from the hands of the Apostle. The first century was the formative period of the Body, a unique time when gifts abounded, and everything was in a state of flux. Alongside the Apostles there were prophets, spiritual teachers and elders. Irenaeus and Eusebius tell us something about the ordination by the Apostles of their direct successors to the sees of Rome, Jerusalem, Ephesus, Antioch, Smyrna, Athens and Philippi. The fact that there are other places that we know nothing about makes no difference to our general understanding of the ecclesiastical structure. The Church leaders relied on the charismatic principle of 'the grace which completeth that which is wanting' (in the words of the ordination rite); they relied on

[136] *Adv. haeres.* IV, 18, 5.
[137] *Eccles. Hier.*, Chap. III, col. 424 C.

the vertical power of the Church, the Sacrament of sacraments, to make up for any technical or temporary deficiency, whether human or historical. In the second century every eucharistic community or local church already had a clearly defined hierarchical structure with a bishop at the head.

From the moment that the Apostolic succession achieved its final form, and was fixed by canon, it continued in history without further interruption. The priesthood took its present form. The hands of the Apostles that were stretched over the world without any differentiation of gifts, as we read in the Acts, became, with perfectly canonical regularity and exact timing, the hands of the bishops over the three degrees of priesthood: bishop, priest and deacon. For the Orthodox (because of the comprehensiveness of the Apostolic succession in respect of the priesthood and the Eucharist) it is clearly not important to prove that each local church is directly descended from the Apostles. The Apostles and charismatic leaders drew their power from the Church, the Sacrament of sacraments; the power of Peter or John or any other Apostle was not in any way personal to him, but came from the Church as a whole – *totus Christus* – which has the power to create such canonical forms as and when it needs them, and mark them as belonging to its own essential nature.

The saying, 'the Church is in the bishop,' means that he has the spiritual quality of embodying the community within himself and making it the Church (that is the symbolism of his '*omophorion*', just as the High Priest bore on his heart the names of the twelve tribes of Israel). On the other hand, 'the bishop is in the Church;' his power is never personal but of *the Church*, and likewise his *potestas magisterii* is a function of the *theandric* reality of the Body. Thus do the bishops act at the same time *in persona Christi* and *in persona ecclesiae*. Similarly, they never speak in their own name, but always *ex officio*; never *ex sese*, but always *ex consensu ecclesiae*. The episcopate uses its doctrinal power to express *the faith of the people of God*. The episcopal college administers the Sacrament of Truth according to the ecclesial *epiclesis* of the Councils – 'It seemed good to the Holy Spirit' – which is why a Council consists of bishops. But the operation of this sacrament is not complete till the moment of reception by the Body. The hierarchy both constitutes the people as the Body, and is set at the very heart of it: 'All true believers united by the holy Tradition of the truth, collectively and successively, are established by God in one Church, which is the sure repository of the holy Tradition.'[138] While the task of theological reception and creative receptivity belongs to us, the task of defining and proclaiming, and of conserving the purity of the deposit, belongs to the bishops. We are all guardians of the faith, but the bishops are divinely authorized to bear witness of it (*charisma veritatis certum*).

---

[138] *Catechism* of Metropolitan Philaret.

26. THE PRIESTHOOD

Whatever continuity there might be between the two Testaments, their priesthoods are different in structure. In the Old Testament we see first the gradual development of worship and ritual, which God afterwards comes to inhabit; so the Church comes into being when the institutions are already in place: 'I will consecrate the tent of meeting and the altar; Aaron also and his sons I will consecrate, to serve me as priests. I will dwell among the Israelites, and I will be their God' (Exod. 29.44-45). But this ordinance, like the law, is only 'a shadow of good things to come and not the true form of these realities' (Heb. 10.1); it is not yet 'the thing' itself, but its anticipation, the foreshadowing. Now, Christ 'abolishes the first [sacrifice] in order to establish the second' (Heb. 10.9). So in the New Testament the order is reversed: at the dazzling noonday of history comes the Incarnation, bringing both the thing and the shadow, and the shadow (the ritual and the institution) *does not precede, but comes after.* The people of God meets no longer in a 'tent of meeting', 'neither on this mountain, nor in Jerusalem' (John 4.21), but in Christ: the Church is the Body of Christ, the fullness of 'him who fills all in all.' Fullness is found from the outset in Christ and *afterwards* its elements are differentiated and set in order according to the canons of the time: '*from whom* the whole body, joined and knitted together by every ligament with which it is equipped, as each part is working properly, promotes the body's growth' (Eph. 4.16). The priesthood, the sacraments, the doctrines, the canon of scripture, worship, all the institutional forms are fixed gradually and together make up the visible aspect of the Body, but everything in these forms is assured by the immutable presence of the ultimate Witness, the Spirit, who reveals the ultimate Priest, Christ. Christ does not communicate his personal powers to the Apostles; that would mean he was absent. The icon of Pentecost, in depicting a special place reserved for Christ at the head of his Apostles, emphasizes the presence of the Head of the Body. The prayer said when hands are laid on a bishop is explicit: 'It is not by the imposition of my hands, but by the communion of thy gifts that grace is accorded.' The hands are indispensable, but only in order to transmit the gifts that come from the divine source. This has nothing to do with the prerogatives of any one Apostle, or of the episcopal college – which would be collective papism – but concerns the presence of the one and only High Priest, Christ. His unique word becomes eventually the four Gospels, the one cup the multitude of eucharistic liturgies; his power extends over his whole Body with its differentiation of ministries, functions and spiritual gifts.

27. THE DIVINE ORIGIN OF THE PRIESTHOOD

The priesthood after the order of Melchisedech is 'without father, without mother, without genealogy' (Heb. 7.3), so there can be no hint of immanent transmission or merely human descent. The priestly power is breathed by Christ into the twelve

Apostles, and its origin is explicitly divine: 'You did not choose me but *I chose you. And I appointed you*' (John 15.16). The *'axios'* and the 'amen' pronounced by the people at the election are certainly indispensable, but only as one of the elements of theandrism, a human condition of a wholly divine spiritual gift.

28. THE PRIESTHOOD OF ORDER AND THE ROYAL PRIESTHOOD

Tradition makes a clear functional distinction between the two priesthoods, based on spiritual gifts and the order of their ministries. While never confusing them, it insists that we are all *equally members* of the people of God, and that out of the very equivalence the differentiation of gifts and functions arises. At the most solemn moment in the rite of the consecration of a bishop something significant happens. The most senior of the bishops takes the place of the deacon and recites the diaconal litanies, while the other bishops, taking the place of the people, sing the response. Thus at the moment of raising the elected person to the highest rank in the priesthood of order, all the bishops put themselves in the rank of the faithful; they are all first and foremost priests of the royal priesthood, equally members of the Body, and it is afterwards that the person elected receives the specific spiritual gifts that he needs for his episcopal function, which is to be his recognized ministry at the heart of the Body. Christ alone is Priest and all share in his priesthood, some being bishops and presbyters. It is noteworthy that in New Testament Greek, the term ἱερεύς – priest – is reserved to the royal priesthood; that of order is designated by presbyter or bishop. Only the royal priesthood is conveyed by unction, first Christ, then all the faithful by ordination with Chrism; ministers in the priesthood of order have been ordained since early times by the imposition of hands.

Clearly there is no sympathy in Orthodox thought for any anti-hierarchical egalitarianism, nor for a clericalism that would cut the one Body in two; there is a strong emphasis on the priestly participation of all, but in two modes, two priesthoods. Both are established by God, rendered by their divine origin part of the sacramental economy, lifted out of the world of sociology, but set as a charismatic ministry in the world and for the world.

What is contained in One person alone – Christ – is distributed through his Body, and fulfilled and completed there: the Priest moves towards the Kingdom, where there will be one priesthood for all. But Easter and the Parousia are not yet one, so there still exist two priesthoods; they are without confusion or separation, and cannot be opposed to each other, for it is in the diversity of spiritual gifts and ministries that the presence of the one Christ is realized.

29. THE MISSIONARY ACTION OF THE CHURCH

The missionary expansion of a church is the natural expression of its vitality. There is no need to speak of the history of Christianity in the first millennium –

in Russia for example – which is well known. While missionary work was still continuing on Russian soil, a further effort was made into Finland. Having conquered the vast land of Russia, the missionary monks went beyond, into China, Korea, Japan, Alaska, Persia and India.

The widespread ignorance of the Orthodox mission comes from its own character. The Orthodox apostolate has never been sullied by any imperialism or proselytism. In his decree of 1702 Peter the Great declared, 'We do not wish to compel any human conscience, but leave to each one the responsibility of saving his soul.' Catherine the Great went further when she addressed the Synod of 1733: 'Just as God tolerated all beliefs on the earth, we wish to act in imitation of his holy will.' When in certain circumstances, a different spirit occasionally showed itself, it was essentially foreign to the spirit of Orthodoxy and came from the secular powers. In 1555 the Metropolitan of Moscow, Macarius, gave directions on the subject of mission among the Tartars to Archbishop Gury of Kazan: 'Win the confidence of the heart of the Tartars and lead them to Baptism only by love, and by no other means.'

In one of his novels, *At the Edge of the World*, the Russian writer Leskov clearly conveys the essential spirit of the of the Orthodox mission. A Government official coming to visit Father Kiriak, one of the missionary priests, is astonished that he is in no hurry to baptize the native people, but eventually he understands the wisdom behind his reluctance: Father Kiriak, who has no interest in administrative tasks, still less in numbers, is concerned above all to serve the people humbly and so make them experience the charity of Christ. 'First let them touch the hem of Christ's garment, let them feel his immense charity, and after that the Lord himself will enrapture them.'

The Apostle of Altai in Siberia, Archimandrite Macarius Glukharev (1792-1847) said in his advice to some missionaries, 'We must share as brothers all that we possess: money, food, clothing, books, and everything else; and this will help to unite our souls in the pursuit of our common end.' Apostolic work flourished in an atmosphere of evangelical poverty, utter self-denial, and brotherly love. 'Christ,' he said, 'poured out his precious blood for the salvation of all,' and, 'there is not a people in which the Lord would not have recognized those who belonged to him.' A contemporary said of Macarius, 'In him the Gospel is personified, alive,' thus revealing the very secret of his radiance.

Wherever they went the first thing the missionaries did was to establish a sanctuary, a chapel, and immediately begin the liturgical life, at once putting the local people in the presence of God. Being concerned to evangelize each people in the manner proper to their particular character, the missionaries translated the Bible and the liturgical books into various languages so as to enable all to participate in the Divine Office and to read Holy Scripture. Time and again they were obliged to create an alphabet and a written language, always respecting the individual nature and freedom of choice of those among whom they worked.

The missionaries engaged intimately in the daily life of the people and encouraged a community to develop round the monastic household. Baptism came only after long and careful preparation (for Macarius this was the true way of expressing friendship for the pagans as fellow human beings). There is nothing spectacular about this approach, which is never concerned with mere numbers. In this infinitely discreet way, Orthodoxy has never ceased to 'missionize'. At the end of the 17th century, before any political conquest, great numbers of missionary monks and priests had spread along the trading routes of Siberia; 37 monasteries were grappling with Islam and Buddhism.

Towards the middle of the 19th century the Academy of Kazan founded a school of missionary studies endowed with chairs in Tartar, Arab, Mongol and Kalmyk. In the space of a half-century it specialized in publishing several million books and pamphlets in twenty dialects. Professor Nicholas Ilminsky (1882-1891), an eminent oriental linguist, was the first Christian to hold an appointment at the Islamic academy of Cairo. His outstanding translations of liturgical books were of great benefit to missionary work among the peoples of eastern Russia.

In 1865 the Missionary Society of Petersburg coordinated and financed innumerable missions under the authority of local bishops. Each diocese had its own missionary committee. In 1913 the Society numbered 20,000 members, with a budget of more than a million and a half roubles.

The Mission of Urmiah was sent to the Nestorians of Persia and Kurdistan, and gained 20,000 adherents.

In Palestine and Syria 'The Imperial Orthodox Society of Palestine' founded in 1882, had established 112 centres of religious activity by 1912.

It was through the missionary expansion of the Church that the vast Russian lands of Kiev and Moscow came to be united. In the 18th century Metropolitan Philotheus Leszinsky sent missionaries into Mongolia and Kamchatka; Innocent Kulchitsky had great success in converting the indigenous people around Lake Baikal. The mission among the Kalmyks proceeded by the building of towns and villages where the baptized could stay while attending schools in which they were taught in their own dialect (as in the town of Stavropol on the Volga). In the northern dioceses of Archangel, among the Samoyeds, travelling churches under the direction of Archimandrite B. Smirnov carried the faith into the most remote corners. Bishop Parthenios worked among the Buddhists of eastern Siberia. Bishop Innocent Veniaminov (1797-1879) converted all the Aleutians and many of the Alaskan Indians. It took him seven years to perambulate his diocese, which was five times the size of France. He sent itinerant chaplains to accompany the nomadic peoples on their constant travels. In 1862 he pressed on to the frontier of Manchuria and installed missions at Vladivostok and among the Ussurian Koreans.

Statistics must always be treated with care; nevertheless some numbers will give an idea of the scale of missionary activity. In the reign of Elizabeth there were 450,000 baptized people in the district of Kazan. After 30 years of missionary work by Innocent there were nearly 125,000 more. Similarly in other places conversions must be counted in tens and hundreds of thousands.

The mission to the Caucasus was active from the end of the 18th century; among those very diverse peoples there were by 1823 60,000 baptized with 67 parishes and several monasteries.

The Mission to China
In 1686 a group of Cossack prisoners asked for a chaplain and converted a Buddhist temple into the Church of St Sophia. In 1715 Peter the Great sent a team of missionaries which tried to convert even the Chinese Emperor. In 1732 they had priests, catechists and a monastery. During the Boxer Rebellion in 1900, 22 Chinese martyrs showed their magnificent loyalty to the Orthodox faith. Before the last war, there were 200,000 Russian and Chinese Orthodox in China with an archbishop at Peking, a faculty of theology at Shanghai, and many congregations and schools. At present, a significant Chinese Orthodox congregation is adapting itself to the new conditions of the country.

The Mission to Japan
In 1861 the monk Nicholas Kassatkine (1836-1912) was sent as chaplain to the Russian Consulate of Hakodate. Having learnt the language, he soon translated the liturgical texts into Japanese, and a congregation was gathered through the influence of the liturgical offices. Attracted by their beauty, a pagan priest, Paul Sawabe, was converted and his son-in-law became the first Japanese bishop in 1941. Archimandrite Nicholas, consecrated Bishop of Tokyo in 1891, governed 20,000 faithful with 33 priests, 146 catechists and many teachers, all Japanese. At present Bishop Irenaeus is responsible for 40,000 Japanese Orthodox with 70 priests, in 194 congregations, with a school of theology at Tokyo.

The Mission to Korea
A mission post was set up in 1900; by 1914, 9 missionary priests were serving 4000 converts and providing important medical and teaching work. At present, an entirely Korean congregation with a church in Seoul is under the jurisdiction of the Exarch of Constantinople.

Missionary Work in Greece
Missionary activity in modern Greece warrants a special mention. A strong renewal of spiritual life has resulted in the foundation of a number of missionary confraternities.
    The most important is the *Apostoliki Diakonia* (the Ministry of the Apostolate). Archbishop Christomos of Athens, and his successor Archbishop Damaskinos, used their influence to bring about the foundation of this body in 1934 and entrusted its direction to a lay theologian, Professor Vellas Basile. The purposes of the institution are the deepening of the spiritual life of the clergy, the religious education of Greek youth, the initiation of the faithful into the liturgical life, and the revival of the traditional idea of Christian womanhood, adapted to the challenges of the modern world. Particular attention is paid to preaching. The *Diakonia* trains preachers ac-

credited and subsidized by the State, and also missionary assistants (who are usually young lay theologians) who are sent, with the agreement of the bishops, on missions inland. A high school at Athens trains teams of catechists who have set up catechetical schools throughout the country with the intention of offering guidance to young pupils and students in their extra-scholastic life. Together with radio broadcasts and written sermons, these 600 men and women catechists (only 240 of whom are priests) have taken on an immense educational activity. The school of deaconesses trains assistants for the priests in their parochial work.

The Zoe Confraternity group of celibate priests and laypeople (150 members, including Professor Trempelas and Fr Kotzonis) is concerned with problems of the laity and the royal priesthood of the faithful. Its lay members work also as preachers, catechists, teachers and missionaries. The confraternity makes very praiseworthy efforts in deepening the liturgical life and brings all its members together every year for a month of prayer and reflection on the monastic pattern.

We must mention again the Orthodox Christian Unions and a movement called Aktines (Rays) for people in academic life.[139]

---

[139] Here are some figures to give a rough impression of the present state of Orthodoxy [i.e., in 1979 when the book was first published – *editorial note*]. The total number of Orthodox must be nearly 170-180 million. The Church of Russia (Patriarch Alexis) comprises very approximately 45-90-125 million of believers, 15,000 parishes, 30,000 priests, 70 bishops, 2 faculties of theology and 8 seminaries, and 80 monasteries. The Russian Church of the emigration is divided between three jurisdictions. The most important is that of Metropolitan Vladimir (Paris), Exarch of the Patriarchate of Constantinople; secondly, the jurisdiction of the Synod of Karlovtzy (Metropolitan Anastasy at Mahopac, USA); and thirdly that of the Patriarchate of Moscow. At the beginning the total number of emigrés came to nearly 3 million. The Church of Greece (the Synod presided over by the Archbishop of Athens) nearly 7 million in 67 dioceses; the Church of Romania (Patriarch Justinian): 14 million; the Church of Bulgaria (Patriarch Cyril): 6 million; the Church of Serbia (Patriarch German): 8 million; the Autocephalous Church of Poland: half a million; the Church of Georgia (Catholicos Melchizedek) about two and a half million; the Autocephalous Church of Czechoslovakia (Metropolitan John): 300,000; the Church of Cyprus (Metropolitan Makarios III): 400,000; the Church of Albania (Archbishop Paissy): 215,000; the Church of Finland (Archbishop Herman under the jurisdiction of Constantinople): 80,000; in Hungary about 50,000 Orthodox; before 1945 the Archdiocese of Estonia had 220,000, and that of Latvia 185,000. The eastern patriarchs: the Patriarchate of Constantinople (Patriarch Athenagoras) exercises jurisdiction over 105,000 Orthodox in Turkey, 170,000 in the islands of the Dodecanese and over Greeks outside Greece: Crete (half a million); the Archbishop of Central Europe in London (70,000), an archdiocese for Australia and New Zealand (15,000); the ecclesiastical province of America (400,000); Mount Athos and the Isle of Patmos.

The Patriarchate of Antioch has jurisdiction over 157,000 Syrian Orthodox and 130,000 Lebanese Orthodox, and the communities in Iraq and Persia.

The Patriarchate of Jerusalem has jurisdiction over 10,000 Orthodox in Transjordan and 40,000 in Palestine.

The Patriarchate of Alexandria has 20,000 Orthodox in Egypt and 150,000 in Africa (there is a native Orthodox community in Uganda).

The Archdiocese of Sinai governs the monastic community of St Catherine's monastery on Mount Sinai.

PART III
The Faith of the Church

1

Doctrine

The Greek word δόγμα means indisputable truth – in Acts, these are the 'decrees' issued by the Apostles and the Elders at Jerusalem (Acts 16.4). According to the Fathers, dogma expresses 'the doctrines of the Lord and the Apostles.'[1] Since the doctrines are the lifeblood of the Scriptures, each one must be referred to the sacred text, thus justifying the Fathers' descriptions of them as 'divine' and 'evangelical'.

The Church affirms the doctrines as the 'pillar and bulwark of the truth' (1 Tim. 3.15) and witnesses to their revealed nature – whence comes the name, 'doctrines of the Church.' Being in themselves absolutely true, the doctrines are *the rule of faith*, constituting and defining it.

The first canon of the Fourth Council states, 'Whoever does not receive and confess the doctrines of the faith, let him be anathema, excommunicated.' By the fact of being cut off from the community of faith, such a one shows oneself to be an outsider, proclaiming one's own non-membership of the Church. The anathema is not any kind of punishment (which would not be applicable to someone outside) but the announcement of a final break: 'such a person is ... self-condemned' (Titus 3.11). Nevertheless it is nothing like the active cursing of the Jewish '*herem*'; once the separation is established, the Church prays, 'Holy Trinity! Bring them to the communion of thy eternal truth.'

Marked with the blood of the martyrs, the doctrines are concerned only with life or death; as we read at the end of St John's Gospel, all is far from being told, but what has been revealed is sufficient for salvation, the 'one thing necessary' of the Kingdom. That is why, on entering the Church, a neophyte confesses the symbol of the faith and says '*Credo*', and a candidate for episcopal orders reads an explicit and complete form of confession of the orthodox faith. On the other hand, faced with the rising tide of erroneous doctrines, the Church has, since the beginning of its existence, been forced to defend the purity and integrity of the teachings entrusted to it and to set against every heresy the *consensus* of the Apostolic sees. Nevertheless, while from the beginning Augustinian Trinitarian theology gained ground in the West, with the greatest confidence in human intelligence, Greek thought, by contrast, was plunged into the silence of apophasis in the presence of the Mystery. The Cappadocians guarded the dogmatic formula,

---

[1] St Ignatius, *Magn.* 13.

but never made it explicit; they spoke of the Trinitarian mystery only in their polemical works. The necessity for this is clearly stated by St Hilary: 'The mischief of the heretics and blasphemers forces us to do unlawful things, to climb inaccessible summits, to speak of what cannot be told, to undertake forbidden explanations. It ought to be enough to accomplish by faith alone what we are commanded to do, i.e., to adore the Father, to worship the Son with him and to be filled with the Holy Spirit. But see how we are forced to apply our humble speech to the most unspeakable mystery. Through the fault of others we ourselves commit that of exposing to the chances of human language mysteries which ought to have been shut away in the religion of our souls.'[2] St John Chrysostom said that it is because of our weakness that we have the written Gospels; the coming of Christ should have been enough to capture the attention of all people and change them for ever.

Even while distinguishing between truth and falsehood, doctrine retains all its positive capacity of affirmation. From the charismatic 'memory' of the Church come the inspired words that correctly define the limits of the mysteries of the Word. Beside liturgical poetry and the imagery of sermons, the Church has created the astonishingly precise metalogical, antinomical language of doctrine. It is never purely philosophical, or even religious, because the doctrines depend not on ideas but on divine realities, and a verbal 'icon' captures the 'interior word', just as the pictorial icon captures the 'interior form'. In relation to logic and thought, every doctrine is *symbolic*; all together they make up the symbol of the faith, the synthesis of the antitypes of existent realities.

1. THE APOPHATIC ASPECT OF DOCTRINE

In affirming a doctrine, we must always have in view the principle of apophatic theology. Every human affirmation is a negation of itself, because it never reaches the ultimate depth, never achieves fullness, and it is this basic insufficiency which denies it. For St Gregory of Nyssa the words, 'no one shall see me and live' (Exod. 33.20), signify the mortal danger of *limiting* God by human definitions. 'For my thoughts are not your thoughts ... my ways are higher than your ways' (Isa. 55.8-9), and 'God's foolishness is wiser than human wisdom' (1 Cor. 1.25). For the 'wholly other' of God there is no scale of comparison; in his radical transcendence he is totally and in every respect different from the world. But on the other hand, in his manifestations, God transcends his own transcendence. Grace reveals the limits of the created and immediately enables us to go beyond them, precisely because it is grace, divine philanthropy. As St Paul teaches, 'There is nothing but yes

---

[2] *P.L.* 10, 51.

in God.' The human yes is placed at the heart of the divine yes of the Incarnation, which is the theandric yes of Christ, his 'intelligence', the place of God's Wisdom.

Thus human thoughts are inadequate, for all human utterance is contradictory in continually purporting to say more than it actually contains; every thought, once put into words, fixed and given objectivity, becomes a lie because of the poverty of its expression. The 'coincidence of contraries' operates only in God. So doctrines are not exactly 'human words'; the law of identity and contradiction is not merely relaxed, it does not even apply. Thus, God is One and Threefold at the same time, and he is 'neither triad nor monad as we know them in numbers;'[3] the two natures are united in the one divine hypostasis of Christ; it is no longer the Apostle Paul who lives, but it is Christ who lives in him; as we see throughout, it is not the same *or* the other, but the same *and* the other simultaneously. In this world of pure evidences, the *tertium* is always *datur*, but to grasp it, we must undergo the evangelical *metanoia*, which, in respect of knowing, signifies 'a reversal of the intellect' so far-reaching that it descends to the very roots of all our spiritual faculties. Baptismal grace comes to our aid, restoring the 'image', and so encouraging us to aspire, by the hesychastic method, to the reintegration of the nature we had in Adam, and its complete openness to the uncreated response. Its essential work is *interiorization*, a return to self, a going back into self, *enstasy*, in order to grasp through purification (ascetic *catharsis*) what was created and now lies 'buried under the fog of passions' (St Simeon): 'the supernatural brightness of our soul' (St Gregory of Sinai), and our original 'identicalness with the heavenly light of our incorruptible Archetype' (St Macarius).

The irreducible transcendence of God – the absolute divine otherness – utterly excludes any pantheist or even panentheist coincidence or identification of the soul with God such as we see in eastern religions. Nevertheless the personal God, and – precisely because he is personal – the Creator of humankind in his image, neither absorbs nor diminishes the soul, but deifies it by his presence. Grace is an end never attained and contains no confusion, even at its limits. That is why *metanoia*, through its power of repentance, destroys first of all the Luciferian aspiration to a state coextensive with the divine essence. The *epectasis* – reaching out – of St Gregory of Nyssa is an impulse of faith which goes beyond time and even ranges through eternity without ever stopping or becoming weary.[4] The chief principle of hesychasm has been well stated by Evagrius: God is the Source and End of all knowing because he is *Unknowable* and only Intelligible. But as with Moses, God grants the vision of himself only while refusing it.[5] The logical intelligence can apprehend God only

---

[3] Denys, *Div. Nom.* 13. *P.G.* 4, 412 C.
[4] According to Origen the fall of the angels was due to their deluded belief that they had had too much of the life of blessedness and needed change. *Des Principiis,* I, 3, 8.
[5] St Gregory of Nyssa, *De vita Moysis.*

in his intelligible attributes (so the fundamental error is *premature identification*).[6] The intellect, joined to the heart and returned to its state of pre-conceptual bareness, transcends discursive reason (*dianoia*), abandons the harmonizing of judgements (the scholastic method) and rises above itself to ever higher positions, till it becomes the 'place of God'. Every such advance is less the act of the intelligence grasping its object than the act of God grasping the intelligence and deifying it, and thereby, in that truth which is greater than it, showing it to be without beginning or end. But its capacity to contemplate the Inapprehensible lasts only while it transcends itself and does not belong to itself at all.

The *Deus absconditus* is inaccessible not because of our limited understanding, but *in himself*; it is the essence of divine liberty to be ultimately mysterious, unlimited, transcendent. And herein is the whole meaning of the real distinction for us between the inaccessible Essence and the uncreated communicable Energies. The synthesis, the heart of all truly mystical experience, of the innermost human spirit where it meets the Spirit, and the absolute transcendence of God, is not speculative but operative, and the irreducible conceptual antinomy is safeguarded, 'thanks to what is known in the unknowing and is beyond all understanding.'[7] God is not the Plotinian One, not the One or the Many, but One and Threefold at the same time. The God-Monad and Unity of Origen is only the absolute of the philosophers. 'We can attain to God not in what he is, but in what he is not' (Clement of Alexandria).[8] God being 'above existence itself' (John Damascene),[9] our words apply only to what 'surrounds' God. Only the grace of the Philanthropist can bring about a true meeting between God who descends in his 'names', his energies, and human beings who are raised in the 'unions'. In that light, the doctrines appear in their true meaning: their negative form renders relative all theology of concepts, makes it a 'theology of symbols', and, on the other hand, their positive form invites change, the *metanoia* of the human spirit in the face of the shadow, at the edge of the divine light. St Simeon says that the theologian is ultimately the channel to the 'theology of the unutterable silences,' to the Silence filled with the Word; the doctrines – divine words – reveal it and trace the path of the ascents.

---

[6] B. Schwarz, *Der Irrtum in der Philosophie*, Münster 1934.
[7] St Denys, *P.G.* 3, 1001.
[8] *P.G.* 9, 109 A.
[9] *P.G.* 94, 800 B.

2. DEVELOPMENT OF DOCTRINE

With the end of the Apostolic age, revelation ceases; the doctrines add no new content to the Scriptures. There is no further substantial dogmatic progress, but a choosing between formulations of the truths contained in the Bible, i.e., an evolutionary process of refinement and a making more explicit of what was there in germinal form. St Vincent says, 'Teach the same things as you have been taught. Speak in a new manner, but do not speak novelties.'[10] The Encyclical of the Eastern Patriarchs of 1848 reaffirms, 'No innovations shall be introduced among you, neither by the patriarch, nor by the Councils; for ... the whole body of the Church ...[11] wishes its doctrine to remain unchanged for ever and to conform to that of the Fathers.'[12] Among certain eastern theologians the clear distinction between the Apostolic age of the doctrines and the post-Apostolic time of interpretations is blurred in the principle of 'veiled truths'. The doctrines can 'implicitly' contain new truths. But Galatians 1.8 says categorically, 'Even if we or an angel from heaven should proclaim to you a gospel contrary to what we proclaimed to you, let that one be accursed!' Similarly, the Fathers of the Fifth Council announce, 'We hold the same faith that the Lord Jesus Christ transmitted to his Apostles and through them to the holy churches and that the Fathers and Doctors have transmitted to the peoples;' and the Fathers of the Seventh Council, 'He who adds anything to the doctrine of the Church or subtracts anything from it, let him be anathema.' As St Irenaeus had already stated, the doctrines are 'the analysis of what has been said.'[13]

The Church 'uses spiritual language to construct her doctrines, which the simple fishermen (the Apostles) communicated in simple speech.'[14] These formulae, bearing the stamp of eternity, join up finite ideas to trace the verbal outline of the icon of truth. The heroism of the martyr Fathers makes us see in the doctrines the crucified words, 'the judgement of judgement' where the Wisdom of God has made his dwelling. The epiclesis of catholicity, 'It seemed good to the Holy Spirit,' introduces us to the age-long way of thinking of the Church.

3. SYMBOLIC BOOKS

Orthodoxy does not possess any 'symbolic books' or texts accorded a quasi-credal authority. The *Professio Fidei Tridentinae*, the '39 Articles' of the Anglicans, the

---

10 *Common.* I, 22. St Vincent of Lerins, *P.L.* 50, 667.
11 That is, the whole people of God, including the hierarchy.
12 Mansi, vol. XL (1909), c. 407-408.
13 *Adv. haeres.* I, 10, 3.
14 Office of the Three Doctors.

Formula Concordiae of the Lutherans, the *Confession* of the Reformed Churches, are the late fruits of the age of the Reformation and the Counter-Reformation in the West. They witness to the frequent confusion between doctrine and its purely theological, academic interpretation, and are evidence of the dangerous tendency to impose a uniform theological system (Augustinianism, nominalism, Thomism, integrationism, fundamentalism). Orthodoxy guards and encourages the greatest freedom of theological opinions within the framework of the one Tradition.[15] The Church is greater than any school and at the same time contains them all. But no text outside of the doctrinal definitions of the Councils can ever pretend to a 'symbolic' status. Doctrine suffices and, because of its supreme importance, rules out any uniformity or 'approved practice' in theology.

The truly doctrinal *texts* are: 1) The Niceno-Constantinopolitan Creed. The Third Council (Canon 7) forbids any other confession of faith, or the alteration of this text which is considered sacred. The Second Council (Canon 1) settled the final version and declared it to be unalterable, a decision formally reaffirmed by the Fourth and Seventh Councils. The text replaced all local creeds. Rome has also held in respect the ancient baptismal creed ('the Apostles' Creed'), which is still the western catechetical creed, but unknown in the East. Its directly Apostolic origins were denied by Mark of Ephesus at the Council of Florence, and in its present version it goes back probably to the 4th century, being the baptismal creed of Rome.[16] 2) The doctrinal definitions of the seven Ecumenical Councils. 3) The doctrinal texts of the new local Councils and the 'Apostolic Institutions' received and affirmed at the Sixth Council (Canon 2) and at the Seventh (Canon 1). 4) The texts of the Synods of Constantinople of 861 and 879, and those of the 14th century (1341-1351) on the subject of the doctrine of St Gregory Palamas on the divine energies.

There are other texts venerated but not regarded as authoritative for doctrine: the Creed of St Gregory the Wonderworker (3rd century) with its clear expression of Trinitarian doctrine (approved at the Sixth Council, Canon 2); the Creed of St Athanasius, the *Quicumque Vult* (which goes back to the 5th century; the Latin text contains the *Filioque*); the confession of faith of St John Damascene; and the very explicit confession of the Orthodox faith read at the consecration of a bishop. Other respected doctrinal but non-authoritative texts include: the *Confession* of Metropolitan Peter Mohyla, strongly influenced by the latinizing theology of Kiev of the 17th and 18th centuries;[17] the *Confession* of the Patriarch

---

[15]In Russian theology, for example, Tareyev, Metropolitan Anthony, Fr. S. Bulgakov and Ternavtzev represent distinct and very personal schools of thought.

[16] See Dom Connolly; St Augustine, *Sermones de Symbolo*, 240.

[17] In Greek and Latin in Kimmel, Ienae 1843; Fr. trans. in *Orientalia Christiana*, vol. X, No 39, Rome-Paris 1927.

of Jerusalem, Dositheus, accepted by the Synod of Jerusalem in 1672, which was sent to the Anglican Church and to the Synod of the Russian Church – a polemical work against the theology of the Reformation; and the great Catechism of Metropolitan Philaret of Moscow, which was approved for use in the schools (the definitive version approved by the Synod is of 1879).

4. THE CREED

From the beginning, it was necessary to extract the essence, first of the oral tradition, then of the first writings, in order to compile an official text of the faith and a rule that would meet the needs of the catechumenate. The heart of the message, its central principle, must be identified,[18] its Apostolic origin guaranteed, and its universal, Catholic authority established, as compared with local texts. This normative text would be equal in authority to the writings of the New Testament. Thus, Tertullian ascribed the baptismal formula to Christ himself and called it 'the Christians' oath of allegiance to the flag.'[19] There even emerged a legend that the twelve Apostles had contributed directly to the text of the Creed.[20]

St Irenaeus speaks of 'the rule of truth' accepted by the neophyte at Baptism, evidence already of a baptismal liturgy.[21] Very soon Baptism was always preceded by the *traditio et redditio symboli* under the form of a baptismal examination – entrance *de fide*. Furthermore, the invocation of the Name constituted the current formula of exorcism, the Church's confession by the mouth of the martyrs, Κύριος Χριστός, corresponding to the civic one, Κύριος Καῖσαρ. The mission of the Church for its part required a very precise confession: 'but one God, the Father ... and one Lord Jesus Christ'(1 Cor. 8.6).

The Christological or bipartite confession always presupposed the fully Trinitarian confession, which came not as the final stage of a progressive evolution but had been tacitly understood from the beginning. Certainly, in the Creeds, it is always the Christological part that is the most developed, the Christological emphasis corresponding to the central fact of the Incarnation which brings us the

---

[18] The Reformers disapproved of the Creeds for not mentioning 'justification by faith'!
[19] *Adv. Praxeam*, 2, 30.
[20] *Const. Apost.* VI, 14. The legend was demolished by the humanist Laurent Valla and by Erasmus; see the most recent works of Caspari and Kattenbusch (1900), Oscar Cullmann, *Les premières confession de la foi chrétienne*, Paris 1943; J.N. Kelly, *Early Christian Creeds*.
[21] *Adv. haeres.* I, 9, 4.

full revelation. But the Trinitarian formula, once it became dominant, counterbalanced the differences in emphasis of the ancient local formulae and set *the
standard*. Eastern theology, with its great capacity for synthesis, clearly expresses
in its doxologies and liturgy the pre-eminence of the name of the Holy Trinity.
The 'sighs too deep for words' of the Christian life do not stop at Christ[22] or at
the Spirit, but are always borne before the Father, which is the precise meaning
of the liturgical 'memorial'.

---

[22] According to the Council of Lyons in 1274, grace flows along only one path, from Christ;
and his Spirit is the Holy Spirit. The eastern Church teaches that by the grace of the Son we
have access to the grace of the Holy Spirit and to the deifying energies that come from the
Holy Trinity. Orthodoxy is fundamentally triadocentric.

2

The Doctrinal Task of the Councils and their Legacy

As we look back over the Councils, we see that together they make up a doctrinal icon of revelation. However, within this essential unity there are different emphases; the most important of these concern the Nicene definition of the consubstantiality of the Son and of the Father, the doctrine of Chalcedon on the unity of the two natures in the divine hypostasis of the Word, and the refinement by the Synod of Constantinople in the 14th century of the Palamite doctrine of the divine deifying energies and uncreated grace.

To form a clear picture of the development of doctrinal consciousness, we must take into consideration the historical background against which it emerges, and also the immense distance between the *doctrine*, a crystallized truth, defined and proclaimed, and the *theology* of the age in which the doctrinal question has arisen. The Fathers entered into dialogue with the heretics and, in living out their faith, even to the point of martyrdom, brought about the revelation of truth.

From the beginning, discussion centred on the Incarnation as the means of salvation: *Cur Deus Homo*? – why God-Man? It is the question of life or death, a theology of Salvation at its most dramatic and historical. The mystery is above all Christological, but not pan-Christic. The discussion originated in the clumsy theological attempts to reconcile the monotheism inherited from the Old Testament with faith in the divinity of Christ, either by making Christ the man *adopted* by God (Theodotus, Artemon, later Paul of Samosatus and Nestorianism) or by speaking of 'two names and one Person', Christ being only a *modality* of the Father (modalism, dynamism, patripassionism: Noetus, Praxeas, Sabellius). The logical human mind always prefers Jewish monotheism, the theism of Aristotle, even Stoic pantheism or Plotinian immanentism. The Trinitarian doctrine, that God is one and threefold at the same time, *crucifies* reason; it pushes its truth in like a splinter, and will always be the perfect example of the 'stumbling-block' to the Greeks[1] and 'foolishness' to the Jews: truly, 'Christ crucified is the judgement of judgements'.

The supreme achievement of the First Council – the term ὁμοούσιος, consubstantial – had settled and condemned the heresy of Arius.[2] In his Godward aspect, in his divinity, the only-begotten Son is consubstantial with the Father: 'Light from Light, true God from true God, begotten not made, consubstantial with the Father'. After St

---

[1] St Maximus, *P.G.* 90, 408 D.
[2] A priest of Alexandria and disciple of Lucian of Antioch. Arius taught that the Word was foreign to the substance of the Father, and was drawn by him out of nothingness into time.

Athanasius,[3] the great Cappadocians (St Basil and St Gregory) advanced Trinitarian theology yet further, using the terminology of Nicaea – one substance and three hypostases – and emphasized the consubstantiality of the Father with the Holy Spirit.[4]

But this explanation in its turn raised another doctrinal question, about the humanity of Christ: what does it mean to say, 'the Word became flesh'? Apollinarius, Bishop of Laodicea, veered towards heresy; he denied that Christ had a reasonable human soul, saying this had been replaced by the divine Word. St Gregory of Nazianzus vigorously defended the integrity of Christ's human nature who 'saves only what he assumes.' But the question proved very complicated and thorny. Dialectically the thesis was put forward by the school of Alexandria (Pantenus, Clement, Origen, Cyril) and the antithesis by the school of Antioch (Lucian, Theodore of Mopsuestia, John Chrysostom, Theodoret of Cyrus). The mystical allegorism of the Alexandrines (a mixture of Apollinarianism and Monophysitism) was opposed to the literal exegesis – with a tendency to moralize – of the Antiochians (a mixture of Arianism and Nestorianism). These latter were hampered by a certain imprecision owing to their mistrust of the dialectic, which was nevertheless essential, between the biblical tradition and dogmatic reason. The emphasis was placed either – at Alexandria – on the unity of the natures in Christ, amounting, in the extreme case, to their monophysite confusion, the drop of humanity being dissolved in the ocean of divinity, or – at Antioch – in order to protect the full humanity, on a radical distinction, even to the point of separating of the two natures (Nestorius). According to St Cyril of Alexandria, Christ, in the hypostatic union, is One, resulting (ἐκ) from two natures; Antioch, on the contrary, goes as far as the duality of two Persons existing in one composite hypostasis (the merely moral harmony of the two Persons).

After the condemnation of the 'Macedonians' (who denied the divinity of the Holy Spirit) at the Second Council (381) and of Nestorius (Antioch) at the Third (431), the supreme achievement of dogmatic synthesis came during the Fourth Council of Chalcedon (451). This was based on *Dei et hominis una persona*, the formula of Pope St Leo in his letter to Flavian of Constantinople (*Tome to Flavian*). He proclaims the existence in Christ of two natures, divine and human, distinct and perfect, united without confusion or mixture or separation in one Person or Hypostasis of God the Word. The impasse in which the two antagonist schools, Alexandria and Antioch, were locked clearly demonstrated the limit of all human reasoning on the divine realities. And the solution came from God, as a miracle, in the form of a simple doctrine of crystalline purity. The synthesis

---

[3] Consubstantiality, the basis of the saving deification of humanity: 'God became human in order that we might become god.' *Against the Heathen, On the Incarnation of the Word, Against the Arians*.

[4] *On the Holy Spirit* of St Basil, the five *Theological Discourses* of St Gregory of Nazianzus, the *Catechetical Discourse* of St Gregory of Nyssa.

was not *theological* (still less was it philosophical as in Hegel's triads), but *dogmatic*, superior to all theological analysis and setting a limit to definition. This explains the long resistance of Syrian and Egyptian Monophysitism, in its attenuated version (still held by the Nestorian and Jacobite Churches) which takes the heretical form of *Monothelism* (only one will in Christ; the great defender of Orthodox Diothelism was St Maximus the Confessor). After the condemnation in the *Three Chapters* (written by Theodore, Theodoret and Ibas) of the Nestorian tendency by the Fifth Council (553), the Sixth condemned Monothelism and defined the existence in Christ of two wills. The human will *voluntarily* follows the divine will. According to St John Damascene, the one who desires is one, so the object of the desire is equally one. The great adversary of the Monophysites, Leontius of Byzantium, adopted the term 'enhypostasization': human nature is 'enhypostasized' in the divine hypostasis of the Word.

But all the Conciliar definitions, however liberating, still could not answer all the questions, and above all this one: how does the same hypostasis live in two natures? The classical simplistic solution – that the humanity of Christ suffers and the divinity works the miracles – is clearly insufficient. It chops and divides the very mystery of the unity and, being too rational, misses the ever antinomic truth. It stops with God *and* man, and suppresses the real mystery of the *God-Man*. The doctrine called *communicatio idiomatum* or the *perichoresis* (St John Damascene), comes very close – the divine penetrates the human and deifies it – but the question about the reciprocal action of the human on the divine remains open. The unknown author of the writings entitled *Celestial Hierarchy*, *Ecclesiastical Hierarchy* and *Mystical Theology*, which have exercised a considerable influence in East and West (translated into Latin by Scot Erigena in 850), which he ascribed to Denys the Areopagite (late 5th century Syrian), in a felicitous turn of phrase explains the divino-human, *theandric energy* thus (in the 4th letter to the monk Gaius): it is the diunity of *two wills* and *two liberties* in one energy. The two natures are united in one theandric consciousness, the human consciousness being contained within the divine consciousness.

The Seventh Council (787) condemned the Iconoclasts and, with its teaching on icons, perfected Christology: the humanity of Christ is the human face of his divinity; the icon of Christ reveals the mystery of the unity, discloses the theandric image.

From the Councils we have inherited the daunting problem of Chalcedon. The toxins of Monophysitism are far from being eliminated. The Western theocracy of the Middle Ages, and that of Byzantium, left little room for the human. The Renaissance took revenge by falling into humanist Monophysitism.[5] The balance

---

[5] Churchmen developed the notion of a 'double truth', divine and human, theological and philosophical. Later, human creativity escaped from the control of religious doctrine and freed itself from every transcendent element; the secularization of the culture is noticeable in humanist drama, such as Shakespeare's plays, which are striking in their lack of any religious content.

of Christological Theandrism is upset. Restoring it is the most pressing problem of today.

* * *

The Creeds make symbolic use of spatial language: the Father is above everything, the Son is *on the right hand* of the Father and the Holy Spirit is *in the Church*. Recent studies of the Apostles' Creed[6] have established the authentic text of Hippolytus of Rome: 'I believe in the Holy Spirit, *in* the Holy Church, *for* the resurrection of the flesh'. Hippolytus adopted a favourite notion of St Irenaeus, who attributed the resurrection of the flesh to the Holy Spirit, and affirmed, 'where the Spirit is, there is the Church and all grace,'[7] and he called every believer to 'hasten to the Church, where the Spirit flourishes.'[8] 'The means of communion with Christ has been distributed throughout the Church, that is, the Holy Spirit.'[9] Similarly, the anaphora of the *Apostolic Tradition* prays, 'that thou wouldst grant to all the saints who communicate, making them one, in order to *fill* them with the Holy Spirit.'[10] He who has 'spoken by the prophets' opens our understanding to the Scriptures and the doctrines – a clear statement of the doctrinal epiclesis .

The κοινωνία τῶν ἁγίων of the Apostles' Creed can mean communion with the *sancta* – that is to say the Eucharist,[11] or equally with the *sancti* – the sanctified ones. It is the sacramental faith transmitted by the Apostles, the *agape* of the Church 'in which the Spirit flourishes.'[12] The same order can be seen in the Nicene Creed where Christology leads into pneumatology and ecclesial sanctification. The reality of deifying grace is at the heart of the philanthropic economy of God.

* * *

---

6 Fr Nautin, *Je crois à l'Esprit saint*, a study of the history and theology of the Creed, Paris 1947.
7 *Adv. haeres.* XXIV, 1.
8 Hauler, LXXVI, 30, p. 117.
9 *Adv. haeres.* III, 24, 1.
10 Hauler, LXX, 27, p. 107.
11 See *op. cit.* de Fr Nautin, p. 67, note 2.
12 The text of Hippolytus, *Hauler* LXXVI, 30, p. 117.

The Synods of Constantinople (1341-1352)[13] canonized the doctrine of St Gregory Palamas as the true expression, even the completion, of the Orthodox faith. It distinguishes in God the three hypostases, hypostatic processions; the one nature or essence; and the energies or the natural processions. The energies are inseparable from God's nature, and God is totally present in them. Inaccessible, radically transcendent in his essence, God is immanent and manifests himself in his energies; so these are the two modes of divine existence: intradivine in him and extradivine in the freely created world. The uncreated energies do not imply any idea of causality, as though grace were the effect of the divine cause. God does not operate as the cause of grace, but manifests himself in it and works in a free reciprocation between the *yes* of the Incarnation and the *'fiat'* of the creature.

Western theologians fail to understand the meaning and the implications of Palamism, which marks a deep doctrinal division between West and East. It is the same tragic contempt that Charlemagne's theologians showed towards the definitions of the Seventh Council. The Palamite doctrine makes no attempt to introduce anything new but synthesizes and completes the Patristic Tradition. Western theology, from the eastern point of view, is not sufficiently reticent before the mystery of the divine ineffability and, lacking the doctrine of *theosis*, can give no clear account of the nature of communion. Communion is neither substantial nor hypostatic, nor in created grace (three impossible cases); to be effective, it can only be *energizing* (Palamism). God communicates himself and deifies by means of the deifying energies; humanity 'participates in the divine nature' without being mixed with the essence of God. The whole eastern doctrine of human nature and grace is implicit in this. The epicletic theology of the Holy Spirit, underlying the whole of Patristic thought, re-establishes the Trinitarian equilibrium, for it sets before the heavenly *Monarchos* the whole economy of creation recapitulated in Christ. With the 'two hands'[14] of the Word and the Spirit, the Father sculpts the age-long face of the 'gods according to grace' of the Kingdom.

---

[13] *P.G.* 151, 679-692, 717-762, 1273-1284. The decree of canonization of Gregory Palamas is in *P.G.* 151, 693-716. The establishment of his feast on the second Sunday in Lent set the seal of acceptance on his teaching, which was inserted into the *Synodikon* of the Sunday of Orthodoxy.
[14] St Irenaeus calls the Son and the Spirit 'the two hands of God' (*Adv. haeres.* IV; *P.G.* 7, 975 B).

3

Canon Law[1]

'Teaching them to obey everything that I have commanded you' (Matt. 28.20).§ Being divinely constituted, the Church is the guardian of the divine law, and possesses the right to establish canons (from κανών – rule), to judge and to punish if necessary: 'Whoever listens to you listens to me' (Luke 10.16). From the beginning the Church was well aware of its responsibility for its historic, incarnate order. The Council of Jerusalem ruled on questions relating to those Christians who had originally been Jewish (Acts 15.22); St Paul, in his epistles, touches on the holding of assemblies, the qualities required of bishops, and the use of spiritual gifts. During the three first centuries, the Church exercised the customary authority that we see in the *Didache* (late 1st century and early 2nd), the *Apostolic Tradition* of Hippolytus (early 3rd century), the *Didascalia of the Apostles* (c. 250) and the *Apostolic Constitutions* (c. 380).

In the 4th century, the Church began to hold regular Councils. The canons are listed in several *Collections* (for example the *Collection* of John the Scholastic in 550). The 'symphony' of the powers of the Church and the Empire explains the presence of ecclesiastical law in the *Collections* of the imperial law of Theodosius or Justinian (*The Digest, News*, etc). Later on, works were published by canonists such as Balsamon and Zonaras.

Orthodoxy does not possess a unified code for all the churches, like for example the *Corpus Juris Canonici* of the Roman Church. There are only local codes of which most date from the Middle Ages and which are not always consistent with each other. Until critical study is undertaken it will be hard to know exactly which canons are still in force and which have become disused through changing historical conditions; there are also canons 'on the back burner' held in reserve in case of future need (for example those which govern the calling of Councils).

Although there is some inconvenience in this state of affairs, the alternative – the imposition on the whole Church of a common standard such as would be

---

[1] Hefele & Leclercq, *Histoire des Conciles*, Paris 1907-1921. Mansi, *Sacrorum Conciliorum nova et amplissima collectio*, Paris-Leipzig 1903-1927. Tardif, *Histoire des sources du droit canonique*, Paris 1997. *Dictionnaire du Droit canonique*, Paris 1957.

appropriate for a local church – would be foreign to the Orthodox spirit. Unity of faith and worship can be expressed very differently in local historical forms.

The Canon of Doctrine

The doctrines represent the unchangeable content of the Revelation, and the canons whatever is adaptable according to historical conditions, and the two must never be confused; above all, the canons must never be treated as doctrine. That being said, there is a need to restore the direct functional relationship between them. The canons are the exterior expression, visible, historical and variable of the unchangeable doctrines. The expression and the existential forms change according to the circumstances of the time, helping the faithful to incarnate the doctrinal *esse* of the Church in their life. So the canonical order is always at the service of doctrinal teaching.

But an institutional form can never fully accommodate doctrine; it can only ever be an approximation to the truth because it must change with time. So it is clearly impossible to absolutize a temporal and contingent canonical form, turning it into dogma. On the other hand, every modification of an element that has become 'tradition' must be justified on the grounds that it better expresses the doctrinal truth. Without ever pretending that its disciplinary forms are exhaustive or all-sufficient, canon law achieves the most correct possible charismatic order in the given historical conditions, so as to avoid any deviation that might affect the immutable *esse* of the Church.

Thus the canons, by their interpretation of the doctrines, seek, display and govern the incarnation of them in the material conditions of life.

While the body of precise canon law outlines the visible form of a local church, of its 'canonical personality', there is a way in which Orthodoxy goes beyond the immediate and aspires to communion in doctrine not only through variable practices and disciplinary rules, but also in the course of transcending them. And this can happen only where there is a settled and unchanging 'doctrinal awareness' that is the same for all the Churches. So canonical awareness will seek not the bygone historic forms of the Apostolic age, but the spirit that animated them and will animate every form in every age, making them perfectly identical to itself.

The Chalcedonian doctrine of the unity of the two natures, its theandrism, is reflected in this canonical awareness and unites the *jus divinum* and the *jus humanum* in the *jus ecclesiasticum*, the doctrinal unity which guarantees that, while empirical forms vary, the source of inspiration is the same. The canons order the relation between the meta-historical *esse* of the Church and its historical body. They share in the doctrinal truths, and from this point of eminence they demonstrate how they are to be used to safeguard the Church from any heretical deviation, i.e., disagreement with the doctrines.

4

The Bible

1. READING IN CHRIST: THE ORTHODOX A PRIORI

The best way of defining the Orthodox spirituality is to say that it is essentially biblical, but in the Orthodox, ecclesial meaning of the term. The Fathers of the Church lived by the Bible, thought and spoke by the Bible to such a degree that their very being was identified with the substance of the Bible itself. Pure exegesis as an autonomous science never existed in the time of the Fathers. Submitting to their instruction, we find out at once that there is no such thing as a school of exegesis, whether historical or allegorical, whether of Antioch or of Alexandria. Within the comprehensive scope of Patristic exegesis every tendency finds its proper place. But underlying them all is the truth that every reading or hearing of the biblical Words is an encounter with the living Person who is the Word. Christ is never limited by the didactic, catechetical or any other meaning of his own words. All our utilitarian and pragmatic senses, all our curiosity and questioning, are subordinated to the fact of the fullest revelation of the Presence and its illumination. St John Chrysostom prays thus before the holy book: 'Lord Jesus Christ, open the eyes of my heart that I may understand and do your will ... enlighten my eyes with your light ... You only, the one light.' And St Mark the Hermit: 'The Gospel is closed to human efforts; to open it is the gift of Christ.' St Ephraem instructs us: 'Before reading, always pray and beseech God *that he would reveal himself to you.*'

We might say that for the Fathers the Bible *is* Christ, because his every word brings us into the presence of the one who spoke it; 'Him do I seek in your books,' says St Augustine.[1] The legitimate desire to understand and to find answers is subject to that fullest revelation, and in the sacramental context. 'The word mysteriously broken'[2] is consumed 'eucharistically'[3] in a form of *communion* with Christ. Providentially, the word *to know* in the Bible, in Hebrew and in

---

[1] *Conf.* II, 2.
[2] Origen, *P.G.* 13, 1734.
[3] All the ancient authors emphasize the strict relation between Holy Scripture and the Eucharist. See, for example, Clement of Alexandria, *Strom.* 1. 1; *In Gen. serm.* 6, 2. St Gregory of Nazianzus, *oratio*, 45, 16. St Jerome: 'We eat his flesh and drink his blood not only in the Holy Eucharist, but also in reading the Scriptures.' See O. Casel, *Le mystère du culte dans le christianisme*, Paris 1946.

194

Greek, means *to know by communion*, in the nuptial sense: the ultimate knowing of God is symbolized in the marriage of the Lamb.

The Gospel of St Luke (24.45) tells us that Christ 'opened the mind of the disciples, showing them how they must read the Bible to discover 'everything written about me' – 'Then beginning with Moses and all the prophets, he interpreted to them the things about himself in all the scriptures.' So the Lord 'opened the Scriptures' (Luke 24.27 and 32), and revealed that *the Bible is the verbal icon of Christ*. Since then, for the Orthodox all reading of the Scriptures has been governed by the *a priori* of 'theandrism', as taught at Chalcedon. God wished Christ to establish the Body in which his words should resound with authority as words of Life; it is in Christ, therefore, within his Body, in the Church, that we must read the Bible and listen to God. When a believer takes hold of the Bible, the *a priori* places them both in the Church, and within that act of 'ecclesiastification' the miracle is accomplished: a historical document becomes at once a Holy Book filled with Presence. As my existence in the Body deepens, so does my receptivity; my life in the Church structures my spirit 'theandrically' so that from the moment the Bible is opened, I know it is the Church that is reading it. Even when we are alone, we read the Bible *together*, liturgically. That is how God wishes it to be, and the real subject of the knowing and of the communion is never the isolated person, cut off from the Body, but the person as a *member*, 'liturgical man'.

2. THE BIBLE AND THE TRADITION

The theologians of the Reformation placed the Holy Bible in violent opposition to Tradition, the divine word to the human word. Real abuses and, in western Christianity, a tragic misunderstanding, have distorted these complementary elements into an entirely artificial opposition.

The biblical books are largely the historical record of the life of the Church preserved by Tradition. Before being collected in the New Testament Canon, the word of Christ was received by the Apostolic community in the form of *oral tradition*. Having rapidly assumed the form of written tradition, it was constantly being added to, and, like every historical record of witness to past events, was at the mercy of the irregularities inherent in humanity. Now, 'no one comprehends what is truly God's except the Spirit of God' (1 Cor. 2.11). The Spirit never ceases to bear witness within the Church, making it 'the pillar and bulwark of the truth' (1 Tim. 3.15). The Church 'full of the Trinity,'[4] selected and kept, out of a multitude of writings, those which were 'inspired', sealed them as authentic, and became their guarantor, while rejecting others as apocryphal and classifying others

---

[4] The expression is Origen's, *P.G.* 12, 1265.

as deuterocanonical. The Bible is given to the Church. It is the Church that has received it, fixing its Canon and bearing it within her womb as the 'Words of Truth'; it can therefore never be taken out of the Church without the danger of distortion.

The witness of the Word to itself is not a formal principle, isolated and self-sufficient; it is in danger of being misrepresented through human insufficiency, as the entirely 'biblical' sects demonstrate. Only 'grace supplies every insufficiency,' and that is why the Church gives the Bible to humanity, together with herself as the fundamental *a priori* of its reading. Even if it opposes the Church, nevertheless it is at the hands of the Church that any sect receives both the Bible and the belief that the sacred texts are inspired. To put the Bible *above* the Church is to misrepresent the will of the Lord, that it should be read *in* the Church.[5]

The powerful meditations of the Fathers, liturgical hymnography, icons – the doctrinal and canonical understanding: all these elements that make up the Tradition form an essentially dynamic world, a realm alive and resonant with the Word, inseparable from the Word itself, being its living continuation, its body originating in the same source of inspiration. This is not a matter of searching for answers among inert historical records, but rather of reaching down to the pure springs of Tradition, appropriating the great experience of the Church and seeing in ourselves the growth of the *instinct of Orthodoxy* which will guide our steps to the heart of the *consensus patrum* and *apostolicum* of the Church. The moment will come when we suddenly understand that through the many forms of the Church, through all the elements of the Tradition, *Christ himself is interpreting his own words*. The Holy Spirit bears witness to it, but this scriptural epiclesis takes place only at the heart of the Catholic Body; it is on the humanity of Christ, which has become the Church, that the Spirit rests.

The witness of the Holy Spirit within the Church has a bearing on the inspiredness of the sacred text. This very particular witness must never be confused with the interpretation of the text. The Church is the whole Christ, and sets within the ever-living context of Christ the words uttered by him during his earthly life. God has spoken and he continues to expound his words. Thus the Bible, divinely interpreted, includes in its fullness the Tradition as its living continuation, continually unfolding. The Tradition bears witness to Scripture, which in turn forms part of the Tradition; however, the Bible retains absolute authority as the primary source of faith. The 'eternal Gospel' (Rev. 14.6) is the benchmark and criterion of truth unequalled by any other. Every tradition and every doctrine must be in agreement with Scripture. Apart from the very limited and precise field of doctrine, Tradition possesses no formal criterion or external mechanism by which it

---

[5] If we do not read the Bible *in* the Church, then, fatally, we shall take from the Bible an external, superficial idea of the Church.

might be able to settle the final interpretation of the text. Only from within its own life can it give guidance as to what is orthodox and what heterodox. However, we can list a few preconditions for all sacred reading.

1) Every passage must be read in the context of the given book, then in the context of the Bible and that of the Church; every part must be interpreted in the light of the whole. Parallels help us to grasp the emphasis of the particular pericope. Liturgical use enriches the text that we read by relating it to the Church's seasonal observance and the commentary provided by the hymns (thus, for example, 1 Cor. 10.1-14 is read at Epiphany, the end of the Gospel of St Matthew at the sacrament of Unction, etc). Liturgical reading draws life from the event recounted and becomes its 'advent' here and now.

2) The only unvarying rule is: anything that contradicts doctrinal truth must be eschewed. For example, any suggestion that Mary had other children contradicts the doctrine of her perpetual virginity. Among hypotheses we must choose whichever agrees with doctrinal truth, for that defines the infallible meaning, given to the Church by God himself, of the most important biblical texts. The understanding of John 14.28 in the sense of subordination is condemned by the doctrine of the equality of the three divine Persons. Any notion of the Son of God as 'child of God' in the sense of universal filiation is in conflict with the doctrine of Monogenesis. Whoever does not believe in the resurrection of Christ as it is *lived* in the Church and proclaimed in the Creed can never read the Scriptures correctly.

3) By contrast, the greatest freedom is enjoined in the study of the historical and human aspects of the Scriptures (language, period, place and surroundings, image and symbolism), using all the discoveries of modern science. The problem of the authenticity of certain texts, their origin and the attribution of the writings to this or that author (Moses, Isaiah, the Epistle to the Hebrews) presents no difficulty at all. Those passages (for example, Mark 16.9-20; John 7.53-8.11; 1 John 5.7) that probably do not belong to the earliest texts, are accepted as variant readings, sanctified by liturgical use; God has spoken through them. And as with variant readings, there are various ways of understanding the texts and commenting on them, which shows that the richness of the content exceeds any stereotyped human understanding. Although the whole of Scripture is divinely inspired (2 Tim. 3.16) the doctrinal importance of certain passages can be distinguished only by means of the doctrinal definitions of the Church. All attempts at a 'Life of Jesus' finish up with a remainder that cannot be reduced to the human; all the 'scientific' reconstructions of essential Christianity (*Das Wesen des Christentums*) fail because of the arbitrariness of subjective choices ungoverned by Apostolic authority.

4) The biblical narratives belong to two distinct realms, historical and metahistorical. Every fact recounted has had its time and place, but is also symptomatic of a metaphysical largeness that transcends pure history. There are passages that clearly display an essentially and deliberately 'mythological' structure (for example, the account of creation and the Fall situated outside chronological his-

tory. Adam's importance is that of the archetype; he is there before time begins and governs it for all humankind[6]). Communion in liturgical prayer with Adam or Lazarus as persons makes it impossible to reduce them to mere symbols. But the liturgical celebration of their feast displays Adam as the universal man, Adam 1st or Adam Kadmon, and Lazarus as the prophetic anticipation of the resurrection. For the Fathers the Old Testament was straightforward concrete history, and also the prefiguration of Christ, the typology of the events of salvation. While a religious picture portrays a historic fact in very realistic terms, an icon, by contrast, reveals its silent depth, its metaphysical face. Biblical reading in Orthodoxy seeks the seamless continuity between the two: as it moves away from the picture, it begins to contemplate the icon.[7]

3. PROBLEMS OF THE INSPIRATION OF THE SCRIPTURES

Divine inspiration is clearly asserted by Scripture itself: 'All scripture is inspired by God (2 Tim. 3.15-17) – 'men and women moved by the Holy Spirit spoke from God' (2 Pet. 1.20-21), but this notion is not easy. The mechanical taking of dictation, the divine inspiration of each letter, makes the authors into passive scribes. A softer form of the same automatism is implicit in the notion of cause: God is the sole author – *causa principalis* – first cause, and the human being – *causa instrumentalis* – second cause; as causalities are multiplied to infinity, genuinely human participation fades away. Eastern synergy, by contrast, offers a solution, a reciprocity that safeguards human freedom and the dignity of the child to whom the Father is speaking. St Basil insists that the Spirit never deprives of reason anyone whom he inspires, that such an effect would be demonic.[8] What properly belongs to humankind is kept inviolate, but enriched, inspired, guided by the inbreathing of the Spirit. Every book of the Bible bears the unmistakable mark of human genius peculiar to each author. The Fathers laid strong emphasis (once the somewhat superficial task of the second century apologists was finished) on the human character of the authors.

When a human being listens to God's voice, he or she is never passive; that person's very receptivity always contains an active and creative element. Indeed, the authors of the sacred books are *prophetic* authors; their work is founded on

---

[6] All demythologizing is obedient to the critical fashion of the time, without reference to any standard authenticated by God (the Church). We ought not to assume that the 'mythological' elements are not desired by God.
[7] See Mgr Cassien, 'L'Etude du Nouveau Testament dans l'Eglise Orthodoxe'. *Bulletin de la Faculté libre de Théologie protestante de Paris*, No 55, 1956. *P.G.* 30, 121.
[8] *P.G.* 30. 121.

an intuitive understanding of the message and arises from spiritual enlightenment, which, true to its nature, fully safeguards all the human reality, never violates it. Every prophet receiving the word must communicate it to the ecclesial community, and the Patristic and liturgical interpretations are proof that, although the revelation is given once for all, the richness of its content is continually enhanced by the creative receptivity of the Church.

The Scriptures are divine utterance in human form, and in their unity are revealed as *theandric*. Nestorianism separates the two: the Word of God *and* the human word. The Monophysite heresy speaks of the Word of God alone *or* the human word alone. But the Bible is the divine-human word. The human being never becomes a medium, there is no room for any spiritual automatism. Apart from the absolute purity of the doctrinal passages and the general inspiration of all the texts, the Bible is a legitimate focus of human interests; it has come to us through the prism of humanity, so all the scientific study of the text and the historical development of this study is entirely justified

Reading the Bible can also be inspired. It is addressed above all to the heart, the organ of wisdom: 'Oh, how foolish you are, and how slow of heart to believe all that the prophets have declared!' (Luke 24.25) The heart includes the intellect, but is greater than it, so that each new reading can discover new depths. Thus, the typological interpretation of the Old Testament in the light of the New unveils the anagogical course of history, showing it to be cyclical. Similarly, a baptized believer traces the figurative curve of salvation and recapitulates in his own life the whole reality of the biblical events. This is the way of life, inspired by the sacramental principle, that the Lord is referring to when he says, 'Let anyone with ears to hear listen!'

5

In Dubiis Libertas

Unlimited freedom is an absurd notion, and 'scientific objectivity' is only a myth. Every human being, however learned, is a creature of passions and instincts, and reason always affected by the heart; science is never free from sympathies and prejudices. And theology, the queen of the sciences, has assumptions of its own.

However, utter faithfulness to doctrine must be accompanied by freedom of theological research. This fundamental principle protects theology from any idolatry of the human and any mechanistic understanding of the divine.

The Fathers say that the Truth was revealed in stages: 'It was necessary that the three-sunned light should enlighten us by gradual anagogies.'[1] During this process the Church has shown a subtlety of judgement that, while taking account of the wide variety of approaches towards absolute truth, has guarded against excessive reverence to any particular approximation to it. While the *consensus patrum* of Tradition is a constant and sure guide, the works of the Fathers contain clearly defective passages, and parts of the Tradition are ambiguous.

Fr Sergei Bulgakov held the radical opinion that doctrine entails freedom of theological thought. Doctrine comes to us as creatures of flesh and blood and so works on our humanity that we can understand the tasks of the age in its light, which presupposes the greatest creative freedom of the spirit. The Ecumenical Councils have left us with unsolved problems, together with the expectation that we shall continue to reflect on them. Theology is called to respond to many questions unanswered in the past and to others that have arisen only in our own time. But Orthodoxy is unwilling to define doctrine unless it is absolutely necessary. Doctrine is kept to a minimum, while opinions, *theologoumena*, are unlimited; *in dubiis libertas* remains the golden rule.

The idea that the Fathers and anything that comes from tradition must be infallible is simply evidence of a rabbinic approach or ignorance of the true situation. The Neoplatonism of Gregory of Nyssa or the *Corpus Areopagiticum*, the alleged Messalianism of St Macarius of Egypt, the Origenism of Evagrius, certain inconsistencies in the writings of St Isaac the Syrian and St Ephraem, the disturbingly exaggerated asceticism of many works of the great spiritual masters and of much of the *Philokalia*, the Aristotelianism of St John Damascene – these are proof that the teachings of even the greatest authorities must never be elevated

---

[1] St Gregory of Nazianzus, *Or.* XXXI, 25, 26.

into dogma. The discoveries of the Fathers must not be allowed to become a neo-Patristic theology which would simply replace neo-Scholastic theology. In dealing with the Gentiles, St Paul had to 'invent'. Through the writings of the Fathers we must discover their creativity, and see how the Church brings us treasure that is always new.

Nevertheless, immersion in the thought of the Fathers, a certain identification with their experience and catholicity, is a *sine qua non* for every theologian of our time: a *going back* to the sources but also and above all *going forward* in eschatology; as St Gregory of Nyssa said, 'We remember what is coming.'

As well as doctrines, the Church holds 'facts' which, while of a doctrinal nature, have not been given the force of Conciliar definitions; these are mostly truths that spring from the *lex orandi* which is an inseparable part of Orthodoxy – such as devotion to the Virgin and the saints, and doctrines of the sacraments and eschatology.

Theology today needs no justification. Scientism or scepticism, not to mention the absurdity of materialism, have nothing to say to people today. In its royal progress theology has pushed aside all obstacles (except perhaps, within its own world, the formidable obscurantism of the 'integrists'). The finest offering the children of God can make to their creator, in the knowledge that they are free, is to sing his praise and serve his glory. In this service theology comes into its own as the real and preferred prayer of the Church: 'a theologian is someone who knows how to pray.'

6

Tradition

With the end of the Apostolic age, revelation ceases. God adds nothing more to the objective content of his word. But with the day of Pentecost, the age of the Church begins; and that presupposes a transmission, a *tradition*. Now what the Church transmits is not an archive for a museum, but the living and ever-present Word: God himself continues to speak it to people in every age.

So Tradition is the Church's consciousness of being the living home of the active Word, that springs up inexhaustibly, endlessly varying its manner of expression.

The vital importance of the *paradosis* was already being emphasized by St Paul: 'So then ... stand firm and hold fast to the traditions that you were taught by us, either by word of mouth or by our letter' (2 Thess. 2.15; 2 Tim. 4.2) – continuity, both by word of mouth and in writing, is assured. The great theologian of Tradition is St Irenaeus who calls it 'the word that speaks;' Scripture remains supreme, but brings us back constantly to Tradition – the living realm where it must be heard. The continuity of love and faithfulness becomes the continuity of interpretation and discernment; the Church is effectively a Council – perpetuated and spread abroad in space and time, but always assembled here and now – always in the act of expressing the Truth lived in its Tradition. Here we see the full force of the teaching of St Irenaeus on the unanimity of doctrine and worship: the Church, however dispersed across the world, maintains the apostolic preaching 'as if it inhabited a single house ... had a single heart ... and a single mouth'.[1] For him the Tradition of the Apostles is visible 'in each church'.

Similarly the *Acts* of the Council of Constantinople in 553 state clearly, 'We maintain and preach the faith which was given in the beginning by our great God and Saviour Jesus Christ to the holy Apostles, and was preached by them throughout the world. That is the faith which the holy Fathers have professed, expounded and *transmitted* to the churches, and in all things we follow them.' What is professed and transmitted goes back to Christ and bears the seal of its divine origin, which is why every aspect of the faith is referred to and founded on Scripture. It is Scripture that yields the seeds that spread out and flourish in Tradition. Now, the 'inspired words' cannot be understood or correctly interpreted unless the

---

[1] *Adv. haeres.* I. 3. See D. van den Eynde, *Les normes de l'enseignement chrétien dans la littérature patristique des trois premiers siècles*, Louvain 1933.

reader is inspired by the Holy Spirit in exactly the same way, and this task is essentially one for the Church – living Tradition. In the Church the past never undermines the present, but inspires it to progress, while staying in the context of Tradition and in obedience to its inner principle: the agreement of catholicity in the same Lord, in the same Spirit.

It is a great paradox that – thanks to the Witness who is present all along – the Tradition assures us that present and future are in agreement, but we find this agreement in the past. 'The Holy Spirit ... has spoken through the prophets,' so the Church, in its prophetic role, draws *from the past*, in Christ, what it announces *in advance* (John 16.15). This immediately explains why there exists no *formal criterion* of the Tradition.

The Gospel, speaking in the midst and from the midst of this world, announces the future age, and the Church, while witnessing to the Messianic past of Christ, witnesses also to his Kingdom already present. It announces and judges, but its task is *to convert*, and the field of its mission is the whole world and the whole of history. It dispenses doctrine, but also *principles of Life*: the Eucharist and the sacraments. The Spirit of Life from this point of view is the Spirit of Transmission. With the ascension to his Father, Christ's mission is ended (John 17.4); and yet he reaffirms, 'I shall come, I shall speak.' From the Body that he has established on earth Christ is not absent, but his presence is of a different kind: he comes again and is present *in* the Holy Spirit. According to Nicholas Cabasilas, 'the sacraments: they are the way ... the door which he has opened ... it is by that way and through that door that he returns to the human race.'[2] Christ comes again in the sacraments, his presence being dependent on the epiclesis. Similarly, the continuity of Christ in the mission of the Apostles and of the Church depends on the coming of the Paraclete. The Spirit bears witness, 'brings to remembrance' all that Christ has said, finishes and completes his mission by realizing in human beings the humanity of Christ, Christifying them. During his earthly life, it is Christ who works, and the Spirit is at the heart of his acts. Now, it is the Spirit who works in order to manifest Christ at the heart of his operations. The age of the Church is the age of the Spirit, and comes between the two parousias of the Lord.

The Church is founded on the historical Christ, in his *acta et passa in carne*, and if 'as yet there was no Spirit, because Jesus was not yet glorified' (John 7.39), that is because the 'sending' is essentially related to the sacrifice of the Lamb.

Mgr Cassien[3] identifies the Johannine Pentecost with the day of the Passover, thus reinforcing the connection between Pentecost and the historical Christ (magnificently portrayed at Vézelay). Similarly, the festivals of Easter and Pentecost are celebrated in a single liturgical season which prepares us for the parousial

---

2 *The Life in Christ*, tr. de Catanzaro, New York 1982.
3 *La Pentecôte Johannique*, Valence 1939.

Easter of the marriage of the Lamb, and unites the historical Christ and the Christ of glory. But the Spirit, throughout the age of the Church, 'plenifies' Christ (Eph. 1.23): in the words of St John Chrysostom, 'The head will be fulfilled only when the body is made perfect, when we are all conjoined and bound together.'[4]The Church is indeed the extension and the fullness of Christ incarnate. What Christ has *given* is supplemented by what is *done* on earth through the Spirit:[5] it *fills* the witnesses, establishes the bishops; the Fathers of the Councils, by their own testimony, are brought together with the Holy Spirit who presides over them and enlightens them;[6] everything is charismatic in the Church, in the diversity of ministries and spiritual gifts; the Spirit works in the epiclesis of the sacraments, and in that of our Christification and adoption by the Father. The *Acts of the Apostles*, Acts of the Church until the end of the world, make up the *Gospel of the Holy Spirit*. Beside the institutional and hierarchical forms which constitute the Body, there are the events of history (St Paul was an 'Apostle by theft', because of an event, but was none the less reckoned among the number of the Apostles); beside the regular mediation, there is the unpredictable mediation of holiness and the mystical life, in which grace cannot be organized. Beside dogmatic theology, there is also the lived theology of the Tradition; beside the structure there is also life. In the whole economy of the realization of the whole Christ, the age of the Spirit is the age of Tradition, with the essential qualification that it must be *Apostolic* and ready for the Parousia. Doctrine agrees with the Eucharist, but the Eucharist is the future age already present, and by that fulfilment it is the criterion of Tradition. It judges every sclerotic, 'rabbinic', state of affairs, every historical arrangement, and it inspires by opening up history and encouraging its movement towards the *eschaton*. In the Eucharist the time of the Incarnation is made present (John 7.39), and the continuity of the historical Christ already flows into the glory of his coming.

Beside the (more or less human) 'traditions', there is Tradition – the transmission of the *Presence of Christ* 'filled with the Trinity' – the One in the diversity of his forms. The revelation given once for all is given again at every moment in history by the Church, and is thus the uninterrupted continuity of a single act which is assured by the *Paradosis*. Even outside the assembled Councils, the epiclesis of conciliarity is constantly at work; it is the epiclesis of the Tradition, of the uninterrupted life of the Church. Some of its elements have already become normative (doctrines, worship); the others are still being reflected on or are in the process of being received. Without hurry, and at the moment chosen by the Spirit, the Body of the faithful comes to a common mind and declares them to be Apostolic.

---

[4] *In Ephes. hom.* III; *P.G.* 62, 29.
[5] Fr Congar, 'L'Eglise, lc Saint-Esprit et le Corps apostolique réalisateur de l'œuvre du Christ,' *Forma Gregis*, June 1925.
[6] Council of Ephesus, Denzinger, 125; St Cyril of Alexandria, *P.G.* 77, 293.

PART IV
The Church at Prayer

1

The Category of the Sacred:
Sacred Time, Sacred Space, the Temple

1. THE SACRED[1]

In everyday speech we may speak of a sacred trust or a holy person. The words 'sacred' and 'holy' have become cut off from their roots and taken on a moral meaning that falls far short of the original ontological one.

Above all, the sacred consists of what is opposed to this world, what R. Otto calls *das ganz Andere*, the absolutely other, different from this world. The Bible gives us the precise fundamental principle: God alone is ὄντως – truly self-existent, the Holy One; the creature's existence is derivative, never sacred or holy in its own nature, in its essence, but only by *participation*. The term *Qadosh*, ἅγιος, *sacer*, *sanctus*, implies total appropriation by God and presupposes a setting apart. The act that makes something sacred removes it from its worldly conditions and puts it in communion with the numinous,[2] changing its nature and immediately making it feel the *mysterium tremendum*, the sacred trembling in the presence of this 'numinous'. This is no fear of the unknown, but the very characteristic mystical terror that accompanies any manifestation of the transcendent, as the divine energies radiate from the inner realities of this world: 'I will send *my terror* in front of you, and will throw into confusion all the people against whom you shall come,' says God (Exod. 23.27); or again, 'Remove the sandals from your feet, for the place on which you are standing is holy ground' (Exod. 3.5).

So among the distortion and fragmentation of this world there emerges a reality that is 'innocent' but sanctified – i.e., purified and returned to its pristine condition, as it was originally intended to be, the pure vessel of the Holy, the abode of the radiant presence of God. Indeed, 'this place is holy' because of God's presence; as was the part of the Temple containing the Ark of the Covenant; as are 'The Holy Scriptures', for they enclose the presence of Christ in his word; as is every church, for God dwells in it and makes it the 'House of God', speaks in it and

---

[1] See M. Eliade, *Traité de l'histoire des religions*. Paris 1948; G. van der Leeuw, *La religion dans son essence et ses manifestations*, Paris 1949; R. Otto, *Le sacré*, Paris 1929; F. Heiler, *La Prière*, Paris 1931; R. Caillois, *L'homme et le sacré*, Paris 1950; C. Baudoin, *Psychanalyse du Symbole religieux*, Paris 1957.

[2] The term was coined by R. Otto, *Le Sacré, op. cit.*, p. 22: 'Since *luminous* has been formed from *lumen*, we can form *numinous* from *numen*.' In German *ominös* is derived from *omen*.

gives himself in it for food. The kiss of peace at the liturgical synaxis was called 'holy' because it sealed the communion in Christ who was present. The angels, the 'second lights', are holy because they live in the light of God and reflect it. The prophets, the apostles, 'the saints at Jerusalem' are holy because of the spiritual gifts of their ministry. It was by a 'setting apart' that Israel became ἔθνος ἅγιος, the 'holy nation'; and in the economy of the New Israel every baptized person who is confirmed is 'anointed', sealed with the gifts of the Holy Spirit; these gifts incorporate us into Christ so that we 'become participants in the divine nature' (2 Pet. 1.4), and in so participating are sanctified, made 'holy'. Those who were bishops acknowledged one another as *sanctus frater*, and a patriarch is called 'his holiness', not for any human qualities but because of his particular participation in the priesthood of Christ, the only Pontiff, who alone is Holy.

In its teaching on this subject the Liturgy is very explicit. Before administering the eucharistic meal the priest announces, 'Holy things for the holy', and the congregation of the faithful, as if awestruck by this precondition, replies by acknowledging its unworthiness: *Tu solus sanctus*, 'Thou only art holy, Lord Jesus Christ.' The only Holy One, who is holy *by nature*, is Christ; his members are holy only *by participation* in that unique holiness. The Church sings, 'The faces of thy saints are radiant with thy light.' 'Christ loved the Church ... in order to make her holy,' (Eph. 5.25-27) and Nicholas Cabasilas says, 'The faithful are called holy because of the holy thing in which they share.'[3] Isaiah (6.5-7) describes it exactly: 'Woe is me! ... for I am a man of unclean lips ... Then one of the seraphs flew to me, holding a live coal that had been taken from the altar with a pair of tongs. The seraph touched my mouth with it and said: "Now that this has touched your lips, your guilt has departed and your sin is blotted out." Humankind has been made holy by purification, for transcendent powers have touched it. The priest after Communion 'calls to mind' the vision of Isaiah: he kisses the rim of the chalice, the symbol of the pierced side of Christ, saying, 'This has touched my lips; take away my iniquities and purge me from my sins.' The spoon with which the priest gives the holy gifts is called in Greek λάβις, *tongs*, the very word used by Isaiah; and the spiritual masters, speaking of the Eucharist, say, 'you consume the fire.'

From the one divine source – 'You shall be holy, for I am holy' – proceeds a whole series of consecrations or sanctifications by participation, which act as 'deprofanations' or 'devulgarizations' of the essential nature of this world. As the sacraments and sacramentals exercise their special task of rendering the world 'porous', we learn that everything in the Christian life is potentially sacramental, for everything is destined to find its fulfilment in the liturgy, to participate in the Mystery. Thus, at the feast of the Transfiguration or Easter, the faithful bring food to the Church to be blessed, so that by extension all 'nourishment' is subject to

---

[3] *Explication de la Divine Liturgie*, ch. XXXVI.

the eucharistic principle of offering and consecration. The element of water is fulfilled by participating in the mystery of the Epiphany; earth by receiving the body of the Lord for its rest during the great Sabbath, and stone in the 'sealing' of the sepulchre and in being rolled away in the presence of the spice-bearing women. Olive oil and water are perfected in becoming conductors of grace to regenerated humanity;[4] wheat and the vine become the flesh and blood of the Lord. Everything clearly points to the Incarnation, all converges on the Lord in a splendid liturgy and recapitulation of human existence. The Liturgy connects the most elementary actions of life – drinking, eating, washing, speaking, moving, living – with their true end: 'Things are at last the furniture not of our prison, but of our temple.'[5]

Humankind becomes accustomed to living in the world of God, in its depths; it can read the world's Edenic destiny, see the universe as cosmic liturgy, the temple of God's glory. It begins to understand that *everything* is potentially sacred and that there is nothing profane, nothing neutral, because everything refers to God (the liturgical 'memorial' signifies reference to the Father, recalling everything to the mind and memory of God). Nevertheless, next to the sacred we see its caricature, the sinister fellowship with the Prince of Darkness, participation in the demonic. Hence St Gregory of Nyssa categorically denies the existence of the exclusively human; there is no such thing for him as pure worldliness. Either the human being is an 'angel of light', the icon or likeness of God, or 'it wears the mask of the beast' and behaves as an ape.[6]

The liturgy teaches us the language of the sacred, introduces us to the world of symbols. Through symbols, such as a cross, an icon or a temple, through their very materiality, we participate in the heavenly.[7] Similarly a fragment of time or space

---

[4] The sacraments of Baptism and Anointing.

[5] Paul Claudel.

[6] *P.G.* 44, 192. These are two modes of existence and two conceptions of the 'profane' world – which should now be called the 'profaned' world, i.e., the world from which all references to the Transcendent have been removed. This perception is of fairly recent origin, the experience of the unreligious person in modern society.

[7] The set phrases taken into the Liturgy, such as *alleluia, kyrie eleison, amen,* were already ancient idioms, not in common use; similarly, *verba certa,* fixed forms, such as the Trisagion, the Sanctus, the Lord's Prayer, the Prayer of the Heart, the Creed, the sacramental formulae. Their power comes partly from their repeated use, and from the formal and heightened delivery of the litanies, chanted prayers and liturgical readings. Just as every act of blessing invokes the grace of the Name, every wish has a real power of its own, which is why we pay full attention to *every* utterance (cf. the texts in the Gospels expressing the wish for peace...). When believers cross themselves, they are performing an act of epiclesis, calling down the Holy Spirit, or more precisely the 'invincible strength of the Cross', and by its penetrative power placing that Sign on their very being, surrounding themselves with it, identifying themselves explicitly with the Cross of Christ; through that figure of crucified love they go back to the cross that stands for the Trinity, and becomes an icon, a living transcription of that sacred hieroglyph.

can become a hierophany, a vessel of the sacred, but without any change in its appearance, which continues to be part of its existing surroundings. But between the sacred and its material support there is a communion of essence (between the matter of the sacraments or the human being, and the energies of grace), sometimes even to the extent of consubstantiality, complete metabolism: the eucharistic bread and wine neither signify nor symbolize the flesh and blood; they *are* them. This is the miracle of 'identity by grace' of which St Maximus speaks,[8] ἡ κατὰ χάριν αὐτότις; St Arsenius was seen by his disciples ὅλος ὡς πῦρ,[9] in the form of fire, man-light, not only receiving but emitting it. But in such extreme cases, the words of the Gospel remind us, 'Let anyone with ears to hear listen.'

2. SACRED TIME

A. Contrary to current opinion, time and space are not pure forms. Space is not simply a kind of sack into which atoms are thrown. Nor are they the *a priori* of transcendentalism, a *subjective* net that our mind would throw round things in order to make sense of them. Space and time exist *objectively*; they are the measure of existence, one of its dimensions; their function is to order and also to *qualify* things which exist only in the forms intrinsic to every creature. They reveal the state of health of things, their ontological temperature.[10] When the Angel of Revelation announces the end of the evil time, it is the end of mathematical time that he announces, the succession of separate moments; it is the end of the unfinished temporal age; there will follow the finished age, set within time that is qualitatively fulfilled.[11] St Augustine expresses himself in biblical terms when he says that the world and time were created *together*: 'the world was not created *in* time but *with* time,'[12] meaning that time is essentially good, that life in Paradise and in the Kingdom of God exists *in its own time*, i.e., in the order that is revealed in the succession of events. 'The first human being was created in such a way that time would have moved on, even if human beings had stayed still,' says St

---

[8] *Ad Thal.*, q. 25; *P.G.* 90, 333 A.

[9] *Alphab.*, Arsenius 27, *P.G.* 65, 96 C.

[10] Breal and Bailly (*Dictionnaire étymologique latin*, sub. V) believe the primitive meaning of *tempus* to be temperature.

[11] For Bergson time is the intuitive experience of duration – which is essentially a succession of conscious states – as opposed to Kant's idea of mathematical 'spatialized' time (*Données immédiates de la conscience*, pp. 74 ff.). Pascal is keen to emphasize the mysterious nature of time, asking how it might be defined. 'We define things only so that we may point to them by name, not so as to show their nature' (*De l'esprit géométrique*, Ed. Brunschwieg, p. 170).

[12] The world cannot exist outside of time, *procul dubio mundus non factus est in tempore sed cum tempore* (*P.L.* 41, 322).

Gregory of Nyssa. Eternity for creatures is not the absence of time, and certainly not our time with its end cut off, but the positive form of it. It is time in which the past is entirely preserved and the present open to the infinite future; it is the 'memorial of the Kingdom,' the state in which everything points to and is totally present to the eye of the Eternal. So we must distinguish between profane time, infected with the negativity of the Fall, and the sacred, redeemed, oriented time of salvation.

B. Of this present time the first thing to say is that although it is divided into regular and identical intervals, that is only an abstraction of our clocks. We are not mere dials on which the hands turn and mark mathematical fractions; we are not subject to time but we live it, having taken possession of it; and lived time consists of the mathematical form and what happens within it interacting closely together.[13] Time modifies us, but we also modify time, making it richer than the mere sum of its moments and capable of being opened on to another dimension.

St Augustine in his *Confessions* brilliantly demonstrates that none of the three parts of time exists: the future, which does not yet exist, moves into the present, a moment so fleeting that it cannot be grasped, which immediately becomes the past and vanishes into what has already ceased to exist.

The first form of this time is ordered by the cosmic seasons; it is the *cyclical time* of the stars translated by our clocks, expressed graphically as a curve closed on itself, the serpent biting its tail, the vicious circle of eternal repetition with no escape. 'There is nothing new under the sun,' cries the pessimistic Ecclesiastes. Closed time, like the God Kronos, devours its own children, the moments, coldly and mathematically timing the repetitions, and provoking terror of the meaningless, like that of Pascal contemplating infinite space.[14] The hands, perpetually in motion, lead nowhere.

'Our earth has probably reproduced itself a million times; it has frozen, cracked open, fallen apart, separated into its elements, and been covered again by the waters. Then it has become once more a comet, then a sun, from which has emerged another

---

13 'The theory of relativity rules out any notion of mathematical, *absolute time*, which has no experiential meaning. Every system of reference has its own time' (see Langevin, *Le Temps, l'Espace et la Causalité*; Poincaré, *La valeur de la science*).

14 The genius of Dostoyevsky in *A Gentle Creature* shows us the unbearable contrast between the infinite depths of suffering and the indifference of time: '"Men, love one another." Who said that? The pendulum ticks callously, with a hateful monotony' (Dostoyevsky, *A Writer's Diary*, vol. II). Time reminds us that everything is passing. In *Crime and Punishment*, the ghost of the woman murdered by Svidrigailov appears and reminds him that 'he has forgotten to wind the clock'! We can stop the clock; we cannot stop time which moves implacably towards the Judgement. One of the most terrible images is that of stopped time. Kierkegaard describes the awakening of a sinner in hell; '"What is the time?" he cried; and with icy indifference Satan replied, "Eternity."'

earth. This cycle has been repeated an infinite number of times, in exactly the same way, down to the last detail. It is incredibly tedious ...'[15]

But this brings us to the second form, which we might call historical time, Bergson's duration; its graphical expression is a line indefinitely produced, and it is measured differently. Its epochs possess their own rhythm, faster or slower. This time is biological, bearing the scars of experience, and varying subjectively according to when the wounds were inflicted – just as time is altered by suffering or joy, so that it seems imperceptible or infinitely long.[16]

The third form is existential: each moment can be opened from within on to another dimension, so that we experience eternity here and now, or 'the eternal present'. This is sacred or liturgical time. Its engagement with the wholly other changes its nature. Eternity is neither before nor after time, it is the dimension on to which time can be opened.

C. St Gregory of Nyssa, to define time, uses the term ἀκολουθία, an ordered succession that governs evolution, distinguishing before from after, and directing seeds towards their end.[17] But the true end, fulfilment, is not simply τέλος, full stop, but τέλειος, the fullness of perfection.

Christ is the axis of time. Before Christ, history was directed towards him, in expectation of the Messiah; it was the time of gestation, of foreshadowings and waiting. Since the Incarnation, all has been interiorized, governed by the categories of empty and full,[18] absent and present, unfinished and perfected, the only true content of time now being the expanding presence of Christ; everything is turning, as on a hinge, visibly or invisibly towards the final perfection of time itself, which, simultaneously is here already and will come at the End. That 'simultaneously' brings out the sheer extent of the real problem of time, which is the mystery of the coexistence of the two natures in a single being, which are living *in different times*: 'though our outer nature is wasting away, our inner nature is being renewed day by day' (2 Cor. 4.16). Christ has broken the historical *continuum*, but he has not abolished time itself; he has only opened it up. 'The Word became flesh,' and as flesh is subject to the *continuum*, 'the child grew and became strong,' as the Evangelist St Luke says (2.40); but as the Word he can be apprehended only by faith, and it is in the eyes of faith that historical time opens on to sacred time, on to a wholly other succession of events: the miraculous Nativity, the Transfiguration, the Resurrection, the Ascension, Pentecost and the Parousia. 'God entered time so that we, humans in time, might become eternal,'

---

[15] Dostoyevsky, *The Brothers Karamazov*.
[16] Lecomte de Noüy introduced the notion of 'biological time' following a logarithmic, not an arithmetical law (*Le temps et la vie*, Paris 1936; *L'homme et sa destinée*, Paris 1946).
[17] *P.G.* 46, 547 D; 45 364 C.
[18] Even in the 1st century St Ignatius of Antioch said that what set Christians apart was the fact that they were Θεοφόροι and Θεοῦ γέμετε, bearers of God and *filled* with God (Magn. 14.1).

says St Irenaeus,[19] thus showing that the temporal culminates in the eternal 'here and now'.

So Christ does not destroy time but he perfects it, gives it a new value and *redeems* it. Real events no longer vanish, but are held in the memory of God (our prayer for the dead is that God should 'keep them in his memory'). Positive time gains the upper hand, banishes the threat of negativity and annihilation, and demonstrates that human eternity is not the absence of time, but its fulfilment; Abraham, Isaac, Jacob, and people throughout history will be guests at the messianic banquet. Nor is historical time wholly negative in character; of its very nature it has a positive, powerful aspect; properly oriented, it is analogous to the homeopathic principle which depends on substances that produce similar effects: *similia similibus curantur*. It allows the natural course of events to be interrupted, steps to be retraced, unworthy aspects of the past destroyed, and life to begin again; 'let the dead bury their own dead' (Matt. 8.22). In the 'second birth' of Baptism (John 3.3) the evil past is allowed to die. This is the basis of Gregory of Nyssa's double interpretation of history[20] as the simultaneous process of growth and decay. Salvation is found in breaking through the levels. Thus, Baptism interrupts the vicious chain of succession and sets up an alternative: in opposition to the order of death God establishes the new order of eternal life. It is the application of St Paul's theology of the two Adams: the first inaugurates the time of perdition and the second the time of the universal recapitulation, the time of salvation.

The evil past is abolished in Baptism and repentance, and the future age is already present in the Eucharist; in that 'oriented' time we already enjoy our rising, our Eternity.

D. Following Kierkegaard, people have spoken of the liturgical power to 'reverse time'; but time is not reversible. It is more accurate to speak of the power to *open time* to what abides. While memory gives us the homogeneous presence of the past as *recollection*, the fixed image of it, the liturgical memorial goes further and contains not images of the past, but events really present, so that we are *contemporaries*. St Gregory of Nyssa speaks of 'progressive order', and the 'regular following of liturgical feasts.' Every liturgical reading of the Gospel places us in the corresponding event. 'At that time,' the sacred formula with which every liturgical reading of the Gospel begins, signifies the 'sacred time' – *in illo tempore* – the now, the contemporaneous. When we celebrate Christmas, we are present at the birth of Christ, and on the night of Easter the risen Christ appears to us who are celebrating it and makes us *eye-witnesses* of the Great Time. There is nothing left here of the dead time of repetitions, but everything happens once and abides for ever. 'It is the same sacrifice that we offer, not one today and another

---

[19] Cf. St Hilary, *P.G.* 82, 205 A; St Gregory of Nyssa, *P.G.* 45, 1152 C.
[20] *P.G.* 44, 1312 B.

tomorrow,'[21] says St John Chrysostom, and Theodore of Mopsuestia says, 'This is not something new; the Liturgy takes place in heaven, and heaven is where we are;' the levels are indeed broken through. All the Holy Communions in the Church are a single and eternal Supper, that of Christ in the Upper Room. The divine act that took place at a precise moment in history is the same that is always present in the sacrament. It has the power to open time and occupy the heart of every moment and become its true content.

In the liturgical dimension, every moment is near because its content is present in all the others. Thus the *kontakion* of the Ascension says, 'Thou didst ascend into heaven, O Christ our God, never to leave us again ... and thou didst say to them that love thee, "I am with you".' Similarly, 'In the tomb with the body, in Hell with the soul, yet as God, in paradise with the thief, and on the throne with the Father and the Holy Spirit, wast Thou, O boundless Christ, filling all things.' And in the prayer before Communion: 'Thou who sittest on high with the Father and art here invisibly present with us.'

Repetition occurs where people enter at intervals into communion with the eternal. We see it for example in the cosmogonic richness of the liturgical commemoration of the New Year. St Ephraem the Syrian[22] says, 'God has created the heavens anew because sinners worshipped the heavenly bodies; he has created the world anew that was stained by Adam; he has built a new creation with his own saliva.' The last statement refers to the healing of the man who was born blind, interpreting it as the great symbol of the healing of *blind time*. Strictly speaking this is not the new creation, but the *regeneration* of time as a whole. We go back through time to the cosmogonic moment of the dawn of the very first morning, and in consequence time recovers its true destiny, and is renewed, redirected, and rejuvenated from within, 'so that your youth is renewed like the eagle's' (Ps. 103.5). That explains why cosmogony and all renewal and true birth are intimately bound up with the element of water,[23] as is the idea of birth and resurrection. The *Talmud* says, 'God has three keys: that of rain, that of birth and that of the resurrection of the dead.'

E. The religious significance given liturgically to the dates of the astronomical calendar makes clear their symbolic and prefigurative function. Thus, the twelve days between Christmas and Epiphany (25 December to 6 January) prefigure the twelve months of the year. (From these twelve days the peasants of central Europe predict the rainfall and harvest for the next twelve months, just as the Jews predict the rainfall for each month from the Feast of Tabernacles.) According to the Fathers of the Church, since the Sabbath is the seventh day of the Jewish week,

---

21 *In Tim.*, hom. , 45; *P.G.* 62, 612.
22 *Hymn* 8, 16; Wensinck, 169.
23 The depths of the world or the foetus surrounded by water.

Sunday does not replace it, but constitutes the eighth day[24] or, in the absolute
and unique sense, the first. While the days of the week symbolize the self-contained cosmic week, or the whole of history, Sunday, by contrast, the day of the
Resurrection, is the eighth day, the weekly Easter, and represents eternity. (St
Basil the Great reminds us that kneeling, the attitude of penitence, is forbidden;
on Sunday we *stand upright*,[25] in the eschatological attitude, the expression of
epectasis, looking for the parousia.)

The forty years in the wilderness, the forty days of Christ's fast, the forty days
of Great Lent, are the days of waiting before reaching the 'promised land'.[26]
Thus the time of Lent symbolically sums up the whole of history. By contrast,
the fifty days between Easter and Pentecost are treated as fifty Sundays (and for
that reason kneeling is forbidden), the time of joy, prefiguring the future age that
has already begun).

Similarly, Christmas is not only a feast but 'a festive time' when light is growing, *crescit lux*. 'Christmas and Epiphany are the solar manifestations of Christ:
"Light of the Nations" and "Rising Sun".' In the future age, says Origen, 'All
will be perfected in one perfect Man and will become a single sun.' While the
astronomical calendar 'orients' people at the times of sowing and harvest, the ecclesiastical calendar is not oriented, but is ordered and ordained time. Each New
Year is universal history in a nutshell, regenerated by the liturgical order, and on
the other hand, each day is a *feria*, open to the future age.

F. A baptized person, being immersed, passes through the Flood, through the
death of vicious time and is reborn into the time of salvation. The prayer of the
Sacrament of Anointing with Chrism, 'that he may please thee in every deed and
word', shows a human being effectively withdrawn from the time of perdition
and sealed by the gifts of the Holy Spirit, consecrated, marked, the whole of life
destined for the *time of salvation*. Therefore, according to St John, if you follow
Christ you will not come to the judgement (for the historical past is already abolished) and if you eat the flesh of Christ you *already* have eternal life, live in
sacred time. Hell, on the other hand, cannot exist in the time of salvation, in eternity. Since it belongs essentially to negative and subjective time, it has no ontological place in the positive and universal time of the Kingdom of God; it cannot
become its content.

G. Joshua, when he stops the sun at the passage through the waters, breaks
through the levels, passes to the time of salvation; 'For the gate is narrow and

---

[24] St Basil, *P.G.* 29, 59 B; St Gregory of Nazianzus, *P.G.* 36, 429 C. See Jean Danielou, *Bible et Liturgie*, ch. 16.
[25] St Basil, *De Spir. Sancto*, 27; Canon 20 of the Council of Nicaea; however Origen observes, 'For the perfect every day is Sunday' (*P.G.* 11, 1549 D).
[26] There is also the traditional belief that the souls of the dead remain on earth for forty days before entering the heavenly spheres.

the road is hard that leads to life, and there are few who find it' (Matt. 7.14) refers to the same passing.

Hesychastic technique concentrates on this narrow gate, by which we enter time of a different quality. Lengthening the intervals between breathing out and breathing in, we experience another rhythm, another time.[27] Time is essentially 'wearing away' and according to Meister Eckhart there is no greater obstacle to union with God than time.

In the vision of the *Shepherd* of Hermas, the Church is eternally young, for its fresh and spring-like nature is beyond the reach of time. The calendar of feasts and saints gives a new value to every fraction of time, makes it sacred time and corresponds here on earth to the eternity that we long for. The liturgy is thus revealed as a sacrament of eternity which integrates time in the Word – the Chronocrator, the Lord of time.

3. SACRED SPACE

As time is to duration, space is to area. Space is not homogeneous; there are amorphous, chaotic spaces, and there is ordered, sacred space. Profane space is subject to the law of mutual exclusion and exteriority by which beings coexist. Sacred space abolishes mere juxtaposition and replaces the unity of simple coexistence with the more profound 'oneness' in Christ, consubstantiality.

When Christ says to the Samaritan woman, 'The hour is coming when you will worship the Father neither on this mountain nor in Jerusalem' (John 4.21) he is speaking of himself as the omnipresent sacred space who abolishes the exclusivity of every empirical space. Ever since then, every visit to a church has been a pilgrimage to sacred space. So although there are many such places, each one is truly a centre, because their centrality is not geographical but cosmic, determined not horizontally but vertically, and therefore united with the transcendent wherever in geographical space they happen to be. Thus, the blessing of oil, bread and corn in any church spreads out from there and consecrates those elements over the whole earth, and similarly with the blessing of the four corners of the world at the feast of the Exaltation of the Cross.

At these points all the levels coincide: the subterranean, the earthly and the heavenly; their image is the Holy Mountain, the cosmic Tree, the central Pillar

---

[27] The yogis emphasize the influence of breathing on the physique and so explain the astonishing youthfulness of the ascetics; during the night they reduce the rate of their breathing to a tenth; so in a day of 24 hours a yogi suffers about half the wear and tear, and therefore the ageing, of other people because he is breathing so much less frequently. And if he eats once in 24 hours, that is equivalent to a meal for every 12 hours of breathing (see M. Eliade, *Images et Symboles*, Paris 1952, p. 112-113).

or the Ladder.[28] Hence Mount Tabor, probably derived from *tabbúr* which means navel,[29] and similarly Mount Gerizim, called 'the navel of the earth' (*tabbúr erez*, Judg. 9.7). That is why, according to rabbinic tradition, the land of Israel was not drowned by the Flood.[30] In one Christian tradition the centre of the world is Golgotha, where Adam was created and the Cross was set up, and at its foot Adam's tomb was found,[31] a common subject in icons. Similarly, the roots of the cosmic tree reach down to hell and its top touches heaven, the branches symbolizing the different celestial levels (the Apostle Paul was caught up to the third heaven). In the *Book of Mysteries*, St Maximus the Confessor emphasizes the possibility of transcending the cosmic levels: 'Today you will be with me in paradise – since what is the earth for us is no different from paradise for him; he appears anew on this earth and converses there with his disciples.'[32]

The rabbinic writings attribute gigantic size to Adam, while in the Apocryphal scriptures[33] and the *Shepherd* of Hermas[34] Christ is the giant whose head reaches above the heavens.[35] Origen says, 'Scripture describes Christ as a tree.'[36] On the other hand, many images, such as the mosaic in the baptistery of Henchir Massaouda, identify Christ with the Cross. The same symbolism is found in 'living' crosses, the extremities of which are covered in branches and end in human arms: one opens the gate of heaven, the other breaks down the gates of hell. At the Exaltation of the Holy Cross we hear, 'The Tree of Life planted at Calvary (the tree in Eden identified with the Cross[37]) which was set up at the centre of the earth ... and which sanctifies to the ends of the universe ... the length and breadth of the Cross reaching as far as heaven'.[38]

St Augustine for his part asks, 'And what is this mountain by which we ascend, if it is not the Lord Jesus Christ?'[39] The *Acts of Philip* call Christ the Pillar of Fire, στύλος πυρός, and in the ascetic writings a spiritual master uses the same image: 'Pillar of fire joining heaven and earth.'[40]

---

[28] See H. de Lubac, *Aspects du Bouddhisme*, Paris 1951; Mircia Eliade, *Images et Symboles*, Paris 1952; van der Leeuw, *La Religion*, Paris 1948.

[29] Eric Burrows, *The Labyrinth*, London 1935, p. 51.

[30] A. Wensinck, *Navel of the Earth*, Amsterdam 1916, p.15.

[31] Adam's body is believed to have been buried where Christ was crucified (Origen, *In Matt.*; *P.G.* 13, 1777).

[32] *P.G.* 91, 1309 B.

[33] *The Gospel of Peter*, v. 29-40; *The Acts of John*, N 90-93.

[34] *Similitude* 9, ch. 6, N 1.

[35] Cf. St Ambrose, *De Incarnatione*, *P.L.* 16, 827 C.

[36] *In Psalm.* 1: Pitra, *Analecta sacra* vol. II, p. 445.

[37] Von W. Mayer, *Die Geschichte des Kreutzholzes vor Christus*, Munich 1881.

[38] *La Prière des Eglises de rite byzantin*, Mercenier, vol. 5., Part 1, p. 39.

[39] *In Psalmum*, 119, n. 1; *P.L.* 37, 1597.

[40] Amelineau, *Etudes sur le christianisme en Egypte au VIIe siècle*, 1887.

But these images are best explained by the biblical one of Jacob's Ladder. The angels ascend and descend upon it. Heaven is opened and the ladder is set up at the centre of the earth, and since the ladder is Christ it springs up in every holy place; the centres are innumerable. James of Sarug says, 'Christ on the cross stands on the earth as on a many-runged ladder.'[41] Catherine of Siena sees it as a bridge between heaven and earth, like the rainbow, a living sign of the Covenant.[42] St Ephraem says in his epiphanic hymn,[43] 'Brothers, contemplate the pillar, hidden in the air, the base of which rests on the waters and which reaches the gate of heaven like the ladder that Jacob saw.'[44]

Finally there is the circle (the church enclosure or city wall) with the power of protection, for it symbolizes eternity. When the trumpets sounded and the walls of Jericho fell down, the town was without heavenly defence. Similarly, when a city is besieged, the clergy go in procession along the ramparts carrying something holy such as a relic or a miraculous icon. Such prayer invokes and reinforces the power of protection. A liturgical procession round the church has recognizably the same intention; it traces the symbol of eternity and reclaims the area as sacred space. As sacred time corresponds to the deep longing for eternity, sacred space corresponds to the thirst for Paradise lost; in these transcendings of the empirical effected by the sacred, humankind partially recovers its original destiny and is guided towards its fulfilment.

4. THE CONSTRUCTION OF THE SACRED: THE TEMPLE

A. An observer can look at each part of a church in turn, classify its architecture and evaluate it artistically, but it will still be a closed book. Only if we appreciate the nobility of the conception of the church as a whole will every stone, every bit of it begin to speak and sing together in a liturgical chorus[45] It is set apart from its surroundings above all in being an organized space, and the rite of consecration lays great emphasis on this fact,[46] carving out a certain area, separating it from profane space, purifying it, and in the epiclesis calling down the Holy Spirit which transforms any given place into a precise point of theophany, a holy mountain, a cosmic centre and Jacob's ladder.

The bishop lights a big torch, 'the first light', and goes in procession round the outside of the church, tracing the circle of eternity and carrying the relics of

---

41 *Homélie sur la vision de Jacob*, n. 95, Zingerle-Nozinger, *Monumenta Syriaca*, vol. 1, p. 26.
42 R.P. Louis Beirnaert, 'Le symbolisme ascentionnel', in *Eranos-Jahrbuch*, vol. 18, 1950.
43 Hymn XI, 11.
44 Similarly Aphraates, in *Homélie sur la prière*; *Patr. Syr.* vol. 1, p. 146.
45 St Gregory of Nyssa: 'Dumb art can speak'. *P.G.* 46, 737 D.
46 *Consécration et inauguration d'une église*, Chevetogne, 1957.

a martyr. In front of the door, the bishop recites Psalm 24: 'Lift up your heads, O gates! and be lifted up, O ancient doors! that the King of glory may come in.' The choir inside the building, in the space not yet organized but about to become so, sings, 'Who is the King of glory?'

The bishop makes the sign of the cross with the relics and proclaims, 'The Lord strong and mighty: he is the King of glory.' The bishop's entrance signifies God taking possession of the place, transforming it into the House of God, so that the Liturgy can rightly be called *divine*. From this sacred centre towards which the eyes of God are 'open night and day' (1 Kgs. 8.29), the Son causes the offering and the incense of liturgical prayer to ascend unceasingly to the Father. Then the bishop *builds* the table of the altar, dresses it and proceeds to anoint it with Chrism and cleanse it with baptismal water, while the angelic alleluia is sung. The church, as a whole, becomes the sculpted face of God's heaven on earth.

'Altar' (from *alta-ara*) means high place; here is the holy mountain of Zion, with its cosmic centre, the holy table, which, in a mystical shift of meaning, represents the Lord himself. St Denys says of the rite, 'It is on Jesus himself, as on the altar ... that the consecration takes place.'[47]

During the ordination of a priest, at the moment of the laying on of hands, the ordinand presses his forehead against the table of the altar, which symbolizes Christ.[48] The tabernacle containing the Flesh and Blood of Christ will be placed on the table, which transforms it into the *tomb broken open* by the power of the Resurrection. Nobody but a priest can touch it, and he, when he comes in, prostrates himself before this living representation of Christ. But the very material of the table on which the tabernacle rests is transfigured by the depositing within it of holy relics or incorruptible bones of the martyrs, an explicit reference to Revelation 6.9, where the angel sees 'under the altar the souls of them that were slain for the word of God, and for the testimony which they held.' Nicholas Cabasilas goes so far as to insist that the bones themselves constitute the true altar. By anticipation the relics, and therefore the table, are the σῶμα πνευματικόν of the future Easter.[49] So the liturgical centre is made out of the material of the Kingdom of God, and the sacred space is organized around a particle of heaven.

B. The architectural term for the lengthened rectangular part of the church is the nave, and the whole building can be said to resemble a ship being steered towards the East. The *Didascalia of the Apostles*, referring to Psalm 68.33, 'God who rides on the heavens of the east,' and Acts 1.11, 'Jesus ... will come in the same way as you saw him go into heaven,' explains the origin of praying towards the East as we wait for the return of Christ. Hence all prayer, when it

---

[47] *Ecclesiastical Hierarchy*, IV, § 12.
[48] This is the image of St John leaning on Jesus' breast (John 13.23).
[49] *The Life in Christ*.

is well 'oriented', is waiting, and therefore ultimately eschatological in intention.

Franz von Doelger has shown how, in basilicas with three apses, the shape of the Cross can be seen, and in it the symbol of Light and Life, the eschatological letter omega, the central letter of the two words Ζωή and φῶς. This reinforces the architectural significance of the church: a ship floating in the eschatological dimension, and sailing towards the East.

C. The perfect ordering of the place does not allow us to enter directly and bring in with us the profane world; the liturgical chant called the *Cherubicon* explicitly calls us, at the threshold of the church to 'lay aside all earthly cares.' The person coming in is introduced by stages marked by the arrangement of the space within the building. The church was formerly surrounded by a circular wall, the symbol of eternity and protection, which also defined the spaces. In monasteries there was often, backing on to the church, a cemetery and a hostel, a demonstration of the unity of the dead and the living in one sacred space. Entering by the gate, we are at once in the 'wholly other'; then we cross the atrium or courtyard and ascend the steps up to the church, as if climbing the holy mountain. We then enter first the external narthex, then the internal one (formerly the place where the penitents stood, the place of funeral ceremonies and also the refectory for the monks). Only after this measured and gracious initiation do we enter the church proper. Here the perspective which is opened up by the arrangement of the constituent parts invites us to resume and complete the ascent, the path that leads to the summit of the Mountain.

D. On the eastern side there is a raised platform, the *solea*, the central part of which is called the *ambo*, from ἀναβαίνω, to mount or scale; this is the upper room, the place of the Communion of the Faithful. As the Church sings in the Liturgy, 'Let us lift up our hearts and find ourselves in the upper room.'

The Royal Doors open directly on the Holy Table, and all this part is the 'high place' – the Holy Mountain proper. The cross behind the table of the altar represents that Jacob's ladder which God uses for his descent to earth and which takes the form of the cross set within the Trinity; it represents the Face of God turned towards the world, the expression of his unutterable love. Between the cross and the table is the seven-branched candlestick, the light from which speaks of the power of the gifts of the Holy Spirit sealing the human race and of the grace of Pentecost making the universe 'sacred'.

E. The organized space of the Temple is surrounded by profane space, which, in so far as it is opposed to the sacred, is demonic. So the whole Temple is designed to stand as a decisive contradiction of the Beast of Revelation and a clarion call to the world to become the temple 'where everything that has breath' enters and forms the *sobor*, the Body of Christ. The cross that crowns the dome, and the dome itself, command the space. By its lines the dome expresses the descending movement of divine love and its rotundity draws humankind together into a congregation, the eucharistic synaxis. Beneath the dome we feel protected, safe from the torment of vicious infinity; similarly the cross, if its branches are infinitely extended, contains the whole of organized space, real infinity. The onion dome of an Orthodox church suggests the image of prayer inflamed by the transcendent elements of this world that link it with the world beyond. It is a tongue of fire, and a church with several domes is like a chandelier blazing with flames. The brilliance of this flame penetrates to the interior of the dome and lights up the vaults, like heaven come down to earth, with the image of the *Pantocrator* at the centre, whose hand holds the destiny of all and every one.

The elongated and soaring figures of the icons and frescos surge ever upwards. Everything individual finds its fulfilment, but is restrained by communion and catholicity. All is united in a liturgical cosmos where 'every creature praises the Lord.' This 'superbiological' joy and peace preaches and proclaims the eternal life that begins here and now.

The sacred art of the Orthodox churches works to incorporate everything into the liturgical Mystery, to such an extent that outside the offices everything in the temple constitutes a waiting for the Holy Mysteries. But this very waiting is already sacred, for it is entirely filled with presence, and that is the ministry of the icon.

Liturgical time and sacred space together provide the setting for the action, the liturgical act of worship in which the Kingdom of God makes itself present in an inauguration of the Parousia.

2

An Introduction to Icons[1]

1. THE THEOLOGY OF GLORY

We behold 'the glory of the Lord as though reflected in a mirror' (2 Cor. 3.18); the truth of God is arrayed in glory because the Lord is the Truth, 'clothed with majesty and honour.' And when he shows the light of his countenance, the heart of the creature responds with a hymn of praise to his kingdom, his power and his glory. God 'has shone in our hearts to give the light of the knowledge of the glory of God in the face of Jesus Christ' (2 Cor. 4.6). He gives the heart the capacity to recognize glory, and also to reflect it: the Church sings, 'The faces of thy saints are radiant with thy light.'

The icon is another hymn of praise, bathed in glory and singing in a way of its own. True beauty has no need of proofs; it is itself evidence that argues iconographically for divine Truth. The intelligible content of the icons is doctrinal, so it is not the icon, the work of art, that is beautiful, but the truth. An icon cannot always be 'pretty'; it demands spiritual maturity to recognize its beauty.

The attribute of glory is light. The halos around the subjects of icons are not the distinctive signs of sainthood, but the radiance of their luminosity. For the saints, the statement, 'you are the light of the world,' actually defines their nature. The truth of every being speaks by the purity with which it reflects the light; every created thing has the marvellous grace to be the face, the mirror of the uncreated. Such a pitch of inspiration is possible only through the spiritual gifts of the 'holy iconographers', by which art is elevated to sacred art. The vision of the iconographers depends on the faith that is the 'conviction of things not seen' (Heb. 11.1). They experiment with that invisible aspect, the 'interior form' of the being, and this inner reality is 'Taboric', spiritually illuminated.[2] There is never a source of light in an

---

[1] *Bibliography*: O. Wulf und M. Alpatov, *Denkmöler de Ikonenmalerei*, Dresden 1922; W. Weidle, *Les icones byzantines et russes*, Florence 1950; E. Trubetskoy, *Altrussische Ikonenmalerie*, Paderborn-Schöningh 1927; P. Muratov, *Les icones russes*, Paris 1927; N. Kondakov, *The Russian Ikon*, Oxford 1927; USSR, *Icones Anciennes de Russie*, Unesco 1958; Paul Evdokimov, 'Initiation à l'Icône', *Bible et Vie Chrétienne*, No 19, 1958, Casterman; L. Ouspensky, V. Lossky, *The Meaning of Icons*, New York 1982; Felicetti-Liebenfels, *Geschichte der Byzantinischenn Ikonenmalerie*, Olten and Lausanne 1956.
[2] Tabor: where the Transfiguration of the Lord took place.

icon, light is its subject, you do not illuminate the sun. We can say that the iconographer paints with Taboric light. It is significant that the painting of the Transfiguration is usually the first icon of every monk iconographer, so that Christ 'may make his light to shine in his heart.' A manuscript of Mount Athos enjoins, 'let him pray with tears, so that God will penetrate his soul. Let him go to the priest, who will pray over him and recite the hymn of the Transfiguration.'[3] The rules of the Councils recommend 'working with the fear of God, for it is a divine art.'

2. THE MARTYROLOGY OF THE ICON

Martyrum signum est maximi caritatis. The Church particularly venerates 'the wounded friends of the Bridegroom,' and iconography is closely bound up with that cloud of martyr-witnesses. It portrays them motionless, with eyes opened wide on the 'flame of things'. They are like tongues of Pentecostal fire in human form. There is something deeper here than resemblance. The icon itself is a martyr and bears traces of its Baptism by fire. The blood of the martyrs is mixed with fragments of broken icons, splashes of light during the relentless battle with the iconoclasts.[4] The deposed Patriarch German, when taking off his pallium, said, 'Without the authority of a Council you, *Basileus*, can change nothing.'[5] And Pope Gregory II said to Leo the Isaurian, 'The doctrines of the Church are not your business ... let go of this madness.'[6] It is nothing to do with mere illustrations. To strike at the icon was to strike at Christological doctrine. How symptomatic it is that heretical iconoclasm immediately turns against the monastic life and undermines the divine motherhood of the *Theotokos*. The rationalization of mystery never stops half way. The veneration of the Gospel, the Cross and the icons is all of a piece with the liturgical mystery of presence that the Church proclaims from the depths of the chalice.

3. THE DOCTRINAL SIGNIFICANCE OF THE 7TH COUNCIL

The law of the Old Testament prohibited images because they endangered the worship of a unique and spiritual God. In the East the sense of the infinite was conveyed through geometrical ornamentation. In Islam non-figurative art, arabesques, polygonal decoration reinforced the notion of the radical transcendence of God.

---

[3] Dom Idefonse Dirks, *Les Saintes Icones*, Prieuré d'Amay 1939, p. 44.
[4] In 726 and 842.
[5] *Theophanes chronogr.*, p. 825.
[6] Similarly St John Damascene in his 2nd Discourse.

But towards the Christian era Judaism itself became less rigorous.[7] Whereas in human nature the divine image is so obscured that the likeness becomes un-likeness, in angelic nature it remains pure, so that God even orders its representation (Exod. 25.18-22; 1 Kgs. 6.23-32). This divine command is of capital importance; it means that, since the celestial world of the spirits has a human face, it can be artistically portrayed: on the Ark of the Covenant, the Old Testament has left us the carved icon of the cherubim.

Christ delivers humans from idolatry, not negatively by doing away with every image, but positively by revealing the true human face of God. While the divinity of Christ on its own eludes every attempt to represent it, the humanity on its own, separated from the divine, no longer means anything; it was the genius of the Fathers of the Seventh Council to proclaim that 'his humanity is itself the image of the divinity.' 'Whoever has seen me has seen the Father.' They affirmed the iconographic purpose of the visible: to be the image of the invisible.

The biblical basis of the icon is the creation of humankind in the image of God, which demonstrates a degree of conformity between the divine and the human and explains the union of the two natures in Christ. God is visible in the human, reflected there as in a mirror, for humankind is made in his image. God speaks the language of humanity. He also has a human face. Indeed, the best icon of God is humanity; when the priest censes the faithful during the liturgy he is doing the same thing as when he censes the icons: it is the Church greeting the image of God in human beings.

4. THE THEOLOGY OF EXPRESSION

By the same process of revelation the icon is also a 'visual Gospel', the Gospel in pictorial form. To the assertion of the iconoclasts, that 'the art of images has no basis in the economy of salvation,' the *oros* of the Seventh Council replies, 'The more the believer looks at icons, the more he remembers those whom they represent and tries to imitate them. He shows respect and veneration (*prokinesis*), without any actual adoration (*latreia*), which belongs only to God' – '*Confounded be all they that serve graven images!*'

The argument of the Fathers is interesting: the icon is the expression or likeness of what exists, whereas an idol represents what does not exist; it is a fabrication, a sham.[8] To idolatrize an icon is to destroy it; shutting up the represented person in a piece of wood makes an idol of it and renders that person non-existent.

---

[7] The Catacomb of the Vigna Randamini, the mosaics of the Synagogue of Hammam-Lif, the funerary chamber of Palmyra, Dura-Europos.
[8] Theodore the Studite. *P.G.* 199, 180; 345. Also Theodoret, *P.G.* 80, 264.

The icon is in no sense an incarnation, or even a place, but a visible sign of radiant invisible presence. 'The image bears the *name* of the original and not its *nature*.'[9] Therefore no ontology is 'graven', let alone defined, in an icon; only the name delineated and thus manifested in perfect reality, but spatially unconfined. The space you enter when you contemplate an icon imprisons nothing, but participates in the presence and is sanctified by it. The icon is nothing in its own right; it simply leads to the beings themselves. To sum up early Patristic thought, the purpose of the icon is to teach, to remind us constantly of God and to arouse in us the desire of imitation.[10] These first three benefits correspond to a real need: 'even someone who is perfect needs the image, just as he needs the book for the Gospel.'[11] Iconoclasm leads to the denial of the visible Church: 'And above all, the body and blood of the Lord, are they not matter?'[12] But the essential nature of the icon emerges only from the theology of presence, and it is here that the West departs from the East.

5. THE FATE OF THE ICON IN THE WEST

The 'Caroline Books', starting from a most unfortunate mistranslation[13] of the Latin text of the Seventh Council, called it *ineptissimae synodi*. Images were only for decoration and whether to have them or not was a matter of indifference. The Councils of Frankfurt in 794, and Paris in 852, decreed that images have no participatory relationship to their prototypes, and furthermore, 'it is not with paint that Christ saved us' ... nor with a book, we might add. Something of this attitude remains and perhaps explains the blind alleys of sacred art today. Even irruptions from the past, however influential, failed to get the upper hand; the doctrinal definitions concerning images were restricted to the merely utilitarian, ranging pedagogically from teaching to consolation.

Till the 11th and 12th centuries the arts fortunately lagged behind theological thought, continuing to view the created world as an 'illuminated book', of which they revealed the *invisibilia*; so we have the miracle of Chartres, of Romanesque

---

9 Seventh Council.
10 'When reason cannot grasp the meaning through words, the icon comes to our help' (Patriarch Nicephoras, *P.G.* 100, 380 D). 'If a pagan asks you to show him your faith, take him to the church and stand him in front of the holy icons' (St John Damascene, *P.G.* 95, 325 C). And finally the most important: 'By means of my bodily eyes which gaze on the icon, my spiritual life plunges into the mystery of the Incarnation' (St John Damascene, *P.G.* 96, 1360).
11 Theodore the Studite, *P.G.* 99, 1537.
12 St John Damascene, *P.G.* 94, 1300.
13 It called the Fathers of the Seventh Council 'worshippers of images'.

art, of Italian iconography, and later the visionary genius of Fra Angelico,[14] Simone Martini and many more besides. By the 13th century little of the 'Byzantine' style remained. Giotto, Duccio and Cimabue renounced the irrational reality of the world of 'the intelligible'. They introduced optical illusion (depth, created by perspective, and lighting) and art lost its transcendence. It broke with the 'canons', discovered its independence, and established itself in the secularized culture of the 14th century. The subjects – even the angels – are ultra-real individuals of flesh and blood. They are dressed and behave like everybody else; the image becomes contemporary with the artist. Before long, a sacred subject became a chance for the artist to demonstrate his skill in the techniques of landscape or anatomy. When he felt the wish to satisfy the desires of the soul, the spiritual voices were indistinct and sentimentality took over; sacred art degenerated into the merely religious. Art was now entirely human; from being firmly centred on the transcendent it was displaced towards portraiture, landscape and ornamentation.[15]

The Council of Trent regulated the honour due to images, explained their usefulness and gave directions for their use in very moderate terms.[16] Bossuet said that images of God 'must be rare, in obedience to the wishes of the Council, which leaves the bishops discretion as to when it might be necessary to forbid them.'[17] The real question remains unanswered: why did the easy solution, the three-dimensional statue, prevail over the infinitely more mysterious two-dimensional image?

Luther tolerated the image as an illustration; Calvin accepted only 'historical scenes' of a general nature. For Protestants, according to a recent commentator, there is no such thing as preaching through art, because art has no real significance.[18]

---

[14] Guilio Carlo Argan, in *Fra Angelico* (Geneva, Skira 1955) shows the angelic painter – alas! – as someone doctrinaire, a perfect Dominican.
[15] The obsession with 'ornamentation' explains the heavy-handed interventions by the authorities: the warnings to Veronese, the 'breeches makers' of the Sistine Chapel, the affair of the Christ of Assy...
[16] *Concil. Trident.* sess. XXV, in Denzinger, n. 986.
[17] *Culte des images*, vol. 1.
[18] Cf. *Réforme* of 5. 1. 1952, article 'les Arts'.

6. THE THEOLOGY OF PRESENCE

Since the time of the Crusades, the western Church, haunted by the vision of the Holy Land and the Holy Sepulchre, has been attracted, mystically, to the Cross. To gaze at length on Grunewald's reredos (which was even at the time practically a sermon by Luther) is deeply moving, but produces a tragic feeling of absence. The eastern Church, which never left Palestine, its native land, deepened its doctrinal understanding and concentrated on the Glory of God.[19] The Byzantine *Pantocrator*, though different from the humble Christ of the Gospels, moves us by his all-pervading presence.

---

[19] In the 4th and 5th centuries, and later in the 9th century, popular art of an emotional kind came out of Syria and Egypt and mingled with sacred art (extreme asceticism, by which every monk became as one crucified, gave rise to forms of piety that almost approached stigmatization and devotion to the Cross). The Byzantine icon, on the contrary, filters out any tendency to particularism and sticks closely to doctrine and liturgy. The essential point is this: western Christianity (especially in the period after the Crusades, which brought it into direct contact with Palestine, and in the cult of the Eucharist and of the Sacred Heart) is deeply devoted to the *suffering humanity* of Christ; eastern Christianity, however, which is more concerned with doctrine, goes infinitely further, only stopping on the threshold of unknowing, in the presence of the *unutterable* mystery of the παθών Θεός, the *suffering God*. The expression comes from St Gregory the Theologian, who, contemplating the Lamb sacrificed *before* the Incarnation, insists strongly on the *Passion* of Being, who is by definition *impassible*. St Cyril of Alexandria is equally insistent, as is St Maximus; and even that model of Antiochian sobriety, St John Chrysostom, says, 'We need the life and death *of a God* in order to live.' If we say that suffering affects human nature alone, are we not in danger of dividing the Person of Christ, like the Nestorians? Whilst keeping well away from any heretical theory of the 'patripassian' sort, we must say that the Passion certainly bears on the *Hypostasis* of the Word, not just on the humanity which is enhypostasized within it and cannot be separated. Eastern Christology is founded on the perichoresis, the communication of idioms. Beyond that we cannot go; further theological analysis is impossible, so the rest must be 'venerated in silence'... Christology certainly comes to a stop, not with a simplistic definition because of the poverty of its subject, but in a silence which according to St Maximus is 'privation by excess' (*Quaest. ad Thal.* XIV). Nevertheless, nothing but a dizzying flight of doctrine can account for the eastern theology of glory. The theology of the Cross has its proper place but does not predominate. The Mystery comes to fulfilment in the sealed tomb and bursts it by the pressure of triumphant life that is already filled with the Parousia. The Cross is the pre-eternal, therefore unutterable, vehicle of the divine love.

While the Roman Mass achieves its purpose in the renewal of the unbloody sacrifice of the altar, the Orthodox Liturgy goes beyond that to announce the Ascension and the Parousia. That is why the crucified Christ of the Orthodox icons will always keep the regal bearing of the *divine* Conqueror, for he has conquered *death itself*, not just the death of a man, Jesus of Nazareth. The raising of Lazarus has no universal human significance except that of prefiguration.

So we are in the presence of a mystery that the icon can convey better than any words; as St John Chrysostom says, 'I call him King because I see him crucified' (*P.G.* 49, 413). The icon of the Nativity is just as profound. The black cave in which the child lies represents hell. In order to triumph *mystically* over the Kingdom of Satan, Christ is born under the earth, at the very heart of the Fall. This deepens our understanding of Baptism: the baptized dies with Christ and *descends into hell* in order to rise again with Christ and enter the Kingdom here and now (see P. Evdokimov, 'L'Icône de la Nativité', *Bible et Vie Chrétienne*, No 20).

Essentially, in the eastern Church the icon is a sacramental of presence, receiving a miraculous character from the rite by which it is consecrated: 'Channel of divine strength and grace,'[20] the place of 'phanies'.[21] The Seventh Council explicitly stated, 'Whether by contemplation of Scripture or by the representation of the icon ... we are reminded of all the prototypes and *are brought into their presence*.'[22] And the Council of 860: 'What the book tells us in words, the icon tells us in colours, and makes it *present* to us.'[23] 'When my thoughts torment me and I cannot savour the reading, I go to the church ... at this enthralling vision my soul rises up to praise God. I think of the valour of the martyr ... his zeal enflames me ... I fall to the ground in adoration and pray to God with the aid of the martyr's intercession' (St John Damascene[24]). For the martyr is present through his office of intercession and communion.

Indeed, the icon is nothing in itself – a wooden board – but, precisely because it derives all its significance from participating in the 'wholly other', it cannot contain anything; it becomes one of a network of points of radiation where the Presence, itself entirely unlocalized, can be encountered. The icon merely communicates it, 'as if we saw it face to face.'[25] Since there is no solidity, there can be no materialism; in western piety a statue may come to life, but an eastern icon never can, for the radiant presence concentrated there comes from outside. Its significance is closely tied to the liturgical theology of presence, which clearly distinguishes an icon from a religious picture. An ordinary work of art is locked into a triangle of aesthetic immanentism: the artist, the work executed, and the spectator whose emotions are aroused. And if the emotion should take a religious form, that is only due to the subjective capacity of this or that spectator to have an experience that could be had anywhere else. St John of the Cross expresses himself in very western terms when he classifies images among 'emotive objects that work through the feelings.' Now, sacred art is precisely opposed to all that is charming and appealing, to any sweet accord with romantic souls; rather, it is marked by a certain hieratic dryness and an ascetical process of stripping away.

The icon, by its sacramental character, destroys the triangle together with its immanentism. It asserts its independence both of the artist and of the spectator, and arouses no emotion; instead of the triangle it introduces a fourth element, the transcendent, *whose presence it announces*. It is the tradition that speaks, while the artist is behind, out of sight; the work of art becomes a springing up of

---

[20] St John Damascene, *On Holy Images*, I, 16.
[21] I.e., 'manifestations'.
[22] Mansi, vol. 13, col. 482.
[23] Mansi, vol. 16, col. 400.
[24] See the exposition of doctrine in his three discourses, *P.G.* 94, 1231-1420.
[25] Nicephoras, *P.G.* 100, 381.

the presence, a theophany,[26] not just a thing to look at, but something before which we must fall down in worship and prayer.

A picture fixes, reproduces visually something which no longer exists (in its concrete form as we remember it) and thereby witnesses to the absence or non-existence of what it portrays; that is what is so striking and poignant about photographs – time is irreversible; the same face can never be captured twice.

An icon, however, provides only the bare necessities for 'narrative' and thereafter abandons any attempt at a copy, which can only be partial and ephemeral, but rather 'presents' – *renders present* – the essential nature of the original. The icon satisfies the only truly biblical desire – that for the absolutely new, the absolutely desirable, the Kingdom of God; it invokes and proclaims a form of the Parousia, here and now. It is truly paradoxical that the visible body of the Church constructed by iconography is really its *invisible* body, its place of manifestation. Apophatic theology and asceticism forbid any image and all imagination in the mystical life, and yet they approve and prescribe the icon. The icon, in its very symbolism, arrives at an apophaticism of its own, suppressing all illustration, never delineating or reifying the transcendent; it delineates the presence, and its strict rules safeguard the spiritual from any sensory objectification. Everything on this side of the boundary of fire is no longer an icon, no longer a miracle. We sink into the most monstrous deformations of the sacred, of a highly dubious nature. There is a world of difference between the Bible and a theological textbook, or between the sacrament as an act and a conference about the sacrament. The human imagination, when not filled with the Spirit, is pathetically impoverished, like paper flowers that have never known the morning dew.[27] The insane attempt to make a portrait of the Holy Spirit shows God the Father as a senile old man and the *Theotokos* as a seductive woman.

7. SIGNS AND SYMBOLS

A sign, such a shop sign or signpost, tells or teaches us something, or points somewhere. A symbol is related to what it symbolizes by belonging to it and communicating with its essence.

In the catacombs we see art that is purely significative. Its simple and immediate purpose is to proclaim and explain salvation in coded signs. These fall into three categories: 1. those related to water – Noah's Ark, Jonah, Moses, the fish,

---

[26] I.e., a 'manifestation of God'.

[27] It is symptomatic that the canons forbid the mass reproduction of icons by printing on paper, and similarly the commercial selling of them – at the most they can be exchanged. Present practice bears the marks of very recent decadence.

the anchor; 2. those related to bread and wine – the multiplication of the loaves, ears of corn, the vine; and finally, 3. images of salvation and the saved – the children in the burning fiery furnace, Daniel in the lions' den, the phoenix, the raising of Lazarus, the Good Shepherd. People are portrayed with just enough realism to demonstrate a saving action, such as the raising of the dead, or the rescue of someone who is perishing. There is a complete disregard of artistic form and no attempt at any theological interpretation. The Good Shepherd in no way represents Christ, but means: the Saviour really saves. Daniel in the lions' den is shown together with the Praying Woman, the sign of the saved soul. They are drawings, economical and striking, speaking of salvation *through the sacraments* of Baptism and the Eucharist. A contemporary Greek inscription clearly explains the art of the catacombs: 'I, Abercius, am the disciple of the holy Shepherd who feeds his flocks on hills and plains ... Everywhere faith has been my guide, and everywhere it has given me for food Fish from the Spring, mighty and pure, which the spotless Virgin caught and offers to her friends, always having sweet Wine mixed with Water which she gives with the Bread ... Let him who understands and believes this pray for Abercius'.[28]

It is all summed up in one message: outside Christ and his sacraments there is no eternal life. All is reduced to the one sign of joy: the resurrection of the dead is engraved on the sarcophagi (meaning 'those who chew the flesh') are vanquished. Art, having completely negated itself, has reached the decisive moment of its own destiny. The perfect form it reached in antiquity, so very recently, is now for the moment useless; it renounces itself, undergoes death, is immersed in the waters of Baptism, and is inscribed and preserved in the graffiti of the catacombs, to emerge from this baptismal font at the dawn of the 4th century in a form never seen before, that of the icon. Art is resurrected in Christ: neither sign nor picture, but the icon, the symbol of presence, doctrine made visible and revealed for eternity.

8. THE ICON AND THE LITURGY

We shall never understand the icon unless we remember the most important thing: that all the parts of the Temple – its architectural lines, frescos, icons – are *integrated* into the liturgical mystery. The Liturgy itself in its entirety is the icon of the whole economy of salvation.

At the singing of the *Cherubicon*, 'We who mystically *represent* the Cherubim and who sing to the life-giving Trinity the thrice-holy hymn'[29] are actually pres-

---

[28] L. Wilpert, *Fractio panis*, p. 116-117.
[29] We might even say, 'We who are the mysterious icon of the Cherubim.'

ent in the divine Liturgy. Christ is attended by angels with innumerable eyes and myriads of rustling wings, the divine Trinity participates in the Mystery, and we also, to such a point that we become icons of the cherubim. The Liturgy here below is the icon of the celestial Liturgy, and people are the icons of the angelic ministry of adoration and prayer. All is participation and presence. Every particle of created being, by virtue merely of existing, repeats the eucharistic prayer, 'Of thine own do we offer to thee.' In this tremendous congregation, the believer contemplates the mystery of God, sees his elders, the Apostles, martyrs and saints, really present, and enters with them into the celestial realm; sharing in the liturgy of the angels, he praises the Spirit of Beauty: 'In thy holy icons we contemplate the heavenly tabernacles and rejoice with holy joy.'[30]

The dome crowned with the cross is the point of encounter with the heavenly world. Heaven penetrates within, fills the dome and reveals the *Pantocrator* between the Angels of Presence. The icon called 'the righteous in the hand of God' shows them ascending towards the open hand of the *Pantocrator* to form the sacred *sobor*.[31] Plants cling to the columns and put forth flowers of Paradise, animals swarm at their bases. With a powerful gesture, the hand of God directs all towards the liturgical heart, the icon of the Lord's Supper over the royal doors.

In the central apse, halfway between the dome and the ground, we see the *Theotokos* as *Orans* or 'Indestructible Wall'. She is *Hodegetria*, the Church on earth which 'guides' all people to join together in the Body of Christ. The icon faces west. Below it, the cross on the wall marks the direction from which Christ of Glory will come to occupy the throne represented by the holy table that stands in the sanctuary; the throne is that of the Judge but also of the Bridegroom celebrating the mystical marriage with his Bride the Church. The icon of the Synaxis shows the host of angels. The eternal Son himself forms the exact centre of the triple circle of the spheres. This is the celestial Liturgy, and the angels reveal Christ – the Great High Priest – so that 'the light of the gospel of the glory of Christ, who is the image of God' (2 Cor. 4.4) may shine in the eyes of believers. The cosmic joy that surrounds the *Theotokos* resolves itself into expectation of the Kingdom. And so, in a church, at every moment and even outside the time of services, everything is in a state of waiting for the holy mysteries, waiting for the Eucharist. The thrilling sensation of unceasing life emanates from these presences reaching up towards the celestial Liturgy.

[30] Office of the first Sunday in Lent.
[31] Sobor or synaxis: the congregation of the faithful celebrating the Liturgy.

9. DIVINE ART

The whole of art is the life of forms, but sacred art deals with forms of the invisible, the life of liturgical forms. The icon is a miracle of faith. The most perfect technique, the most daring new style is always affecting, but by itself it remains a 'human document', human in its religion, ephemeral. The power of an icon comes from its content, it reveals the Spirit. The iconographer introduces us to the supra-sensible; empirical reality becomes indistinct compared with the prototypes of the divine. It is because of its 'divine' character that this art requires such apparently rigid canons to govern it. These, combined with ascetic preparation, train the imagination so that its visions are never at odds with true doctrine. The very conservatism that ensures the continuity of the archetypes also liberates the imagination to find the best form of expression and the richest interpretation. 'The Guide for Iconographers,'[32] which sets out the rules of sacred art, keeps the icon from becoming bland and protects it from subjective piety and the fluctuation of shallow fashions.

Architecture is concerned with space, the liturgical memorial with time, the icon with the invisible. So the proper business of the icon is the 'essences' present in it; it reveals the hidden spiritual order. It is not abstract; it is figurative, but in no sense a portrait. It appeals to the eyes of the spirit, making them see the 'spiritual bodies' of which St Paul speaks. Every emotional flourish, dramatic gesture or attitude, all agitation is utterly suppressed. The key to all icons is the 'acheiropoietic' (not made by hands) icon of the Holy Face of the Saviour; it is on a veil held up by angels for us to see, precisely not a portrait of Jesus, but the icon of his presence. Similarly any narrative content is reduced to a bare reminder, for what is represented transcends history. The martyrs do not carry the instruments of their torment, they are already above earthly history – they are there, but in a different way. An icon depicts a saint as he exists in the mind of God. According to St John Climacus, a hermit represents 'the earthly form of an angel.' Sacred art does not disembody, but dematerializes the essences and reveals the transparent matter as subject to the service of the spirit.

Profane art follows optical laws that cast their net over things, pulling them together into a homogeneous vision of the world. These are the laws of the world that is fallen, external and atomized. Unity of action gathers time together; unity of perspective gathers space; the eye sees everything through a grid formed of *a priori* assumptions. It is a 'point of view', an optical illusion, useful for daily life; but there is far more to the eye than this, and there are many points of view.

---

[32] There is a similar 'guide' dating from the 11th century on Mount Athos, entitled Ἑρμηνεία τῆς Ζωγραφικῆς. A French translation was published in 1849 by Didron (Paris, Imprimerie royale) under the title, *Manual d'iconographie chrétienne*.

By an ingenious hoax the eye is deceived by the converging lines of a picture into seeing a depth that is entirely false. Cubism and modern art seek to escape from these laws, but they dissect and rearrange everything and do not reconstruct. The iconographers are perfectly aware of 'techniques' but never make them the condition of their own art. Their art is perfectly oblivious of material reality as everyday sight perceives it, but insists on its own principles and teaches the spectator true vision. It is a complete science that makes us aware of the 'intelligible' world, so that we can almost 'touch' it. Thus, the relative dimensions of material objects play no part in an icon; nature is not imitated, but traced in its essential interior form and shown subdued to the human spirit. Space and time are treated with complete freedom and all the innovations of the abstract painters left far behind. Everything is deployed outside the space-prison; the proper importance of each subject is apparent to the eyes of the spirit according to the way it is arranged and the splendour in which it is depicted. The flat technique allows the position of each part to be considered independently while safeguarding the balance of the whole composition.

There are icons in which the perspective[33] is reversed, where the lines converge towards the onlooker, creating the impression that the people are coming out to meet him. Instead of the two physical eyes with their dual vision ruled by the 'vanishing point' of fallen space, the eye of the heart sees spiritual space expanding into infinity (the good infinity which expands, not the bad infinity of the vanishing point which closes in). The precise point from which the reversed perspective springs is in the heart of the person looking at the icon. Weights and masses disappear, and the gilded lines, penetrating everywhere like rays of deifying energy, spiritualize the bodies. *Homo terrenus* becomes *homo caelestis*, light, carefree, winged. The bodies seem to merge into the ethereal gold of divine light. The gold background replaces three-dimensional space.[34] At the same time, the freedom to arrange each figure independently leaves room for marvellous flexibility in subordinating everything to the centre of the composition. In a church, the bodies are accommodated to the lines of the vaults, and modified accordingly, becoming elongated where necessary with a vigorous movement towards the centre. By catholicity it all becomes a harmonious and ordered assembly.

The absence of natural forms brings the spiritual dimension astonishingly close in all its depth. The body is traced lightly, and is divined rather than seen through the stately folds of the vestments; their linear near-dryness does not draw attention to the anatomy but directs the gaze towards the inner reality. Moreover

---

[33] W. de Grunlisen, *La perspective, esquisse de son évolution des origines jusqu'à la Renaissance*, Ecole fr. de Rome, Mélanges d'arch. et d'hist., 1911 (XXXI), p. 393.
[34] For the significance of the gold background, see Worringer, *Griechentum und Gotik*.

all is dominated by the face. The iconographer begins with the head, which determines the size and the position of the body and governs the rest of the composition. Even the cosmic elements have a human face, humankind being the cosmic
word.[35] The much enlarged eyes are fixed on the transcendent world. The fine
lips lack all sensuality (for the passions or eating); they are for singing praise,
consuming the Eucharist and giving the kiss of peace. The nose is merely the
finest curve, the forehead broad and high, lightly distorted to emphasize the preoccupation with contemplative thought. The dark tint of the faces suppresses
every realistic and sensual note. The frontal position does not distract the sight
with dramatic attitudes or gestures. Whereas the profile interrupts communion,
and soon becomes absence, the full face establishes communion by plunging the
gaze into the eyes of the spectator. The motionlessness of the bodies, which is
however never static, concentrates all the dynamism in the expression of the face.
All anxiety, care and restlessness vanishes in the presence of inner peace. By
contrast, demons and sinners are shown in profile and exhibit great agitation,
which is to say incapacity for contemplation. The landscape consists of the most
perfunctory geometric forms, no more than a suggested cosmic background
against which the man-*pneuma* is displayed. Plants and buildings have no intrinsic importance but are useful in drawing attention to the arrangement of the bodies and contributing to the symbolism of the composition.

The colours are never drab or gloomy. Except for some (gold, purple, azure,
etc.) they can lighten or darken as they follow the linear pattern. They leap out
to strike the eye, astonishing in their joyful intensity. Pale blue, vermilion, clear
green, pistachio, ultramarine, purple and scarlet are used in many varying shades
which, speaking to one another in an infinite shimmering, reflect the divine light.
The Transfiguration streams with gold, but where Christ's humanity predominates, other colours are used to signify kenosis.[36] There is a whole science of
light. There is never any chiaroscuro, nor any shadows to show relief, for in the
world of the icon the sun never sets; it is day without dusk, the brilliant noonday
of the Incarnation, without shadow or darkness. Every gradation is achieved
purely by the contrast of colours, without any artifice of lighting or point of view.
The artist separates the important from the secondary by patches of different density. In the whole work he follows the method of progressive 'clarification', going
from dark to bright. The source of the light is absent, for the light is within the
icon, which itself illuminates the details of its composition.[37]

---

[35] It is interesting to note the prohibition by the Synod of 692 (canon 82) of the symbolic representation of Christ – as a lamb or fish – 'because the thing itself' has supplanted its prefig-
urement.
[36] Kenosis or self-emptying: when Christ humbled himself in taking on humanity.
[37] The success of Rublev's 'Trinity' lies in the equal radiance of the three angels – the trisolar
light illumines whoever contemplates it.

Paradoxically, it is the outward immobility of the faces that creates the strong impression that everything is moving within: 'We advance because we have come to a stop,' 'the well of living water,' 'unmoving motion' – the icon perfectly illustrates these paradoxes in mystical language, in which all description is powerless. The material surface seems absorbed in expectation of the message, the gaze alone translates all the tension of the energies into life.

'Divine art' presupposes grace, the gift of prophecy: 'To those who know and accept the prophetic visions, in the shapes and forms that God himself has given them and that the choir of prophets profess to have seen, who also hold the tradition, written or oral, that has come from the Apostles down to the Fathers, and who, for that reason, represent holy things in images and venerate them: memory eternal.'[38]

10. MODERN ART AND THE PRESENT STATE OF THE ICON[39]

The present crisis in sacred art is not aesthetic but religious. From the royal door at Chartres to the Archangel Michael, from the icon of Rublev to the Italianizing Russian schools of the 17th century, we can see a progressive waning of the sense of the sacred. The sacred is displaced by the aesthetically 'beautiful', the genuinely religious is eclipsed by the narrative or anecdotal, the pleasing, the portrait, the complicated. Instead of the sacred, we have works of art with religious subjects.

There also exists an intellectual iconoclasm which turns the Bible into the Koran. It is a crisis of growth, of sensibility still in search of balance. Apophaticism – the negation of every form of expression – means nothing unless it is balanced by positive cataphaticism, to which the former gives its true meaning.[40] Psychological and sociological theories of art explain only those parts of it that are not artistic. On the other hand, reducing art to pedagogy is ruinous and leads to the

---

[38] The Greek Synodikon – Office of the first Sunday in Lent.
[39] The Academy of Sciences in Soviet Russia undertook the publication in 12 volumes of a History of Russian Art. The first three volumes were entirely given up to church architecture and iconography. Since it was a scientific work, the history had to begin in a objective way with the iconography which alone could explain all the later forms of the culture of old Russia. Exhibitions and films in modern Soviet Russia portray icons and churches as 'historical monuments'! But the material is explosive and full of surprises. 'If people should hold their peace, the stones would immediately cry out,' says the Evangelist. Where apostolic work is forbidden and the word reduced to silence, the stones, the 'monuments' begin to cry out, to preach...
It is surely symptomatic that UNESCO, wishing to produce something of its own to the USSR brought out a wonderful book of icons!
[40] True knowledge is possible only because of things that we shall never know. So, for example, a geometric point occupies no space, for it is by nature metaspatial, metaphysical, despite the mysterious 'locus'. (Zero and place value are more mysterious still.)

pompous realism of Soviet art. To understand a work of art we need to discover, not its human origin, but its miraculous element; this cannot be deduced from looking at the materials in front of us; these are only the 'debris' of an unpredictable process of creation. We are looking for an inner purpose, its mysterious birth.

The phenomenological method effectively challenges the subjectiveness of the emotions, which can never be relied on as a measure of beauty. Indeed, art reveals the 'essences', introduces humanity to them, and so reveals it to itself and perfects it, convincing it of non-intellectual principles of truth. Reality is never represented or imitated, but expressed. Art, therefore, contains within itself its own expressive truth. In music there is neither concept nor image, but its world is eminently true. Hegel's assertion, that art had been killed by thought, is now being contradicted. The truth is quite the opposite: art goes beyond thought; we can even say that in the perpetual conflict between the philosophy of the true and the philosophy of the good, art offers a unique synthesis.[41] By a roundabout way – despite the fear of Platonism – metaphysics is returning: we already recognize that a work of art does not *have*, but *is* metaphysical significance. The phenomenological method in art leads to a metaphysic in action – to beauty. It is increasingly believed that because art belongs partly in the realm of transcendence it involves 'pure creative activity'; we hear of the 'superessential *aura*' that surrounds it.[42] The surrealists – poets and artists – invent a world by stripping this world of its objective reality, in order to discover whether there is another realm of existence beyond it. Thus has art led to a longing for transcendence, to a presentiment or expectation of it – *eros* stops at its threshold. Something more is needed before that realm can be revealed. Art is overtaken by art.

But today we must again distinguish between the form and the formless, between passing fantasies and the growth of the sacred style of atheism – the 'positive nothingness' of existentialism comes with a supporting ideology. Art seems to have been emancipated from any 'canon' and aspires to the resounding title of 'theurgic', in the same way as spells and enchantments and other forms of occultism, with their false metaphysical coating – hence the fashion for negro masks, Mexican blood-magic, the ecstatic effect of mescaline, the masonic symbolism of the anti-Church, compositions inspired by reinforced concrete, or the atom or fusion, plastic images of pure speed, wire sculpture. Oppressed and suffocated by the universe around us, we are driven to seek protection where there is none to be had, or to make excuses that cannot be justified. The immense long-

---

[41] In the Old Testament (as opposed to Hellenistic society) what is heard takes precedence over what is seen, but in the Messianic period vision becomes pre-eminent: *Hear, O Israel* becomes *Lift up your eyes and look*. In the New Testament, from the Resurrection of Christ onwards events are already in the realm of eschatology, and the 'blessed shall see God'; similarly Revelation puts vision, iconography at the centre (see G. Kittel, *Die Religionsgeschichte und das Urchristentum*).
[42] M. Souriau, *L'Ombre de Dieu*, Paris.

ing at the heart of our shut-off existence flings itself into the frenzy of modern dance, the procession that leads nowhere.

The falsities and disguises are denounced, but the accuser goes away feeling that he too is playing a role – that of the 'Juge-pénitent' of Camus.[43] The clear-sightedness, the 'optimistic hardness' of a stricken conscience sees only an endless solitude in which to be observed by others is a hindrance and a restriction. It is born in the ontological breach between a world that cannot bear to be watched and the biblical world watched over by God. 'Your eye is the lamp of your body ... if it is not healthy, your body is full of darkness. Therefore consider whether the light in you is not darkness' (Luke 11.34-35). Here is a whole philosophy of art. The eye does not only capture, it emits and lightens. Every artist has the terrible power to remake the world in his image, to project on to it the devastated landscape and shadows of his own soul, to impose on others the vision of an immense sewer teeming with deformed monsters...

Recent exhibitions have demonstrated clearly that the clever decompositions of Picasso or the mannered games of Salvador Dali are now superseded; they already seem old-fashioned – modern forms do not outlive their fame. Art today is the arrangement of pure forms and colours without any content. So painting is like modern music that has no melody and conveys only desolation (cf. *musique 'concrète'*). Although it has no content and is essentially cerebral, art is glutted with countless earthbound forms, without any symbolism or key by which to make sense of them, and so therefore meaningless. True art expresses what cannot otherwise be expressed; there is always communication, revelation, presence. Reducing it to a new language without roots in the past – pictorial Esperanto – without any depth of culture to give it meaning, without anything to say, turns it into pure sound, mere amusement; or rather, into a cry of pain which is false as soon as uttered, because going to the trouble to express pain aesthetically is nonsense. The emptier the pure form, the more varied the ways it can be used in compositions; but as soon as it is required to say something, there will be one and only one composition that fits the content so perfectly that it can be represented and embodied in its very structure, and properly reclothed with what we call beauty. The absence of melody in music, and of the human subject in art, the abolition of boundaries, unrestricted freedom of expression, demonstrate the drastic shrinking, the *limiting of the soul*: these eruptions are going on outside the intolerable littleness of the soul. To be unlimited within the limits of the closed world really transcends nothing. It is the art of the 'in camera', of arabesques which have not even the Islamic grandeur of translating the terrible transcendence of God. The divine unlimitedness, however, takes very precise form in the Incarnation – it limits itself to human forms. The hieratic character of the saints, their al-

---

[43] Camus, *The Fall*, Paris 1956.

most rigid immobility, their exterior limitedness conveys *the true unlimitedness of their spirit*. 'From the image of Christ we lift the eyes of our spirit to the unlimited image of God.'[44] 'By thy nature, certainly, thou art unlimited, but thou Lord hast desired to reduce thyself under the veil of the flesh.'[45] In this transcendence-immanence God is present, but all the humanity is there.

Modern art, however, is very significant as a phenomenon. Its titanism on a human scale has brought liberation from every prejudice, it has destroyed the horrors of recent centuries, and for that reason is refreshing; it has killed off the bad taste of the 19th century. The exterior form has been defeated. But here, just as in the time of the catacombs, art has reached its intrinsic limit and, obeying its inner dialectic, now faces the inevitable ultimate choice, not between life and death, but between living in order to die and dying in order to live. No more evolution is possible, for the key to understanding the correspondences is lost; the breach between sacred transcendence and 'religious immanence' is so radical that there can be no straightforward evolution from one level to the other. Access to the inner, eternal form is barred by the angel with the flaming sword. It is necessary to pass through Baptism, which is death, in order to rise again, not this time in the earthly light of the Gospel and kenosis, but in the apocalyptic brilliance of the human face of God; not this time the face of the gentle Jesus, but the tremendous and dazzling human features of the Trinitarian God.

What makes the situation of art even worse is that iconography itself has not yet emerged from its own crisis of four centuries. After the rediscovery of the icon at the end of the 19th century, the conservatism of the 'copyists' brought the art to a standstill, turned it into a petrified art, without posterity. Modern iconography must take account of all the techniques down to the present, then from within its own time contemplate the 'wholly other'. The 'real life situation' of iconography today requires an unforced receptivity to the new sanctity, the spreading abroad of the abundant mercy that we associate with the charity of the *bowels of Christ*; it requires initiation into the 'brotherhood of the crucified ones.' From charismatic inspiration, from the prophecies of the last days, there must arise a wholly new eschatological interpretation of destiny. The King has come, but his Kingdom has not; the last mystery of the 'grain of wheat' will be the return of the world to its inner, royal shape. This going back to the source will be neither in the present with its modern techniques, nor exclusively in the past, but essentially in the glory to come. The new icon will rediscover its origins and will close its sacred circle on the parousial Gospel of Glory.

The liturgy teaches us today more than yesterday that art decays not because it is the child of its time and a sinner, but because it is demonic in its renunciation

---

[44] Theodore the Studite, *P.G.* 99, 1193.
[45] Office of the first Sunday in Lent.

of its priestly functions, in its Luciferian refusal to perform the sacrament: that of making theophanic art. It is the office of the Paraclete, when the shadow of death is at its darkest, to set the icon of the Angel of the Presence in the midst of the graveyards of buried hopes. It is for the human being – 'the labourer of the eleventh hour' – to understand the vocation to be 'priest and prophet of the heavenly mysteries,' in the magnificent words of St Macarius of Egypt.

To give a taste of the richness of the iconosophic vision, to understand how the icon is drawn speech, we give a very brief commentary on the famous icon of the Holy Trinity of Rublev.

11. INTERPRETATION OF THE ICON OF RUBLEV

1. In 1515 the Cathedral of the Assumption at Moscow had just been decorated with splendid icons executed by the pupils of the great master Rublev. When the metropolitan, the bishops and the people entered, they all cried out with one accord, 'Truly, the heavens are open to reveal the glory of God.' We can well understand their reaction to the icon of icons, the icon of the Holy Trinity, executed in 1425 by the monk Andrei Rublev. About 150 years later the 'Council of the 100 Chapters' upheld it as a model of iconography and of all representations of the Holy Trinity.

In 1904 the commission of restoration removed its metal ornaments, and when the later coatings had been stripped off, the icon was displayed in such brilliance that the members of the commission literally fell back in amazement. There is certainly nothing anywhere else to equal it, in its power of theological synthesis, its rich symbolism or its supreme artistic beauty.

2. There are three distinct superimposed planes. The first recalls the biblical account of the visit of the three pilgrims to Abraham's house (Gen. 18.1-15). The liturgical commentary decodes it thus: 'Blessed art thou Abraham, who in seeing them hast received the one and threefold divinity.' And already the omission of the figures of Abraham and Sarah invites us to penetrate more deeply and move to the second plane, that of the 'divine economy'. The three heavenly pilgrims constitute the 'eternal Council', and the significance of the landscape changes: the tent of Abraham becomes the palace-temple; the oak of Mamre, the tree of life; the cosmos is shaped symbolically into a cup, a gentle reminder of his presence; the calf on a dish is replaced by the cup of the Eucharist.

The three angels, light and slender, possess very elongated bodies (fourteen times the head, rather than the normal seven). The angels' wings, like the landscape, are somewhat diagrammatic, giving the immediate impression of something immaterial, the absence of any terrestrial heaviness. The inverted perspective abolishes depth, in which everything disappears in the distance, and works in the opposite direction to bring the figures nearer, showing that God is there and everywhere. The group forms a winged vision of joyful lightness, which is the secret of Rublev's genius.

The three persons are in conversation – their subject ought to be the text of John: 'God so loved the world that he gave his only Son.' And the Word of God is always an act; it takes shape in the cup.

The third plane concerns the inner divine life, which is only suggested, being transcendent and inaccessible. It is present, however, inasmuch as the economy of salvation stems from the interior life of God.

3. God is love in himself in his threefold essence, and his love towards the world is only the reflection of his Trinitarian love. The gift of himself, which is never a loss, but the expression of the superabundance of love, is symbolized by the cup; the angels are gathered around the divine food. The work of restorers has revealed the contents of the cup. A cluster of grapes had been painted over the original design, the Lamb – which connects the heavenly Meal to the words of the Revelation: the Lamb slain from the foundation of the world. The love, the sacrifice, the immolation precede the act of creation of the world, they are there at the beginning.

The three angels are in repose, enjoying the sublime peace of the self-existent being, but this repose is 'intoxicating' – it is genuine ecstasy, 'going out of oneself.' This ecstasy alone contains the whole mysterious paradox, of which St Gregory of Nyssa remarks, 'The greatest paradox of all is that that rest and movement should be the same thing.'

The movement leaves from the left foot of the angel on the right, continues in the inclination of his head, passes to the angel in the middle, sweeps the cosmos – the rock and the tree – irresistibly along with it, and is resolved in the vertical position of the angel on the left, where it comes to rest, as in a receptacle. Beside this circular movement, of which the completion governs all that precedes it, as eternity governs time, the vertical element of the temple and the sceptres indicates the yearning of the earthly for the heavenly, where the upward momentum reaches its end.

4. This vision of God shines out from the transcendent truth of doctrine. Rublev's conception of the angels breathes unity and equality – and one angel could be mistaken for another; the difference comes from the personal bearing of each one towards the others; however there is neither repetition nor confusion. The gold gleaming on an icon always indicates divinity, the overflowing richness of God; the angels' wings overspread everything, the soft blue underneath emphasizing the unity and the heavenly character of the one nature. One only God and three perfectly equal Persons, symbolized by the identical sceptres, signs of the royal power with which each angel is endowed. The divine form of the threefold unity looks at us, transcends our divisions and our separations. This imperial call acts by virtue of the divine reality alone, by virtue simply of its existence.

5. The geometric forms in the composition are the rectangle, the cross, the triangle and the circle. They form the internal structure of the image and they have to be

discovered. At that time the earth was thought to be either octagonal or rectangular; we see a rectangle, the hieroglyph of the earth, on the lower part of the table.[46] The upper part of the table itself is also rectangular, signifying the four sides of the world, the four cardinal points which, according to the Fathers of the Church, symbolized the four Gospels in their fullness, to which nothing can be added and from which nothing can be taken away; it is the sign of the universality of the Word. This upper part of the table-altar represents the Bible offering us the cup, the fruit of the Word. If we extend the line of the tree of life (behind the angel in the middle) it descends across the table and dips its roots in the rectangle of the earth; it is announced by the Word and fed from the cup. So the mystery – why it bears the fruits of eternal life, why it is the tree of life – is explained. On Christmas Eve we hear, 'The angel with the fiery sword goes away from the tree of life' for its fruits are given in the Eucharist.

There is a movement in the angels' hands converging towards the sign of the earth, the point at which the divine Love is communicated. The world, being of a different nature, is outside God, but included in the sacred circle of the 'communion of the Father'; it describes a circular path through the heavenly space from the rock to the palace-temple, where its circle is completed. The temple is like the extension of the Angel-Christ, of his incarnation. It is his cosmic body, the Church, the bride of the Lamb united to him 'without separation and without confusion.' The temple remains immobile in the repose of the great Sabbath – the end of the Trinitarian movement. The cycle of the cosmic liturgy is closed. It is the eschatological vision of the new Jerusalem. The gilded part of the temple which juts forward, offering protection, symbolizes the maternal protection of the *Theotokos* and of the priesthood of the saints; it stands for the Virgin's veil, the *Pokrov*.

According to tradition, it is from the tree of life that the wood was taken for Christ's cross. It is only implicit in the composition, but very evident nonetheless. An invisible vertical line passes through the aureole or luminous circle of the Father, the cup and the sign of the earth, dividing the icon in two. It forms a cross with the horizontal line that joins the luminous circles of the angels at the sides. So the cross is inscribed within the sacred circle of the divine life; it is the living axis of the love of the Trinity. 'The Father is the love that crucifies, the Son is love crucified, the Holy Spirit is the cross of love, its unconquerable power'. There is movement through the branches of the cross, which, like the outstretched arms of Christ, enfold the universe: 'And I, when I am lifted up from the earth, will draw all people to myself' (John 12.32). The Son and the Spirit are the two hands of the Father. If we join the extremities of the table to a point just above the head of the angel in the middle, an equilateral triangle is formed, signifying the unity and equality of the Trinity of which the apex is the πηγαία Θεότης, the

---

[46] Cosmas Indicopleustes, the great voyager of the 6th century, asserts in his *Christian Topography* that the world is oblong.

The Church at Prayer

Father. And finally, the line that follows the external outlines of the three angels forms a perfect circle, the sign of divine eternity. The centre of the circle is the hand of the Father, the *Pantocrator*.

6. There is something monumental in the attitude of the Father, conveying hieratic peace and stillness, pure act, completeness, changelessness and eternity; but in striking contrast, the crescent-shaped movement of the right arm, its powerful curve corresponding to a similar power in the inclination of the neck and head, displays energy. This synthesis of immobility and movement sums up the ineffable mystery of God: the Absolute of the philosophers, the Pure Act of the theologians, and the living God of the Bible, 'our Father which art in heaven.'

The Creed begins, 'I believe in God the Father Almighty;' the divine power is the paternal power of the love of the Father, as we see in the gaze of the angel in the middle. He is Love, and precisely because of that he can reveal himself only in communion and be known only as communion. 'No one comes to the Father except through me' (John 14.6); and on the other hand, 'No one can come to me unless drawn by the Father who sent me' (John 6.44). There is no evangelical exclusiveness in this, only the most moving revelation of the essential nature of love. We can have no knowledge of God at all outside the communication between humankind and God, and that is always Trinitarian and admits us to the communion between the Father and the Son. That is why the Father never reveals himself directly. He is the Source, and because of that he is Silence. He reveals himself eternally, but only through the biunity of the Son and the Holy Spirit. The icon shows that communion of which the burning heart is the cup.

The lines, from the right side of the middle angel, are amplified little by little as they approach the angel on the left. In the symbolic language of lines, the convex curves always indicate expression, speaking, movement, revelation; concave curves, by contrast, signify obedience, patience, humility, receptiveness. The Father is turned towards his Son. He speaks. The movement which runs through his being is ecstasy. He expressed himself entirely in the Son: 'The Father is in me. All that the Father has is mine.'

7. The Son listens, the parabolas of his robe express close attentiveness, the abandonment of self. He effaces himself in order to be only the Word of his Father: 'The words that I say to you I do not speak on my own; but the Father who dwells in me does his works.' His right hand reproduces the gesture of the Father: benediction. The two fingers that are separate from the whiteness of the table-Bible signify that salvation-union is by the two natures of Christ, who brings the world, the human, into the communion of the Father.

8. The lowered hand of the angel on the right indicates the direction of the benediction – the world; it seems to cover, protect, 'brood over' (as in the biblical narrative of creation) the rectangle of the world, like the stretched-out wings of the pure dove.

There is something maternal in the gentleness of the lines of the angel on the right.[47] He is the Comforter, but also the Spirit, the Spirit of Life. It is he who gives life, and in him all life originates. He is the third term of the divine Love, the Spirit of Love. His attitude is subtly different from that of the two other angels. By the degree of inclination and the essential energy he conveys, he comes between the Father and the Son; he is the Spirit of communion and of circumincession. That is clearly shown by the remarkable fact that the movement originates in him. The Father moves into his Son in his breath, and thus the Son receives his Father and the Word is uttered. As St John Damascene says, 'Through the Holy Spirit we recognize Christ, the Son of God, and through the Son we contemplate the Father.' At Epiphany, it is in the movement of the Dove that the Father descends towards the Son.

9. Colours in iconography have their own language. With Rublev, they achieve a supreme richness, total harmony, the fine nuances of which echo throughout the composition. However, there are no polychromatic effects, for nothing must be allowed to disturb the depth of divine contemplation. Shadow is absent and every particle is lighted only by its own light, which springs from secret roots. The density of the colours of the central figure is heightened by the contrast with the whiteness of the table and is reflected in the silky shimmering of the angels on either side. Deep purple (divine love), and opaque blue (heavenly truth) with the gleaming gold of the wings (divine abundance) form the perfect harmony which is repeated in softer tones as a gradual revelation, initiation by degrees: light rose and lilac on the left, softer blue and silver-green to the right. The gold of the thrones, the divine council, signifies the overflowing life of the Trinity. The blue called 'Rublev's blue' represents the colour of the heavens of the Trinity and of Paradise, becoming clearer little by little; it is like the celestial light of the icon itself.

Thus the Father, inaccessible in the density of his colours, in the darkness of his light, is revealed in softened form, accessible in the luminous cloud of the Son and the Holy Spirit. From far off, this composition gives the impression of a blue and red flame. Everything blazes in the dazzling air of Noonday: 'The one who is near me is near the fire.'

The Father's hand stretched over the cup holds the beginning and the end. The Lamb slain from the foundation of the world and the Lamb-Temple of the new Jerusalem, the holy Supper of Christ and his promise about drinking the fruit of the vine in the Father's Kingdom, bring time into eternity. The cup is radiant in the dazzling whiteness of the Word which reflects all the colours of the Truth; it is the radiation of the divine heart, the reciprocal gift of the three divine Persons.

---

[47] *Ruach*, Spirit, in the Semitic languages is also feminine. Syriac texts when speaking of the Comforter, often use the feminine form.

10. From the icon a powerful call is heard: 'Be one, as my Father and I are one.' Humankind is in the image of God the Trinity, and the Church-Communion is by its very nature charged to be his ultimate truth. All are called to join together round one and the same cup, to be raised to the level of the divine heart and share in the messianic Banquet, to become one only Temple-Lamb. 'And this is eternal life [the Spirit], that they may know you, the only true God, and Jesus Christ whom you have sent.'

The vision ends on this eschatological note – the anticipation of the Kingdom of Heaven, all bathed in the light which is not of this world, all bathed at last in pure disinterested divine joy, because of the simple fact that the Trinity exists and that we are loved and that all is grace. Astonishment springs up from the heart and falls silent. The mystics never speak of the summit, the inner light that silence alone can discover.

3

The Liturgy

1. INTRODUCTION

Orthodox churches are full of light, warmth and intimacy; the walls throughout vividly represent heaven, bringing human beings into communion with their elders in the faith: the angels, prophets, Apostles, martyrs and saints; they are truly visiting God and entering heaven. Through icons, liturgical worship, and rites bound up quite naturally with daily life, the Bible becomes astonishingly alive, and heaven almost near enough to touch. It is a kind of 'theomaterialism', a vision of nature in God who makes everything transparent, allowing us to grasp his invisible presence. Long familiarity with these presences creates an unsatisfied longing for the pure and the absolute; the candles crowned with flames speak of burning faith, and the lives of the saints whom we praise in the canticles and see in the icons teach us that the divine imperatives in the holy Gospels are addressed to all and not beyond the reach of any.

The unbroken continuity of the material and spiritual planes of existence is seen in the cloud of incense that prolongs the movement of the priest's arms as he lifts them to 'collect'[1] the general energy of the souls and direct it into communion. Similarly when he blesses the four cardinal points of the universe with the cross he gathers all the material world under the sanctifying energy of grace. At Orthodox vespers, the blessing of oil, wine and wheat sanctifies the fertility of the earth and teaches human beings that the earth they cultivate is holy, that the crops drawing nourishment from the depths of the earth are not just aggregations of chemicals but a living presence that shares in the eucharistic mystery, and that even the fertility of the earth is linked directly not only to the fertilizers and the seasons but also to human spirituality.

When breaking bread humankind recites the Benedicite; the act of eating is always a reminder of the eucharistic mystery. When it is in contact with the spirit, matter becomes supple and malleable; from a lifeless and heavy lump emerges a beauty engraved all over with signs and pulsating with life. It is the human vocation to draw from things the most wonderful prayer of all, a temple. 'Behold the King of glory entereth. Behold the mystical sacrifice, all accomplished, is brought forth. Let us with faith and love draw near, that we may become partakers of life everlasting.'

---

[1] Liturgical term: a prayer of intercession which gathers the intentions of the congregation.

2. THE LITURGY, TYPE OF ALL PRAYER

The word liturgy means the work of the people: λειτουργία = ἔργον τοῦ λαοῦ. While individual prayer responds to the needs of the moment, liturgical prayer always springs from the whole body of truth, overcomes any particularity and sentimental excess, and forms the Catholic conscience. Its emotional life is powerful but wholesome, any subjective tendency being filtered out, and the whole subordinated to liturgical conventions that have taken many centuries in a life of grace to perfect.

The Liturgy teaches us the true relationship between the individual and the community, between the member and the body: 'Love your neighbour as yourself'. In the liturgical offices these words come to life, take us out of ourselves, and help us to make the prayer of humanity our own. Here our own circumstances are embraced together with those of all people. The litanies, like powerful waves, draw the worshipper beyond self and his or her family circle out to the congregation present, then further out to those who are absent, those who are suffering and in pain, and the dying. Then the prayer encompasses those in holy orders or in authority, town and country, nations and peoples, and finally the whole human race; it asks for orderly seasons and abundance of the fruits of the earth. The prayer ends with the universal petition for peace and the unity of all.

Refreshed and renewed by the energetic charity of this communion human beings rediscover the essential truth about themselves and the world around them. Solitude is abolished, and even nature, longing to be set free, bursts into cosmic liturgy: 'Trees, plants, birds, earth, sea, air, light, all tell me that they exist for man, that they witness to the love of God for man; everything prays, everything sings the glory of God.'[2]

Thus the Liturgy brings home to us the evangelical truth that no single soul can be saved by itself. In the Liturgy the pronoun 'I' never means just one person. A priest is not supposed to celebrate the Liturgy alone; there must be at least one other person, who then represents the whole world. Thus liturgical prayer is regarded as the canon or measure of all prayer. The Fathers simply called it 'prayer', without qualification, meaning the eucharistic Liturgy.

The priestly college and the people together make up a single liturgical body in which each member fulfils its own function. That is why Orthodoxy has never allowed the use in church of musical instruments, of sounds without words, because only the human voice possesses a suitable dignity for responding liturgically to the Word of God, and a 'choir', even of a single person, is the fullest expression of the Body, in union with the choir of angels.

---

[2] *Récits d'un Pélerin*, Les Cahiers du Rhône, 1948, p. 48.

3. THE CONTENT OF THE LITURGY

The round of liturgical offices consists of passages of Holy Scripture, with related paraphrases and commentaries. Beside psalms[3] and parts of the Old Testament, the whole of the New Testament is read in the course of the year following the official lectionary. In addition to these there are the litanies and various chants and sacred prayers with their historical and doctrinal content.[4]

The daily cycle of the Hours – Vespers, Compline, Nocturns and Matins – is centred on the eucharistic Liturgy and the preparation. The annual cycle follows all the events of the life of the Lord. The weekly cycle provides a special commemoration for the offices each day: Wednesday and Friday, the suffering and death of the Saviour; Monday, the Angels; Tuesday, St John the Baptist; Thursday, the Apostles; Saturday, the *Theotokos*. The book called the *Typicon* governs the movable parts of each office. The whole body of the offices is a liturgical treasure-house of amazing richness, containing the most vigorous and clearest doctrine of the Fathers. We are borne along by its regularity and marvellous composition, which encompasses every part of revelation and meets all the needs of spiritual life. The lyrical and emotional element is so grafted on to the doctrinal element that any individual, schismatic tendency is at once corrected, and the balanced presentation of the Truth is never put in danger.

4. THE ETERNAL AND THE TEMPORAL

History unfolds in time and is deposited in the memory. This capacity to transcend the fragmentation of time is at the basis of the liturgical 'memorial', but its mystery goes further. During the Liturgy, by its sacred power, we are raised to the point where eternity and time meet, and at this point we become real *contemporaries* of the biblical events from Genesis up to the Parousia, experiencing them here and now as eye-witnesses. During the liturgy, when we hear, 'This is my Body', these are the very words of Christ resounding across time. This is no human repetition, but liturgical contemporaneity; we communicate beyond time with him who is now and always the same, so the office draws its strength from the divine life, whose appointed setting the temple becomes. The Christians of the first centuries, with the realism so characteristic of the age, contemplated the invisible world quite *naturally*, and saw the temple filled with transcendence:

---

[3] The whole Psalter is read during the week.
[4] The Liturgy is nourished by the Bible; it contains 98 quotations from the Old Testament and 114 from the New Testament. In the first part, 49 from the Old Testament and 38 from the New; in second part the New Testament predominates: 76 New Testament and 49 Old Testament.

'Now all the invisible powers are present with us.'[5] They saw the cloud of angels, and, in the officiant, Christ in person. So we can understand that holy fear, that infinite respect, that intense awareness that 'this place is holy,' a precious tradition transmitted from generation to generation from the beginning of Christianity.

When the royal door opens the Kingdom of God is already among us. Heaven descends and humankind joins with the choir of angels to greet worthily the one who comes: 'Behold the King of Kings who draweth nigh.'

During the Office of Christmas, the birth is not something we remember but an event at which we are really present; Christ is born before our eyes. And during the night of Easter, the risen Lord appears to the faithful and confers on them the honourable status of eye-witnesses, equal to the Apostles. Similarly, the reading of the Gospel during the office is clothed in the power of the event itself.

5. THE DRAMATIC ACTION[6]

The Liturgy is a *mystery* which unfolds in the sacred setting of the Temple and sweeps the congregation up into its action. It is a dramatic dialogue directed by the priest, assisted by the deacon, messenger or herald and by the χορός, the choir drawn from the faithful. In this cooperative enterprise the people make their offering to God and God graces it with his approval and his presence. The movable barrier formed by the doors of the iconostasis controls access to the heavenly realm. Standing between the sanctuary and the nave, the deacon angel-messenger announces what is being done and directs the common action, he intones the liturgical dialogue, guides the prayers of the congregation and governs the demeanour of all and of everyone.

The highly sophisticated psychological and aesthetic clothing of the rite is in tune with the heavenly content. The *Sanctus*, for example marks the moment when the people join with the choir of angels and sing the hymn which has come to them by revelation. Some things are repeated (for example the *Trisagion*) but this hymn, unique in its fullness, is sung only once. Similarly, the liturgy imposes a certain sobriety: the text of Lamentations 3.41, 'Let us lift up our heart with our hands unto God in the heavens,' is refined by a wonderful economy of style into ῎Ανω σθῶμεν τὰς καρδίας, *Sursum corda*. The action is centred on the 'entrances' (the 'Little' and the 'Great' during the Liturgy) and so heightens the attention and participation. Many biblical texts testify to the importance that has always been given to entrances. A person who knows how to come in and go out 'worthily' is capable of holding in his hands his own destiny and that of the world.

---

5 Liturgy of the Presanctified.
6 K. Holl makes much of the analogy between the Byzantine Liturgy and ancient drama (*Die Enstehung der Bilderwand in der griechischen Kirche*, *Archive für Religionswiss.*, 1906 5, IX, p. 365).

The Liturgy as a whole is the visual representation of the biblical events in the historical life of Christ. The hieratic symbolism is very condensed and the faithful are at once witnesses and participants in this liturgical drama. 'Those who exercise the priesthood know that what is done in the liturgy shows *figuratively* the coming of the Saviour and the economy of salvation.'[7] 'The whole of mystagogy is like the representation of a single body, in order to know the economy of the life of the Saviour, bringing before our eyes, from beginning to end, all the members of that body in their interdependence and harmony.'[8]

During Vespers, we are present at the events from the time of Genesis onwards. The invocation at the beginning is not explicitly Trinitarian: 'Blessed be our God' (but the office leads us from the Old Testament to the New and ends with the *Trisagion* and the prayer of the Trinity). The royal doors open like the sky opening on to Paradise. The priest makes a tour of the church, preceded by the deacon carrying a lighted candle. The incense symbolizes the Spirit who moves over the depths at the moment of creation, and the flame of the candle the command, 'Let there be light!'

Psalm 103 which sings the praise of the creature to his Creator, returns to an age when humankind, not yet crushed by sin, could go joyfully to meet its God. At the next stage Psalms 129, 140, 141 mark the fall and the banishment from Paradise. The royal doors close.

In the solitude, face to face with personal sin, the individual prays that the Lord will turn his face towards him or her anew: 'Lord, I have cried unto thee.' The choir and the reader, in a dramatic dialogue in which the two Testaments meet, alternate in cries of distress and of joy at the promises. Then God bends over the world and the mystery of the Incarnation is proclaimed in the chant called the Dogmatic Hymn of the Virgin. The priest comes out of the sanctuary saying, 'Wisdom,' which is the greeting to the Word coming into the world.

Immediately afterwards there is the moving hymn attributed to the martyr Athenagoras who confessed his faith under the Emperor Severus in about AD 169: 'O gladsome light' – φῶς ἱλαρόν. Christ has been revealed to the world and we have seen the radiant light of the holy Glory of the Eternal Father. Then comes the Song of Simeon, the humanity of the Old Testament disappears, giving place to that of the New Testament. Vespers finishes with the greeting of the Archangel to the Blessed Virgin Mary; the Saviour of the world rests in the arms of humankind. Thus Vespers, like Matins,[9] leads into the eucharistic Liturgy.

---

[7] Theodore D'Andida, *P.G.* 140, 417.

[8] Nicholas Cabasilas, *Commentary on the Divine Liturgy*, trans. J.M. Hussey and P.A. McNulty, SPCK 1960.

[9] Matins begins with the invocation of the Trinity.

6. THE EUCHARIST

Historically the Liturgy revolves round the Lord's Supper. Revelation gives us the vision of what is happening during the Liturgy simultaneously on earth and in heaven: 'Then I saw ... a Lamb standing as if it had been slaughtered ... and I heard the voice of many angels ... singing with full voice, "Worthy is the Lamb that was slaughtered to receive ... glory and blessing! Then I heard every creature ... singing, "To ... the Lamb be ... glory ... for ever and ever!" And the four living creatures said, "Amen!" And the elders fell down and worshipped' (Rev. 5.6,11-14).

The cosmic planes, human and angelic, meet in the one Eucharist. 'From nothing, thou hast called us into being, and thou hast not ceased to act before raising us to heaven and opening to us the Kingdom of the age to come.'[10] The beginning joins the end, Genesis is answered by Revelation. Truly the world was created for the Messianic banquet: 'Then the angel showed me the river of the water of life... On either side of the river is the tree of lif' (Rev. 22.1-2). In that vision of the future Kingdom the Fathers see the image of the eternal Eucharist; but already here on earth, 'Those who eat my flesh and drink my blood have eternal life' (John 6.54). The Eucharist in the world is already and wholly something other than the world: 'Let his grace draw near, and let this present world pass away', says *The Didache*. Faced with the eschatological announcement, time is utterly alert: the Incarnation, the Atonement, the Resurrection and the Parousia are announced from the depths of the same chalice. This is the essence of Christianity: we see the mystery of divine life to be the mystery of human life, 'that they may all be one. As you, Father, are in me and I am in you' (John 17.21).

That is why the establishment of the Church at Pentecost is followed immediately by the revelation of its nature: 'They devoted themselves to the apostles' teaching and fellowship, to the *breaking of bread* and the prayers' (Acts 2.42). That eucharistic expression became the description of a whole way of life: 'All who believed were together and had all things common' (Acts 2.44). By the bread-Christ, the faithful become that same bread, that same love one and threefold, the priestly prayer lived by the human race.

This is far from being a bare commemoration. Every time Orthodox believers come to the Holy Communion, they say, 'Of thy Mystic Supper, O Son of God, *today* admit me a partaker.' Memory reproduces, but the liturgical memorial invites us to share in the One who abides. St John Chrysostom says, 'Every Eucharist has been offered once and has never been exhausted. The Lamb of God is always eaten and never consumed'.[11] And Nicholas Cabasilas: 'The bread becomes the Lamb.'[12]

---

[10] Prayer of oblation, Liturgy of St John Chrysostom.
[11] *In Epist. ad Hebr.*, hom. 17; *P.G.* 63, 131.
[12] *Commentary on the Divine Liturgy*, ch XXII.

Worldly material as it changes touches heaven and becomes part of it. St Ignatius and St John Chrysostom call the Eucharist 'the Body of Christ', 'Leaven and bread of immortality.'[13] We can now understand the whole meaning of the words, 'Those who eat my flesh ... have eternal life' (John 6.54). In this lies the ultimate mystery of the Church: 'Thou, my Creator, who thy flesh for food hast freely given me, who art a fire that the unworthy burns, consume me not, but rather my whole substance penetrate, my every member, and my reins and heart. Burn my iniquities like crackling thorns; cleanse thou my soul, hallow each pondered thought; make firm my knees and my whole frame.'[14]

Until the 9th century, respect for the eucharistic mystery was so great that no one ever questioned it. It was only after St Ambrose (*De Sacramentis*), in the 9th and 11th centuries in the West, that the question of 'what' and 'how' was asked for the first time. In the discussions that followed, the verb 'to be' took the meaning 'to signify'. 'This *is* my body' became 'this *signifies* my body.'[15] Now, the Orthodox have never asked that eucharistic question, quite simply because they have never accepted the verb 'to signify'. Faithful to the sacred text of the Scriptures and keeping some distance from the mystery, they affirm the amazing identity, 'This is my body,' and accept it as an integral part of the unutterable miracle of the divine love. On the other hand the eastern tradition is rich in reflection on the Epiclesis and the pneumatology of the Eucharist.

7. THE MIRACLE OF THE EUCHARIST

Fr Sergei Bulgakov, in his masterly study *Eucharistic Dogma*, clearly expounds the Orthodox understanding. When the water is changed into wine at the Marriage of Cana, one earthly material is replaced by another, but both are still of this world: the miracle is *physical*. The bread and wine of the Eucharist become, are metamorphosed into, a reality that is not of this world: the miracle is *metaphysical*. The eucharistic antinomy crucifies our reason; it transcends, but does not break, the law of identity, for it is the identity of the different and the difference of the identity. It is not a transformation within the limits of this world, but μεταβολή, metaphysical *transensus*, the transcendent and the immanent coinciding. So the wine at Cana was apprehended by the senses, but the eucharistic blood is the object of faith: 'I believe and I confess ... this verily is thy most pure Body, and that this verily is thy precious Blood.' And faith immediately affirms that the evidence is utterly real, and with immediate effect: 'Not unto judgement nor unto

---

13 Eph. 20, 2.
14 Prayer of St Simeon Metaphrastes after holy communion.
15 Calvin joins Zwingli in opposing Luther and his doctrine of *consubstantiation*, and interprets 'is' in the sense of 'signifying': 'the bread and wine are visible signs.'

condemnation be the partaking of thy Holy Mysteries to me, O Lord, but unto the healing of my soul and body.'[16]

St Thomas's doctrine of transubstantiation, and similarly Luther's doctrine of consubstantiation, turn a philosophical conception of the relations between substance and accidents into a dogma. The miracle is in the persistence of the accidents joined to another substance (transubstantiation), or in the penetration of the bread, which then possesses two realities (consubstantiation): the bread that is replaced by or to which is added a spiritual or corporeal presence = substance. The substance is *Christus totus et integer*. Without leaving heaven, he is present at the same time on earth and constitutes the eucharistic substance. As far as the heavenly body of Christ is concerned, transubstantiation and companation are only variants of the same thing: the substantial presence of Christ in and under the species of bread (*in pane, sub pane, cum pane*), or under the accidents of forms of bread. But the metabolism of the bread and heavenly flesh to be consumed is one thing, and the presence of Christ in the species, i.e., his descent to earth, is quite another; because the latter leads logically to the cult of the adoration of the earthly, physical presence of Christ, and therefore the denial of the Ascension.

The heavenly body of Christ no longer belongs to this world. It is not 'everywhere', for it is outside and above space; it is not spatial, but he can be in any specific place and reveal himself there, just as he wills. This localization is necessary for us, for otherwise we should not be able to communicate with the invisible. But the heavenly body is in no way beneath, with, or in the bread (consubstantiation), nor does it take the place of the bread (transubstantiation), but it *is* the bread: 'This verily *is* my flesh'. According to St Irenaeus, the eucharistic bread does not conceal or replace another reality, but, through the epiclesis, unites heavenly and earthly food in one identity, and that is the miracle.[17] When the priest plunges the Lamb in its blood, it is the living body and not a sign or an illusion of accidents. It is not a reincarnation of Christ in the species, but the total *metabolë* of both substance and accidents into heavenly flesh. It is not the accidents of the bread that are maintained, but the state of our eyes, which are incapable of contemplating the heavenly flesh while keeping the illusion of the appearances. The doctrine is at fault in being concerned with the object and not the subject, with the bread and not the person. There is no need to analyse the miracle quasi-chemically according to our senses; we should rather accuse our senses of not perceiving the real miracle, the heavenly reality. There is an analogy in the miracle of the Transfiguration of the Saviour on Mount Tabor. The change is not in Christ, but in the eyes of the Apostles that are opened for an instant. St John Damascene says, 'The epiclesis effects what is accessible only to

---

[16] Prayer before communion.
[17] *Adv. haeres.*, IV, 34.

faith.'[18] It is therefore useless to philosophize about it. Western theologians try to penetrate to the heart of the miracle and to explain what it *means*; those of the East look with the eyes of faith and from the beginning see the flesh and the blood, and nothing else.

The Eucharist is given 'as food' to be consumed. Adoration of the gifts reifies the manifestation of the heavenly and contradicts the Ascension. Orthodoxy does not *expose* the gifts but *keeps* them for Communion alone. Adoration in the course of the liturgy is simply a part of the liturgical adoration of the whole mystery of Christ. We prostrate ourselves not before the gifts but before the Spirit in the gifts, before the *liturgical* advent of Christ which the Spirit manifests and which possesses full reality only within the liturgy.

St John Damascene expresses the doctrine of the Church when he says, 'Not that the body which was received up into the heavens descends, but the bread itself and the wine are changed into God's body and blood.'[19] Similarly the Encyclical of the Eastern Patriarchs says, 'The bread becomes *one* with the Body which stays in heaven.'[20]

Bishop Benjamin of Arzamas in *The New Tablet* speaks of the three *proskomidiës*, three offerings in the course of the liturgy: the first offering comes from the world when the bread and wine is placed on the table of sacrifice; the second is the transfer of these presanctified gifts to the table of the altar; the third and final one is the transfer of the gifts from the visible altar to the invisible altar of the Holy Trinity, their elevation to heaven by the invocation of the epiclesis and their metabolism into the flesh and blood of Christ offered anew on the visible altar of the Temple. Thus the bread and the wine are united with the heavenly reality of Christ, and so become part of him: 'The immolation of the Lamb is not indefinitely repeated, but the bread becomes the Lamb.'[21]

After the consecration the bread is more than bread. Human beings do not perform subjectively, by the power of faith, the miracle in their mouths. Sacramental operation is always transubjective; the person consumes subjectively what exists objectively, whether to salvation or to condemnation.

The eucharistic presence is subjected to the command, 'eat and drink', it is therefore to be consumed. Christ is present and gives himself in Communion during the Liturgy (Communion of the sick is an extension of the Liturgy, never an extra-liturgical act). While an icon is a point radiating presence and provides a place for veneration, the gifts offer a heavenly-bodily presence for the sole purpose of consumption.

---

[18] *De fide orth.*, IV, 13.
[19] *Ibid.*
[20] § 17.
[21] Nicholas Cabasilas, *Commentary on the Divine Liturgy*, Ch. XXXII.

8. THE SACRIFICIAL NATURE OF THE EUCHARIST

In the words of the Liturgy, 'Here is the true oblation'; this oblation or sacrifice is graphically represented in the *proskomidië*.[22] Time plays no part and causes no real difficulty. The Supper of the Lord given to the Apostles before the crucifixion and every Eucharist since then are one and the same Supper in relation to the Lamb slain *before* the foundation of the world, *before* all time. The heavenly, eucharistic Body is not *ubiquitous* – omnipresent – but trans-temporal and transspatial; it does not exist everywhere and always, but *can* be present in any place and at any moment. The best explanation is given by Nicholas Cabasilas: 'The state of being slain, which, because of the change, would normally apply to the bread, exists no longer in the bread, which has disappeared, but in the body of Jesus Christ, into which it has been changed ... this sacrifice takes place not by the actual slaying of the Lamb but by the change of the bread into the Lamb already slain. The change is repeated, but that into which the bread changes remains one and the same.'[23]

Already in the prefigurative practices of paganism and of the Old Testament, identification with the victim that had been offered was realized in the act of consumption. The life of the victim passes into that of the sacrificer and of the people. In the eucharistic identification we die with Christ and are raised with him. Christ is victim and Saviour, he reveals himself to us as 'our victim', but the miracle of 'the sacrifice that is one and not many'[24] touches in a personal manner every concrete situation in time. What happened once for all and is not reproduced objectively, is realized subjectively for each communicant, for the body is one:[25] 'Sanctify us as you have already so many times sanctified the people of our race,'[26] for the one sacrifice is, the liturgical phrase, 'on behalf of all and for all,' The anamnesis is not of platonic ideas but of the real event of the one sacrifice. We 'memorize' it by participation (in Slavonic the eucharistic act is 'participation'). 'Do this in remembrance of me' refers to the divine Memory which renders the act eternally present and announces the end of this world and the Parousia: 'Come, you that are blessed by my Father.' 'The Day of the Lord', the day of the Eucharist, is the day of judgement and of the marriage of the Lamb (which is the double meaning of the icon of the *Deesis*). Christ is both the victim and the one who offers, the one who offers and the one who receives: in the words of the

---

[22] Preparation of the sacrificial elements, or prothesis, which precedes the Liturgy proper.
[23] *Commentary on the Divine Liturgy*, Ch. XXXII; *P.G.* 150, 440 D-441 A.
[24] St John Chrysostom, *In Epist. ad Hebr.*, hom. 17; *P.G.* 63, 131.
[25] St Cyril of Jerusalem, *Catech. mystag.*, *P.G.* 33, 115-118; St John Chrysostom, *P.G.* 61, 361.
[26] Nicholas Cabasilas, *Commentary on the Divine Liturgy*.

prayer before the epiclesis, 'Thine own, of thine own, we offer unto thee, on be-half of all, and for all.' Nicholas Cabasilas says emphatically that the complete-ness is such 'that one cannot go further, or add anything to it.'[27]

9. THE EPICLESIS

The prayer 'for the precious gifts which have been offered and sanctified' sums up in a few words the essence of the eucharistic miracle, 'that our God, who loveth mankind, will accept them upon his holy, heavenly and invisible altar ... and will send down upon us in return his divine grace and the gift of his Holy Spirit.'

Nicholas Cabasilas sees in the rite of the *zeon*[28] the eucharistic Pentecost.[29] The words that accompany the rite, 'the warmth of faith, full of the Holy Spirit,' reaffirm the epiclesis that follows the anaphora.

Every sacrament has its own Pentecost, the descent of the Holy Spirit, working at its heart. Thus the Orthodox faith testifies to the role of the Holy Spirit in the economy of salvation and Trinitarian balance. Christ the Word pronounces the words of institution and the epiclesis asks God to send down the holy Spirit, the sanctifying power, on the gifts and on the Church.[30]

Even by the end of the 4th century the Antiochene anaphoras were invoking the Holy Spirit to come and transform the bread and wine into the body and blood of Christ. The heresy of the Pneumatomachi had perhaps provoked a desire to place greater emphasis on the action of the Spirit; this emphasis agreed particu-larly with the rapidly evolving eastern theology of the Paraclete. In the West the Byzantine influence affected only the Mozarabic liturgy. To understand the pro-found reason for the conflict between East and West (the essence of which con-cerns not only the eucharistic epiclesis but the epiclesis as the expression of the theology of the Holy Spirit) we must remember that, for the Greeks, the whole canon of the liturgy is one inseparable Mystery, and no analysis could possibly

---

[27] *The Life in Jesus Christ.*

[28] The pouring of boiling water = the water and the fire, images of the Holy Spirit in the chalice before communion.

[29] *Commentary on the Divine Liturgy*, Ch. XXXVII; *P.G.* 150, 452. The epiclesis is the eu-charistic Pentecost. In the 15th century a very late addition was made to the epiclesis, the Troparion of the Third Hour. The logical progression of the marvellous text was thus inter-rupted and its meaning and unity fragmented. Fortunately, the Greek editions now in use no longer contain the troparion.

[30] There is ample, even irrefutable, evidence of Orthodox practice; see Fr Cyprian Kern, *The Eucharist* (in Russian), p. 240.

identify a central quasi-isolated moment. For the Latin Church, the _verba substantialia_ of the consecration, the institutional words of Christ, are pronounced by the priest _in persona Christi_, which immediately gives them consecratory power. Now, for the Greeks the identification of the priest with Christ, _in persona Christi_, was quite unknown, and strictly unthinkable. Rather, the priest invokes the Holy Spirit precisely in order that the word of Christ _reproduced, cited_ by the priest should acquire all the efficacy of the word-act of God.

The eastern Fathers place the _ontological_ relation of the Word to the humanity of Christ alongside the _dynamic_ relation of the Holy Spirit witnessing to and manifesting the humanity, on which he is sent as unction. Human nature subsists ontologically, and finds support in the hypostasis of Christ, but is sanctified and suffused with divine energy by the dynamism of the Spirit. Christ is the incarnate Word, but he acts and reveals the Father in and through the Spirit (_dynamis_, by definition power: Luke 1.35 and Rom. 15.19). The parousia of Christ in the Eucharist takes place in and through the parousia of the Holy Spirit (John 15-17) which operates the _metabolë_ of the gifts and of the very communicant.[31] The integral pneumatization of the nature – φύσις – of the Saviour continues in those who partake of his 'sacred flesh'. Consanguineous and concorporate, they are not only conformed to Christ, but are actually _Christified_ (Col. 2.9ff). There is a transfer and infusion of vital, deifying energy, often called by the Fathers φάρηακον ἀθανασίας, the cure or leaven of immortality. The communicant 'is transformed into the substance of the King,'[32] not, according to St John Chrysostom, by anything 'deposited' in him, but by catching fire and sharing in the divine love.[33] This is the hidden meaning of perichoresis. According to Innokenty, Bishop of Tauride, 'We are in communion with Christ, but Christ is in communion with us.' God takes flesh in humankind and humankind is spiritualized in God. The Incarnation, the humanization of God, meets the pneumatization, the divinization of humankind. From the beginning the love of God has found its response in the love of the Son of Man, and 'we remember the Lord' (in the liturgical memorial) because 'he remembers us' (keeps us in the divine memory). 'The Spirit and the Bride say, Come, Lord.' This is what the epiclesis means above all; it leads to the πνευματικὸν γάμος, the mystical marriage of Christ with every soul, represented in the _Deesis_: the Bridegroom-Lamb is between the Bride-Church and the Paranymph, the Friend of the Bridegroom; the angels and the Apostles are the honoured guests and witnesses.[34] As Theodoret of Cyr says,

---

31 Maximus the Confessor, _Mystag._ 24; _P.G._ 91, 170 A.
32 Nicholas Cabasilas, _The Life in Jesus Christ._
33 Cf. St Cyril of Jerusalem, IV _Cat;_ Cyril of Alexandria, _Comment. in Lucam_ IV. See Fr Kern, 'Homothéos' in _l'Eglise et les Eglises_, V. II, Ed. Chevetogne 1955. p. 15.
34 Cf. Jean Danielou, 'Eucharistie et Cantique des Cantiques', in _Irénikon_, 1950.

'When we eat the flesh of the Betrothed and his blood, we enter into nuptial *koinonia.*'[35]

* * *

The Christian Liturgy borrowed from the rites that already existed; thus the synaxis of the Word, the first part of the Liturgy, comes from the synagogue worship on Saturday morning centred on the reading of the Bible, and the eucharistic synaxis corresponds to the family supper on Friday evening or the supper of the *Chaburah* (brotherhood) with the cup of blessing. At the end of the supper, after the giving of thanks, there was an invocation – the *epiclesis* in fact – which referred to the eschatological coming of Elijah, the restoration of the kingdom of David, the restoration of the Temple and the confirmation of all in the faith. Ἐκκλησία has the same root as *qahal* in Hebrew, but in the New Testament, the congregation of YHWH becomes the people of God *met together in Christ.* The congregation is called together by the heralds of the heavenly King. The Apostle-bishops (κήρυκες, heralds) call the people together by the word, then the congregation listens to the kerygma and feeds on the same Word-Eucharist. So the subject and object of the liturgical worship is God. The Word calls people together and is given as food. This divine initiative dominates the worship from beginning to end and makes it plain that the form of worship, the liturgical order, is not unimportant; being divine, it is eternal in character, and not the product of free human inspiration. The tradition goes back to the Apostles. Consisting of adoration and thanksgiving, worship is essentially theocentric.

One thing that stands out is the strict connection between the two parts of the Liturgy. *The Liturgy of the Catechumens* is the liturgy of the Word. The Gospel is placed in the middle of the altar table. The reading of the *Apostle* ('the *schaliach,* the *apostolos* of someone is like another self' – an aphorism from the *Mishnah*) is followed by the reading from the Gospel, and then a sermon. *The Liturgy of the Faithful* is the Liturgy of the Eucharist, and for this the chalice is at the centre. To separate or oppose the two would clearly be unthinkable. 'God speaks and it comes to pass;' what the Word announces is immediately realized. The action of the 'Word made flesh' is immediate; the believers are transformed into 'the substance of the King.'

---

[35] *P.G.* 81, 128 A.

10. THE LITURGY[36]

Outline of the Liturgy

I THE PROTHESIS or PROSKOMIDE
1. Preparation of the oblations, bread and wine intended for the sacrifice.

II THE LITURGY OF THE CATECHUMENS
1. Great Litany: a long prayer in the form of a dialogue between the Deacon and the people, concluding with a Trinitarian doxology.
2. Psalm 104.
3. Little Litany.
4. Psalm 146.
5. Troparion: *O Monogenes* (O Only-begotten Son).
6. Singing of the Beatitudes.
7. Little Entrance.
8. Chant: 'O come, let us worship.'
9. *Trisagion.*
10. Epistle.
11. Gospel.
12. Diaconal Litany.
13. Prayer for the Catechumens and their Dismissal.

III THE LITURGY OF THE FAITHFUL
Before the Anaphora:
1. Prayer for the Faithful.
2. *Cherubicon.*
3. Offertory Prayer.
4. Great Entrance.
5. Litany of the Offertory.
6. 'Let us love one another.'
7. Kiss of Peace.
8. Creed.

---

[36] See A. Salaville, *Les liturgies orientales*, 3 vol., Paris 1932; A. Baumstark, *Liturgie comparée*, Chevetogne 1933; Mercenier et Paris, *La Prière des Eglises du rite byzantin*, 3 vol., Chevetogne 1937; *L'Office divin de saint Jean Chrysostome* (Greek and French), trans. M. Rodocanachi, Paris 1955.

Anaphora or Canon of the Eucharist:
　　Call to attention: 'Let us stand in fear.'

A. The Great Eucharistic Prayer:
　　1. It is meet and right that we should worship thee (*dignum et justum est*).
　　2. *Sanctus.*
　　3. Commemoration of the Lord's Supper.

B. The Consecration:
　　1. Words of Institution.
　　2. Oblation of the Body and Blood. Chant: 'We praise thee.'
　　3. Epiclesis or invocation of the Holy Spirit.

C. The Great Prayer:
　　1. Commemoration of the Saints and the Diptychs (commemoration
　　　of the living and departed), Megalinarion of the *Theotokos*: 'It is meet
　　　indeed that we should glorify thee, O Virgin.'
　　2. Litany before the Lord's Prayer, Priest's secret prayer.
　　3. Lord's Prayer.

D. Elevation, Fraction and Communion:
　　1. Blessing, prayer over the people.
　　2. 'Holy things unto the Holy.'
　　3. Fraction.
　　4. Prayer of Preparation.
　　5. Communion of the Priest and Deacon.
　　6. Blessing of the people with the chalice.
　　7. Communion of the people.
　　8. Prayer of Thanksgiving.
　　9. Transfer of the sacred species to the prothesis.
　　10. Dismissal of the people and distribution of the *antidoron* or blessed bread.

The Liturgy properly so called or the Mass represents the three stages in the economy of salvation. The first act represents the Messianic link between prehistory and history; the second, the Liturgy of the Catechumens, reproduces the whole of the work of Christ; and the third, the Liturgy of the Faithful, represents the passion, death, resurrection, ascension, parousia and eternal reign of Christ. We can see clearly that the Liturgy sets out, as Theodore of Andida[37] says, 'all the

------

[37] *P.G.* 140, 417.

mystery of economy,' and, according to Theodore the Studite, it is 'the recapitulation of the whole economy of salvation.'[38]

The Prothesis[39]

The first act or Prothesis, the preparation of the bread and wine, is a highly condensed and realistic little drama that rehearses the sacrifice of the Lamb, thus
providing in advance a summary of what is going to be done during the Liturgy.

The priest takes the prepared altar bread and with the spear traces on it the
sign of the Cross three times, then thrusts the spear into the right side and makes
a cut while saying, 'He was led as a lamb to the slaughter' (Isa. 53.7). He makes
a similar incision in the left side, saying, 'and as a lamb without spot before his
shearers is dumb, so he opened not his mouth' (Isa. 53.7).

After two more incisions the priest lifts up the bread, from now on called 'the
Lamb', and says, 'For his life is taken away from the earth.' He puts it on the
paten, upside down, to signify the kenosis. The deacon says, 'Sacrifice, Master.'
The priest then cuts right through the bread in the form of a cross, saying, 'Sacrificed is the Lamb of God who taketh away the sins of the world, for the life of
the world and for its salvation.' Then he turns it over again and the deacon says,
'Pierce, Master.' The priest pierces the bread with the spear, on the upper right
side, saying, 'One of the soldiers did pierce his side with a spear, and straightway
there came forth blood and water' (John 19.34).

The deacon pours some wine and a little water into the chalice and says,
'Bless, Master, the holy union.' Taking a particle of another altar bread the priest
puts it on the right of the Lamb, saying, 'On thy right hand stood the Queen,
clothed in a vesture wrought with gold' (Ps. 45.10). A particle from a third altar
bread commemorates the Forerunner and the Angels (as in the icon of the *Deesis*,
the marriage of the Lamb); successive particles represent the Prophets, the Apostles, the Saints, and the living and departed, each being presented by name.

Thus, on the paten of oblation, there is symbolized the perfect and universal
Church encompassing heaven and earth, extending to those who are absent and
even the dead, the Church-Lamb who recapitulates in himself all the living, 'as
thou thyself knowest it, in the way known to thee alone.'

It is the image of the Body of Christ: the whole communion in the whole
Body, the vision that transcends time. During the censing the deacon says, 'O
Christ, thou wast present with the body in the tomb, and with the soul in hell; as

---

[38] *P.G.* 99, 340 C.
[39] The present office of the Prothesis or Proskomide dates from the 12th century. Before the 7th
century it came before the Great Entrance, i.e. at the beginning of the Liturgy of the Faithful.

God, in Paradise with the thief and on the throne with the Father and the Holy Spirit: thou, the infinite, who fillest all things.' It is the vision of perfect fulfilment: 'Everything that is accomplished for us, the Cross, the tomb, the Resurrection, the Ascension, the presence at the right hand of the Father, the second coming in glory.'

It is the vision of the world in God, when the whole world becomes a theophany, the threefold God present in his creation. All is accomplished and all is united in a theandric *Sobor*. Over and above time, *before* history, the Lamb already contains in himself the end and the beginning. The concentrated symbolism of the Prothesis thus lifts us up to participate in the prologue of the heavenly drama of 'the Lamb slain from the foundation of the world' (Rev. 13.8 and 1 Pet. 1.19-20).

From eternity, from pre-existence, we now descend by means of the liturgical action in an unfolding of history. The Lamb enters space and time, taking the form of the child at the Nativity. The priest covers the paten with the particles, placing over it the metal star and says, 'And the star came and stood over the place where the young child was' (Matt. 2.9).

The prayer addressed to the Holy Spirit, 'O heavenly King, the Comforter...', equivalent to the *Veni Sancte Spiritus*, is the general epiclesis at the threshold of the Mystery.

The Liturgy of the Catechumens

The second act is opened by the deacon, who stands in front of the holy doors and says, 'Bless, Master.' The priest pronounces the doxology-blessing, 'Blessed be the kingdom of the Father, and of the Son, and of the Holy Spirit,' placing us at the very start in the kingdom of the Holy Trinity. The deacon begins the collective prayer of the whole congregation by calling down upon them *Shalom*, the highest form of peace: 'In peace let us pray to the Lord'... Ἐν εἰρήνῃ – whence comes the name *irenika* given to these litanies.

The choir sings the 'typical' Psalms 103 and 146, which recount the longing of the people of the Old Testament as they wait for the promised salvation. This part finishes with the solemn hymn[40] to Salvation itself, to the only-begotten Son, *Monogenos*, which affirms the essence of the Christian faith according to the doctrine of Chalcedon. Then the singing of the *Beatitudes*[41] reminds us of the distinguishing marks of the soul that lives according to grace.

---

[40] The author of this troparion was probably Emperor Justinian.
[41] In the order of the text of Matthew 5.3-12. Troparia are interpolated to give the whole section an antiphonal character.

The door of the sanctuary opens like the Kingdom of God opening at the coming of Jesus; this is the *Little Entrance*. The priest solemnly carries the gospel at head height, preceded by a lighted candle. This symbolizes Christ announcing his word, preceded by John the Baptist, 'a burning and a shining light' (John 5.35).

The 'Prayer of the Little Entrance' mentions the angels who celebrate the eternal liturgy in heaven and are now joining with the faithful to concelebrate with them: 'O Master, Lord our God, who hast appointed in heaven ranks and hosts of Angels and Archangels for the ministry of thy glory: cause that with our entrance may enter also the holy Angels with us serving thee, and with us glorifying thy goodness. For unto thee are due all glory, honour and *worship.*' The last word lays stress on the whole point of the rite: worship. It explains this incursion of the heavenly into the earthly at the Little and Great Entrances. The angels celebrate the eternal liturgy in heaven and participate in the liturgy of human beings which is only an insertion into time of that perpetual adoration which is the normal condition of every creature. In the elaborate icon called the 'Divine Liturgy' Christ is depicted in pontifical vestments at the altar, surrounded by angels concelebrating and vested as priests and deacons.

'Blessed be the entrance of thy Holy Ones,' says the priest, calling all the holy powers of the Church to the worship of God. The saints and the whole human race bow down together, united in a liturgical synaxis by their common participation in the holiness of God and of all the angels. Thus God the Holy One, concealed within the mystery of his brightness as in a cloud, is worshipped by all the powers of his own holiness, 'reflected in the face of his saints.'

After the blessing of the Entrance, the deacon lifts up the Gospel and proclaims, 'Wisdom!' This is the call to the faithful to avoid all distractions and to devote themselves completely to the act of worship. The choir sings *Venite adoremus*, 'O come, let us worship and fall down before Christ. Save us, O Son of God, who art wonderful in the Saints.' In the pontifical rite, this is the moment when the bishop begins his priestly, liturgical office: this concentrated act of adoration marks the beginning of the Liturgy. The canticles that follow commemorate the saints of this particular day and church. The whole occasion is awe-inspiring in its richness of meaning; a universal obeisance greets the entrance of Christ surrounded by the cloud of witnesses and ministers of his glory; the sanctity of God radiates in its human capacity through the assembly of the saints.

The deacon bows and addresses the priest: 'Bless, Master, the time of the Thrice-Holy.' The priest gives the blessing, saying, 'For holy art thou, O our God … now and ever.' 'To everything there is a season,' says Ecclesiastes (3.1). God 'has made everything beautiful in its season; moreover he has set in human hearts the thought of eternity' (Eccles. 3.11).

So we come to the liturgical time of the *Trisagion*, the time of worship. The priest says the prayer of the *Trisagion*: 'O Holy God, who inhabitest the holy of holies; who art glorified by the Cherubim and worshipped by all the heavenly powers; … thou who hast vouchsafed unto us, thy humble and unworthy servants, here at this hour, to stand before the majesty and the glory of thine altar and to render unto thee the *adoration* which is thy due: do thou, the same Lord, accept from the mouths of us sinners the Thrice-Holy song, ... for holy art thou, O our God, and unto thee we ascribe glory, to the Father, and to the Son and to the Holy Spirit.'

The priest prostrates himself three times while saying the *Trisagion* and the choir sings, 'O Holy God, Holy and Mighty, Holy and Immortal, have mercy upon us;' from the porch open to the mystery of the Triune God, Christ emerges and appears to the faithful in the fullness of liturgical worship.

Before the end of the chant, the deacon calls for *dynamis* (strength), inviting the choir to sing more loudly. At a pontifical liturgy, the bishop comes forward during the song, holding in his left hand the *dikerion* (the candlestick with two candles crossed, symbolizing the mystery of the two natures in Christ) and in his right hand the *trikerion* (the candlestick with three candles, symbolizing the trisolar light), and blesses the people while crossing the Christological and trinitarian symbols. This crossing expresses the sheer ineffable density of the divine holiness. There follows 'the ceremony of the throne', or the blessing of it, which symbolically indicates the throne of the thrice-holy God who has just been just praised in the *Trisagion*.

Christ has abolished enmity and banished the shadows, and now he speaks in the reading[42] of the *Epistle* (the pericope taken from Acts or the Epistles is called *Apostolos*) and the *Gospel* of the day. The synaxis of the catechumens has its own *epiclesis*: the prayer before the reading of the Gospel asks for the gift of enlightenment, which refers to the text of Luke 24.45,49: 'Then he opened their minds to understand the scriptures ... I am sending upon you what my Father promised'; that is the Spirit, who will 'guide you into all the truth' (John 16.13). The reading of the Scriptures undergoes the eucharistic metabolism into the Word of God, the scriptural Eucharist of the Catechumens. The readings used to be followed by a sermon or instruction from the bishop. This part of the liturgy was completed by the litanies which caught up the worshippers and carried them along together. Then the deacon announced the 'dismissal of the catechumens'[43] and the penitents and catechumens left the temple and the Liturgy of the Faithful began.

---

[42] The Orthodox keep to this line of readings: for the Sundays of the Pentecost season (Eastertide) the Acts and St John's Gospel are read; after Pentecost and through to Holy Week, St Paul's Epistles – Romans, 2 Corinthians, Galatians, Ephesians, Colossians, Timothy and Hebrews; the Gospels of Matthew, Luke and Mark.

[43] According to St Maximus of Chrysopolis the custom of the dismissal fell into disuse in ancient times but was revived in the 7th century (*P.G.* 4, 141).

The Liturgy of the Faithful

In the Liturgy of the Faithful, there is the proclamation of the witnesses of the risen Christ and the Kingdom. The royal doors are sacramental, they symbolize Christ: 'I am the gate' (John 10.7). They are not opened except by Baptism and the anointing of the Spirit. The Old Nature dies at the threshold of the Temple and the New Nature, risen in Christ, enters and stands in the Temple of Glory.

'Let us stand with fear and wisdom,' says the deacon, and the choir, taking their spiritual cue from him, sings the *Cherubicon*: 'We, who mystically represent the cherubim, and who sing to the life-giving Trinity the thrice-holy hymn, let us lay aside all earthly cares, that we may receive the King of all, invisibly escorted by the Angelic hosts. Alleluia, alleluia, alleluia.' The soul is emptied and enters into harmony with the song of the heavenly powers; taut in every fibre as it waits for the advent.

The Great Entrance or Offertory Procession is the liturgical dramatization of Christ's entry into Jerusalem. The faithful bow before the Priest and Victim, who appears in the midst of them, and surround him in celebration. It is all as depicted in the *divine liturgy* icon.

The chant on Holy Saturday makes the entry even more tremendous: 'Let all mortal flesh keep silence and stand in fear and trembling, and meditate nothing earthly. For here the King of Kings and Lord of Lords, Christ our God draweth near to be slain and give himself to the faithful for food. He is preceded by the Choir of Angels, with all the Principalities and Powers, the many-eyed Cherubim and six-winged Seraphim, veiling their faces and singing the hymn, *Alleluia*.'

When the procession re-enters the sanctuary the priest prays in the words of the penitent thief, 'Remember-me, O Lord, in thy Kingdom.' Then he places the chalice on the altar, saying, 'Noble Joseph, when he had taken thy pure body from the Cross, wrapped it in a clean linen cloth, then laid it in a new sepulchre ... '

This is the Passion and death. The great veil again covers the oblations like the shroud, and the incensing recalls the spices. The door of the sanctuary is shut like the entrance of the sepulchre. This is the moment of the Offertory and the eucharistic Canon. The curtain is drawn back again as if by the force of triumphant life, as the door will always open at the push of living faith; the angel with the fiery sword goes away from the Tree of Life. Heaven is opened and the awesome mystery draws near, urging the soul to a total self-offering so that it may totally receive God. The prayer at the Offertory anticipates the epiclesis: 'May thy spirit of grace, author of every good thing, descend upon us, on these gifts here prepared, and upon all thy people.' And the words of the deacon resound in the silence of contemplation, 'Let us love one another, that with one heart and mind we may confess our faith.'

It is only when rooted in love and in the very unity of the faith, with all the saints, that the human being shares in the mystery of divine love;[44] only love can know Love, the divine Fellowship, the Holy Trinity. That is why it is the *kiss of peace*, sealing the most amazing act of *unity* in Christ, that introduces the singing of the Creed, proclaiming the Love that comes down, gives itself, suffers and saves. The words that accompany the kiss of peace explain it perfectly: 'Jesus Christ is in the midst of us ... The Church has become one body and our kiss is the pledge of this union, enmity has been cast aside and brotherly love has penetrated everywhere.' Visible and invisible in the Church interpenetrate and change the very nature of things. During the singing of the Creed, the celebrant gently agitates the veil over the chalice and paten, symbolizing the descent of the Holy Spirit.

'Let us stand in fear, let us attend, that in peace we may offer the Holy Oblation,' calls the deacon. The most sacred moment approaches: '*Sursum corda!* Lift up your hearts!' – 'We lift them up unto the Lord.' Worldly cares having vanished, the heart lifted up, human beings can surrender themselves to the mounting current of praise. The priest invites the congregation, 'Let us give thanks unto the Lord.' With a grace appropriate to this action devoted to praise and called 'the Eucharist' – Εὐχαριστήσωμεν τῷ Κυρίῳ – the choir's response goes beyond simple recognition and becomes adoration, contemplation, exaltation, resounding in a truly Trinitarian Eucharist: 'It is meet and right that we should worship thee, Father, Son and Holy Spirit, the consubstantial and undivided Trinity.' The sacrifice contained in the one act of Christ is threefold.

The prayer of the Preface acknowledges God in all his titles and concludes with the *Sanctus*: 'Holy, holy, holy, Lord of Sabaoth.' The angelic Eucharist in the liturgy of the synagogue ends with, 'Blessed be the glory of the Lord from his place' (Ezek. 3.12). The Liturgy changes this to, 'Blessed be he that cometh in the name of the Lord' (Ps. 118). The rabbis, after the Exile, taught that where two or three were gathered together to read the Bible, the glory, the *Shekinah*, was in the midst of them. Christ applied this saying to himself: 'Where two or three are gathered together in my name, there am I in the midst of them.' So the *Shekinah*, the mysterious presence of the Trinitarian God, fills the temple.

The sacrifice is explicit in the *anamnesis*, the commemorative passage that immediately follows the words of the institution of the Holy Communion: 'This is my Body... this is my Blood.' After recalling the great mysteries – the passion, death, resurrection, ascension, and coming again – the priest makes the oblation according to the formula, 'Thine own, of thine own, we offer unto thee, on behalf of all, and for all.'

---

[44] The Liturgy teaches us unmistakably that the Eucharist completes and crowns what has gone before: the indispensable confession and communion in the one true faith, expressed in the common repetition of the Creed and final Amen.

In the Syrian Liturgy of St James the words of the priest convey an extreme spiritual intensity: 'How noble is this hour and how awe-inspiring this moment, brethren! For the life-giving Holy Spirit descends from the heights of heaven and rests on this Eucharist to consecrate it ... Stand therefore in fear, pray that peace may be with you, and the protection of our God. With a loud voice let us say three times *Kyrie Eleison*.'

The response of the faithful, bowing low, sums up the whole theme of the Eucharist: 'We praise thee, we bless thee, we give thanks unto thee, O Lord, and we pray unto thee, O our God.' This is the moment of the consecration of the gifts, the *epiclesis*, the prayer of invocation to the Holy Spirit for the eucharistic miracle: 'Send thy Holy Spirit on us and on these gifts present, and make this bread the precious Body of thy Christ, and of what is in this chalice the precious Blood of thy Christ, transforming them by thy Holy Spirit' – μεταβαλὼν τῷ Πνεύματί Σου τῷ Ἁγιῳ. 'Amen, amen, amen' sounds like the Trinity ratifying the miracle that has been performed. The unifying power of Christ enfolds the universe and makes it the Church: 'Unite us all'. The threefold commemoration of the saints, the dead and the living is attached to the epiclesis and to the universal offering of everybody and everything. This is the Church's great prayer of intercession. 'Remember, O Lord, those whom each bears in the spirit, and everybody and everything ... and send thy mercies upon us all.'

Like children, we are all united in one great offering before the Father. The priest continues, 'Grant that with one mouth and one heart we may glorify and praise thine all-honourable and majestic Name, of the Father, and of the Son, and of the Holy Spirit ... Vouchsafe that we may partake of the terrible mysteries of this holy table;' and to that end, and most important of all, he solemnly calls upon the Father hidden in the luminous cloud of the triune God: 'Vouchsafe, O Lord, that boldly and without condemnation we may dare to call upon thee, God the heavenly Father,[45] and say, "Our Father...".'

The deacon arranges his stole in the form of a St Andrew's cross on his back and chest, symbolizing the seraphim who veil their faces with their wings before the unfathomable mystery of divine love. This acts as a sign to the congregation, recalling them to devotion.

As the Communion approaches the feeling of expectancy is intensified by the majestic chant of the Lord's Prayer. Coming just before the Communion, this prayer identifies the supersubstantial – ἐπιούσιον – daily bread with the bread of the Eucharist. As the moment of union draws near the feeling of unworthiness, the *mysterium tremendum*, runs through the congregation: *Sancta Sanctis*. 'Holy things for the holy,' says the priest, as he elevates the Lamb, the Bread of life; and everyone replies, 'One only is holy, one only is the Lord, Jesus Christ.' The

---

45 Or 'beyond the heaven', Ἐπουράνιον; this marks the apophatic moment of the invocation.

faithful come near to one another like the holy women at the tomb. The door opens wide, in silence, the symbol of the Angel Gabriel rolling away the stone from the sepulchre. The worshippers bow themselves as the priest appears, holding the chalice. The risen Christ is coming to offer eternal Life. The grave and death are broken up. The dawn of the Resurrection bathes everything in a light that will never fade.

'In the fear of God, and with faith and love, draw near.' The Communion witnesses to the presence of Christ that is real and constant till the end of the world. But at the same time, the elevation of the chalice after the Communion and the spirals of incense enveloping the holy gifts as they are brought back to the prothesis to be consumed ('as they were watching, he was lifted up, and a cloud took him out of their sight,' Acts 1.9) symbolize the Ascension of Jesus into heaven, from whence already rays of light are falling, the precursors of the light of the Parousia and the new Jerusalem. The Liturgy ends on an eschatological note; the meal is messianic, the faithful stand around looking at the one who comes: 'O Christ, Passover great and most holy, grant that we may more perfectly be admitted to the communion of thy mystic supper in the day without evening of thy Kingdom.' The priest prays, 'Be thou exalted above the heavens, O God, and thy glory over all the earth.'

The mission of Christ is finished: 'O Christ, who hast accomplished the mystery of thy divine economy, fill our hearts with joy and gladness.'

The world must become one Christ: 'We have beheld the true light; we have received the heavenly Spirit; we have found the true faith in worshipping the undivided Trinity, for he hath saved us ... Blessed be the name of the Lord, now and for ever.'

The Liturgy ends with the final blessing and the distribution of the *antidoron* or blessed bread, a reminder of the primitive agapes. In this act of *eulogia* (blessing) the Church extends its liturgical action beyond the walls of the temple to the very ends of the world. The worshipper carries away, as an offering to the world, this spiritual witness of unity and love.

Having eaten and drunk at the source, each person is now like a cup filled with the presence of Christ and offered to humankind and to the world.

* * *

The liturgy is not a means but a way of life that is an end in itself, that displays its *theocentric* character for all to see. The focus of human attention in the liturgy is not self but God in his splendour. Human concern during the Liturgy is not so much with self-perfection as with coming into the full light of God. And this is the joy which, quite impartially, showers back again over a human being's nature and changes it. It acts of itself so that the human adds nothing to the splendour of God, to the sheer fact of his presence. There must be times when human beings are not anxious to find a reason for what they are doing, times of adoration when their instinctive nature is unconstrained, such as when King David danced before the Ark; let the moralists join with Michal in the chorus of disapproval.

We do not always have to be thinking about our woes, to be fixed on our sins; the Lord's Day is surely the time to accept the gift of his grace, to relax for a little while and be filled with simple and transparent joy.

'The wedding-guests cannot mourn as long as the bridegroom is with them, can they?' (Matt. 9.15) 'The friend of the bridegroom, who stands and hears him, rejoices greatly at the bridegroom's voice.' moreover, his joy has been 'fulfilled' (John 3.29).

And in the end these friends are the witnesses of the 'terrible mysteries', so terrible and so great that, according to the liturgical expression, the angels tremble, cover their eyes, and 'are astonished' as they see the divine purposes at work. And this astonishment is the beginning of wisdom, of that capacity for wonder that renders the human being completely open to receive the Truth when it comes and is offered in pure grace.

In the Liturgy, we find the Kingdom of God; it has come upon us, it is already among us, in the midst of and within us, and whatever remains will be given us when the time is right, as a bonus. In seeking the Kingdom, we are obeying the Lord and becoming his child; when we find it, we rejoice as one who has found a 'pearl of great price' or a 'treasure hidden in a field', and our joy is fulfilled.

4

The Sacraments

1. INTRODUCTION

'The sacraments: they are the way our Saviour has laid down for us, the door he
has opened ... and they are the way and the door by which he comes back to the
human race.'[1] Christ returns in the sacramental economy of the Holy Spirit and
so continues to be present in history. In addition to this, the sacraments of the
Church now occupy a place equivalent to that of the miracles in the time of the
Incarnation,[2] or, according to the more classical definition of the *Orthodox Confession*, 'The sacrament is a holy action in which, under a visible sign, the invisible grace of God is communicated to the believer.'[3]

The union of visible and invisible is inherent in the very nature of the Church,
which, as the extension of Pentecost, overflows with grace in every manifestation
of its life. But the institution of the sacraments (making them 'lawful', canonically
'valid', and 'effective' in conveying sanctifying grace) establishes an order which
sets bounds to any disorderly sectarian 'pentecostalism', and at the same time
provides an unshakeable foundation, objective and universal, for the life of grace.
The Spirit blows where it will, but through the sacraments, under conditions set
by the Church, and in virtue of the Lord's promise, the gifts of the Holy Spirit
are assuredly conferred with the Church's endorsement.

Academic theology, under Latin influence, recognizes *seven* sacraments: Baptism, Anointing with Chrism, the Eucharist, penance, extreme unction, priestly
ordination and marriage. This doctrine originated in the West in the late 11th century, was confirmed at the Council of Trent and spread to the East. But the seven
sacraments had already been mentioned in the *Confession* of Michael Paleologue
in the 13th century and cited at the unionist Council of Lyons (1274). Disputes
with Protestant theologians at the time of the Patriarch of Constantinople Jeremiah II (d.1595) resulted in the affirmation of the same number seven (the Calvin-
ist Cyril Lucaris accepting only two). The *Encyclical* of the Eastern Patriarchs[4]
also lists seven, adding for emphasis, in keeping with the polemical purpose of

---

[1] Nicholas Cabasilas, *The Life in Jesus Christ*.
[2] See O. Cullmann, *Les Sacraments dans l'Eglise Johannique*, Paris 1951, p. 35-48.
[3] First part, 99.
[4] § 15.

269

the document, 'neither more, nor fewer.' But in the 15th century, Joasaph, Metropolitan of Ephesus, was still speaking of ten sacraments, St Denys of six and St John Damascene of only two. Some lists include monastic profession, the office of the dead, and the great blessing of the waters. By 'Baptism' the Fathers often mean the three great sacraments taken together.

Broadly speaking, everything in the Christian life is within the Church and therefore sacramental in nature, for 'I will pour out of my spirit upon all flesh' (Acts 2.17); everything is a spiritual gift or ministry put at the service of the Church. However, while personal holiness, acts of faith, witness or charity, and the sanctification of every form of life and being are within the Church, they constitute a realm that cannot be formalized, regulated or objectified, and that therefore neither needs nor can be given explicit authority by the *consensus* of the Body. The most one can say is, 'To each is given the manifestation of the Spirit for the common good' (1 Cor. 12.7).

There are also a great many sacramentals (*sacramentalia*): the consecration of churches, crosses and icons, the blessing of water and of the fruits of the earth, funerals and monastic vows, liturgical and priestly blessings, the sign of the cross, prayer. All these rites also confer the grace of the Holy Spirit.

Fr Nicholas Afanasiev[5] refines the distinction. While every sacrament includes a sanctifying act, not every sanctifying act is a sacrament. The latter comprises the will of God that this act should take place, the act itself, and thirdly its authentication by the Church, so that the gift is known to be conferred and received. Thus, in ancient practice every sacramental act was accompanied by the *axios* of the people, and all the sacraments led up to the Eucharist, the crowning example of the assurance that the Church gives of every sacrament – that the Spirit is actually conveyed. This *consensus* belongs to the inner truth of the Church. A sacrament is always an event *in* the Church, *by* the Church and *for* the Church; it excludes any individualization that isolates the act or him who receives it. Every sacrament affects the Body of *all* believers. Everyone baptized and confirmed is born into the Church, enriching it by one member; every pardon and absolution gives the penitent back to the Church,[6] to the 'communion of saints'; every Eucharist unites 'all of us who partake of the one Bread and the one Cup, one to another in the communion of the Holy Spirit' (Liturgy of St Basil), 'after which we make mention of the sky, the earth and the sea; the sun, moon and stars; every creature reasonable and unreasonable, visible and invisible; and the angels and archangels.'[7] The consecration of a bishop ensures the Eucharist, the manifestation of the Church. Before anything else a husband and wife will join the

---

[5] 'Sacramenta et Sacramentalia', in *La Pensée Orthodoxe*, No 8 (in Russian).
[6] Clement of Alexandria, *P.G.* 9, 649.
[7] St Cyril of Jerusalem, *P.G.*, 33, 1119.

congregation at the Liturgy in their new married state. So every sacrament transcends the particular in favour of universal significance, and the gifts are manifested for all to see.

As the extension of Pentecost, continuing the revelatory work of the Holy
Spirit, the Church is constantly revealing itself as identical with Christ who is the
Way, the Truth and the Life, so that the Church is itself a sacrament of the Truth
and the Life. The spiritual gift of Truth governs the work of the Councils. Their
doctrinal definitions have an almost sacramental character. Their formula, 'it
seemed good to the Holy Spirit and to us,' is realized in two stages: first, 'it seemed
good to us', and afterwards the reception by the Body, the proclamation of the
consensus, if the Council is recognized as Ecumenical: 'it seemed good to the
Holy Spirit'. The Council is Ecumenical because the Spirit of Truth has spoken.[8]

'Our teaching agrees with the Eucharist.'[9] Every sacrament goes back to the
institution of the Eucharist, is included in it. There is no need to find a statement
of the Saviour explicitly instituting every sacrament. There must certainly always
be scriptural support, but every sacrament derives its power from the Sacrament
of sacraments which is the Church-Eucharist. And there is no formal or legalistic
principle governing the sacraments. If, for some good reason, when a sacrament
is ministered, the canonical conditions are not met, 'grace supplies human weakness,' and close association with the Eucharist can testify to the descent of the
Spirit and the reception of the gift. That is why in ancient times every sacrament
was celebrated as an integral part of the eucharistic liturgy, and was perfected in
the Lord's Supper.

Every sacrament is preceded by its epiclesis and springs from the economy
of the Holy Spirit: 'For as the bread of the Eucharist by invocation (epiclesis)
becomes the Body of Christ, so the Chrism by invocation (epiclesis) becomes
Christ's gift of grace, and, by the operation of the Holy Spirit, is enabled to convey his divinity.'[10]

Sacrament, μυστήριον, means something secret or hidden. 'The mysteries of
Christ are hidden from the profane, even from the prophets, for Christ has communicated them only in parables.'[11] It is a mystery also, because while God performs it, he does so through the action of the priest. 'When the priest baptizes, it
is not he that baptizes, but God, who is invisibly present, holding the head of the
baptized.'[12] And St John Chrysostom: 'God works through the priests, even un-

[8] According to St Gregory of Nazianzus the Father is the True, the Son is the Truth and the
Holy Spirit is the Spirit of Truth – Πνεῦμα τῆς Ἀληθείας (*P.G.* 35, 1164 A).
[9] St Irenaeus, *Adv. haeres.* IV, 18, 5.
[10] St Cyril of Jerusalem, *P.G.* 33, 1089.
[11] Clement of Alexandria, *Strom.* I, V.
[12] *P.G.* 57, 507.

worthy ones, to save the people.'[13] Moral excellence is of course always desirable in the minister, but it is not an absolute requirement; similarly, the faith of the recipient has no effect on the objective validity of the sacrament; this is always efficacious either to salvation or to condemnation, depending on whether faith is present. The sacraments are not merely signs that confirm the divine promises, or means of quickening faith and confidence; they not only give grace but *contain* it; they convey immortality and nourish us for it, being both instruments of salvation and salvation itself.

2. THE EUCHARIST

The theological manuals describe the Eucharist as if it were one sacrament among others. In so doing they distort ancient tradition and commit the fatal error of considering that 'the mother of all the sacraments' is no longer the Eucharist, but the ordination of priests.[14]

Now the institution of the priesthood is included in the institution of the holy supper, for the bishop is above all the one who has the power to say with assurance, 'The Word was made flesh,' and, 'This verily is the flesh and blood of the Lord;' and it is he, acting *in nomine Christi*, who transforms a gathering of people into a eucharistic congregation and a manifestation of God's Church. However, the witness cannot take precedence over what is being witnessed. There is no possible scale of comparison: the Eucharist is neither the most important nor the most central among the sacraments, but in it the Church is fulfilled and manifested; every sacrament depends on the power of the Eucharist, which is that of the Church itself. Wherever the Eucharist is celebrated, the Church is there, and a member of the Church is one who takes part in it, for it is in the Eucharist that Christ 'is with us to the end of the world,' according to his own promise. Excommunication, on the other hand, is above all the removal of the chalice, the cutting off from the *koinonia*.

Through communion the faithful are made consanguineous and incorporate in Christ, 'transformed into the substance of Kings' (Nicholas Cabasilas),[15] into Christ's heavenly body, of which Fr Sergei Bulgakov says, 'In the present age, the Church as the Body of Christ is, in its ultimate (but invisible) reality, that eucharistic body into which the eucharistic gifts are changed.'[16] This is one meaning of the Pauline expression, 'the mystery hidden for ages in God who created all things' (Eph. 3.9). If the mother of the sacraments had been the priesthood, the

---

13 *P.G.* 62, 609.
14 *Theol. dogm.* by Bishop Macarius.
15 *The Life in Jesus Christ*; St Maximus stresses the metamorphosis of the communicant into Christ.
16 'Le dogme eucharistique', Review *Voie* (in Russian), 1930.

Pontiff of Rome with his universal jurisdiction would take precedence over the Eucharist, and the whole hypostasis in the pope would take precedence over the parts – the local churches. Now the Eucharist, source of all the graces, is the foundation of the eucharistic conception of the Church, and reveals every local church under its bishop as the 'Church' of God. The Church is the omni-sacrament and performs every sacrament by its power, because it is the Eucharist, which includes everything, and 'further than that we cannot go...'. At the end of the Liturgy the Church utters this glorious testimony to its fullness: 'We have seen the true Light, we have received the Heavenly Spirit'.

3. GRACE

In his *Homily on Pentecost* St Gregory of Nazianzus says, 'We celebrate the coming of the Spirit, the conclusive fulfilment of the promise ... The works of Christ according to the flesh come to an end ... the works of the Spirit begin.'[17] Nevertheless, while, according to St Basil, 'in all its activity the Spirit is inseparably united to the Father and the Son,' St Irenaeus sees the economy of salvation proceeding from the Father, through the Son, to the Holy Spirit: beginning with the creation, and continuing through the Incarnation, everything is directed towards Pentecost; then on that first morning of the Church the movement is reversed: in the age of the Church, the Spirit gathers and incorporates all the faithful into the Body of Christ which the Son will finally put into the hands of God. The mystery of salvation is *Christological*, but not *pan-Christic*; the epiclesis is always a preliminary act done for the purpose of Christifying. So as the age of the Church begins, the sanctifying power of the Spirit, *grace*, assumes the work of salvation. At Epiphany the Dove, in its descent, traces that bringing to birth which is the Father going towards the Son and sending his Spirit upon him: 'Today I have begotten you.'[18] To receive the Dove into ourselves, to be opened to the Spirit, is to be opened to the birth of Jesus in our hearts. By the movement of the Dove we are carried towards Christ, to that Nativity when the creature 'gives birth' to its Creator (so continuing the universal mystery of the *Theotokos*), and thus 'the Creator puts himself at the heart of creation.' The Holy Spirit accomplishes that birth of Christ which is the Christification of humankind.[19]

   Gratia, χάρις, is the power of God: 'You will receive power when the Holy Spirit has come upon you' (Acts 1.8). The agent of that power is 'the Spirit of grace' (Heb. 10.29). The kenosis of the Spirit will not allow any conceptual definition of grace; academic theology deals with its phenomenology and very little

---

[17] *P.G.* 36, 437.
[18] Luke 3.22 (variant); Psalm 2.7.
[19] 'The Spirit renders the soul fertile, Virgin and Mother at the same time,' and unceasingly begets Christ in her womb (St Maximus, *Expos. or. dom.*, *P.G.* 90, 889 C).

with its ontology. The *Encyclical of the Patriarchs*[20] distinguishes between enlightening, prevenient grace which is addressed to each individual, and sanctifying and justifying grace. It is the latter that is at work in the sacraments and brings
about the deified state.

Human nature, being created in the image of God, is predestined, and therefore predisposed, to communion with God, open to inner grace. This conformity
is fundamental, for it preserves human freedom of choice. Grace must be present
to provide freedom with its content, the *what*, and freedom must be real to provide
grace with its *how*. Without such interaction and complementarity, the message
of the Gospel would be in danger of becoming as rigid as the Koran.

As a consequence of the Fall, the action of the Spirit became *external* to nature
(so that in Old Testament times, the Spirit, like a tangent that does not penetrate
the circle, spoke through the prophets, but was not within them). But at the
anointing in the Jordan he came down upon Christ's humanity and filled it, and
on the day of Pentecost he became active *within* human nature. Ever since, according to the Patristic saying, the Spirit has been 'more familiar to us than we
ourselves.' The Council of Chalcedon recognized Christ's humanity as *the* human
nature (the second Adam).[21] The doctrine of the two wills in Christ explains how
they interact: the human will is not automatically subordinate to the divine will,
but *freely follows it*, 'without confusion and without separation.' This interaction
determines from eternity the structure of our own personality – St Maximus calls
it 'identity by grace'[22] – so that the more it is itself, the less it belongs to itself.
That is the essential mystery of the human being, its heavenly, liturgical predestination; only in God can it be truly itself and at peace. The call is not from outside, acting by violence or force, but from within humanity's very being (which
is theandric, in keeping with the image); it identifies itself with the person's deepest desire, so it is freely accepted as the ultimate destiny ordained for the person
from the beginning. This is *creative grace*: humankind, according to the Fathers
of the Church, is endowed with a grace implicit in the very act of creation. Utterly
human nature, pure and simple, does not exist; if it were neutral it would tend
inevitably towards demonic autonomy, but it cannot rid itself of its deiform structure. Even in evil, the human being retains its freedom; its grace is perverted, but
still a gift – the fevered outpouring of a god of evil; and even if a human being
can turn itself into a demonic monkey, this deformity has no reality except by
reference to the image. Negation must always be secondary, subordinate to affirmation; in God there is only *yes*, according to St Paul. The 'Son of Man', the

---

[20] § 3.
[21] The whole nature is infused with divine power. Western theology is far more preoccupied
with the salvation of individuals, humanity being seen rather as the *massa peccati* (see St Leo
the Great, *P.L.* 54, 192 C-193 A).
[22] *Ad Thal.* V. 25; *P.G.* 90, 333 A.

'heavenly Man', refers enigmatically to the mystery of the human image in God: it was necessary for creation to be crowned by the Incarnation, even if there had been no Fall. And the Incarnation leads into Pentecost, the age of the Church, the age of participation, by the various means of grace, in the divine life.

Prevenient grace renders our nature sensible to 'the breathing of the Spirit', it makes us attentive and thus entirely safeguards our *freedom of choice* (Acts 14.16); 'If you hear my voice and open the door, I will come in to you and eat with you, and you with me' (Rev. 3.20). Its attention aroused by the Spirit, the human being can then utter the decisive *'fiat'* for its destiny.

4. THE MYSTERY OF PREDESTINATION

While emphasizing the sovereign way of the sacraments, we must not overlook 'extraordinary grace', fundamental as it is to the teaching of St Paul. A 'natural Old Testament' (Rom. 1.18-21) was certainly offered to the pagans, and the Fathers refer to early encounters with the Word that foreshadowed the Incarnation; the pre-Christian saints mentioned in the Bible came within the scope of God's glorious and universal covenant.

In defining the relations between God and his creation, the Latin approach is to use the terminology of causation. God is the first cause, the divine motor that sets in train movement, life, existence; everything is traced back to its first cause. The consequence of this is that human freedom is only a second, instrumental cause; it originates in the first cause and is determined by it. If the second sins, the first tolerates it. Causal determinism is inevitably within time, and so, necessarily, is the first cause, which is thereby the universal pre-cause of everything, the prefix 'pre' signifying that time is introduced into the eternity of God. Thus humankind can be nothing more than the object of divine action. The jurist Calvin took Augustine's unfinished notion of causality and pursued it with iron logic to the very end: *Praedestinatio ad gloriam, reprobatio ad gehennam.* The circle is closed, there is no possible way of escape.[23]

In eastern theology God is never the first cause, but the Creator. Creation 'in the image' places liberty outside the confines of mechanical causality, and the Patristic conception of humankind as *autexousia* signifies exactly its mysterious capacity to transcend every constraint of nature, even to the point of approaching divine freedom, to appear as *microtheos*. We can even say paradoxically that God the Philanthropist is himself much more determined by his creation and his covenants ('The Lord has sworn and will not change his mind', Ps. 110.4) than

---

[23] 'Thus, in view of the end for which human beings were created, we say that they are predestined to death or life' (*Institution*, ch VIII, p. 62).

the creature by its Creator. The Incarnation is seen as the inevitable response of God to his own premise: the deiformity of his creature. And the Fall of humankind reveals the enormous scope of its freedom to determine its own fate. Satan was not lying when he said, 'You will be like God'; humankind has created something that had never existed till then; it has created evil and introduced it into its own innocent nature. Even more, humankind determines the *form* of the Incarnation as *crucified Love*. The divine blood was poured out precisely to safeguard freedom under grace; for God, according to the Fathers, 'cannot force anybody to love him.'

But autonomy pushed to its breaking-point is always against nature, for it imprisons the human being in its sub-nature, hardens its 'ipseity', destroys its deiform ontology. On the other hand, when a human being ceases to see itself in its pure subjectivity and sees itself in relation to the divine Other, then it discovers its identity to be the gift of grace, its personal being to be received from eternity; its hellish isolation is abolished and it moves beyond it to rejoice as the friend of the Bridegroom and to pronounce the *'fiat'* of the Handmaid.

'I am standing at the door, knocking,' says the Lord, and he knocks at his own image in humanity; his waiting is real, *kenotic*, and nothing is predetermined. The decrees of God, even the predictions of Revelation can be seen as *conditional*;[24] human freedom can change them. The *'fiat'* of the human, its prayer, the miracles of its faith, the absolute newness of sanctity introduce a synergetic causality that far transcends any preliminary necessity of a general law; this 'creative causality' is absolutely new, not part of any previous causal chain, and generates a new effect and leads us to a nuptial relationship ruled by love in its sovereign freedom, where submission and subordination lose all meaning and become 'wholly other'. The whole mystery of the icon of the *Deesis* it that it gives us simultaneously the image of judgment and the image of the marriage of the lamb.

True faith is never a simple signing up to something, but a dialogue, the merest hint of an invitation, an almost imperceptible call, which is never irresistible: 'Not by might, nor by power, but by my spirit, says the Lord of hosts' (Zech. 4.6). God puts himself 'at the heart of his creation,' or rather, *in* the heart of his creation, and so 'redeems' spiritual relationships, frees them from our categories of time. The vice of *pre*destination, of *pre*science, is that it introduces into God the Creator a temporal before and after; the first cause is thus placed within time so that it *pre*views, and therefore *pre*destines, determines everything.[25] Now, divine eternity and religious faith rooted in freedom do not include our distorted divisions of time. By introducing the 'pre', the past and the future, we distort the

[24] See texts such as Jeremiah 18.7-10; 26.2-3 and 13.
[25] There were theologians who carried determinism even to the extent of denying that Adam was free before the Fall. He was *predestined* to fall, and Christ was *predestined* to shed his blood for the elect!

'eternal present'[26] of God and the very capacity of faith to pass beyond everything that is 'pre' into that divine present, thereby debarring the temporal creature from its access to the realm of timelessness. Thus it becomes all the more important to emphasize that the essential nature of freedom, its one necessary quality, is revealed in the exercise of choice. And it is large enough to allow for the most tremendous choice of all, that of deciding to oppose God. The only thing it cannot do is exercise choice without reference to God, because choice is the function of the image, which alone can answer questions of theodicy and explain the origins of evil; even *before* any temptation, 'being in the image of God' carried with it a certain abstract, theoretical knowledge of evil, such as must exist in God himself, since he is omniscient. It explains the first Luciferian choice *before* any evil really existed and shows that, even in that state of innocence, freedom was preserved intact, and that it was God who protected it against his own omnipotence.

According to Patristic thought, Lucifer – 'Day Star, son of Dawn' (Isa. 14.12) – was a true *alter ego* of God, set in a relation of particular intimacy between God and his created image. His will and love, concentrated at first on the very being of God, then lighted upon the entirely theoretical idea of evil and turned aside, was perverted by changing its object: from the One God it turned towards his attributes; love of God became the inordinate desire for his own glory. Likeness turned into a sinful longing for equality and identity, and this was the Fall. Instead of being content with a pure reflection of God's glory, the perverted creature claims the glory for itself, resulting in self-worship.

The notion of God as 'first cause' imprisons God within the world; now, dependence on God – as we are reminded in the Liturgy – creates a relationship not of cause and effect, but of likeness; the *Archetype* marks the *type* with his imprint – freedom – which sets it beyond the reach of any determinism.

Time is contained within eternity; it can come out of it and set itself in opposition to it in absurd and hellish repetition, and equally can re-enter it: 'Before Abraham was, I am' (John 8.58). The beginning, the first 'moment' of time – the *in principio* of Genesis – is in itself, according to St Basil, non-temporal, but at the instant of its occurrence time was set in motion. So it is impossible to speak of what 'existed before' that moment, but we can imagine and even anticipate the expansion and breaking out from time into eternity of all creation.

Sunday is truly the 'first day' of all time, the first and only – μία – and the eighth day of the week, the day after the seventh day of the Jews, outside the worldly week, or history, of which it is the beginning and the end; it is the instant when eternity gives rise to time and it is the parousial instant when eternity receives it back again. For want of a deeper understanding of the relation between time and eternity, for want of a firm doctrine of creation *ad imagem*, rather than

---

26 See Louis Lavelle, *La dialectique de l'éternel présent*.

one of causation *ex nihilo*, western theology, faced with the fearsome theory of double predestination, stops half-way and speaks only of the better case, that of predestination to salvation. In any event this is to elevate an exclusive soteriology into eschatology. Enslavement to sin is turned into submission to grace, for the original freedom of choice has become transcendent. This simplification presents such insurmountable difficulties that the classical call to the unutterable mystery cannot even be heard. There is nothing really mysterious about the arbitrariness of the divine choice of the elect and the damned.

In modern commentaries on Romans 8.9, predestination depends on the foreknowledge of God, and the 'we' of Ephesians 1.3-12 and everywhere else is understood in the limited and absolutely arbitrary sense of the 'elect' only. Now, for St Paul, to be called is synonymous with being Christian. On the other hand, Paul often uses anthropomorphic and temporal notions; indeed, his terminology is often confused and inadequate to his thought, his theology is strongly voluntarist. The great theme of the Epistle to the Romans is salvation by faith *and* by the life full of grace and conformed to faith. The great and fundamental Pauline antithesis is not between faith and works, but between the works of faith and the works of the law. More importantly, and setting aside all doctrinal prejudice, predestination, if we wish to use that concept, is only a conventional way of formulating the mystery of 'the love of God', the love that determines – predestines – not humanity but God. It is highly symptomatic that in Romans 5.19, 'as by one man's disobedience the many were made sinners, so by one man's obedience the many will be made righteous', the terms used are παρακοή (disobedience) and ὑπακοή (obedience), which occur very rarely, even in classical Greek. Their rarity points to an unaccustomed meaning: corresponding to the depth of disobedience there exists a depth of obedience. To transgress that boundary is a matter not of law but of ontology. The obedience of Christ is that of the Word to the Father, leading in its utter completeness towards the nudity of Adam, the 'other humanity'[27] of St Gregory of Nyssa, the metamorphosis of the human being.

In Romans 1 and 8 St Paul speaks of the historio-sophical mystery of Israel, which, like the story of Jacob and Esau (so beloved of the Reformers) is much more about the paradoxes of providence, and about the course of history and its meta-historical meaning, than about salvation. Similarly, the image of the potter illustrates *only one* of the many aspects of divine wisdom, and does not pretend to describe *the whole* relationship between God and humankind. St Paul is sufficiently aware of the nature of the mystery not to fall into such a simplification. Certainly, 'it is God who is at work, enabling you both to will and to do;' but this immediately follows the contradictory command, 'Work out your own salvation

----

[27] *P.G.* 44, 1225. See Dom O. Rousseau, *Monachisme et Vie religieuse*, Chevetogne 1957, p. 131, notes 1 and 2.

with fear and trembling' (Phil. 2.12-14). According to the Fathers, the virtues belong to God, but the sweat and labour, the fear and trembling, belong to humanity: 'God has imprisoned all in disobedience so that he may be merciful to all.' To all restrictive rationalization Paul replies with the confession of the true mystery: 'his ways are past finding out.' It behoves human beings to honour them with silence. *Docta ignorantia* is the reverse of taking refuge in ignorance. The Saviour's plan, 'that everyone should be saved' (1 Tim. 2.4, Rom. 8.32), is infinitely more mysterious and more impenetrable than the impoverished foursquare human logic of double predestination.[28] The 'chosen people complex' is an unhealthy state that indicates an unquiet conscience, haunted by the fear of hell.

5. THE SACRAMENT OF BAPTISM. ENTRY INTO THE CHURCH

St Peter's hearers asked what they must do. 'Repent, and be baptized every one of you in the name of Jesus Christ so that your sins may be forgiven; and you will receive the gift of the Holy Spirit' (Acts 2.38). There is a clear progression from the abolition of the past to the present age of spiritual gifts which heralds the Kingdom. Entry into this Kingdom-Church entails undergoing death and being reborn by 'water and the Spirit' (John 3.5). The neophyte receives the seal, σφραγίς, of membership of the people of God united in Christ and living in the new age-Eucharist. Regeneration by 'water and the Spirit' is an early indication that the 'Christian initiation' conferring salvation already consisted of a package of the 'three major sacraments' – Baptism, Anointing and the Eucharist.

There is evidence for the practice of child Baptism in the Lord's words, 'Let the little children to come to me' (Mark 10.14), and in the Baptism by the Apostles of 'houses' or entire families, which presupposes the inclusion of children (1 Cor. 1.16). The tradition is very strong: Origen,[29] Irenaeus, Tertullian[30] testify that in the 2nd century the Church was baptizing children, and by the end of the century it had become the usual practice; in the time of St Cyprian we see Baptism administered even before the eighth day.[31] In the time of the Apostles preaching was addressed to adults in order to form the first generation of members of the Church; the question of the age for Baptism arose only in the next generation. The tradition needs to be examined in its historical context.

Baptism is analogous to circumcision (Col. 2.11) and replaces it with its own sign non manufacta of anagenesis and of belonging to the new age. 'Repent, and

---

[28] In his *Church Dogmatics* Karl Barth offers a more balanced doctrine, outlining an alternative but profound approach that preserves the Mystery.
[29] *P.G.* 12, 496.
[30] *P.L.* 1, 1221.
[31] Fourth Council of Carthage; *P.L.* 3, 1015.

believe in the good news' (Mark 1.15), the act of faith precedes the operation of the Spirit and follows it as the condition of sharing in the Eucharist. This require-ment of faith in children is satisfied by the biblical understanding of the close connection between the generations; children can never be dissociated from the spiritual bond they have with their parents or (if the parents are unbelievers) more distant relations. In every case the godparents and the spiritual family of the Church confess the faith required by the sacrament. At the same time, the general rule of sacramental economy applies: everything depends on God; nothing is ex-pected of humanity but a readiness to receive the energies of grace. In any case the person's state of awareness, the ability to understand will never be equal to the unutterable immensity of the event. The mystery will always remain impen-etrable to anyone at any stage of life; the angelic innocence of the child gives place to the 'trembling of the soul before the door of Paradise.' Borne on the faith of the Church, a human being can only say, 'I believe; help my unbelief!' (Mark 9.24) The human element is completely subordinated to the sacred; all is con-centrated on God and designed to reveal him, hence the name μυστήριον. The Council of Carthage in the 5th century declared, 'Adults and children are equal before God'; they are at the same level of pure receptivity. Any knowledge that humankind can have of God does not depend on its own power of thought, but is given to it as evidence. However, this knowledge is never coercive, but requires a willing response of receptivity and of active confession. The absolutely gratu-itous divine revelation can be rejected. But the initiative lies always with the pre-venient love of God: 'The Master stooped to earth and recognized his image.'[32]

The Holy Spirit is πανάγιον, holiness hypostasized, not by appropriation, but by his very nature. St Cyril of Alexandria explains that it is of the very nature of divine holiness to work directly on the creature to sanctify it. The latter possesses no gift that does not come to it from the Spirit (St Basil). The Spirit is present in substance in the sanctified soul (St Cyril). As the Giver, he comes into the human being and makes a 'gift' of it to the Father. The work conceived by the Father and executed by the Son is perfected by the Spirit. The Spirit recreates the human being and makes it a Christ-bearer, Christlike, because first of all he makes it a Spirit-bearer. He is ἅγιον and ζωοποιόν, but also ἐκφαντορικός: he reveals the Father and the Son and unites us to them. St Cyril of Alexandria sees in this the spiritual gift of divine filiation.[33] The Spirit transforms the sacraments into ves-sels for the collection and dispersal of the breathings of divine grace, so that Nicholas Cabasilas, in his treaty on the sacraments, can even paraphrase Acts 17.28 thus: 'By these sacred signs we live and move and have our being.'[34]

---

[32] Nicholas Cabasilas, *The Life in Jesus Christ.*
[33] *P.G.* 33, 372. 445. Similarly St Athanasius, *P.G.* 25, 473.
[34] See M. Lot-Borodine, 'La grâce déifiante des Sacraments d'après Nicolas Cabasilas', in *Revue des Sciences philosophiques et théologiques*, vol. XXV, 1936.

Symbolism
Baptism is the 'bath of eternity' and hence ἀναγέννησις, the total refashioning of the human being, its remoulding truly according to the image of God. Our Adamic nature summed up in Christ is restored by his work of salvation. The death-and-burial and life-and-resurrection of Christ are expressed in the symbol ism of Baptism.[35] The term βαπτίζω means plunging, immersion, which in ancient times was the only permissible method of administration,[36] and Hermas speaks of 'going down into the water.'[37] The profound connection with the descent into hell[38] disappears entirely when Baptism is done by pouring or sprinkling. This sacrament represents symbolically the whole course of our salvation: the triple immersion is our passage through the *triduum* and the descent into hell;[39] emerging, we return towards endless noonday. The baptismal water takes on the sacramental value of the purifying blood of Christ, and so the Cross is set up at the threshold of the new life.

The Matter of the Sacrament
Regeneration is effected *ex aqua* and *ex Spiritu sancto* (John 3.5-7). Liturgically the feast of the Epiphany celebrates the general sanctification of all matter.[40] The sanctifying power in person, the Holy Spirit, in his sacramental parousia bestows his energies on the baptismal water, the living water, ὕδωρ ζῶη, making it the vehicle of grace, procreative, μήτρα ὕδατος.[41] Referring to the great biblical prefiguration of the Flood and the Ark, Hermas says, 'the Church is built on the waters,' and St Cyril of Jerusalem, '*The Spirit of God moved upon the face of the water*. Water was the beginning of the world, and the Jordan the beginning of the Gospel tidings.'[42]

By the epiclesis-invocation the water is purified of all evil influence and is given the power of sanctification. The Spirit does not simply raise up the water to be the agent of his work, or an instrumental cause, but infuses himself within it. According to St Cyril of Jerusalem, the water is now united to the Holy Spirit who works in it and by means of it.[43] Similarly, oil, μύρον, χρῖσμα, prepared for

[35] St Cyril of Jerusalem, *P.G.* 33, 444; St Basil, *P.G.* 32, 129; St Gregory of Nyssa, *P.G.* 45, 85.
[36] *Didache* 7, 1, 3. Exceptions were allowed only if there was not enough water, or in the case of sickness or emergency.
[37] *Mand.* IV, 3.
[38] St John Chrysostom, *P.G.* 61, 347.
[39] See Dom O. Rousseau, 'La descente aux enfers, fondement sotériologique du baptême chrétien', in *Mélanges Jules Lebreton*, II, 273.
[40] St Ignatius of Antioch, Eph.18, 2; St Ambrose, *P.L.* 15, 1583.
[41] Clement of Alexandria, *Strom.* IV, 25; *P.G.* 8, 1369; *Didache*, VII, 1.
[42] *Catech.* III, 5; *P.G.* 33, 432.
[43] *Catech.* III, 3; *P.G.* 33, 429.

Unction by the epiclesis, becomes 'Christ's gift of grace, and, by the advent of the Holy Spirit, is made fit to impart His Divine Nature.'[44] The Holy Spirit is in the Chrism as it is in the baptismal water; he works in it and by means of it. Thus the Chrism is the antitype – ἀντίτυπος – of the Holy Spirit: it is no mere image or symbol, but really contains and constitutes the element within which the work of the Spirit is concealed. Our fleshly element participates in grace for the same reasons as our spirit, so that the two reflect the image of the incarnate Word. That is why, in sacramental symbolism, the sacred sign not only operates but *is* the thing signified; here *signum* equals *res*.

The Operation of the Sacrament

Before the 'promise' of Baptism, 'the great and blessed profession of faith in the Trinity,'[45] the oath that truly binds us to Christ, the soul must be made ready by exorcism and the renunciation of evil; the priest breathes on the face of the 'dead', breathes Life on it, as life was breathed into Man at his creation; facing west, the neophyte 'mimes' the struggle that will last throughout his Christian life and solemnly renounces the power of the enemy.[46]

The rite of unclothing and reclothing with the white garment signifies the return to innocence: 'We leave the garments of skin and go back to the royal robe ... We give up one existence in order to regain another ... The baptismal water destroys one life and produces another.'[47]

The invocation of the name of the Trinity (which is why it is called the sacrament of the Trinity) and the pouring of the consecrated oil into the baptismal font consecrates the water for the sacrament. The anointing of the body recalls the preparation of Jesus' body for burial: 'We offer to the Lord the imitation of his death.'[48] God responds to it by the resurrection. We receive our essential nature and, like a statue, the creature is 'remodelled' according to its divine archetype; the integrity of the image is restored. The baptismal water effaces the imprint of the Enemy, the smirch of original sin, and imprints the σφραγίς, the seal or indelible stamp by which the angels recognize the faithful.[49] The creature comes out of the 'bath of eternity' branded like a sheep by its shepherd, rendered without blemish; the soul receives the grace of predisposition to holiness.

---

[44] *Cat.* XXI, 3.
[45] St Athanasius, *P.G.* 26, 1197.
[46] St Cyril of Jerusalem, *P.G.* 33, 1068; Denys, *P.G.* 3, 396.
[47] Nicholas Cabasilas, *The Life in Jesus Christ.*
[48] Nicholas Cabasilas, *Ibid.*
[49] Pseudo-Basil, *P.G.* 31, 432.

The presence of the Holy Spirit at Epiphany is manifested in the great light of the Jordan, whence the name of φωτισμός,[50] illumination, that the Fathers give to Baptism, as well as to the Parousia-Advent. The 'Feast of Lights'[51] celebrates our birth to the divine light: 'Baptism reveals the Creator to the creature, truth to the intelligence, and to the *heart* the only desirable being.'[52]

Christ works by the sacred influence of the Spirit which he sends on earth, and this is emphasized by the role of the priests in the administration of the sacraments which convey the active power of the Church: 'It is not the priest who baptizes, but God whose invisible power holds the head of the baptized,' as St John Chrysostom explains.[53] Instead of the indicative western form, *Ego te baptismo*, the more ancient form, in the third person, is used in the East: *Baptisatur servus Dei*. It dates from early tradition and has been fixed since the 16th century.[54]

The image of God is restored, and with it, the capacity to recognize grace; the spiritual senses are set free to allow the growth of spiritual understanding, the apprehension of uncreated grace and the communication of the divine. 'And all of us, with unveiled faces, seeing the glory of the Lord as though reflected in a mirror, are being transformed into the same image,' says St Paul (2 Cor. 3.18). 'As soon as we are baptized, our soul being cleansed by the Spirit shines more brightly than the sun, and we not only behold the glory of God, but also receive from it a kind of splendour,' says St John Chrysostom.[55] 'So if anyone is in Christ, there is a new creation' (2 Cor. 5.17).[56]

6. THE SACRAMENT OF ANOINTING WITH CHRISM[57]

Anointing immediately follows Baptism. According to the pattern of Epiphany, Unction is an integral part of Christian initiation.[58] The connection of the two

---

[50] Justin, *Apol.* 1, 61; *P.G.* 6, 420; Denys, *P.G.* 2, 392.
[51] St Gregory of Nazianzus, *Or*, XI, 46; *Or.* XL, 24; *P.G.* 36, 392.
[52] Nicholas Cabasilas, *The Life in Jesus Christ.*
[53] *In Mat.* hom. L, 3.
[54] Theodorus Lector, *P.G.* 86, 196.
[55] *In Ep.* II *Cor.*, hom. VII.
[56] Speaking of those who die unbaptized, Hermas says the Apostles come to them after their death to preach the name of the Son of God to them and give them the σφαγίς, the seal of Baptism. (*Simil.* IX, 16). Clement of Alexandria repeats the passage (*Strom.* II, 9; *P.G.* 8, 980). Icons showing St John the Baptist as the forerunner of Christ into the underworld lend an extra depth to the subject.
[57] The term 'Confirmation' is Latin, used by Leo the Great, the Council of Orange and that of Arles (455).
[58] St John Damascene, *De fide orth.* IV, 262.

sacraments is very ancient.[59] The Patristic teaching about the meaning of this link is quite explicit: Baptism re-imprints the obliterated divine *image*, Anointing restores the *likeness* of God. It is the gift of perfection ('be perfect, therefore, as your heavenly Father is perfect') and of holiness ('be holy, for I am holy'). Chrism (μύρον or χρῖσμα), Unction is 'the very symbol of our participation in the Holy Spirit'. It incorporates us in the humanity of Christ, opens us to holiness; it is the direct infusion of uncreated divine grace in souls.[60] The giving of the Holy Spirit is the giving of the Kingdom here and now: the Spirit is called the Kingdom and he inaugurates the reign of God in us.[61] Baptism reproduces in the life of every neophyte the Passion and the Passover, and Chrismation is our Pentecost. Our awakening to life in Baptism is followed by the bestowal of the *Pneuma*, of his energies, to realize the gift within us. First we receive the essential nature, then the unction gives us strength and movement, the δύναμις, the energy to act. It arms us as the soldiers and athletes of Christ. We are commanded, and by God's grace and love enabled, 'to bear witness without fear or weakness,' as the Synod of Elvira put it. Christ the spirit-bearer sends the Spirit on us to consecrate us as witnesses and prophets. According to Nicholas Cabasilas,[62] the Spirit confers on us 'the power to act for the glory of God.' 'Do not forget the Holy Spirit; at the moment of your illumination he is ready to mark your soul with his seal; he will give you the heavenly and divine σφραγίς which makes the devils tremble; he will arm you for the combat; he will give you strength ... he will be your guardian and your defender, he will watch over you as over his own soldier;'[63] 'clothed in the armour of the Holy Spirit you will stand firm against every opposing power.'[64] The prayer over the Chrism asks for 'a divine and heavenly energy that renders firm and invincible.'[65] The Apostolic Constitutions call the Chrism the βεβαίωσις τῆς ὁμολογίας.[66]

The Matter of the Sacrament
The consecration of the Holy Chrism composed of olive oil and precious balms (57 in number) is celebrated on Holy Thursday by the Patriarch himself, which

[59] 48th Canon of the Council of Laodicaea.
[60] See St Cyril of Alexandria, *Thesaurus* and *De Trinitate*.
[61] St Nil of Sinai, *De Oratione*, 58, n. 1.
[62] Cf. M. Lot-Borodine, 'La grâce déifiante des Sacraments d'après Nicolas Cabasilas', in *Revue des Sciences philosophiques et théologiques*, vol. XXVI, 1937.
[63] St Cyril of Jerusalem, *P.G.* 33, 996, 1009.
[64] *P.G.* 33, 1092.
[65] *Sacramentary of Serapion*, Brightman, *Journal of Theological Studies*, London 1900, vol. 1, p. 215.
[66] *P.G.* 1, 797.

underlines the importance of this event, the oil being not an instrument, but the vehicle of the Spirit that manifests Christ.[67] The epiclesis equivalent to that of the Eucharist[68] asks the Father to send down the Spirit in 'Royal Unction'; this is not just a virtue emanating from the Spirit (as in the Latin prayer) but Christ coming in the Spirit, his parousia by which he communicates himself to us. 'May fear and joy, may a holy burning desire quicken us ... in that day, a venerable mystery is accomplished ... In that moment, the whole company of the apostles comes to us with hands stretched over us.'[69]

By the epiclesis, the oil becomes 'the gift of Christ that produces the Holy Spirit by the presence of his divinity' (St Cyril, *Catechesis*). This teaching on the real presence of the Holy Spirit is common to the Fathers.

The Operation of the Sacrament

The Chrism is the element under which the Spirit hides his presence. 'While thy body is anointed with visible ointment, thy soul is sanctified by the Holy and life-giving Spirit.'[70] The unction is not merely a signing on the forehead but is applied to all parts of the body; it is in the body as a whole that the human being is *'sealed* by the seals of the gifts of the Holy Spirit' and becomes *totally* charismatic. Far from simply confirming the promises of Baptism, the Anointing activates all the powers of divine grace. Chrismation is inspired by the consecrations of the Old Testament, and χειροτονία, the laying on of hands, is done only at the signing with Chrism.

The Sacrament of the Royal Priesthood [71]

Under the conditions of the Old Testament, Israel was a chosen people, holy, set apart to be a 'kingdom of priests' (Exod. 19.6). Nevertheless, the priesthood was exercised only by the tribe of Levi (Deut. 10.8). The universal priesthood was only a promise which would be fulfilled when the New Testament took effect.

---

[67] See Goar's *Euchologion.*
[68] The Fathers insist on it: St Cyril, Cat. XVIII, 3; St Gregory of Nyssa, *P.G.* 46, 481.
[69] Prayer at the consecration of Chrism, which makes it clear that the imposition of hands is included in the chrismal consignation; as Denys says, 'The holy oils which convey Jesus Christ, complementing the hand.'
[70] St Cyril of Jerusalem, *3rd Catechetical Lecture.*
[71] For the Orthodox point of view see Fr Afanasiev, *The Ministry of the Laity in the Church* (in Russian), Paris 1955; Y. Congar, *Jalons pour une théologie du laïcat*, Paris 1953; G. Philips, *Le rôle du laïcat dans l'Eglise*, Paris 1954.

By the blood of Jesus, all, by following the divine Forerunner, are admitted to the sanctuary (Heb. 6.19-20). So the faithful are raised to the priesthood and concelebrate with the High Priest Jesus, after the order of Melchizedek. Mgr Cassien, in his study *Jésus le Précurseur*,[72] has demonstrated that our liturgical ministry, introduced by Jesus, begins *here and now*. Henceforth the faithful constitute in Christ 'a holy priesthood' (1 Pet. 2.5-9), 'that you may proclaim the mighty acts of him who called you out of darkness into his marvellous light.' Our concelebration with Jesus is a sharing in his priesthood and in his royalty. The unction (1 John 2.20) restricted in the Old Testament to kings, priests and prophets, is extended in the Church to *all* the faithful. It is no longer exclusive to a particular people or place (the temple at Jerusalem) (John 4.21-24) but belongs to all who are united by Baptism in Christ into the people of God – λαὸς Θεοῦ – and every baptized person is λαϊκός, a member of the laity or people, a member of the royal priesthood – βασίλειον ἱεράτευμα, a *priest*.[73]

The sacrament of Anointing with Chrism, which is the sacrament of the universal priesthood, establishes *all* on exactly the same priestly footing, under the single sanctifying grace of personal holiness. Out of this general priesthood some are withdrawn and appointed bishops and presbyters by a divine act. Difference of ministries is functional and has no ontological significance.[74] So for example, according to the tradition that goes back to St Ignatius of Antioch,[75] the divine fatherhood is represented by the bishops; in all that he does, every bishop or priest is 'father'. As the *Didascalia Apostolorum* says,[76] 'The bishop is, after God, your father, having regenerated you by water and the Spirit to divine sonship.' But a priest who is interdicted, cut off from the Church which is the source of his authority to operate, can no longer exercise his ministry, and so no longer receives the gift of *ministerial grace*. Another tradition goes back to the 'Desert Fathers'. These are charismatics whose *spiritual gifts are personal to themselves*, and to their own holiness; they have the gift of seeing into the heart and discerning spirits and thoughts. They are *pater* or *abba*, so that the collections of their sayings and their deeds have always been called *Paterika*. Regardless of clerical status,

---

[72] In *Théologie*, vol. XXVII, Athens 1956.
[73] See Fr Afanasiev, *op. cit.*.
[74] The Council of Trent decreed that it was impossible to reduce a cleric to the lay state, and thereby established an ontological separation between those who are 'consecrated' and those who are not. The priestly state of the laity is thus equated to the state of being outside the Church. When, exceptionally, a member of the Roman regular clergy is laicized, he retains the 'character' of the priesthood and in no circumstances is allowed to marry. An Orthodox cleric reduced to the lay state can marry.
[75] Magn. 3.1; Trall. 3.1; Smyrn. 8.1.
[76] II, 26, 4.

the essential thing for a 'spiritual father' is to become himself 'spiritual', or charismatic.[77]

Orthodoxy is remarkable for the utterly homogeneous nature of its spirituality. There is only one spirituality for all, without any distinction between bishops, monks and laymen, and the spirituality is *monastic*. Orthodoxy has never accepted the difference between the Commandments of the Church and the Counsels of Perfection; all the requirements of the Gospel as a whole are addressed to every single person. So it is in the light of this one spirituality that we must seek to understand the dignity of the lay state as a royal priesthood.

If we go back to the end of the 3rd century and beginning of the 4th – the monastic period – we find that St Anthony and St Pachomius were laymen who took to the desert in search of the conditions most favourable for the perfect practice of the spiritual life and of utter obedience to the demands of the Gospel. Among the anchorites and hermits, and later in the monastic communities, priests were there only to provide sacramental absolution and to feed them with the Eucharist. The *igoumen* or abbot elected by the community was more often than not a simple lay monk. During the iconoclastic period the monks demonstrated their steadfastness, and people came from the world at large to seek spiritual advice from these *staretz* or *gerontes*, who in the *Paterika* are always called *prophets* (such as Zenon the Prophet, or John the disciple of Barsanuphius). Theirs was a ministry of counselling; not the sacramental power of 'binding and loosing', of effacing sin, but the therapeutic way of avoiding it in the first place.[78]

One feature of this spirituality emphasizes its unity even further. While in every other sphere the woman was considered inferior to the man, in spiritual matters she was treated as perfectly equal. Clement of Alexandria says, 'Virtue and good conduct are exactly the same thing for men and women.'[79] Theodoret[80] mentions women 'who have struggled not less than men, but even more ... though weaker by nature they have shown the same resoluteness as men.' Their special strength was 'divine charity' and the particular gift of passionate devotion to Christ. Nobody took them for spiritual inferiors. They were considered just as capable as men of giving spiritual direction to nuns, and under the same conditions. A spiritually gifted woman, θεοφώτιστος – illuminated by God – was called *amma*[81] or spiritual mother. Such a one would usually be the mother of her

---

[77] 'Πνευματικὸς πατὴρ anderer kann nur sein, wer πνευματικὸς geworden ist', as R. Reitzenstein aptly says (*Historia Monachorum und Historia Lausicaa*, Göttingen 1916, p. 195; see *DC fasc.* XX-XXI, col. 1015).

[78] Cf. B. Poschmann, *Paenitentia secunda*, Bonn 1940.

[79] *P.G.* 8, 260 C.

[80] *P.G.* 82, 1489 BC, 1504 AB.

[81] *Vitae Patrum*, v. 18, 19.

monastery as Pachomius was father of his. People from the outside world sought
out such people as St Euphrosyne and St Irene to ask advice. In about 1200 the
monk Isaiah made a collection of sayings of the mothers and called it the *Me-
terikon*,[82] by analogy with *Paterikon*. Except for the power to administer the
sacraments and the authority to teach in the Church (which was reserved to the
episcopate) the mothers had the same rights and duties as the fathers had among
the monks. They were not Mothers of the Church, but were genuinely spiritual
mothers, with the right to disseminate sound doctrine; liturgical texts mention
some, such as St Helen and St Nina, as 'equal to the Apostles.' *The Banquet of
the Ten Virgins* of St Methodius is further evidence, where there is a parallel to
the life of St Anthony in the *Life of St Syneletica*, and the sayings of the mothers
take their place in alphabetical order among the *Sayings* of the Fathers. St Pachomius sent his sister the rule of his monastery so that the nuns might be formed
'according to the same canons.' Similarly the *Rules* of St Basil presuppose the
presence of a feminine element in the virtues to be looked for in monks.[83]

We shall appreciate the importance of these aspects of the monastic life if we
think of them as books of piety that, along with the Holy Scriptures, have been
the means of spiritual formation for many generations. It is why letters of spiritual
direction addressed to laymen are no different from the advice given to monks
(see the counsels of St John Chrysostom, the letters of Barsanuphius and John,
of St Nilus, and so on). 'Christ's commandment to follow the narrow way was
addressed to *all*. Religious and secular alike are called to the same standard.'
What at first seems paradoxical is that the one spiritual discipline designed for
everybody was developed by lay monks. It is in the light of this that we can form
the most accurate idea of the quality and importance of the lay state.

Monks, according to St Nilus,[84] 'lead the ascetic and apostolic life according to
the Gospel,' they are 'the ones who wish to be saved,' and to that end, 'do violence
to themselves in everything.' The universality of these principles is obvious; they express the perfect equality of all Christians when faced by the demands of the Gospel.

In the words of St Theodore the Studite, τά πάντα ἐπίστης; this unity agrees
with Tradition.[85] It is all a matter of adaptation. While the laity do not make vows
of chastity and poverty, they must still practise their exact equivalents. 'People
who live in the world, even if they are married, must in every other way resemble
monks;'[86] 'you are entirely mistaken if you suppose that there are some things
required of secular people and others of monks ... they must all give the same

---

[82] Translated into Russian by Theophan the Recluse, Moscow 1891.
[83] *P.G.* 31, 664 D, 625 A.
[84] *P.G.* 79, 180 D.
[85] *P.G.* 99, 1388 D.
[86] St John Chrysostom, *Hom. in Epist. ad Haebr.*, 7, 41.

account of themselves.'[87] Wisdom for the laity consists in being like the monks,[88] sharing their 'eschatological maximalism', living in ardent expectation of the Parousia. The ways are always the same for all: the supreme power of prayer, fasting, reading the Scriptures and the exercise of charity. All the monastic practices are imposed on everybody without distinction.[89]

So the unanimous tradition throws into relief an important fact: a special theology or spirituality for laypeople is a very modern invention. Even if there is support for it in the conditions of the modern world, it never existed in the early tradition and would have been regarded with deep astonishment. One theology or spirituality for the episcopate, and a quite separate one for the laity, would be quite incomprehensible to the Fathers of the Church. The Fathers speak constantly of the people of God, and of the universal priesthood, without ever making a distinction between clergy and laymen.

The distinction arose not in the thinking of the Fathers or in the spirituality of the deserts and monasteries, but in the towns and parishes, and the first worrying signs were already noticeable in the 4th century. Laypeople abandoned their dignity as priests, impoverished themselves, emptied themselves of their priestly substance, while the bishops became more and more the points of concentration of the sacred and the priestly. This by no means amounted to a separation, still less an opposition, but a distance was set up which indicated among the laity a dreadful refusal of the gifts of the Holy Spirit. By abdicating their priestly state the laity became mere βιωτικοί, or even ἀνίεροι (deprived of the sacred, profane). But by the sacrament of Anointing with Chrism everyone is made a member of the universal priesthood, introduced into the ἱερὰ διακόσμησις, holy order or ministry.

During the Liturgy every participant is λειτουργός, a co-minister with the bishop. All, *as people*, take an active part in the Mystery, the eucharistic anaphora, the epiclesis. Although only the bishops have sacramental power, they nevertheless celebrate the Liturgy and govern and teach only with the *consensus* of the people, who must use their own gift of discernment to 'judge, test and hold fast to what is good' (1 Cor. 14.29, 1 Thess. 5.21). 'The guardian of piety is the whole people of the Church.' However, the exercise of this gift assumes that the 'people' properly exists, for the liturgical importance of a person is always linked to the Body. Individualism, the decadent fragmentation of the priesthood into individuals, causes the gifts of grace to run dry, and destroys the priestly nature of the laity, so that the *consensus* no longer works.

When the bishops delegate liturgical and pastoral authority to the priests who represent them in the parishes, they are proceeding in accordance with the sacrament of the priesthood of order, in which every priest is appointed to his minis-

---

[87] *In Epist. ad Haebr.*, 7, 4.
[88] St Nil, *P.G.* 79, 273 D.
[89] St Nil, *Epist.* I, 167, 169.

terial function by a divine act. If necessary, laymen, teachers of theology, can also be deputized to teach and even to preach, and this is possible by virtue of the universal priesthood in which they already share – their status as 'anointed by the Spirit'. In neither case is the delegation ever purely human; anything essential for the order of the Church is always a priestly matter.

The laity are the level or perhaps the point in church order at which the World and the Church coincide. They have not been given the power of dispensing the *means of grace* (the sacraments); on the contrary, their sphere is the *life of grace*, its penetration in the world. The royal priesthood possesses the power to consecrate the world in a 'cosmic liturgy' by the simple presence of 'sanctified beings' who are 'dwelling-places of the Trinity'. Here the gift of prophecy comes into action, displaying to the laity the immensity of the world together with their particular task of lifelong apostolate and mission, which is to be accomplished *by their priestly nature* that will purge the world of every profane element. It is through their social life, through their relationships with other people, through the structures of this world, that they carry the 'three-sunned light', revealing the truth of doctrine in their lives, offering to the world the grace they have received in the Church .

'O Saviour, as thou hast given grace to the prophets, to kings and to pontiffs, give it also by this holy oil to those who receive its unction.'[90] By means of this 'oil of gladness' we are 'anointed by the Holy Spirit.' Reflection on this state, and especially on the words, 'we have become partakers of Christ' (Heb. 3.14), leads the Fathers to deduce that every Christian is invested with a threefold office: royal, sacerdotal and prophetic.[91]

The prayer at the heart of the sacrament asks for the seal of the gift of the Holy Spirit explicitly 'so that he will be pleased to serve you in every act and every word.' His whole life is consecrated and sealed for the ministry of the royal priesthood, without any possible omission, keeping nothing back from the 'terrible jealousy of God.' The totalitarian nature of this is expressed in the ceremony of the *tonsure*, identical to that at the entry into the monastic life. The prayer of the rite says, 'Lord, who hast taught us that we ought to do everything to thy glory, bless thy servant who is come to offer thee a first offering shorn from the hair of his head.' The eschatological direction of the prayer reinforces the completeness of the consecration: 'May he ascribe glory unto thee, and behold the *good things of Jerusalem* all the days of his life.'

The bodily anointings are accompanied by the formula, 'Sealed by the gift of the Holy Spirit,'[92] and they symbolize the tongues of fire of Pentecost.

---

[90] Office of the Holy Chrism.
[91] There is a rich collection of quotations from the Fathers of the Church in the book by Fr Dabin, *Le sacerdoce royal des fidèles dans la tradition ancienne et moderne*, Brussels-Paris 1950.
[92] Σφαγὶς ὄωρεᾶς Πνεύματος ἁγίου (Can. 7 of the Council of 381, can. 95 of the Council of 692, called the Quinisext.

Human beings, by the power of the Holy Spirit, 'put on Christ,' are rendered Christlike. Praying for those who are to be confirmed, the bishop says, 'O God, mark them with the seal of the spotless Chrism; they will bear Christ in their hearts, and be dwelling-places of the Trinity.' Here the Trinitarian balance is magnificently clear: sealed by the Spirit, made bearers of Christ, to be temples 'filled with the Trinity.'

In the final words of St Matthew's Gospel we read, 'Go and make disciples of all nations'. This passage, read during the sacrament of Chrismation, is a call addressed to *every baptized person*. It signifies that, alongside the missionaries officially appointed by the Church, every confirmed or anointed Christian is a missionary, an 'Apostolic person' in his or her own way. Such persons' whole life is an inner liturgy in a Trinitarian dwelling-place; they are called to bear witness unceasingly with their whole being. It for this end that they are totally consecrated: they are the priests of their entirely new existence as an oblation and sacrifice to their Lord.

The Triple Dignity of the Royal Priesthood

We may think liturgical and Patristic expressions are flowers of poetry, but they are utterly plain and realistic, because they bring us to the heart of the mystery where the most beautiful utterance can only be a very poor sign.

St Macarius of Egypt says, 'Christianity is far from mediocre because it is a great mystery. Consider your own nobleness, and the fact that you have been called to a royal dignity. The mystery of Christianity is quite removed from this world.' And he adds, terrifyingly, 'If we are not yet the royal priesthood, we are still serpents and the brood of vipers.'[93]

St Cyril of Jerusalem calls the sign that the priest traces on the newly confirmed, 'the antitype,' because it corresponds with the sign with which Christ himself was marked. St Macarius adds, in a profound comment, 'Just as, in the time of the prophets, unction was something extremely precious, because it set apart priests and prophets, so now, spiritual people, anointed with heavenly Chrism, become by grace kings, priests and prophets of the heavenly mysteries.'[94] And Arethas of Caesarea says, 'God gives us the kingdom and the glory of becoming priests and prophets.'[95]

But what does it mean for us all to be kings, priests and prophets?

---

[93] *Homil.* XXVII, 4; *P.G.* 34, 696 BC.
[94] *Homil.* XVII, 1; *P.G.* 34, 624 BC.
[95] *P.G.* 106, 509 B.

1. *Royal dignity*

In the Syriac anaphora of St John Chrysostom the priest asks for 'a pure spirit that aspires to royal glory.' These words immediately suggest the mastery of spirit over matter through ascetic discipline, which is to say freedom from all subordination to the world, to concupiscence in all its forms, or to the demonic powers: 'The ruler of this world is coming. He has no power over me' – the free utterance of a King. By the power of this transforming grace, a human being can say, I am master of my instincts, I reign over the flesh and over every worldly impulse; we are kings, as Ecumenius says, 'because we control our passions.'[96] And St Gregory of Nyssa says, 'The royal nature of the soul is shown in the free disposition of its desires, such as befits only a king; it belongs to royalty to rule over all.'

But every freedom *from* is at the same time freedom *to*. While freedom is the 'how' of humankind and its existence, it moves us to consider the 'what' of human life, its positive content, and so we turn to priestly dignity.

2. *Priestly dignity*

The creature is brought into being as the subject not only of God's thought, which gives it logical and abstract existence, but also of his love. 'God first loved us,' as St John says, and it is in that love that humankind is spoken, expressed, named; only through divine love does the human creature become a concrete being, truly existing.

The essence of humankind, created in the image of God, is communion, and that is why the Church, responding as a living body to that nature, is never an institution imposed on the human race from outside, but is its very truth, indelibly printed on its nature and revealing it to be the humankind-Church.

When humanity is seen for the mystery it really is, it appears as communion open to the world. Thanks to the great spiritual masters we must always pass from having to being. It is not enough to have poverty and prayer; we must become poverty and prayer. 'Blessed are the poor in spirit' means, perhaps, not, blessed are those who *have* the spirit, the proprietors or possessors of the spirit, but blessed are those who *are* the spirit. Here we touch on the change that the sacrament brings about in our nature, making it priestly.

In Romans 12 St Paul exhorts us to present our bodies a living sacrifice, which is our 'reasonable service'; service (λατρεία) refers to the sacrifice of the Eucharist. The 4th century *Epistle to the Tarsians* says, 'Honour virgins as priestesses of Christ.' Similarly, Minucius Felix (2nd century) says, 'To pluck someone from danger is to sacrifice a fat victim. That is the service that we offer to God:

---

96 *Comm. in Ep. ad Cor.*, 11; *P.G.* 118, 932 CD.

the worship of innocence and love of truth.'[97] And Origen clearly links the grace of Unction to the priestly offering by faithful people of their whole lives: 'All those who have been imbued with the Unction of Holy Chrism, are now priests ... each bears within the self a burnt-offering, and personally puts fire to the altar ... so that each is burnt endlessly. If I renounce all that I possess, if I take up my cross and follow Christ; or if I give up my body ... if I love my brethren to the point of giving my life for them, if I fight for justice and truth till death, if I mortify myself ... if the world is crucified to me and I to the world, I have offered a sacrifice on the altar of God and I become the priest of my own sacrifice.'[98]

This is all to do with ascetic *catharsis*, preparing to become sacrificial victims.[99] St Gregory of Nazianzus thus describes the correct approach to the Liturgy: 'Nobody can participate in the sacrifice who has not himself been offered as a victim beforehand.'[100] 'We are kings by mastering our passions and priests by offering ourselves as spiritual victims.'[101] St John Damascene,[102] meditating on the sword that pierced the soul of the *Theotokos* (Luke 2.35), calls it the 'ointment poured forth' (Song of Solomon 1.3).

During the Liturgy, the celebrant says when presenting the offering, 'We offer to thee of thine own.' The faithful member of the royal priesthood continues this action *extra muros* – each celebrates the Liturgy in everyday life, so responding to the prayer of the sacrament, 'That he may be pleased to serve thee in every deed and every word.' A glass of water offered to the thirsty becomes a miracle, takes on the spiritual value of the wine at the Marriage of Cana. St Ephraem the Syrian wrote hymns on the epiphanic Marriage of Cana making exactly the same point: that the essence of sanctity, the essence of priesthood, is the intense desire for God, the thirst for God which transforms the human being into a pure offering. Pure hearts will see God, and God will be visible through them.

---

[97] *Octavius*, c. 32; *P.L.* 3, 339-340.
[98] *In Lev. hom.* IX, n. 9; *P.G.* 12, 521-522.
[99] The dignity of the confessor is so great that the 'Hippolytan' Canons (3rd-4th centuries) extraordinarily extended the priesthood of order to the martyrs without their having undergone ordination.
[100] *Oratio* II; *P.G.* 35, 498.
[101] Anonymous manuscript of the 6th century (Hoskier, *The commentary of Oecumenius in the Apocalypse*, Michigan 1928, p. 37).
[102] *Homil.* II *in Nat.*; *P.G.* 96, 693 B.

3. *Prophetic dignity*

Being a prophet has nothing to do with divining or predicting; biblically, a prophet is one who is aware of 'God's design' in the world, who discerns and announces God's will, the inexorable movement of his grace.

Eusebius of Caesarea, in his *Demonstration of the Gospel*,[103] writes, on the subject of the priestly anointing, 'In every place we burn the incense of prophecy and sacrifice to him the sweet-smelling fruit of a practical theology.' That is an excellent definition of the lay state in its prophetic aspect. Every member of the royal priesthood is revealed as living, theophanic theology. Similarly St Oecumenius says, 'We are kings by ruling over our passions, priests for the sacrifice of our bodies, prophets in being instructed in the great mysteries.'[104] And the last of these in the words of Theophylact: 'Prophet, because he sees what the eye has not seen.'[105]

Christianity, in the splendour of its confessors and its martyrs, is messianic, revolutionary, volcanic. In the Kingdom of Caesar it is ordained that we should seek and find what is not there: the Kingdom of God. And precisely in so doing we must refashion the world, change its transient face. Changing the world means transforming it into what by its very nature it cannot yet possess, and thereby turning it into something different, the Kingdom.

The central and final call of the Gospel is the call to Christian violence that takes the Kingdom of God by force. St John the Baptist is not only a witness of the Kingdom of God; in him already the world is conquered and the Kingdom is present. He is not only a voice announcing it, he is its voice. He is the friend of the Bridegroom, who decreases and becomes transparent so that the Other may increase and appear. That is the prophetic dignity: to be the one who, by his life, being already present, announces the one who is to come.

7. THE SACRAMENT OF CONFESSION

'Repentance and forgiveness of sins is to be proclaimed in his name to all nations, beginning from Jerusalem. You are witnesses of these things' (Luke 24.47-48); more than witnesses, for the Lord confers on the Apostles the power of forgiveness: 'Receive the Holy Spirit. If you forgive the sins of any, they are forgiven them; if you retain the sins of any, they are retained' (John 20.22-23).

The practice of the Church is clearly described in the classical text of St Cyprian: 'Let each confess his or her sin while the sinner is still in the world,

---

103 *P.G.* 22, 92-93.
104 *Comment. in Ep.* II *ad Cor.*; *P.G.* 118, 932 CD.
105 *Expos. in Ep.* II *ad Cor.*; *P.G.* 124, 812.

while the confession can be accepted, while the satisfaction and the remission agreed by the bishops are agreeable to the Lord.'[106]

The bishop is the 'steward' of penitence; he hears the confessions of sinners and gives absolution.[107] As congregations multiplied, the bishop delegated the ministry of confession and the stewardship of penitence to the priests. At Constantinople in the 4th century there was already a priest functioning as a penitentiary – πρεσβύτερον ἐπι τῆς μετανοίας.[108] And there was a period (10th and 12th centuries) when even religious – monks who were not priests – occasionally assumed the role of confessors, especially in the monasteries.[109]

The institution of the *startzy*, 'spiritual fathers',[110] who were much more than 'spiritual directors', is evidence that the Orthodox have always looked for spiritual grace, not only in the formal hierarchical system, but wherever it is made living and present by an authority that is not simply functional, but comes directly from God, and in which the Holy Spirit is manifested. Πνευματικός πατήρ is above all one who is himself born of the Spirit. The great spiritual masters are often given the title of prophet; such people have been given the grace of 'burning prayer', of knowledge of the heart and of διάκρισις, the discernment of spirits and thoughts. Being wise doctors, they know that gifts by themselves are not enough, and they insist on the importance of discipline and the right direction of the human faculties. Some of them have engaged in experimental psychology, even psychoanalysis. Modern psychiatrists find scientific material of an astonishing richness in the works of Origen, Evagrius, Diadochus, Macarius, John Climacus ... these were well aware of the existence of the subconscious and fully understood the danger of repression. 'Many passions are hidden in our heart and remain unnoticed. Temptation reveals them.'[111] They distinguish nicely between the various psychological zones, never confusing physical, psychological, moral and demonic causes. Their psychogenesis is remarkable; evil can be traced back through a whole range of 'suggestions' to its origin in deadly *philautia*, pride. 'It

---

[106] *P.L.* IV, 489.
[107] St Gregory of Nyssa, *P.G.* 45, 221, 233; St Basil, *P.G.* 32, 661, 716, 723; St John Chrysostom, *P.G.* 47, 644.
[108] *Apostolic Canons*, Canon 51; Socrates, *P.G.* 67, 613-616.
[109] Holl, *Enthusiasmus und Bussgewalt beim griechischen Mönchtum*, Leipzig 1898 (Clement of Alexandria, *P.G.* IX, 645; Origen, *P.G.* XI, 528). For very rare exceptions see Poschmann, *Paenitentia secunda*, Bonn 1940, which corrects the exaggerations of Holl.
[110] The relation between spiritual father and spiritual child is peculiar to Christianity and it is always a homage to the unique divine paternity (see *Theological Dictionary of the New Testament*, G. Kittel, Michigan 1964, for the word 'Abba'; S. Smirnov, 'The spiritual father or staretz', in *Bogosl. Vestnik*, vol. 2, 1904 (in Russian); N. Suvorov, *The problem of confession and the spiritual teachers in the eastern Church* (in Russian), Moscow 1906.
[111] Evagrius, *Centuries* VI, 52; also St Maximus on the subconscious, *P.G.* 90, 997 B; St Nil on the psychology of the demonic, *P.G.* 79, 1201.

is the hidden thought that destroys the heart. If we hide we shall make ourselves ill ... If we blush to reveal a thought to our master, we know for certain that it comes from the devil.'[112] Opening the heart brings complexes into the light and destroys them before they are formed,[113] and heals sickly scruples. Like Elijah and Elisha before him, the spiritual father transmits the Spirit to his disciples. According to St Gregory of Nazianzus, he is 'the storehouse of divine philanthropy.'[114] *Startzy*, who were simple monks not priests, were often 'spiritual fathers' of bishops. According to St Simeon the New Theologian this special dispensation is justified by the monastic state, which is essentially the state of penitence; the *startzy*, being masters of that art, can help others.[115] Nevertheless, in the 12th century, the canonist Balsamon distinguished clearly between the counselling ministry and the power of absolution and reaffirmed the classical tradition of the bishop and the priests charged with the ministry of absolution.

Confession is called 'exomologesis', εξομολόγησις, the admission of guilt followed by absolution. For Clement of Alexandria the confessor is like 'the angel of God' or 'the angel of penitence,' able to penetrate and open the heart of the sinner. Above all he is a doctor who heals the sick, 'God's physician'. The Greek term *metanoia* expresses better than the Latin *paenitentia* the basic idea of spiritual therapy. The prayer before confession says, 'Take heed lest, having come to the physician, thou depart unhealed.' And the task of the physician was precisely defined by the Trullan Synod (692): 'Those who have received from God the power to bind and loose will, as conscientious doctors, apply themselves to finding the particular remedy for curing each penitent and each of his or her faults.'[116] Anastasius the Sinaite (7th century) advises the faithful to make their confession 'to God by the means of the priests' and at the same time to 'find a spiritual, experienced man, capable of healing us ... so that we may confess to him as to God and not as to a human being.'[117]

Through a thousand years of experience the Church has learnt the saving value of confession.[118] A fault, rooted in the soul and poisoning it from within, requires a surgical operation to cut the roots and externalize it, and this necessi-

---

[112] *Cassian, P.L.* 49, 162.
[113] Dorotheus, *P.G.* 88, 1640 C.
[114] *P.G.* 35, 593 C.
[115] See Holl, *op. cit.*, p. 119 and 120.
[116] *Canon* 102; Mansi, vol. XI, col. 987.
[117] *P.G.* 89, 833; 89, 372.
[118] Protestant theology talks of the 'cure of souls', '*Seelsorg*'. But in reaction against individualism this notion has been modified and has lead to the affirmation of the need both for consciences to be guided and for a sacramental view of penitence (see J.D. Benoit, *Direction Spirituelle et protestantisme*, Paris 1940; Max Thurian, *La Confession*, Paris 1953; W. Stählin und Ritter, Kirche und Menschenbidung, Kassel 1950; E. G. Léonard, *Le protestantisme français*, Paris 1953).

tates a witness who will listen, break the solitude and restore the penitent to the communion of the Body. It is the great discovery of psychoanalysis that the patients must be brought to accept their need for dialogue – be helped to overcome their very ineptitude for it, be cured of the anxiety that makes them reluctant to approach someone else, then to have their diseased solitude operated on so as to restore them to communion. The historian Sozomen said in the 5th century, 'Before you can ask forgiveness you must confess your sin.'[119] A fault confessed is removed; but how to render it non-existent? Bad conscience is not only remorse for the fault committed, but also regret for lost innocence. The human being seeks forgiveness, but from the bottom of its heart it yearns for the annihilation of the evil, and this can be achieved only by sacramental absolution. A fault externalized, even when it has been told and thus objectified, remains as a taunting presence on the outside. Only by sacramental absolution can it be utterly destroyed and a complete cure effected. Psychiatrists who are believers are familiar with this sacramental act of total freedom, and often send their patients to finish their treatment in the ecclesiastical 'clinic' of grace. To become free again we must know how to use our past to create the present, no longer to see the past as the automatic cause of our behaviour. Escaping from this predetermination we become masters of our fate, freely shaping and dominating our circumstances.

The act of forgiveness puts us at the heart of the relationship between God the Holy and humankind the sinful, and we must appreciate the infinite gravity of this act. The emphasis here is not on the omnipotence of God who can efface and annihilate, but on the Lamb slain from the foundation of the world, who, as St Paul says, 'he forgave us all our trespasses, erasing the record that stood against us with its legal demands. He set this aside, nailing it to the cross' (Col. 2.13-14). The creation of the world is rooted in sacrifice, and the power of forgiveness is bought at the price of the blood poured out by the crucified Lamb. It is because Christ takes *on himself* the sins of the world, responds to the love of the Father by his inexpressible love on our behalf, that he has the 'moral' power to wipe clean and forgive and make us children of the Father. The Lord's Prayer makes our forgiveness dependent on an 'imitation' on our part whereby we are invited to descend to the underworld of universal culpability where all are guilty, which every believer confesses before Communion: 'Of all sinners, I am chief.'

In the 12th century the canonist Balsamon said that the age for first confession was seven years,[120] and that is the practice today. While, according to St John (1 John 5.16-18), there is a distinction between sins *ad mortem* and others, there are no explicit lists of venial and mortal sins. The prayer of the sacrament asks for

---

119 *P.G.* 67, 1460.
120 This agrees with the observations of psychologists and educationalists. It is the age of 'moral awareness' in a normal infant.

forgiveness of faults 'voluntary and involuntary, in word or deed, witting and un-witting, by day and night, in spirit and in thought'; all are included in the same act of the *heart* without any attempt at analysis or classification; the offence is against God and his mercy. For an Orthodox penitent to be asked whether he or she is in a state of grace or not would be an impossible question. The person comes in poverty as a beggar seeking salvation. Even after confession, at the moment of communion, such persons confess that they are the 'chief of sinners,' and when the celebrant announces, 'holy things for the holy,' they simply reply, 'only the Lord is holy!'

Public penitence continued alongside private penitence in some places, but eventually fell into disuse.[121] The latter rigorously preserves the principle of the *sigillum* of absolute secrecy of the confessional under pain of excommunication.

Absolution

After the confession and, when appropriate, a penance (a penitential exercise) according to the discretion of the confessor, the formula of absolution is pronounced. The penance, the making amends, is in no sense a punishment; there is no such thing as a juridical moment of 'satisfaction'. It is a remedy, and the spiritual father is seeking to find the right cure for the sick person, the object being to remove the penitent from temptation. St John Chrysostom says, 'Time is of no consequence. We do not ask how often the wound has been dressed, but whether the dressing has done any good. And we discover this at the moment of taking it off, when we see the state of the wound.'[122] So it is a question not of atoning for past deeds, but of stopping them at the source. 'Open the door of penitence, grant me tears to wash the impurity of my heart, O Christ.' The state of penitence and tears is already a gift, it is why purification ends in consolation and joy. The indicative form is recent among the Slavs; it comes from the Latins via Pierre Moghila who inserted it in the public ritual at Kiev in 1646, and it was adopted by the Russian Church in 1757. The classical Orthodox form which is also that of the Greek Church today, is imploratory: 'Whatsoever thou hast said to my humble person, and whatsoever thou hast failed to say, whether through ignorance or forgetfulness, whatever it may be, may God forgive thee in this world, and in that which is to come ... Have no further care for the sins which thou hast confessed, depart in peace.' The priest is merely a witness of Christ's

[121] St Simeon of Thessalonica, *P.G.* 115, 357.
[122] Sick nature is healed by the antidote of salvation (St John Damascene, *P.G.* 94 1332); Origen was the first to see salvation in relationship to the parable of the Good Samaritan-Healer (*P.G.* 13, 1886-88; 14, 656 A).

presence; 'the clergy are hidden, so to speak, under the sacraments,'[123] their power is that of transmission; it is God who is the author of the sacraments. The prayer before confession and the reading of Psalm 51 witness to the re-attachment, the re-union of the sinner to the Church. It is when they know they are back in the bosom of the Church that persons can confess their souls and receive healing, for every sin puts a person outside the Body of Christ. Penitence is seen as the continuation of the waters of Baptism, and is the 'trembling of the soul before the gate of Paradise.'

8. THE SACRAMENT OF MARRIAGE[124]

On the face of it, monasticism and marriage are utterly opposed. But at a profounder level, where our life is intertwined with the life of the Spirit, we can see that they are intimately related and complementary. The sacrament of marriage internalizes in its own way the monastic state; indeed, it originally included the specifically monastic rite of the tonsure. Two aspects of the same mystery are both directed towards the supreme and universal human value of spiritual virginity.

As St John Chrysostom says so strikingly and clearly, 'When Christ commands us to follow the narrow way, he is talking not only to monks, but to all ... it follows that the same standard is expected of monks and laypeople,' and, 'Use marriage with moderation, and you shall be first in the kingdom, and enjoy all good things.'[125] St Amphilocus, Bishop of Iconium (d.394), sums up the Orthodox understanding when he says that from the religious point of view, marriage and virginity are both highly honourable estates, equally instituted by God.[126]

Spiritual chastity-integrity goes beyond physiology and concerns the very structure of the human spirit. It is normal in Christian thinking to affirm the diversity of ministries and therefore of vocations. There is no point in asking whether anyone in particular would make a better monk than a married person, or vice-versa; all must ask themselves how they personally measure up to their own standard of sanctity. The vital thing – and this is the precise meaning of humility – is to reach one's personal standard, as set by God. The two slopes of Tabor, those of monastic sanctity and conjugal sanctity, meet at the summit; either, no less than the other, is the way into 'the rest of God' and 'the joy of the Lord'.

For Orthodox clergy who were not monks, marriage was even compulsory until very recently, and celibate priests (over the age of 40) were not allowed into

---

[123] Androutsos, *Dogmatique*, D. 383-38.
[124] See P. Evdokimov, *Sacrement de l'Amour*, Epi 1962.
[125] *Adv. oppugn. vitae monist.* III, 14; *In Epist. ad Haebr.*, hom. VIII, 4.
[126] *P.G.* 39, 44-45.

Russia till the 19th century. It is highly significant that at the time of the First
Ecumenical Council it was the Bishop Paphnutius, one of the most severe ascetics, who defended the marriage of priests. Similarly, there are innumerable
canons that categorically and severely condemn those who consider marriage to
be incompatible with priesthood, or display the least scorn towards its holy institution.[127] 'Marriage and the relations between the couple are by nature honourable and *pure*. The relationship of husband and wife can be a chaste
relationship.'[128] Accordingly the Trullan Council (691) stated, 'In the Roman
Church, those who wish to receive the diaconate or the priesthood promise to
cease marital relations. We for our part observe the Apostolic canons and allow
married life to continue.'[129]

A married clergy thus demonstrates that the married state is no hindrance at
all to participating at the very heart of the liturgical life, the priestly celebration
of the Eucharist. The greatest ascetics (St Macarius, St John Cassian, etc) speak
of the possibility of fornication in the heart and imagination of monks. On the
other hand they insist that real marriage is a state of chastity. The monastic state
and marriage therefore culminate in spiritual chastity, in purity of spirit, and thus
meet and complement each other.[130]

In the words of the marriage service, 'Marriage is honourable and *the marriage bed undefiled,* for Christ blessed them when he changed the water into wine
at the Marriage of Cana.'

The Paradisal Institution of Marriage

According to ancient and constant tradition, marriage was instituted in Paradise.
The Lord, speaking of marriage, refers to the Old Testament: 'Have you not
read?' (Matt. 19.4; also Eph. 5.31). 'The Son has done nothing but confirm what
was established by the Father,' says Clement of Alexandria, and he sets out the
fundamental idea of the *paradisal grace* of marriage τῆς τοῦ ψάμου χάριτος.[131]
While he sees the creation of humankind as Baptism (birth), the love of the first
couple 'in one flesh' is the sacrament of matrimony. So it is no accident that the
Edenic Church originates in the marital bliss of the first couple, or that in the
Fourth Gospel the first manifestation of glory shines forth in the joy of the bride
and groom at the Marriage of Cana.

---

127 Hefele, *Histoire des Conciles*, V. I, p. 621.
128 The words of Bishop Paphnutius.
129 Canon 13.
130 The remarkable Pauline discussion of circumcision (Rom. 2. 26-29) puts the problem on
exactly the same spiritual level and outlines an identical point of view for the discussion of
virginity.
131 *Strom.* III, 4; *P.G.* 8, 1096.

Clement goes even further: 'God created humankind, man and woman; man is Christ, woman is the Church'.[132] Marriage as an archetypal image existed before the couple, for Adam was created in the image of Christ and Eve in the image of the Church. St Paul later formulated the principle: 'This is a great mystery, and I am applying it to Christ and the Church' (Eph. 5.32). Thus, marriage goes back to before the Fall and this is explicitly stated in the text of the rite: 'Neither original sin nor the Flood detract anything from the sanctity of holy wedlock.' St Ephraem the Syrian adds, 'From Adam to the Lord, true married love was the perfect sacrament.'[133] That is why, according to rabbinic wisdom, the single channel by which grace was poured upon the pagans was precisely that of married love.[134]

The remembrance of Paradise, 'paradisal grace' fills us with joy: 'Let us rejoice and exult... Blessed are those who are invited to the marriage supper of the Lamb' (Rev. 19.7-9). Deuteronomy (24.5) says that every newly married man is freed from all public duties in order to 'cheer up his wife'. The heart of marriage ceremony is joy, but the deeply spiritual quality of that joy points to the true hidden nature of the celebration. All the light contained in it can be fully released only when the joy mounts up to equal that of the martyrs and confessors, the joy that bursts into life only at the moment of total self-offering. In the light of this, we know instinctively that without the married love of the first couple Paradise itself would lose something of the fullness that the Incarnation bore in its womb, even that it would no longer be Paradise! Through the 'memorial' of this sacrament, love brings Paradise back to earth and makes it accessible; this 'paradisal grace' invites love to transcend everything earthly and stand in its sheer beauty as a powerful witness to truth, simply by the fact of existing. The soul rises up, says Claudel[135] 'not like a cow in calf that stands chewing the cud, but like a filly, her mouth burning with the salt she has taken from her master's hand ... who sniffs through the cracks in the door the scent of heavenly pasture, borne on the dawn wind.'

In eastern tradition, Christ, at the Marriage of Cana, merely confirms with his presence the sacramental institution of Paradise. The Gospel narrative is full of deep symbolic meaning to which Patristic exegesis pays close attention. The heart of it is the transition from water to wine, prefiguring the Eucharist and symbolizing vividly the metamorphosis of animal passion into the noble wine of charismatic love.[136]

---

[132] *2 Cor* XIV.
[133] *Commentary on Ephesians*, 5, 32.
[134] Zohar, I.
[135] *La Ville*.
[136] St John Chrysostom, *P.G.* 62, 380; St Gregory of Nazianzus, *P.G.* 37, 373.

The Image of Marriage
The creation of humankind, the institution of marriage and the foundation of the
Edenic Church are united in a single creative act of God, which shows their intimate relationship. This explains the matrimonial terminology that the Bible uses
to describe the mystery of the relation between God and human beings – betrothed, married, the Marriage of the Lamb.

'It is not good that the man should be alone,' says Holy Scripture, for solitary
existence does not reflect God. In the judgement of St Ambrose, the human race
is not 'good' except as the unity of male and female. Adam-Eve, man-woman is
the human dyad reflecting that plurality in God who, although he is 'one', speaks
of himself as 'us' (Gen. 1.26). 'When husband and wife are joined together in
marriage, they form an image not of something earthly, but of God himself,' according to St John Chrysostom.[137] The man and the woman are joined together
in a third term which is God, just as the divine and human are expressed in the
hypostasis of the Word, and as the Father and the Son are united in the Spirit.
Unity in multiplicity is a statement of Trinitarian doctrine that says as much about
marriage as about the Church. Clement of Alexandria applies to marriage the
saying, 'Where two or three are gathered in my name, I am there among them'
(Matt. 18.20).[138] By this profound interplay of archetypal values, marriage is a
parable of the age to come. 'Whoever is not bound in the marriage bond is not a
whole being, but only half.'[139] Or as St John Chrysostom says repeatedly, 'The
man and the woman are not two, but a single being.'[140] Here we have a scaled-
down image of unity, no longer of couples (for in the Kingdom 'they neither
marry nor are given in marriage, but are like angels in heaven') but of male and
female in their wholeness integrated in the humanity of the Kingdom – Adam
reconstituted and bearing Eve in his side. St John Chrysostom calls the family
ἐκκλησία μικρά,[141] thinking of the *ecclesia domestica* of St Paul, and seeing it
as a living cell of the Church, the prophetic image of the Kingdom.

---

[137] *P.G.* 61, 215; 62, 387.
[138] *P.G.* 8, 1169.
[139] St John Chrysostom, *P.G.* 62, 387.
[140] *P.G.* 61, 289.
[141] *P.G.* 62, 143.

The Chief End of Marriage

The Orthodox approach is basically *personalist*.[142] Matrimony is a particular vocation for attaining the fullness of being in God. 'Love changes the very substance of things,' says St John Chrysostom,[143] and he adds, 'Only love can make two beings into one.'[144] Only love recognizes Love. 'Only love unites creatures to God and unites them to one another.'[145] Love becomes a form of grace designed to overcome the sinful condition of selfish separation and isolation. We learn the astounding truth that the love that God bears to humankind is of the same quality as the love that humankind bears to God and that people experience from the bottom of their hearts when they are pure and open towards others. The Song of Solomon makes this clear of human love: 'Its flashes are flashes of fire, a raging flame of the Eternal' (Song of Solomon 8.6). Married love is essentially spirit-bearing. The matter of the sacrament is mutual love which is an end in itself, for the gift of the Holy Spirit makes it 'the union of indestructible love,' prompting St John Chrysostom's fine definition, 'Marriage is the sacrament of love.'[146]

As against *prolis est essentialissimum in matrimonio* and *Matrimonii finis primarius est procreatio atque educatio prolis*, Orthodox teaching asserts the primary meaning or the highest end of marriage to be conjugal love, the fullness of the unity of the spouses which makes it a domestic church. Marriage may be useful to society, but it retains its intrinsic sovereign value. The Pseudo-Areopagite writes, 'The Athenians called marriage τέλος, because it crowns man for life.'[147] Children bring to it a new quality, that of paternity and maternity, but this is an outpouring from that fullness which remains self-contained. Even sexual differentiation, while it pervades the whole human being and goes far beyond the strictly sexual, is independent of humanity itself and of quite secondary importance.

The Meaning of Marriage

The Fall has perverted human ontology, separating it into flawed masculinity and flawed femininity and throwing them into a perpetual to and fro of attraction and repulsion. The separation is not only between men and women but in the heart

---

[142] In Catholic theology this is limited by the primacy of physical virginity (see some of the somewhat hesitant and yet already clearly defined suggestions that have been put forward: Doms, *Von Sinn un Zweck der Ehe*, Breslau 1935; N. Rocholl, *Sei Ehe aks geweihtes Leben*, Dülmen 1946; D. von Hildebrand, *Le Mariage*. Ed. du Cerf; A Fayol, *Notes sur l'amour humain*, Desclée de Brouwer).

[143] *P.G.* 61, 273.

[144] *P.G.* 61, 280.

[145] Thalassy, Moscow 1893 (trans. in Russian), hom. I, ch. 1.

[146] *P.G.* 51, 230.

[147] *P.G.* 3, 1184.

304 The Church at Prayer

of every human being and it creates a incessant tension that begets conflicts and neuroses. The sacrament of matrimony supplies 'paradisal grace' and unites the beginning to the end. St John Chrysostom, as always the great teacher of marriage, points to the underlying truth, amply confirmed by modern psychiatry: 'Love is born of chastity,' while, on the contrary, 'perversion (debauchery and pornographic prurience) comes from an insufficiency of love.'[148] The most powerful remedy is 'love – *amor magnus* – which makes people chaste.'[149]

There is a succession of scriptural texts, by no means accidental, which reveals a dazzling truth about humanity and shines a bright light on its destiny.

The Epistle to the Hebrews (2.7) depicts human beings in the splendour of innocence at the dawn of their life: 'You have crowned them with glory and honour.' The Revelation of St John describes the other end of existence, its conclusion, and we are told that the nations and peoples on the threshold of the new Jerusalem *do bring their glory and honour into it*; when humankind at last reaches the shore of fulfilment it does not come empty-handed, but brings the gifts of the Spirit. In the end, the same formula which serves to sum up the initial promise and final accomplishment – Paradise and the Kingdom – serves to sum up also the sacrament of marriage: the bridal pair are *crowned with glory and honour*. So marriage is an evident point of conjunction, prophetically offered as an image of the wholeness of the age to come.

The Signs of the Last Times
St Clement of Rome cites a very mysterious agraphon: 'For the Lord himself, being asked when his kingdom would come, replied, "When two shall be one, and when that which is without shall be as that which is within, and when the male and female united shall be neither male nor female".'[150]

The coming of the Kingdom coincides thus with the maturing of matrimonial love into one perfect being, into the pan-human reality recapitulated in Christ; matrimonial chastity (which is prayed for in the epiclesis of the sacrament) abolishes the gap between the interior and the exterior which is precisely where concupiscence finds its lodging; closed-off vicious masculinity and femininity gives place to the infiniteness of the first integrity recovered and made really present. The Lord says, 'Behold, I make the *last* like the *first*;'[151] alpha meets omega in the entirely new creature. The state of matrimony, just like the monastic state, is

---

[148] *1 Cor.*, hom. 33, 6.
[149] Ibid.
[150] *2 Clementis ad Cor.* 12 2. See Resch, *Agrapha* 71, p. 93; Clement of Alexandria. *Strom.* III, 3, 92.
[151] Agraphon from the Epistle of Barnabas.

a problem not of ethics, but of ontology. Before ever it could realize its greatness, love was instantly profaned. True marriage, at its noblest, is a rare ascetic achievement, which the rite emphasizes by the hymn of the martyrs that accompanies the couple the whole length of their progress along the narrow way; thus the state of matrimony is raised to the level and the dignity of the 'wounded friends of the Bridegroom.' When marriage is finally revealed, free of all the profanations of history, we shall know that the last days are upon us. Only then will its truth emerge into the light of day, and it will recognize itself, as in a mirror, for what it really is, the true monastic state.

Above the tension between shame and cynicism there floats, beyond the reach of mere natural strength, the harmony of the children of liberty and grace who have no need to hide. When the Angel of Revelation announces, 'there shall be time no longer,' he also announces 'the destruction of the robe of shame'[152] (the garment of skins of the Fall) and signals the approaching virginal restoration of the human being. In history, without holiness, marriage is nothing but the sociological unit, the peaceful coupling of innumerable respectable people, terrifying in its utter sufficiency. Marriage in its fullness concerns not human beings but the human being in its totality and will be revealed in its amazing nobility, according to the Saviour, only *at the end*, at the moment of the future Passing-over/Passover.

The *ars amandi* is entirely compatible with the enjoyment of the eternal newness of the *Maranatha*. The lovers look together towards their fulfilment, and say: 'O Lord, vouchsafe that loving each other, we may love thee.'

9. THE SACRAMENT OF THE ANOINTING OF THE SICK

'Are any among you sick? They should call for the elders of the church and have them pray over them, anointing them with oil in the name of the Lord. The prayer of faith will save the sick, and the Lord will raise them up; and anyone who has committed sins will be forgiven' (Jas. 5.14-15. Cf. Mark 6.13). The presbyters represent the faith of the Church, so their prayer is clearly the intercession of the Body of the Church, of its communion. The moment of death – and every disease is mortal – seems to be the moment of absolute solitude. It is at that moment that the Church gathers round the member in the sacred circle of communion. In Russia the name of this sacrament is derived from the word 'conciliarity', for it must be celebrated by the *sobor*, a synaxis of seven priests. It includes the reading of seven passages of the Gospel, and seven times the priests recite the prayer, 'Holy Father, physician of our souls and bodies, who didst send thine only-begotten Son our Lord Jesus Christ, which healeth every infirmity and delivereth from

---

[152] Clement of Alexandria, *Strom.* 13, 92.

death: Heal thou, also, thy servant N. from the ills of body and soul which do hinder him (*her*), and quicken him (*her*) by the grace of thy Christ.' To the spiritual healing of the soul there is added the prayer for physical healing. Everybody is in effect sick and dying, and that is why in Greece the sacrament of Unction is often given to the communicants. In Russia on Holy Thursday it is administered to all the congregation. The sacrament can be repeated and so is not 'extreme' in the [former] Latin sense, i.e., only for the dying.

The rite goes according to the order of Matins with readings from the Apostle and the Gospel. At the end, after the reading of the last Gospel, the priest places the book on the head of the sick person and says, 'I do not put my sinful hand on the head of the sick, but thy strong and powerful hand which is in the holy Gospel.'

The *Gospel of Nicodemus*[153] speaks of 'the oil of the tree of mercy.' While the Tree of Life in Eden yields its fruits in the Eucharist, the same tree offers 'the oil of mercy' to those who are reborn by water and the Holy Spirit. Unction is thus juxtaposed with Baptism and joins the forgiveness of sins, which is the condition for the healing of body and soul.

Origen quotes the text of St James and mentions unction.[154] Eusebius of Caesarea speaks of it in his commentary on Isaiah,[155] St Ephrem mentions it,[156] St John Chrysostom[157] also quotes St James; all of which proves that the sacrament belongs to a very ancient tradition. The anaphora of Bishop Serapion includes a prayer over the water and oil and asks for 'a healing power to banish every fever, every demon and every disease.' St Cyril of Alexandria[158] speaks of a rite in current use.

The sacrament of unction, however, occupies a particular place in the economy of the sacraments; we can even say that it is on the very edge. For while in the sacraments generally the gifts of the Holy Spirit are *conferred* and the sacrament is certified to have been accomplished, the sacrament of unction only *asks for* the grace of healing without prejudging anything as to the fact. We cannot envisage a permanent ministry of healing, because healing depends on the miraculous power of God who sends it according to his good pleasure. The Church, therefore, prays for healing, but without proclaiming it.

---

153 Trischendorf, *Evang. apocryphes*, Leipzig 1853, 325.
154 *P.G.* 12, 418.
155 *P.G.* 24, 268.
156 Tisseront, *Histoire du Dogme*, Vol. II, 1909, p. 219.
157 *P.G.* 48, 644.
158 *P.G.* 68, 472.

PART V

The Eschaton or the Last Things

1

The Church in the World and the Last Things

1. THE CHURCH AND THE WORLD

'Go therefore and make disciples of all nations,' says the Lord (Matt. 28.19). While the Church concerns herself with individual souls, she also deals with whole peoples. The Church can be drawn by historical circumstances to the heart of the nation's life so that she becomes the expression of its self-understanding, or equally can be pushed to the margin where she becomes an alien presence; in any event, she can never renounce her *theocratic* mission without betraying her true nature. As the salt of life, she adds savour to all events, reveals their hidden meaning. 'The one who rejects me and does not receive my word has a judge; on the last day the word that I have spoken will serve as judge' (John 12.48). That word remains in the world as its ever-present judgement; the Church constantly proclaims it by her very existence.

Every people adopts a particular historic mission, around which it shapes itself, but sooner or later that mission encounters God's plan. This plan is the subject of the parable of the talents (Matt. 25), which demonstrates that no task assigned by the Master is ever abandoned; if one of the servants lets him down, the task is entrusted to another; this results in a long delay, and the souls of the martyrs cry, 'Sovereign Lord, holy and true, how long will it be before you judge?' (Rev. 6.10)

All power comes from God; it can be perverted, but it exists only in relation to the Absolute. There is nothing autonomous about history; every moment of it refers to Him who possesses 'all power in heaven and on earth.' This fundamental relationship loses none of its force, even when it is consciously denied, for even secularization, being a fact of history, is inherently and immediately liable to the judgement, according to which no event is neutral. History cannot escape from its 'pre-destiny'; its trans-historical coefficient judges every event and straightway marks it as positive or negative. Even an apparently simple saying like 'render to Caesar the things that are Caesar's' has a religious content and demands an act of faith.

This religious aspect of the State, society, civilization or the culture, the fact that they depend on the transcendent, does not oblige them to become the Church, but invites them to come to their fulfilment in organic reciprocity with their counterpart, the Church. Only in that womb of divine wisdom can they be brought to birth in their true nature. Any Manichaean dualism or Nestorian separation, any Monophysitism of the solely divine or the solely human, dries up the very

309

lifeblood of biblical thought, and we are lost in the sand of heretical inventions. The Gospel is categorical: the whole of human existence is for one end only, the Kingdom of God. Social life can be founded only on doctrine; 'Christianity is the imitation of God's nature.'[1]

There are those who desire a secularized eschatology, one deprived of its *eschaton*, just as they desire a Communion of Saints without the Saintly and a Kingdom of God without God. This notion is of no interest in itself, but it is important to understand why it appeared, the spiritual context and philosophical context it springs from. Only when we have understood why it has become so strident and what devilish substitutions are involved can there be a satisfactory Christian response. Western Christianity has neglected the Kingdom for the sake of a City firmly grounded in history, whereas we know that every historical city is only a prophetic sign and parable of the Kingdom. Eastern Orthodoxy, for its part, has lost itself in the society of angels and the liturgical contemplation of heaven. Marxist eschatology reintroduces the spiritual problem of history in all its forcefulness, while also obliging us to avoid any Protestant breach in the mysterious continuity between history and the Kingdom. It is precisely in this closed world here below, where we are imprisoned apparently without hope, that our firmly assured faith must make tunnels for escape, so that we can reveal the invisible, raise the dead and move mountains, bringing down the fire of hope for the salvation of others and connecting the emptiness of this world to the 'Church full of the Trinity'.[2]

Now, if the servants of the Good begin to lose heart, their task is taken over by forces of a very different kind, and with very different motives, and confusion breaks loose. The evangelical command to 'seek the Kingdom of God' (Matt. 6.33) is de-spiritualized and diverted towards utopian earthly paradises. The frightful totalitarianism of the beast of the Apocalypse is starkly revealed against the teeming masses of humanity.

Today Christianity no longer makes history, but watches it from the sidelines while it breaks loose and threatens to reduce the Church to the size and significance of a self-engrossed sect, on the margins of the world's destiny. Social and economic reforms, the setting free of peoples and social classes, are now the work of secular activists, people no longer connected with the Church.

Nowadays, almost everywhere, Christians live under governments founded on the principle of the separation of Church and State. The Church can adapt itself to this new situation only by keeping alive its universal and totalitarian aspirations, which are inherent in its nature. But as its theocracy becomes more internalized, its vocation becomes that of an ubiquitous *conscience* speaking freely to those who are free, without relying on any secular authority to back it up. What

---

[1] St Gregory of Nyssa, *De profes. christiana*, *P.G.* 46, 244 C.
[2] Origen, *Selecta in Psalmos*, 23; *P.G.* 12, 1265.

it loses in immediate effect, for want of State support, it gains in moral authority by its new sovereign independence. In a climate of indifference or open hostility, having lost any formal claim to be heard, the Church must rely only on the genuine people of God, whose loyalty is uninfluenced by any wish to compromise or conform.

At every moment of history, we are forced to choose between satanocracy and theocracy, a choice that is more imperative today than ever before, as the two cities define themselves ever more sharply over against each other. There is no question here of how or whether to adapt to social conditions; the important thing is doctrine, a rule of faith that cannot be affected by any sectarian or non-incarnational theology. Those who have approached history from a too human point of view have tried to do what even the Fall could not do, which is to minimize God's original plan of the Incarnation, blunting the impact of the most explosive texts of Scripture. But it is these that most strongly support the eschatological maximalism of the monks. Whoever cannot accept their maximalism, complete with the angels and the immediate end of everything, and our sudden passage into the new age, will have to explain history some other way, but positively, that is to say biblically, from its own depths, transforming it into a 'ladder' for the Coming, because that voice still cries in the wilderness, 'Prepare the way of the Lord, make his paths straight' (Matt. 3.3). 'The temptation of St Anthony,' in its most profound interpretation, vividly portrays the power of the Spirit ripping the life out of the demonic forces; the victory won in the desert was more tremendous than the 'triumph' of the Empire of Constantine. The monks confined themselves to desert places, abandoning the Empire and a life that was too safe and overshadowed by compromise. Today the desert, 'the dwelling-place of the demons,' has moved into the very heart of the peoples 'having no hope and without God in the world' (Eph. 2.12). Monks no longer need to leave the world, and every believer can follow his vocation in an entirely new, inward form of monasticism. The problem of eschatological Man is posed by history itself.

There is a permanent tension between essence and existence; when this is salvific it raises being beyond being, inviting it to plunge into the heart of God. The 'transcendence' of existentialists does not come close to transcending the dimensions of this world and loses itself in the darkness of human bankruptcy, in falseness and tragic error. Complete fullness can come only from God; no one can acquire it by simply claiming it; it is *always* received as a gift. That is why life truly blossoms only within the Eucharist, praise and worship. The theology of the Last End entails the crucifixion of thought itself, and owes nothing to human philosophy: 'But, as it is written, "What no eye has seen, nor ear heard, nor the human heart conceived, what God has prepared for those who love him"' (1 Cor. 2.9). This theology embraces every aspect of revelation, confronts the mystery of eschatological Man – *Filius sapientiae* – and leads us into that magnificent definition of all Christians, 'all who have longed for his appearing' (2 Tim. 4.8). For these lovers of the Parousia the future is the present, the Coming

determines all that has gone before and all that will come after. In its light even
the greatest sinner, like the thief crucified on the right hand of Christ, can repent
and be immediately transported into eternity. The Wicked One, however, the
'Prince of Darkness' beloved of occultists, rots away – and also rots the fabric of
life itself into selfish materialism, which is hell. Both, by their determined choice,
bring the end nearer, while everything in between falls into the category of 'the
chaff of history', of whose lukewarmness Revelation says it is fit only to be
'spewed out'. Saints, heroes and geniuses, as they approach the truth, each in his
or her own way, converge eventually on the one and only reality. Sophiology,
true art, the icon, the liturgy, all forms of true creativity are immediate ways into
Paradise. All worship of perversion, however, leads immediately to hell; it is our
privilege in apocalyptic times to see hidden things. Evil is now revealed as constant static immensity, infinite depravity; the Kingdom as constant growth, infinite reality.

St John's Gospel records the Lord's teaching on this immediacy, which is possibly the most important message for the Church to hear: 'Whoever receives one
whom I send receives me; and whoever receives me receives him who sent me'
(John 13.20). When the world, humankind, our neighbour, receives a member of
the Church, one of us, that person is immediately taken into the gradual movement of communion, and is no longer outside the sacred circle of the Communion
of the Trinity, beyond the reach of the Father's blessing. The fate of the world
depends on the Church's imagination, its ability to make itself welcome. It may
be that hell depends not so much on the anger of God as on the universal charity
of the saints: 'To see the Lord in your brother', 'to feel yourself constantly hang-
ing on the cross', 'not to cease till death from adding fire to fire.'[3]

In the first Epistle of John, the love of God is a beginning, it comes before
everything else, it exceeds every response. At its deepest, love is disinterested,
the pure offering of the handmaid, the joy of the friend of the bridegroom, the
joy that has always existed, like the pure air and the sunlight; joy *a priori* for all.
In John 14.28 Jesus tells his disciples to rejoice with that immense joy that exists
not for any human reason but because it springs from the very existence of God
himself. And from this limpid and pure joy comes the salvation of the world.

2. THE HOLY SPIRIT IN THE LAST TIMES

According to the interpretation of the Seventh Ecumenical Council, the Gospel
defines mortal sin as the terrible and wilful resistance to the working of the Holy
Spirit, resistance that reduces God's wisdom to absurdity. The mystical tradition

[3] Sayings of St Simeon and St John Climacus in *Philokalia*, London 1951, p. 111, 127, 229.

of the 'eternal Gospel' of Joachim of Flora (died 1202) was an attempt, perhaps not entirely successful, to give due weight to the decisive importance of the Holy Spirit for the destiny of the world. Later, Fr Baader, Jacob Boehme, and even Georges Sand spoke of three testaments, three historical epochs.[4] But there is no incarnation peculiar to the Holy Spirit; the 'Paracletophany' manifests Christ, the presence of the Paraclete is fully realized only in Christ. The age of the Spirit was in no sense a period of history, an epoch, but the state of inwardness that lasted till the establishment of Trinitarian communion. There is a seamless and precise progression, which cannot be broken down, from the *Deus absconditus* to the Spirit through the Son, and from the Spirit, through the Only-Begotten, to the ineffable depth of the Father. The history of the Church, ever since the day of Pentecost, is the last age here and now, the beginning of the end; so during this age we should expect the action of the Holy Spirit to be all the more discernible (Acts 2.17-21). *Veni Creator Spiritus* is our *eschatological epiclesis*; the Holy Spirit works within history, preparing the coming of the Kingdom of God. Mortal sin is in effect resistance to the Kingdom. But here great care must be taken to avoid any simplification. We live in a time of terrible confusion; no longer the crystalline, transparent atmosphere of the Gospel, but the time foretold of false prophets, false words, falsified values, when established things are overthrown and corrupted.

The scepticism of extreme modern aesthetics is in keeping with the injunction, 'Love not the world, neither the things that are in the world' (1 John 2.15); it assumes that sooner or later every creation of human culture is destined to perish in the flames.

Historically, Greek culture was the vehicle for the exposition of Christianity. Perhaps its role is already finished? Hence after the coming of Christ, virginity came to be more admired than procreation. The uncomfortable fact is that culture comes with conditions attached, and does not become an organic part of Christian spirituality. It is always an intruder, however respectable, and always suspect. It clearly has its uses in the propagation of faith; it has been widely employed for apologetic purposes, to attract souls. But when culture begins to feel that is only tolerated, that it is a foreign body made use of when convenient, it takes itself off and becomes autonomous, secularized, atheist. But then it comes face to face with another difficulty, a contradiction that arises logically out of its own nature.

The source of our culture is Graeco-Roman. Its principle aim is the expression of perfection in finite forms. In the beginning Christianity dominated culture, then culture in its turn deeply suffused Christianity, but there was always an element that would not be absorbed: culture, whether in its classical or romantic

---

[4] The theory has been supported in modern times by D. Merejovsky (see *Le Mystère des Trois*, 1925).

form, is essentially hostile to eschatology, to the Apocalypse. Because of its rejection and horror of death, culture can never be resigned to its own end; by its very nature it must remain in history.

No human activity in history derives its importance from mere passage of time; its meaning can be seen only in relation to the end. 'The present form of this world is passing away' (1 Cor. 7.31); and this is also a warning not to create idols, not to be deceived by earthly paradises, or even by the utopian identification of the Church with the Kingdom of God.[5] The fashion of the Church Militant passes away just like the fashion of the world.[6] The end of history is the necessary moral condition of history itself.

There is also a hyper-eschatology which leaps over history to the end of the world, there to meet ascetic negation; history thus loses its meaning, and the Incarnation is impoverished; history is disincarnated.

The Christian attitude is never negation, whether eschatological or ascetic. It is *eschatological affirmation*. Culture cannot develop indefinitely; it is not an end in itself. Within its own limits, its problem is insoluble. Objectified, it becomes a system of constraints. It is indeed the sphere in which humankind creates values and expresses 'theurgic' truth,[7] but this truth transcends the present moment, the fashion of this world; that is why culture, at its most sublime, rises above itself and becomes essentially symbolic, a sign of the 'wholly other'. Sooner or later, art, thought, moral awareness, social affairs, arrive at their own boundaries, and then they are faced with a choice: to settle down in the pernicious infinity of their own cut-off existence, to become intoxicated with their emptiness, or to overstep the bounds that threaten to strangle them and, in the transparency of their clear waters, reflect the transcendent. God's Kingdom is intended to be accessible only through the chaos of this world; it is not something foreign planted here, but the revelation of the hidden eternal reality of this world itself.

Today the horsemen of the Apocalypse scour the earth. The rider of the white horse is Christ the conqueror, and his strange fellow-riders represent war, famine and death. Is it not tragic that Christianity should have sunk into sleep at the very moment when the world is falling apart and decaying? Christian heresies are rife in the world because Christians have no idea how to demonstrate the triumphant presence of Life. Israel – *gens prophetica*, the symbolic race – was intensely aware of being a theophanic people, but Christianity has lost that sense of itself. The apocalyptic Christ, not the Christ of history, carries into every corner of the

---

[5] '*Ecclesia et nunc et regnum Christi, regnumque coelorum*' (St Augustine, *De Civitate Dei*, 1, 20, c. 9, n. 1). 'The Church is even now the Kingdom of Christ and the Kingdom of Heaven'!
[6] Loisy said, 'They were expecting the Kingdom of Heaven and it was the Church that came' (*L'Evangile et l'Eglise*, 1902, p. 111).
[7] The term was misused by Soloviev to mean a human act that affected God, whereas the divine energies work synergetically with the creative spirit of humanity towards the Kingdom.

earth the last judgement, a judgement in whose light we shall stand surprised, a judgment as unexpected as that which was delivered upon Job and his friends.

The bridges fall, the ties that bind are breaking. What is happening is even more distressing than at the first tower of Babel: the difficulty now is not the confusion of languages but the impossibility of understanding each other even when we speak the same language; the confusion is of spirits. The world is turned in on itself and may never again hear the voice of Christ; Christianity is turned in on itself and no longer has any purchase on history. It is too comfortably settled in time and in the littleness of daily life, heedless of the fact that others are now busy remaking the world and trying to construct a grand new comprehensive destiny for it. That is the harsh truth. The pre-destiny contained in the breathing of the Spirit is quite different. *Expectandum nobis etiam et corporis ver est*[8] ... The message of the Resurrection plunges the peoples of history, and all their culture, into the expectation of the last spring.

As in the time of the catacombs (as we know from the art they contain), we have to choose between living in order to die and dying in order to live. Modern art cannot evolve, for it is nothing more than a cathartic reaction after centuries of decadence. At its best, abstract art brings freedom, an innocence of all preconceived notions of form. But even as the *exterior form* disintegrates, the way to the *interior form* is barred by the angel with the flaming sword, and will not be opened again except by Baptism, which is death. Artists will recover their priesthood only by performing a theophanic sacrament: by drawing, carving and singing the name of God, and so creating a locus for his presence.

The stagnation of the copyists, petrified, mummified art, is fortunately a thing of the past. Having left copying behind, and come through impressionism and the utter destructiveness of abstract art, the artist now has the creative task of articulating the interior form. But its truth can be apprehended only by mystical sight: 'The glory of the eyes is to be the eyes of the Dove.'[9] What has to be incarnated now is not an idea, or a point of view, or a school, but the very breathing of the Holy Spirit; art must be sophianic. In returning eschatologically to the source we find the absolutely new: 'We remember what is to come.'

Meanwhile science, seeking explanations of particular phenomena, shifts the difficulty further into the distance. 'The greatest mystery is in the possibility of science itself.'[10] 'The most incomprehensible thing in the world is that the world is comprehensible.'[11] It is science as a whole that is mysterious. Even agnostics can see the mystery and draw from it a certain religious feeling. 'The most beau-

---

[8] Minucius Felix, *Octavius* 34.
[9] St Gregory of Nyssa, *In Cant.* hom. 4; *P.G.* 44, 835 CD.
[10] Einstein, quoted by P. Franck, *Einstein, His Life and Time*, epigraph.
[11] L. de Broglie, *Continu et Discontinu*, p. 98.

tiful emotion that we can experience is mystical emotion. Therein lies the seed of all true science.'[12] In an honest, objective scientist the Holy Spirit can arouse the astonishment that Plato felt; he can convey to the most instructed of minds the astonishment of the angels and reveal 'the flame of things' in the very matter of the world.

Existentialist philosophy achieves its own kind of freedom by insisting that nothing in life has any meaning; but then it loses its distinctive purpose of thinking about thought,[13] and in its aimless wandering eventually comes up against the 'closed fist of death'.[14]

The most useful tool in any consideration of the Absolute is perhaps existential phenomenology. Phenomenology observes the conditions under which things appear and relates them to the structure of human subjectivity to which they appear. For Husserl and his school philosophical reflection entails a process of phenomenological reduction, which distinguishes the immediate intuition from what hides it, revealing it through a process of refinement, stripping away the accidental and the artificial and so arriving at the essence. Beneath the outward diversity, the fundamental common structure, the *Eidos*, is laid bare. When we have got behind experience and thought, only the transcendent remains. The transcendent subject discerns the essences; before its clear gaze and unerring intuition the world is present as a phenomenon. This pure 'I', can be apprehended only through transcendental reduction. But we must go further than that, working back through the process of perception until we have penetrated to the original act of intuition. The transcendent, while it is always distinct from the psychological consciousness, must nevertheless work through it. And we know from experience that it always acts with intention (thought must be *about* something, directed to some end), and the external effects produced by this activity reveal what is happening within. By the process of reduction we see that intuition creates the essences. But the transcendental consists of a multiplicity of relationships, subjective and objective; the distinction between subject and object always remains; the transcendental creates the essences, but is not *one* of them. So the *cogito* cannot be ultimate reality, the Absolute.

Reduction turns its gaze upon the world in its entirety; it also 'suspends' or 'brackets out' everything that pertains to me, but which is not myself, including even my feelings and my inmost life, in so far as they are immersed in historical

---

[12] *Ibid.*

[13] The philosopher Rene le Senne (*Obstacle et Valeur: le Devoir*), sees the 'theandric relationship' as a metaphysical state in which philosophical discourse and meditation become prayer. It is the same as the 'total presence' of Lavelle, the precondition for the praying attitude (see P. Evdokimov, 'L'adoration liturgique dans l'Eglise de l'Orient', in *Verbum Caro*, No 35/36. 1955).

[14] Leon Bloy, *La Femme pauvre*, Paris 1951, p. 279.

time. The *cogito*, thus isolated, is beyond time and experience. My extra-temporal essence is revealed; to be set free like this from the world of experience is an exhilarating experience in itself. But this freedom, containing, as it does for Socrates in the *Phaedo*, an 'immense hope', is not simply comfortable, but is as bracing as rarefied mountain air; it is the condition of detachment and total engagement, the imaginative anticipation of a spiritual adventure, the invitation to the encounter with Absolute Value... Does this mean that the process of reduction can ultimately be pursued to its conclusion? Yes, provided that reduction does not mean abolition, but the imposition of order. If there is a multiplicity of interrelated subjects, there must be unity at the top. If we stop at the earlier stages of reduction, we shall look too soon for the Absolute, and be left with *Deus non est, Deus est*: whether it be the Universal Spirit of Hegel, the world of essences of Husserl, the world of ideas of Plato, the absolute me of Fichte, the absolute nature of Spinoza, the absolute matter of the materialists, the absolute society of Marx, the earthly paradise of the utopians, or the absolute freedom of Sartre. The last example is typical of all the others. Because humankind enjoys absolute freedom, and is the origin of value-judgements, because it is itself the union of essence and existence, *Deus non est, Deus est*. But even for Sartre, the very inability of humankind to realize the union of the in-itself and the for-itself draws attention to the God who is missing.

The reality of the existence of God for human beings is the proper subject of the philosophy of evidence, a study that has not even begun. When it achieves recognition it will certainly prove to be the philosophy of revelation. Evidence is perhaps *the very type of apophatic knowing*. It invites the spirit to overstep its own limits, to go beyond itself and discover the hidden reality. *Evidence is always a revelation*, and that is perhaps the only possible definition. It presents and imposes itself with an absolute certainty that has nothing in common with intellectual certainty. Questions of the possibility of illusion or whether the revelation is of something real become pointless. This kind of religious experience is not preceded by a state of reflection; quite the reverse: all that is required is a state of bare receptivity, a spaciousness in the self totally open to grace. Religious experience is the immediate presence of God, before any question can be asked, or indeed conceived.

Evidence reached at the end of an argument is not really evidence, but proof, the conclusion of a process of reasoning. It is actually the opposite of evidence. Even to the strongest intelligence, evidence of the transcendent does away with the need for any proof or intermediate process. It depends neither on credibility nor on reason, but only on the light that comes from the object itself. That is why the most truly evident is always the most incomprehensible, for it is beyond proof, and needs no justification of any kind. Direct mystical illumination is pure grace of the Parousia. A voice comes from the circle of silence above the abyss that surrounds the Father, and says in my heart, I am I, Me. Far from being a definition, this is the apophatic formula that conveys the transcendence of the personal God; a name that hides more than it reveals, demonstrating that human beings cannot truly name God, and it is at the same time a Name-Place where God is immediately present: you who are inaccessible and near.

The world is precarious, God is absolutely certain and evident, and it is only in a living relationship to God, that I also, by virtue of being his icon, am absolutely certain and evident. The Incarnation of our Lord *has united the two apophatic evidences* without confusion and without separation, *Deus absconditus et homo absconditus*: 'I am I, Me', and facing Him, this other being, this *sum*, or rather this *sursum*, also saying, 'I am I, Me'; the one who reflects on himself in himself, and the one who reflects on himself as a human being, in his or her own human form, a consciousness both created and theandric. The Name – the Name in itself that cannot be uttered, the apophatic Nothing, and the uttered Name, *Ecce Homo* – is always threefold.

Humankind could never invent God. If human beings can conceive of God, if they can have an intuition of what is utterly beyond their imagination, it is because they are already within the divine thought, and that thought is already in them.

Even atheists, if they are honest and sincere enough with themselves, if they retain the capacity to look at themselves in the heart of their own mystery, while staying free of any intellectual preconception or prejudice and with a mind undistorted by the passions, can easily say with Pascal: In truth, humanity infinitely transcends humanity; indeed, not to believe is a violation of my nature... Someone has sculpted my face, someone has put these infinite longings in my heart, this ability to see another and call him 'thou', and through this humble love, to perceive the 'wholly Other', and call him 'Thou', the Absolute.

All logical or speculative argument is merely relative. People, however, know that their minds are profoundly and innately drawn towards the absolute. This undeniable and experienced fact is stronger than any process of reflection. We shall never find God through regressive analysis, by working back through the series of finite causes; that would compromise the absolute by mixing it with the relative and reified, bringing it down to the empirical and objective level. Between the absolute and relative dimensions there is an unbridgeable abyss. But there is no such thing as an idea of God, an abstract notion of him; on the contrary, God is from the very outset the one who is the most intimately known.

God exists for me by the fact of making me exist; it is a vital certainty, 'gut-knowledge'. 'The image' borne by human beings refers not to any explanation or proof of God's existence, but to the manner in which God freely chooses to be present. His essence is totally beyond our knowledge, his *existence* is known immediately and intuitively.

Because humanity is made in God's image, the human mind is inherently drawn towards him, but *the content of its thinking about God is no longer the product of its own thought*. In all thinking about God, it is God himself who is thinking within the human mind and thereby bringing about the religious experience of his immediate presence. The human being cannot yet say anything *about* God, but it can *say* God, it already *knows* the nearness of God which entirely surrounds it.

God is always one and the same, identical with his love. Humans continually vary in their attentiveness to that inner attraction which carries them towards God's presence. And this attraction is never irresistible, never restrictive. It is a scarcely perceptible call, the beginnings of a dialogue, a breath of the Spirit.

'Where does humanity come from and where is it going?' Pascal's question clearly assumes that there must be a source. And it seems that the Lord has heard the question and given an astonishingly precise answer: 'I came from the Father and have come into the world; again, I am leaving the world and am going to the Father' (John 16.28). There is the absolute evidence of the source, the testimony to the depth of the Father, beyond all creation and all thought; I can come only from him and can return only to him. The Holy Spirit, the presentiment of the Father in every person, says beforehand, '*Abba*, Father.' It was to make us understand that he is Love, and to live it out, that God 'thought' the Incarnation and offered us, not only his presence, but the grace of his death, the historic faith and the Kingdom.

The Lord said, 'You are gods,' on the sole condition that we should acknowledge ourselves to be 'children of the Most High;' and the two are separated by the *hiatus irrationalis*, the apophatic limit revealed when the process of reduction is taken to its conclusion. The limit demonstrates and preserves divine freedom, for there exists no internal necessity that would oblige God to go out of himself. Only his love oversteps it. Love that is always beyond understanding, and the only thing the human heart desires.

The Russian philosopher Soloviev, commenting on the text that refers to the preaching of the Gospel in every place as a sign of the last times, interprets it in this way: at a certain moment in history, the neutral, agnostic attitude is going to disappear; faced with the evidence, everybody will be forced to choose sides: to be with Christ or against him. But even then the perverted will remain as mysterious as ever. Evidence will never force the will, which can receive grace only while it keeps its freedom. When we reflect on the action of the Holy Spirit in the last times, we can perhaps see 'the finger of God', the *Witness* at work, addressing itself persuasively to human culture in all its forms, with a strong invitation to recover its original purpose: that of transcending the limits of this world and finding fulfilment in the ultimate choice of the Kingdom.

'The faith I love the best, says God, is hope.'[15] For Péguy, and according to the Epistle to the Hebrews, faith is the substance of things hoped for. Hope is the eschatological aspect of faith, it is faith turned towards what is coming. While faith is the acknowledgement of origins, a return to the source by way of tradition, hope finds the source by going forward, in eschatology.

---

[15] C. Péguy, *Le Porche du Mystère de la deuxième Vertu*, Paris 1929, p. 15.

Revelation gives us a rich description of the new Jerusalem to which the nations shall 'bring their glory and honour' (21.24) – they will not be coming empty-handed. We can imagine the noblest expressions of the human spirit, its art and its learning, its highest intellectual achievements, entering the Kingdom of Heaven, to be united with their true reality as a true image matches the original.

Even the majestic beauty of the snow-clad peaks, the caress of the sea or the gold of the cornfields will become that perfect language of which the Bible often speaks. The suns of Van Gogh, the longing of the Venuses and the sadness of the Madonnas of Botticelli will find their adequate expression when the thirst of the two worlds is quenched. Plato will rediscover Socrates, eternally young and beautiful, at the messianic banquet of the divine *Eros*.

And does not music, the purest and most mysterious element of culture, take us even now into a transfigured and more real world? At its highest point, the music itself vanishes and leaves us in the presence of the Absolute. In the Mass of Mozart we hear the voice of Christ; such sublime music is equivalent to the divine presence in the Liturgy.

When it is true, culture, having ceased to be part of worship, returns to its liturgical source. And a cultural form overflowing with the Presence cannot be confined within time, any more than the eucharistic presence or the light on Tabor. 'Seek the Kingdom of God;' culture is essentially that search in history for what cannot be found in history, for what overflows it and leads it beyond its limits. In this way, culture becomes the sign and expression of the Kingdom through the medium of this world.

As the coming of the historical Christ sets in train the coming of the Christ of glory, as the Eucharist both proclaims the end and, in that very act, causes the here and now to explode in anticipation, so culture at its highest point renounces itself, dies mysteriously like the grain of wheat, follows the example of St John the Baptist, the herald and forerunner, whose star was doused in the dazzling light of Noon. Culture becomes the sign, the arrow pointing towards what is to come. With the Bride and the Spirit it says, 'Come, Lord.'

While every human being in the image of God is his living icon, *culture is the icon of the Kingdom of Heaven*. At the moment of the great passing-over, the Holy Spirit will gently touch that icon, and something of it will last for ever.

In the eternal Liturgy of the world to come, human beings will sing the Lord's praises using all the elements of culture refined in the final purifying fire. But already here below, the practising Christian, the scholar, the artist, all the priests of the universal priesthood, celebrate their own liturgy in which the presence of Christ is realized according to the measure of the purity of its receptacle. Like iconographers, using the material and light of this world, they trace the signs through which the mysterious shape of the Kingdom slowly appears.

3. THE THEOLOGY OF HISTORY[16]

What is the meaning of the period between the Ascension and the Parousia? The relation of the gift of the Kingdom and human effort is a mysterious one. Human beings must indeed work out their own salvation with fear and trembling; they must find within history the one thing necessary, also for 'hastening the coming of the day of God' (2 Pet. 3.12). But the precise balance of divine and human activity can never be known. The divine presence is veiled by kenosis and its irruptions will not fit into any simple pattern. In the current discussion between 'incarnationists' and 'eschatologists' the theology of history is quite properly placed in the realm, not of reason, but of faith.

Historical material is now seen to be very complex. We can no longer classify it simply as sacred or profane, as in the *City of God* of St Augustine, or according to a simplistic threefold scheme such as Bossuet's division into Creation, Fall and Salvation. Nothing progresses in a straight line. So, for instance, scientific progress, at the level of synthesis, is sporadic, and the work of Eduard Meyer, Spengler and Toynbee has clearly demonstrated the discontinuity between civilizations. Even between immediately succeeding ages the rhythm is sharply broken; in one period historians may record progress, and in another observe it taking place against a general background of regression. Moreover, no historian can be completely objective; there will be various interpretations of the same event.

In the secularized view there is no place for an original act of creation, so all the emphasis is put on the final stage: the ultimate perfection of humanity and the triumphal march towards the inevitable materialist utopia. As the liver secretes bile, matter has the inherent power to secrete human consciousness, which eventually emerges as the *Logos*. Humankind bursts the chains of alienation and takes command of its own destiny. Generally speaking, historians have not accepted such an absurd account of existence; this innocent view of the End offers only the disappointment of a dubious Marxist paradise or the existential angst that leads nowhere.

For Nietzsche, Pascal's saying, 'humanity infinitely transcends humanity' becomes an axiom, and from it he derives two possible forms of madness from which

---

[16] See H. Marrou, *De la connaissance historique*, Paris 1954; R. Niebuhr, *The Nature and Destiny of Man*, Scribner's, New York 1943; O. Cullmann, *Christ et le temps*, Neuchâtel 1947; K. Lowith, *Meaning in History*, Chicago Press 1949; L. Bouyer, 'Christianisme et Eschatologie', in *Vie Intellectuelle*, 1948; G. Thils, *Théologie des Réalités terrestres*, Paris 1955; J. Danielou, *Essai sur le Mystère de l'Histoire*, Paris 1953; J. Danielou, 'Christologie et Eschatologie', in *Das Konzil von Chalkedon*, Würzburg 1954; J. de Senarclens, *Le Mystère de l'Histoire*, Geneva 1949; Articles by I. Malevez in *Nouvelle Revue théologique*, LIX, LXXI (1937, 1949); R. Mehl, 'Temps, Histoire, Théologie', in *Verbum Caro* No 6, 1948; E. Brunner, 'La Conception chrétienne du temps', in *Dieu Vivant*, 1949; Fr Ricœur, 'Le christianisme et le sens de l'Histoire', in *Histoire et Verité*, 1955; Fr S. Bulgakov, *The Bride of the Lamb*, Eerdmans, Grand Rapids 2001.

we have to choose – the madness that enables us to accept 'eternal recurrence', or the madness that enables us to accept the St Paul's 'folly of the Cross':[17] devilry or sanctity, these are the only ways to transcend our present existence and encounter the Other. And the underlying dilemma is always the same: whether to stay locked in a merely earthly reality or to be open to the beyond.

Which is the true point of view? There are many points of view, but the Gospel speaks of the single eye that is the light of the body (Luke 11.34). What matters is not the particular angle from which we look, but that we should see the whole scene in the light of the Bible, which conveys the one revelation to us in its own way; our awareness being thus deepened, we can only respond to the mystery in silence. No attempt to treat Revelation as history, to 'date its events,' can ever succeed. In our right and left hands we hold the two ends of the chain, providence and progress, meta-history and history, completing the circle in which there is neither beginning nor end, but which allows plenty of space for the mystery that cannot be put into words.

The philosophy of history, so fashionable in the 19th century, gives way to the theology of history. The ethical principles of good and evil are replaced by God and Satan. From the idea of God we pass to his living presence: from the God *of* history to God *in* history.

For the Greeks divinity was changeless. The world of human beings is the moving image, in this world, of the changelessness of God, and the movement causes events to repeat themselves. 'There is nothing new under the sun,' says the world-weary Ecclesiastes (1.9), and St Paul replies, bursting with energy, 'Everything old has passed away; see, everything has become new!' (2 Cor. 5.17).

In eastern thought, the Fall, the Incarnation, the Parousia are not simply irruptions of the heavenly, but interior events which mark the passing (Pasch) of human nature into a different state, and which are mysteriously present and working in history. The Fathers are interested not only in the human Jesus of Nazareth, but in the Christ who by his coming effects an ontological change in earthly existence. The historical, phenomenological narrative conceals the noumenal reality. The Parousia has already begun; it is present, directing the course of history, and only by it can history be truly interpreted.

Ἅπαξ in Hebrews 9.26, 'once', expresses the unique, irrevocable and irreversible nature of the Incarnation. The Ascension brings the human into the eternal depths of the Father and puts the authoritative seal on salvation. History is focused on the uniqueness of Christ. All that went *before* is only 'prefiguration' or typology. In Romans 5.14 Adam is τύπος, the form of Christ, and by this ty-

---

[17] Nietzsche signed his letters 'the Crucified' (see K. Jaspers, *Nietzsche et le christianisme*, Paris 1949, p. 102).

pological method the Fathers decipher the meaning of historical events.[18] All that has happened *since* is the extension of the Incarnation; the time of the Church is the time of the subjective appropriation by everybody of the objective salvation. The Church is thus revealed as a new dimension of life and a new definition of history, because it is focused on the unique, and opened on the *eschaton*. Eschatology, so much neglected in history, yet utterly fundamental to Patristic thought, is the great discovery of our time. Using the typological method, the Fathers demonstrated that the Old Testament was the prefiguration of the age to come in Christ, so that history might be interpreted in its light. The age which is Christ is at the same time the *eschaton*: in Christ history is perfected. Nothing new can occur in history, we cannot overtake Christ. Revelation has come to an end, because the Parousia has already begun with the Resurrection. The Parousia is imminent, but its hour is unknown, which is why, according to St Gregory of Nyssa, history 'goes from beginning to beginning by way of beginnings without end;'[19] nevertheless history as a whole is moving towards its end. While its expectation is expressed in a manner always new, its content is determined by its end, so history becomes sacred. The order as usually understood must be reversed: it is universal history that is sacred, and profane history, which is only its phenomenological aspect, is contained within it. Without adding anything, Christ, in his second coming, fulfils history in the sense that kenosis has come to an end, and his glory is universally manifested. This glory (the *Holy* of Isaiah 6.3) secretly fills the present even now and, while commanding us to look ahead, obliges us just as forcefully to come to terms with the present in which salvation is already coming to pass. This is really the work of the Holy Spirit, through the medium of preaching and the sacraments, by which the historical visibility of Christ is extended and constantly manifested.

In this connection it must be said that history, while not being determined by non-historical elements, is none the less conditioned by them. History is not autonomous; it possesses its edenic prehistory and will have its post-history in the Kingdom. The first, passing through history, is perfected in the second. These metahistorical forces are alive and active in history, and condition its task. So it is clear that while eschatology has an essential historical human component, it also explicitly entails the participation of the heavenly, angelic and demonic powers.

History can neither last indefinitely nor arbitrarily stop. Its final resolution will be effected jointly by its transcendental element, the will of the Father, and its immanent element, the inner maturity of history itself. On the immanent level, it is not given to human beings to change the theme of their existence, to escape their fate; at most they can decide to interpret their experience of life positively

---

[18] See Dom Celestin Charlier, *Typologie ou Evolution*, Ed. Maredsous; *La lecture chrétienne de la Bible*, Brussels.
[19] *Hom. Cant.*, *P.G.* 44, 1043 B.

or negatively. We have to remember that history has already been summed up in Christ's words, 'it is finished.' The Messianic reign, the day of the universal res-urrection and the final consummation of the Parousia culminated in the unique person of Christ. He is the Messiah and he is YHWH, *Christos* and *Kyrios*, God and Man, the beginning and the end; and the end is not merely the last stage of an evolution, but fulfilment. The end of the pre-eternal counsel of God is already accomplished, and beyond the hypostatic union of the divine and human in Christ there is nothing more. According to the Fathers, Christ represents the 'first fruits'.[20] 'He has assumed human nature in its wholeness ... in order to cure it as a whole.'[21] He is the firstborn of the new creation. So the history of the world clearly belongs within the history of salvation, the history of the Church. In the sacraments, all the events of the *eschaton* are already present and at work.

To the ἀκολουθία of the Fall (successive regression) God has opposed the ἀκολουθία of salvation (ordered succession, progressing according to its inherent energy). History, thus, is a dialectic of the initiatives of God and the responses of humankind, the interaction of the two Adams, the dialogue of the two '*fiats*'. The ascending and descending movements have already found their ultimate syn-thesis in Christ, and only Christ possesses the key to the meaning of history. The discrepancy between the norm and existence, between fallen nature and its deified state, will be the object of the Judgement, revealed on the last day. Christ is the absolute measure of universal theandrism. The doctrine of Chalcedon illuminates the whole theology of history: the absolute subject of history is Christ and it is only by reference to him, by being in Christ, Christified, that humankind can also be the subject of history. Christ assumes human nature in all its forms; in him there is neither Greek nor Jew, because every nation and every culture sees its own face reflected in him. Truth employs all means of expression and speaks all languages (Rev. 7.9). The Church is clothed in a 'coat of many colours' (Gen. 37.3; 1 Pet. 4:10).

Christ is also the meeting-point between West and East, between the biblical and extra-biblical religions. A symptom of this is the convergence of genuine mysticism in all the religions, but we must take care to discard all agnostic relativism, and the syncretism of occult beliefs – 'tradition' as defined by Guénon. That still leaves the great fact of the central importance of the interior spiritual life in the extra-biblical re-ligions (Hinduism and Buddhism) and the fundamental affirmation of the transcendent and personal God in the biblical religions (Judaism, Islam and Christianity). Now, the universalism of the Christian revelation, which is its miracle, proclaimed by the Fa-thers, encompasses all traditions, never mutilating them, but bringing out their essential character so that it is seen as their distinctive truth. We see this at work in St Paul when

---

[20] St Gregory of Nyssa, *Against Apollinarius*, *P.G.* 44, 1152 C.
[21] Theodoret, *Adv. haeres.*, V, 11; *P.G.* 83, 492 A-B, 429 D.

he stood before the monument to the unknown god at Athens. The real dialectic of the religions shows that where serious attention is given to the interior life, awareness of the transcendent cannot be far behind, and so it is that in the case of Amidism, or faith-oriented Buddhism, Fr de Lubac wonders if Amida is not a distant substitute for the Saviour;[22] similarly Ramanuja, the Hindu mystic of the 11th century, came to the conviction that the Buddhist identification of humanity with the divine makes the 'meeting' between humanity and God – and therefore love – impossible, which is why Ramanuja affirms his belief in the personal God; Fr Monchanin, telling of his most recent experiences, speaks movingly of the expectancy of India as it waits for the mystery of the Trinity to be revealed; finally there are the astonishing words of Al Hallaj, the Muslim mystic, crucified at Baghdad in 922 but held in veneration ever since, who prayed like a true Christian, 'Praised be God, who has revealed in his humanity (Christ) the mystery of his radiant divinity.'[23] Crucified for having confessed the Incarnation, he implants that truth at the very heart of Islam.

For the Jews, there is God but no Resurrection; the Greeks had a notion of resurrection but they did not have God; in Christianity, God dies and rises again. Between the fanaticism that separates and the syncretism that confuses, there lies the mystery of Christ which distinguishes without separation and unites without confusion. Certainly, the interior life by itself does not produce grace, but it prepares us to receive it. Biblical monotheism implies an initiative of God, his descent towards the creature, and on the part of humanity a going out, its ascent towards the Other. The state of enstasy expects and prepares us for that moment when we are opened up to God in love, when 'the invisible perfections of God ... will burst upon the eyes of him who knows how to look at his works' and we shall see history filled with the '*mirabilia Dei*'. And the precise centre where the perfect interior life converges with absolute transcendence is Christ. From the theocentric direction of the Old Covenant the Spirit leads us to the Christocentric revelation: 'God ... desires everyone to be saved and to come to the knowledge of the truth. For there is one God; there is also one mediator between God and humankind, Christ Jesus, himself human, who gave himself a ransom for all' (1 Tim. 2.4-6).

Only Christ, holding the whole of human nature within his hypostatic unity, keeps every creature from disappearing, brings it into the light of God's presence and reveals through the interior life the transcendent presence of the One in Three.

Is Christ the King of history? Yes, but kenotically, in the way that he entered Jerusalem, unperceived by historians, but more than visible and unmistakably apparent to faith. The parable of the wheat and the tares illustrates the confusion in history of appearances and hidden depths (Matt. 21.22-30).

---

[22] H. de Lubac, *Amida*, Paris 1955, p. 306.
[23] Cf. A. Cuttat, *La Rencontre des Religions*, Paris 1957; Louis Massignon, 'Hallaj, martyr mystique de l'Islam', in *Dieu Vivant*, No 4.

The conflict that polarizes the world is not between spirit and matter, but between different kinds of spirits (Rev. 12.7). Chapter 13 of Revelation speaks of the two enormously destructive demonic attributes: unlimited power like that of a totalitarian State over its inhabitants, and false prophecy.[24] The 'notes' of the anti-Church become apparent – its imposture, its parasitic and parodical character; evil steals the being and feeds on it, demonically recomposing its elements in imitation of God, but inverting the sign to negative, which is the essence of all parody. Conversely, the doctrinal affirmation of Chalcedon defines the positive aim: the recapitulation of humanity in the royal fullness of Christ. The opposition of these two claims to exclusive sovereignty can only end in catastrophe. Straightforward evolution there cannot be, but only a 'catastrophic progression',[25] the advance of involution towards the final reckoning.

Without needing to be precise about dates, names and ages, we can trace this double process through history: on the one hand a progressively intense dehumanization, and on the other the preaching of the Gospel throughout the world, the crystallization of the ages which will force the choice upon us, sanctity in new forms of witness and martyrdom, the conversion of Israel. We have reason to expect that one of these two currents will be crowned by Christ in his Parousia, and that the other will find its fulfilment in the antichrist.

4. THE CHURCH, THE ESCHATOLOGICAL COMMUNITY

Most of the Bible is taken up with the chronicle of God's people, united in one congregation. When the paschal lamb was sacrificed (Exod. 12.6-11): 'the whole assembled congregation' received very precise instructions on how to behave: 'This is how you shall eat it: your loins girded, your sandals on your feet, and your staff in your hand; and you shall eat it hurriedly. It is the passover of the Lord.' Joined together at the Messianic meal, looking for the coming of the Messiah, this community of pilgrims is always on the march. 'The times of refreshing' have come (Acts 3.19), but the attitude of the community of the new Israel stays the same: 'For here we have no lasting city, but we are looking for the city that is to come' (Heb. 13.14). The King is come, but his Kingdom is yet to come.

In Christ the whole expanse of history is directed towards his Kingdom. Christian civilization closes the cycle of cultures, it is the last of them. Its character is

---

[24] Cf. Mgr Cassien, *The Kingdom of Caesar judged in the light of the New Testament* (in Russian), Paris 1949.

[25] The expression is of W. Ern, a Russian philosopher who has conceived a whole theory of catastrophic progression. The subject is one that comes naturally to the Russian mind (see P. Evdokimov, 'Les courants apocalyptiques dans la pensée russe', in *Foi et Vie*, No 4, 1954; also B. Zenkovsky, 'L'eschatologie dans la pensée russe', in *La Table ronde*, No 110, 1957).

antinomian. It is indeed the place of the incarnations of the Wisdom of God and, at the same time, having reached its highest point of culture and worship, it always avoids becoming rooted in history, freeing itself from its grasp by progressive acts of self-transcendence. 'To possess as one who does not possess', 'let the dead bury the dead'. This is the light-hearted detachment of someone climbing the Holy Mountain. This is the original meaning of Christian vigils: we must be standing upright to meet the Lord. *Homo viator* is a traveller who is fed on the bread of the Eucharist.

The Peace or *shalom* announced in the Bible is often confused with peaceful existence; the *Comforter* with the comfortable life. According to the Gospel, the faithful will be persecuted and the Church will be founded on the blood of the martyrs. 'Do not think that I have come to bring peace to the earth; I have not come to bring peace, but a sword' (Matt. 10.34). 'came to bring fire to the earth,' announces the Prince of Peace (Luke 12.49). '*My* peace I give to you. I do not give to you as the world gives' (John 14.27). The Messianic peace bursts the bounds of history and makes it overflow its frame. It is like El Greco's use of perspective; he composes the picture, but is himself outside it. The Messianic peace poses the fundamental question for every church: this peace that overturns the foundations of history and ends the world, is it rooted in history or is it incarnated? If the former, the Church is essentially a historical institution; either settled and self-contained, existing only for its members, 'seated at table' and rejoicing in all the joys of the mystical banquet, but lacking that quality of yeast or any power to influence the destiny of the world; alternatively, penetrating the world, but consequently tempted by ambition for secular power, and therefore no longer possessing the 'fire which salts'. Eschatology without history (the eastern temptation) or history without eschatology (the western temptation) – these lead, in desperation, to hyper-eschatology (the Protestant temptation) which leaps over history into the final moment. In all these cases, history and the world are devalued of their proper meaning, which is to be the object of divine love, the place of the incarnation of the Kingdom. The other, incarnational definition of the Church is determined by Christ and his priestly prayer: the Lord is come into the world only for his Apostolic mission, 'that the world may believe' (John 17.21). Only the Church that lives in the light of the Parousia, meaning not so much the end of the world as its *salvation*, is really in history, for the Day of the Lord is by no means the last day, but Fullness. So we can see that the Church lives under a double regime: the historical one of the Incarnation and the eschatological one of the Parousia. 'The Church consists of penitents and those who are perishing,'[26] and at the same time, as Nicholas Cabasilas says, 'We cannot go beyond, or add any-

---

[26] St Ephrem of Syria, quoted by Fr Florovsky, *The Eastern Fathers of the 4th century* (in Russian), Paris 1931, p. 232.

thing ... after the Eucharist, there is nothing more to strive for; we must stop there.'[27] And yet, after Communion the priest says, 'O Christ, Passover great and most holy! O Wisdom, Word, and Power of God! Vouchsafe that we may *more perfectly* partake of thee in the days which know no evening, of thy Kingdom.' It is at the heart of history, with all the realism entailed by the Incarnation, and specifically through the medium of earthly matter, that the Church celebrates the Eucharist, transforming that matter into the Bread of the Kingdom, and it is that Messianic Supper which displays the Church as inaugurated eschatology and parousial expectation.

Monasticism stays on the margin of the secularized Christian city precisely so that it may be the maximum measure, the salt of the Kingdom, revealing by its light the meta-history of historical existence. In former times, the crowd would come to gaze for a moment on the stylites, then carry away that inspiring vision in their hearts as a standard by which to measure their own life. Those who leave the world oblige us by that very act to see them in a different way, to pay attention to their message, and thus to find the spiritual key to existence.

The ascetics use their science to experiment on the Pauline distinction between the *soma*, bodiliness that is innocent in itself, because it is natural, and the *sarx*, the sinful carnality which entices us away from the normal use of earthly goods towards their anti-natural enjoyment. The purpose of ascetic discipline is the spiritualization of the whole human being. The transformation of the body, of its somatic element, which began with the saints, is evidenced by the well-known phenomena of levitation, luminescence and supernatural power. During earthly life, it is by no means the soul only, but the body also, that is washed by the tears of penitence and rendered ethereal and light, and bathed in the 'fire of divinity'.[28]

Monastic asceticism, when thoroughly purified and concentrated exclusively on love, maps out a rule of conduct applicable equally to monks and to the world at large and all who live in it; once internalized, it yields its most precious secret. 'Those who live in the world, even if they are married, must in every other respect be like monks.'[29] The root of all existence is the love of God, 'whom we must love as we love our betrothed.' Which comes first, knowledge and understanding or love? That is a question that never occurs in the East. We can neither know God without loving him, nor love him without knowing him. In all our knowing there is an exercise of charity; our secret intuition is equipped with cognitive properties, gifts of the Spirit. To have a conception of God and to love him is one and the same act of mystical union. The condition of the couple in Eden united

---

[27] N. Cabasilas, *The Life in Jesus Christ*.
[28] St Simeon, *Hymns of Divine Love*.
[29] St John Chrysostom, *Hom. in epist. ad Haebr.*, 7, 41.

to God by organic grace remains the standard. By a process of appropriation and participation, human love 'memorizes' the divine philanthropy and is satisfied only in God. *Eros* ascending is magnetized by *eros* crucified and sacrificed. *Philtron*, the enchanting name that Nicholas Cabasilas gives to love, is extended beyond itself in 'epectasy' (St Gregory of Nyssa) as offering and sacrifice; this human love for God is the response to the summons, the ascent towards the Beloved.[30]

In the face of this mystery irradiated by the light of Christ we understand the profound truth of Péguy's words: 'In order not to believe we must do violence to ourselves.'[31]

[30] 'Perfect is the soul whose desire is directed wholly towards God' (St Maximus, *Cent. Car.*, 3, 98; *P.G.* 90, 1048 A).
[31] *Porche du Mystère de la deuxième vertu*, Complete Works, p. 175.

2

Eschatology

It is fortunate that the Church has never, from pedagogical motives, attempted to set out all its eschatological teaching in a systematic form. Apart from the articles of the Nicene Creed concerning the Parousia, the Judgement and the Resurrection, there are no authoritative statements of Orthodox doctrine. We affirm a series of events, and refer them to Scripture, but the theological commentary on these, and the tradition itself, are not always entirely clear or even consistent. There are some questions which even theologians skirt round respectfully... However, 'if the essence of wisdom is the apprehension of reality, and since prophecy includes the knowledge of things to come, nobody can be thoroughly wise who does not include in his knowledge, by the aid of prophecy, the future as well.'[1]

The eschatological reckoning is the final statement not only of history, but also of the wisdom of God, that wisdom which, according to St Paul, is incompatible with human wisdom. Indeed, it may be that only human folly can hope to make sense of the unpredictable ways of God. But the great mystery at the heart of the divine economy, how the love of God can be reconciled with his justice, is quite beyond our understanding. While the judgement requires us to *think antinomically*, the schematic approach of the theological manuals remains rationalist and anthropomorphic. Fr Sergei Bulgakov regards 'penitential theology' as the simple-minded solution; just when we are on the very verge of the mystery of God we are offered instead a legalistic code. This may seem to make everything clearer, but the clarity is misleading. We must return to the words of St Paul: 'O the depth of the riches and wisdom and knowledge of God! How unsearchable are his judgements and how inscrutable his ways!' (Rom. 11.33).

'The present form of this world is passing away' (1 Cor. 7.31), 'and the world and its desire are passing away, but those who do the will of God live for ever' (1 John 2.17). Something disappears, while something else remains. The nature of the elements will undergo a change, which notion is as familiar to science as to mythology. The image most commonly used to illustrate this is that of fire; fire cleanses and alters at the same time, but when it has done its work, that will not be the final stage of an evolution; everything will come to a pause, not a pause in time, but a gap or stopping-off point. The last day will have a character all of its own; it will never become yesterday, because it will have no morrow; it will

---

1 St Gregory of Nyssa, *Against Eunomius, P.G.* 45, 580 C.

not be one day among others. At that moment the whole of existence will be raised to a level at which the old standards of measurement no longer apply. St Gregory of Nyssa says that the hand of God will seize the closed circle of phenomenal time and lift it to a higher level.[2] The last day that rounds off historical time does not itself belong to it; it is not in the calendar, so cannot be predicted. When a person dies, the date of his death has meaning only for those who are left behind, who are still in time; but at the end of the world, those other people who would have remained in time will no longer exist, because historical time itself will not exist. We might think of illustrating the emptiness with the image of an empty bottle, forgetting that in the general emptiness the bottle will not exist either. When we read that 'one day is with the Lord as a thousand years, and a thousand years as one day,' that is not a mathematical proportion of 1 to 1000, but a way of expressing the impossibility of comparing times that are inherently incomparable. The transcendent character of the end can be apprehended only by faith and revelation, so some people are bound to be sceptical: 'Scoffers will come ... saying, "Where is the promise of his coming?"' (2 Pet. 3.3-4).

For such as Auguste Comte, the world is peopled more with the dead than the living. The silence of this immense speechless crowd weighs heavily upon the living. The State 'organizes' death, beautifies or ignores it, exerting itself benevolently to banish its distressing reminders. But death will not allow itself to be organized and enclosed in a finite, and therefore false, world. It is a great paradox that while death is the greatest anguish of our existence, it is also what saves human beings from banality and consequently preserves their dignity. Ever since Christ, death has been Christian, no longer an intrusion, but the great initiator. It gives meaning and depth to the mystery of life. To profess atheism entails a double absurdity: life is deduced from nothingness, from inexistence, and the living are annihilated at the moment of death. But life is not an element of nothingness; death is an element of life. We can understand the problem of death only in the context of life. Nothingness and death cannot exist in themselves; they are only an aspect of life, of being, a secondary phenomenon, just as negation is posterior to affirmation and is, in a sense, parasitic on it.

Death cannot be considered as a failure of God, for it does not destroy life. What happened was that the balance was upset, and from that moment death became, as a logical consequence, the common fate of all. Death became natural, even while remaining against nature, which accounts for the agony of the dying. Death is planted like a splinter in the heart of existence. The wound is so deep that healing entails *the death of God* and, in due course, our own passage through the *catharsis* of death. Christian *athanasia* by no means implies the survival of the soul, and nowhere does the Bible teach that the soul is naturally immortal.

---

[2] St Gregory of Nyssa, *In Ps.*, *P.G.* 44, 504 CD.

We must distinguish between a certain survival which, while not a return to nothingness, is a lesser mode of existence – because it is outside God and under the control of *Thanatos* – and on the other hand, eternal life, to which the whole human being will be surrendered, body and soul, under the control of the divine *pneuma*. The Eucharist that we consume is the flesh and blood of the Saviour, the very substance, heavenly but *complete*. In the Creed we confess explicitly, 'I believe in the resurrection of the body'. But before the coming of Christ, the state of death, although not a disappearance, was a disintegration, precisely because it was separation from God; as St Athanasius teaches, 'After the dissolution of death, they rested in death and corruption.'[3] It is the borderline state between being and non-being.

The Word joins itself to 'dead' nature so as to quicken it. The Incarnation was itself *redemption*; its culminating point was the union of God, at the moment of his death, with the state of supreme disintegration; this state of the corpse and the descent into hell mark the end of the work of salvation. 'He took a body capable of dying so that, suffering for all in that body into which he had come, he reduced to nothing the Master of death.'[4] 'He came so far within the grasp of death as to reach a state of deadness, and then in his own body bestowed on our nature the principle of the resurrection.'[5] 'He destroyed the power of mortality and transformed the *body* to make it incorruptible.'[6] 'Christ has changed sunset into sunrise.'[7]

Patristic thought is very explicit: the immortality of the whole human being is the gift of God; it is pervaded and raised to life by the quickening energies of the divine *pneuma*. St Ignatius was already speaking of the Eucharist as φάρμακον ἀθανασίας, the medicine of immortality and the antidote to prevent us from dying – ἀντίδοτος μὴ ἀποθανεῖν (Eph. 20.2).

The saints greet death joyfully, in the knowledge that they are to be freed from the burden of earthly existence. When we die, we are born into the true life of the resurrected state. Consequently, according to St Gregory of Nyssa, death is to be welcomed, ἀγαθὸν ἂν εἰν ὁ Θάνατος,[8] not something to be frightened of. And a martyr may even passionately desire it: 'There is within me a water that lives and speaks, saying to me inwardly, Come to the Father.'[9] We should read the whole wonderful account of the death of Macrina by her brother St Gregory of Nyssa: 'The day was already far spent and the sun was beginning to set,

---

[3] *De Incar.*, 5.
[4] *De Incar.*, 20.
[5] St Gregory of Nyssa, *Catech.* 32, 3.
[6] St Cyril of Alexandria, *In Luc.*, 5, 19; *Hom. Pasch.*, XVII.
[7] St Clement of Alexandria, *Protreptic*, c. 114.
[8] *Or. de Pulcheria, P.G.* 46, 877 A.
[9] St Ignatius, Romans 7.3.

but she remained as lively as ever. And the nearer she approached to her end, as if she saw more clearly the beauty of the Bridegroom, the more she hasted towards her Beloved. Indeed her bed was turned towards the sunrise.'[10] When 'the heart is wounded by the splendour of God,'[11] 'love overtakes all fear.'[12] As the Church sings at Easter, 'Thy tomb, O Christ, is fairer than Paradise.'

The liturgical expression for death is 'falling asleep'; part of the human being falls asleep and part remains conscious; certain psychological faculties attached to the body are lost – all the senses as well as awareness of time and space. The spirit is separated from the body. The soul no longer exercises the function of animating the body, but as the organ of consciousness, it remains in the spirit. It must be emphasized that nothing like disincarnation takes place; the body becomes separate but is in no way lost, for at the resurrection the whole human being is reintegrated and restored.

Although the Orthodox may refer to what comes between death and the last Judgement as *purgatory*, that is not a *place*, but an intermediate *state* of purification. This distinction alone marks the division between two different kinds of spirituality. St Anselm's theology of redemption with its juridical notion of satisfaction has always been foreign to eastern thought, and likewise the penal and satisfactory aspect of the state of penitence (either in this life in the sacrament of confession or after death), and devotion to the Sacred Heart, which is similarly concerned with expiation. These entirely different notions of soteriology are clearly demonstrated in the theology of the *Communion of Saints*; in the West this concerns the Church and has provided it with the doctrine of merit – the merits of some contributing to the forgiveness of others and the good works of some being profitable for others.[13] In the East, however, it concerns the Holy Spirit; it is the extension of the eucharistic communion, in which the Holy Spirit performs the particular work of uniting people and making that unity not merely an additional benefit, but something essential to the Body[14] – the 'naturally supernatural' expression of mutual and cosmic charity, holiness. We are companions of the saints, *sanctorum socii*, because we are in the society of the Holy Trinity. Christ is the mediator, the saints are intercessors and faithful co-operators, *synergoi* and fellow-worshippers, united with all for the ministry of salvation. Charity in heaven becomes more alive and the holy souls of the dead mingle with the congregation at the Liturgy. The saints in heaven join with the angels in the work of

---

[10] *P.G.* 46, 984 B.
[11] St Macarius, *Homil.* v. 6.
[12] St Anthony the Great, *Philokalia*, v. 1, p. 131. See also Oskar Pfister on love and fear in *Das Christentum und die Angst*, Zurich 1944; Paul-Louis Landsberg, *The Experience of Death and the Moral Problem of Suicide*, Living Time Press, Shrewsbury 2002.
[13] St Ambrose, *P.L.* 15, 1723; 16, 511; St Augustine, *P.L.* 33, 87; 38, 1044.
[14] St Basil, *Liber de Spiritu Sancto*, c. 2, 6. n. 61.

the salvation of the living.[15] The purpose of eastern ascesis is not expiation, but deifying spiritualization, and although the Greeks speak of purification through suffering, they never speak of penal satisfaction; even the term 'purificatory expiation' is absolutely unheard of. While they may mention punishment, this is never allowed to have any propitiatory effect; there is no fire before the judgement, and the *ignis purgatorius* and all Roman teaching about purgatory in its juridical form is formally condemned. But while eschewing penal satisfaction, the Orthodox teach purification after death, not in the sense of pain that purges, but as the working out of destiny through progressive purification and liberation, *healing*. The waiting between death and the Judgement is creative; the prayer of the living, their offerings for the dead, the sacraments of the Church, take up and continue the work of the Lord's salvation. The waiting has a pronounced communal and collegiate character; it is communion in the shared eschatological destiny; *far from being reparation for a fault, it is the repairing of nature*. The image often used is that of passing through customs, where we hand over to the demons what belongs to them and, thus freed of our burdens, go on our way with what belongs to the Lord. Eastern eschatology is always an integral part of the economy of the Mystery of God. Purgatory is not a subject of metaphysics or eschatological physiology, still less of any physical science of souls after death; the fate that awaits us between death and judgement is in no sense a *place* (souls are divested of their bodies, so neither space nor astronomical time applies to them) but a situation, a *state*. Torture or flames do not come into it, only a bringing to maturity by the stripping away of every impurity that weighs on the spirit.

The word 'eternity' in Hebrew comes from the verb *alam*, which means *to hide*. God has wrapped in obscurity our future state beyond the grave, and it is not for us to pry into the divine secret. All the same, the Fathers are positive that the interval is not empty; as St Irenaeus says, the souls 'ripen'.[16]

Liturgical prayer for the dead is a very ancient and firm tradition. We know from the example of Moses and Elijah at the Transfiguration, and from the parable of Dives and Lazarus, that the dead possess perfect awareness. Life continues, even as it passes through death (the question, what happens to deformed children and pagans is answered by the 'preaching in Hades'[17]) and, according to the profound words of St Paul (1 Cor. 3.22), death is itself a gift of God put at the disposal of the human race.

---

[15] Origen, *De Orat.*, *P.G.* 11, 553.
[16] *Adv. haer.*, *P.G.* 7, 806.
[17] This doctrine was accepted by almost all the eastern Fathers: Origen, *Contra Cels.*, II, 43; St Irenaeus, *Adv. haer.*, V, 31, 2; IV, 27, 2; St Clement of Alexandria, *Strom.*, VI, 6, speaks also of the preaching of the Apostles; St John Damascene, *De fide orth.*, III, 29; also the two Gregories, St Maximus, etc.

1. THE HEAVENLY EXPECTATION OF THE SAINTS

About the interval between the ages, the Fathers keep a contemplative silence. St Ambrose calls it the *locus caelestis* where the souls live. Tradition identifies it with the third heaven of St Paul, the heaven of the *arcana verba*. However, the approaches to the Kingdom are much more like an age-long state of being than a geographical place. According to St Gregory of Nyssa[18] souls enter the intelligible world, the city of the celestial hierarchies, above the canopy of the ether and the stars. It is Eden, now become the portico of the Kingdom, also called 'Abraham's bosom'; it is 'the place of refreshment, light and peace' referred to in the prayers for the dead.

That existence is the anagogical way of perfection and purification, past the flaming sword of the cherubim which burns only the wicked. The purified souls ascend from one dwelling-place to the next (the *mansiones* of Ambrose), are initiated by degrees into the heavenly mystery and draw near to the Temple, the Lamb. The Fathers also call the Kingdom the Holy Spirit. There, angels and humans first enter into communion, then, to the chant of *Sanctus*, together begin the ascent to the portico of the 'House of the Eternal'. That is the sanctuary into which the Lord enters (Heb. 9.24) and where the 'wounded friends of the Bridegroom', the *Communio Sanctorum*, are assembled around the pierced heart of the *Theos-Anthropos*.

This is still a discarnate existence, wrapped in the presence of Christ, whose glorified flesh supplies the souls' nakedness. The spirits are attuned to the invisible through their inward senses. At the heart of the preliminary 'Sabbath rest' there is a memory at work, without which there could be no communion with the Church on earth: 'they will rest from their labours, for their deeds follow them' (Rev. 14.13). During this active waiting the Church is clothed in clean linen, the works of the saints (Rev. 19.8). 'I slept, but my heart was awake' (Song of Solomon 5.2), refers to the waking sleep of the 'little resurrection'. The souls ascend by degrees, while always waiting for the Day of the Lord, 'for there is only one body that awaits ... perfect bliss.'[19] The mystical unity between Christ and his Church is the mystery of the Body as a whole, of the 'bound sheaf of harvested wheat' (St Cyril of Alexandria), and only this fullness will gain access to the depth of the Father; the gaze of all is directed towards this crowning moment. The Eucharist is already preparing us for it, and the very name *Ecclesia* will take on its full meaning only at the moment of the universal resurrection, with the establishment of the *totus Christus*. Meanwhile the waiting is filled by the prayer

---

[18] Cf. Jean Danielou, *Platonisme et Théologie mystique*, Paris 1944; ch. III, 'Le Paradis retrouvé'.

[19] Origen, *In Levit.*, hom. 7, n. 2.

of the living for the dead and the prayer of the dead for the living, which is the proper work of the *Communio Sanctorum*. History is the eschatological Advent, which is by no means simply a looking ahead to the future, but the sanctification of the present by the participation of all – the living, the dead and the angels – in the unique destiny of humankind in Christ. This is not evolution, but involution carried to its fulfilment. The chief end of the saints is not merely to be united to the Holy Trinity, but 'to express the unity of the Holy Trinity itself.'[20]

2. THE PAROUSIA

The Ascension presupposes the Parousia. Christ is the same, but there is no more kenosis; Christ will come in dazzling glory, unmistakably. It will no longer be possible not to recognize him. His coming will bring immediate judgement on all who doubt, but those who experience it will have undergone a change in human nature. The cataclysmic events of the last days will be still within history, but the world that sees the Parousia will not be the world of history. At that very moment it will be transformed: 'we will all be changed' (1 Cor. 15.51) – 'we who are alive, who are left, will be caught up in the clouds together with them to meet the Lord in the air' (1 Thess. 4.17).

The Resurrection is universal and applies to 'all who are in their graves.' (John 5.28) Some wait with joy, others with fear or even resistance. For St Paul it is like the energy that God puts in the seed to make it spring up: 'It is sown a physical body, it is raised a spiritual body' (1 Cor. 15.44) – having 'put on immortality', bearing 'the image of the man of heaven.' The soul recovers its body – but what form that will take, exactly what condition it will be in, how old it will be, are all questions which deal with transcendental experience. Rather than try answering such questions, we should maintain a respectful silence. The resurrection is an ultimate lifting up – ὑπερ-ὑψωσις – which frees the being from its former limits. The hand of God seizes its quarry and lifts it to an unknown dimension.[21] The most we can say is that the risen body will flourish as it was intended to while perfectly retaining its identity. St Gregory of Nyssa[22] speaks of the seal or stamp which marks the body so that the familiar face can be recognized. The body will resemble that of the risen Christ; no longer heavy and impenetrable.[23] Already in this life, we can by ascesis gradually enter the pre-resurrection state (2 Cor. 3.18). St Paul speaks

---

[20] St Maximus, *Amb.*, *P.G.* 91, 1196 B.
[21] St Gregory of Nyssa, *C. Eunom.*, *P.G.* 45, 697 C.
[22] *De opif. hom.*, cap. 25, 27.
[23] The energy of repulsion, which makes everything opaque and impenetrable, gives way to the energy of attraction and interpenetration of all and of each (see V. Lossky, 'The Bodily Resurrection', in *Anglican Theological Review*, 1949).

of the ability to see oneself 'with unveiled face,' and the judgement consists in the exposure of the entire person. St Isaac speaks also of judgement by the love that burns: the same love 'brings suffering to the condemned and joy to the blessed.' 'Sinners, even in hell, are not deprived of the divine love,'[24] but their remoteness from the source, their poverty and emptiness of heart, render them incapable of responding to the love of God, and this causes torment, because, since God has revealed himself to them, they still cannot but love Christ.

In the Gospel there is the image of the separation of the sheep and goats (Matt. 25.32). There is no such thing as a perfect saint, just as, in every sinner, there is at least some good; so, like Fr Sergei Bulgakov,[25] we can interiorize the image, understanding the separation to be not between people, but within each person. Similarly, according to this point of view, destruction, annihilation and the second death refer not to groups of human beings but to the demonic elements within each one. Fire signifies not so much torture and punishment as purification and healing. The cutting off of a limb is not the destruction of the person, but the pain that is suffered in losing part of oneself. According to strict justice we should all go to hell, but in every person there are elements of Paradise and of hell.

The divine sword penetrates the depths of human nature in its work of separation, revealing that what was given by God as a gift has not been received and actualized; and this emptiness constitutes the essence of hell's torment: love that has not been realized, the tragic discrepancy between the image and the likeness. Good and evil are so inextricably mixed during earthly life that ordinary notions of law cannot apply; we are left with the unfathomable mystery of the divine wisdom.

Is hell eternal? Eternity is above all not a measurement of time, and it is certainly not vicious infinity, mere endlessness. Eternity is divine time; it has a direction and a purpose, and we can say that the eternities of Paradise and of hell are different, for it is impossible to conceive of eternity as an empty form independent of its content (Matt. 25.34-41). To the Hebrew mentality there is no such thing as autonomous nature; it was created for the use of human beings, it is part of their history. There is no purely cosmic evolution, only existential *involution* centred on humankind and open to humanization. Biblical time is not objective; temporality is part of the framework that human destiny requires in order to follow a consistent direction. Humankind is not subject to it, but imposes its purpose on it. Because Messianism is the axis of history, time is subordinate to prophetic and priestly action. Human beings make history in the course of realizing values that transcend time. Everything is directed towards the messianic appearance of Christ, when time will intersect with eternity and be thereby changed in nature.

---

[24] Wensinck, XXVII, p. 136.
[25] *The Bride of the Lamb*, ch. 3, on eschatology.

The general view of eternal torment is only a textbook opinion, simplistic theology (of the penitential sort) which neglects the depth of texts such as John 3.17 and 12.47. Can we really believe that, alongside the eternity of the Kingdom of God, God has provided another eternity of hell? Surely, this would amount to a failure in the divine plan, even a partial victory of evil? Now, St Paul, in 1 Cor. 15.55, states quite the opposite. St Augustine did indeed oppose the more generous interpretations of the *tender mercies* of God, but that was out of a concern to avoid libertinism and sentimentality; besides, fear would not only be useless in pedagogical argument today, but would make Christianity dangerously like Islam. A healthy trembling before holy things keeps the world from becoming bland, but real fear is driven out by perfect love (1 John 4.18).

Perhaps we should say that hell is neither in eternity, nor in objectively measured time, but in subjective isolation, and is consequently ghostly and unreal, a form of subjective inexistence.

The Fifth Ecumenical Council did not occupy itself with the duration of the torments of hell. The Emperor Justinian (who for a while resembled Jonah, who was righteously angry because the wicked escaped punishment) presented his personal teaching to the Patriarch Menas in 543. The Patriarch used it to elaborate some arguments against neo-Origenism. Pope Vigilius confirmed them. By mistake, they have been attributed to the Fifth Ecumenical Council itself, but the teaching was only a personal opinion, and the contradictory teaching of St Gregory of Nyssa has never been condemned. The question remains open, the answer depending perhaps on human charity.[26] St Anthony's explanation is one of the most profound: apocatastasis, the salvation of all, is not a doctrine, but a *prayer* for the salvation of all except me, for whom alone hell exists.

In the end Satan is simultaneously robbed of the world, the object of his concupiscence, and confined within his own being, which is not unlimited: pure Satanism, the subject, is exhausted when it has no object. By contrast, the heart of the Church, in its maternal intercession, is boundless. St Isaac speaks of the heart that burns with love for the reptiles, even for the demons. Atonement is at work over the whole face of God's creation. The second death is the consequence of the forces of evil unwinding in space and time, but eventually these forces work themselves out and unwind completely and disappear for ever. Although, as a function of our freedom, the world has been allowed to deteriorate for a season, everything will be judged by God at the last Assize. The Hebrew name Jesus or

---

[26] St Gregory speaks of the redemption even of the devils (*In Christ. res. or; P.G.* 46, 609 C-610 A). St Gregory of Nazianzus mentions apocatastasis in *Oratio* 40, 36; *P.G.* 36, 412 AB. St Maximus the Confessor invites us to 'honour it in silence' because the subtlety of the concept would be lost on the crowd (*Qu. ad T.* 43; *P.G.* 90, 412 A); it is not wise to speak to all and sundry about the mysterious depth of God's mercy (*Cent. gnost.*, 2, 99; *P.G.* 90, 1172 D).

Saviour also means Liberator, and, in the splendid words of Clement of Alexandria, 'as the will of God is a work, and this is called the world; so his counsel is salvation, and this is called the Church.'[27]

3. MYSTERIUM CRUCIS

The world is saved only in Christ, 'the only name the heart desires', 'There is salvation in no one else, for there is no other name under heaven given among mortals by which we must be saved' (Acts 4.12). And so, 'Whoever has understood the mystery of the Cross and the tomb has grasped the essential content (logos) of all the things [we have mentioned]; and whoever, in addition, has been initiated into the mysterious meaning and power of the Resurrection knows the primordial purpose for which God created the universe.'[28]

But 'the death of Christ on the cross is the judgement of judgement.'[29] One must lose oneself to find oneself, and there is no final salvation except in common adoration. 'O you who are alone among the alone and are all in all! ... The Indivisible divides himself so that all may be saved, and so that even the infernal regions should not be deprived of the coming of God ... We pray to you ... stretch your great hands over your holy Church and over the holy people who are yours for ever.'[30] 'Stretching his two holy hands on the wood, Christ has extended two wings, the right and the left, calling all believers to him, and covering them as the mother protects her young.'[31] This is the wish of the divine philanthropy. 'God exercises patience' and grants a strange delay, for it falls to humankind 'to hasten the Day of the Lord' and to enter now into the heart of the Parousia, like the angels of salvation of whom we sing in the *Cherubicon*. So much depends on 'the intensity of our charity,' on our own 'births' by faith which prepare the world for the coming of the Lord. A secret germination takes place, followed by 'the spring of the Spirit,'[32] the springing up of the saints. Paschal joy is poured out in 'new harmonies',[33] and in the face of the pessimism of the weary world there soars, as it always will, Origen's sublime declaration: 'The Church is filled with the Trinity...'[34] 'Brethren, I know a man who wept about this person, groaned

27 *The Instructor*, 1, 6.
28 St Maximus, *Gnostic Centuries*, 1, 66; *P.G.* 90, 1108 AB.
29 St Maximus, *Quaestiones ad Thalassium*; *P.G.* 90, 408 D.
30 St John Chrysostom, *6th Easter Sermon* (probably the work of St Hippolytus); *P.G.* 59, 743-46.
31 St Hippolytus, *On the Antichrist*, c. 61.
32 St Gregory of Nazianzus, *Discourse. P.G.* 36, 620 D.
33 St Clement of Alexandria, *Protreptic*, c. 1.
34 *Selecta in Psalmos*, 23, 1; *P.G.* 12, 1265.

because of that person, to the point that he even assumed their character and ascribed to himself the faults they had committed... I know a man who so ardently desired the salvation of his brethren that he often, with heartfelt tears, and inflamed with a zeal worthy of Moses, asked God that either his brethren should be saved with him, or he should be condemned together with them. For he was bound to them in the Holy Spirit with such love that he did not even wish to enter the Kingdom of heaven if by so doing he would be separated from them.'[35] This is the miracle of the hope that works the salvation of others. *Our* faith in Christ flows into *his* faith in his Father; in the πρὸς τὸν Θεόν of the prologue of St John we see the Word *towards God*, facing God, gazing into his face and saying, '*Behold, here am I and the children whom God has given me.*'[36] Thereafter everything is new, for our faith is now *his* faith, 'So I tell you, whatever you ask for in prayer, *believe that you have received it*, and it will be yours'[37] (Mark 11.24).

Such faith transcends history; the Son and the Holy Spirit, the hands of God, carry the destiny of all to the very brink of the depths of the Father, the silence of which resounds with his burning proximity. St Peter says, 'The Lord is not slow about his promise, as some think of slowness, but is patient with you, not wanting any to perish ... Since all these things are to be dissolved in this way, what sort of people ought you to be in leading lives of holiness and godliness waiting for and hastening the coming of the day of God...?' (2 Pet. 3.9-11) That Day is by no means a mere goal or conclusion; that day is Fullness.

[35] St Simeon the New Theologian, *Discourse 22*; *P.G.* 120, 423-425.
[36] St Cyril of Jerusalem, 1, *Cat.* n. 6.
[37] Cf. Mgr Cassien, 'The Mystery of the Faith', in *Le Messager ecclésial*, No 66 (in Russian).

3

Orthodoxy and Heterodoxy

Before the great division between the Christians of East and West, there were many churches but they were all local manifestations of the One, Holy, Catholic and Apostolic Church of God. After becoming detached from the Eastern Orthodox Church, the Church of Rome separated into Catholic and Reformed.

In the early stages of the conflict, theological and non-theological factors were entangled; during the subsequent long period of mutual isolation positions hardened on various points of dispute; the reason that the separation persists today is *now* above all *doctrinal*.

The Assembly of Amsterdam in 1948[1] had to take account of the fact that at the heart of the ecumenical movement there were two coexisting traditions, 'Catholic' and 'Protestant'. There is a whole body of Protestants for whom the dividedness of Christianity is an ethical problem: we must exert ourselves in charity to make up for our sinful disobedience and lack of brotherly love. The Word judges the disorder and invites the churches to open themselves to one another, so that they will then naturally wish to gather round the same table. But a Protestant Lord's Supper 'open' to all can never be the answer to the problem of ecumenism because it is acceptable only to various kinds of Protestant. This is emphatically not a matter simply of legal prohibitions, or any lack of desire for unity. The fact is that for a 'Catholic' the Protestant Lord's Supper does not contain certain elements that are essential for a 'Catholic' Eucharist, and one of these elements is the Apostolic succession and the episcopate – which guarantees the Apostolic nature of the Eucharist. To participate in a sacrament of the Church, those concerned must be already fully in communion in the whole faith. Even in the earliest years of Christianity, St Ignatius of Antioch insisted that communion with God is impossible unless there is already communion in the rule of faith; communion in the bishop's teaching is intrinsically necessary; this communion in the faith is the only basis for unity and consequent access to the Eucharist.[2]

For 'Catholics' the ethical evil is only an expression of another evil that lies deeper down. And it is by tackling this that we shall come to the threshold of the Church and for the first time face up to the *doctrinal* problem in the context of the whole Apostolic tradition, for being merely united is beside the point; we are called to be *one*.

---

[1] The first Assembly of the World Council of Churches.
[2] Ephesians 3, 4.

It is not quite true to say that unity already exists and that all we have to do is reveal it. We know of course that unity is given to us in Christ, but only as a task that is yet to be accomplished; for the time being our unity is only virtual while we wait for the Christification of Christianity. It is impossible to reveal what does not really exist. The unity we have now is woefully insufficient, being based on the lowest common denominator of the plain text of the Bible, the Creed, Baptism, and expectation of the Kingdom. Agreement based on these minimum requirements can only be political in nature; the universal, Catholic faith necessarily demands *the confession of the fullness of faith in one spirit*. The sacramental and hierarchical structure of the Church, the authority of the councils and acceptance of their defined doctrines are the *sine qua non* of unity.

The Church, of its very nature, cannot be divided; yet we see that Christianity is severely fragmented. We acknowledge the same God, but we do it in very different ways, and the difference goes right down to our experience of the faith, and our experience of God in the Church. 'You will know the truth, and the truth will make you free' is tantamount to, 'Know the truth, and it will teach you true charity,' which is exactly what the priest calls for before the confession of the Creed: 'Let us love one another so that with one accord we may confess...' True charity eschews compromise and concentrates entirely on the fullness of faith.

1. THE HISTORICAL DIMENSION

The visible body of our Church is constrained and defined by canonical obedience. In the historical life of the Church governed by the economy of the Incarnation, this obedience has been supplanted by a kind of zealotry; so long as there is no hostility in it, this is no more than a thoroughgoing loyalty to our own tradition, our ancestral faith: 'It is zeal for your house that has consumed me' (Ps. 69.9). Here we see how important it is for salvation that we distinguish sharply between orthodoxy and heterodoxy. This is the opposite of the famous 'branch theory', according to which each ecclesiastical tradition possesses only part of the truth, so that the true Church will come into being only when they all join together; such a belief encourages the 'churches' to continue as they are, confirming them in their fragmented state, and the final result is Christianity without the Church.

Each church, in its more pronounced form, displays, according to its own native spirit, a particular version of the unique revelation. So, for example, Roman Christianity is characterized by filial love and obedience expressed towards the fatherly authority hypostatized in the first Person of the Trinity: the Church is there to teach and to obey. For the Reformed Churches the vital thing is sacramental reverence for the Word: it is the Church's duty to listen and reform itself. The Orthodox treasure the liberty of the children of God that flowers in liturgical communion, while the Church hymns the love of God for the human race. But, for centuries before any separation took place, the Councils were taken up, in the eastern Church, with the discussion and doctrinal definition of the mysteries of God, and in the western Church, with the relation between grace and liberty; the temperament of the one was contemplative and mystical, that of the other social and active. In the West St Augustine established the principles of anthropology, St Anselm of soteriology, and St Thomas of gnoseology, but in the East the same sciences were founded on very different principles by St Athanasius, the Cappadocians and Clement of Alexandria. 'In my Father's house there are many dwelling-places' (John 14.2). When the House of God, the Church, was still one, these differences merely represented different aspects of the same fullness. There is no sin whatever in diversity in itself; the sin lies in the perverse fact that instead of one Church there are 'many', that at a certain moment the love of unity, the very desire to be one, ran dry. For this human failing the eastern and western churches are alike to blame, and for this shared culpability there must be the most profound repentance. The truth will ultimately be clear for all to see, but there must be a readiness on all sides to acknowledge and welcome it.

The conviction, at the heart of each church, that it holds all the fullness of the revelation accessible to human beings, is the paradox at the bottom of true ecumenism. It leaves no room for any trace of the 'branch theory'. Indeed, only when we become aware, as Catholic Christians, of the absolute nature of our church, knowing it to be the only true Church of God, can we feel the full force of scandal of disunity and really begin to understand what will be entailed in overcoming it. Where doctrinal relativism and minimalism are accepted as normal, the proliferation of sects follows as a matter of course, and the lack of organic unity never presents itself as a problem at all. For this outlook the only possible answer is a federation of churches, free to organize themselves and formulate their beliefs as they wish, while true unity, the *Una Sancta*, is shifted on to the 'invisible' Church. There is a radical difference: either the palms are alive with the life of the one trunk from which they have sprung, or the branches are cut off and put in a pile at the foot of the tree – these are two alternative ontological realities (a similar image is used by St Augustine).[3] Only somebody who is aware of the fullness of his church can truly feel the pain of separation, for that pain is not simply a longing to supply something that is lacking, but is the pain inflicted by the truth itself, driving us to seek true unity without compromise. The truth does not belong to us personally; it is not something that we construct; truth is self-subsisting and self-perpetuating, it exists before unity and will govern its development. That is why every ecumenical encounter requires the greatest maturity of spirit, a self-conscious loyalty to one's own spiritual culture, and absolute faithfulness to one's church. But ecumenical experience continually brings us up

---

[3] *Serm.* 46, c. 8, n. 18; *P.L.* 38, 280-281.

against the mystery of the Church which is so much greater than any differences arising merely from history or philosophical outlook. From a purely historical point of view the Roman attitude is quite logical; it demands the unconditional surrender of independent thought and unreserved submission to the historical institution. But such straightforward conversion and submission to institutional authority results only from historical missionary activity on behalf of that particular church, whereas proselytism obviously has nothing to do with ecumenism. On the other hand, ecumenism is often confused with negotiations between groups from the same religious tradition, for example, between Lutherans and other reformed churches. By the 'criterion of heresy' these meetings must be disregarded; the necessary condition for a full ecumenical meeting is that intercommunion between the participants is *doctrinally* impossible; there must be Catholics, Orthodox and Protestants taking part.

We are not seeking to complement our faith because we are poor; it is the very abundance of our church, the outpouring of Orthodoxy, that drives us, the Orthodox, irresistibly to 'go out of the city' and seek fellowship with the heterodox. This urge is quite free of any desire to proselytize or to increase our church with converts. We rejoice fully in our freedom, which enables us to bear witness to our Apostolic faith, and in the charity of that faith we hold the freedom of others in deep respect.

Nevertheless, on the historical plane, alongside the fullness of the Apostolic Tradition, we experience the incompleteness of truth that characterizes the Church as a human institution. The growth of ecumenical fellowship is a powerful help in recovering humility and becoming better Orthodox.

2. THE ESCHATOLOGICAL PLANE

The Orthodox Church, without denying any part of its faith or the ancient canons[4] which forbid all spiritual association, even prayer, with non-Orthodox, does in fact associate with them, prays with them, joins in theological discussion, and cooperates in social activity. This attitude, so different from that of the Roman Catholic Church throughout history, is possible only when we remember that we stand at the point of intersection between history and the transcendent. Only by recognizing these two dimensions, the historical and the eschatological, shall we understand what the ecumenical movement can hope to achieve, while at the same time avoiding both disobedience to the canons and simplistic proselytism.

Knowing that we possess the fullness of the faith, we rightly insist that 'outside the Church there is no salvation' and oppose sentimental attempts to water

---

[4] *Apostolic Canons*, 10, 11 and 45; can. 33 of the Council of Laodicaea.

the faith down, but this knowledge should never make us complacent. The steady resolve to be 'Catholic' will burst out of any constraints, especially the frightening spiritual tendency known to the Fathers as 'autorhythm' or self-sufficiency. Anxiety about the fate of the world will never be assuaged in purely historical terms, but must be focused on the approaching 'days of vengeance as a fulfilment of all that is written' (Luke 21.22). The eschatological epiclesis, the maranatha is a call for the gifts pertaining to the last times – Veni Creator Spiritus: the Lord says that he will 'be with you for ever;' nevertheless, 'I still have many things to say to you, but you cannot bear them now' (John 16.12). Since then, certain things have fallen precisely into place, revealing ancient truths with a new and radiant clarity.

Part of being Orthodox is knowing for certain that you belong to the *Una Sancta*; anybody can join this grace-filled body at any time, but the difficulty for ecumenism is that all three Christian traditions continue to exist separately just because each believes itself to possess the whole truth. Now, the whole truth will be fully revealed only on the Great Day of YHWH: 'Let us then go to him outside the camp and bear the abuse he endured. For here we have no lasting city, but we are looking for the city that is to come' (Heb. 13.13-14). The Apostolic call to go outside the 'camp' is an invitation to go outside history, and being freed from purely historical categories, to see everything in the light of eternity and grasp the ultimate meaning of the priestly prayer of Christ. The correct expectation of the *eschaton* takes full account of the historical reality of the Church, for it is only when the Church has accomplished its fulfilment through history that we then look for 'the resurrection of the dead and the life of the world to come,' but it is precisely the finality of that stage that shows that our hope lies not in the extension of time, but in escaping from time altogether.

There is perhaps a sense in which ecumenism is guilty of impatience, by *pre-judging* what its end ought to be and making it part of history: that all will be united in a single historical Church. 'There have to be heresies among you, for only so will it become clear who among you are genuine'... Fragmentation was quick, but reunion takes a long time and is blocked by the *non possumus* of conscientiously held belief. The priestly prayer of Christ is explicit on one fundamental point: 'That they may be one... that the world may believe' (John 17.21). Ultimate unity in the very image of the Father and the Son is subordinate to the Apostolic purpose – the salvation of the world. God, according to his good pleasure, can bring about the miracle of unity, but this is a bonus, pure grace. The ultimate witness, without which the Church will lose its vocation to be the salt and the light of the world, is the witness that arouses in the world the thirst for salvation and for the Lord, the voice that cries in the wilderness, 'Prepare the way of the Lord, make his paths straight!' (Matt. 3.3)

The Lord's Prayer speaks of the final bringing of the human will into agreement with the Father's will. So the theological basis of ecumenism is the Father's love for humankind, and the prayer itself is the ecumenical epiclesis. But the Lord's Prayer is essentially eschatological.[5]

3. THE IMPORTANCE OF ECUMENISM TODAY

Ecumenism among theologians is already a practical reality; without this reciprocal enrichment, theological reflection might have become stuck in intolerable provincialism. On the other hand, ecumenism, in its deep anxiety about the fate of the world, is in effect an urgent question addressed to every church, holding up a mirror and asking it to look conscientiously at its role in history. The common witness to God's existence and the common attentiveness to his Word can create exceptional conditions in which God can speak not only to his Church, but to Christianity as a whole, making it the setting for his final message. As well as the *mystery of union*, we may even speak of a *mystery of disunion* which must be worked through first.

4. AN URGENT TASK

We are all united around the same closed Bible. As soon as we open it, we follow our separate traditions and arrive at different interpretations. Ecumenism, which is originally derived from οἰκουμένη (the populated territory of the Christian Empire), organizes meetings across geographical space, gathering together those who have been scattered far apart. The difficulty we face today is that of meeting across time. Time means tradition, and its careful study is perhaps the most direct way to approach the essential mystery of the Church. The task of overriding importance for ecumenism is to bring a set of real questions to the attention of *every* church, and compel it to answer. To start a true ecumenical dialogue we can formulate some of these as follows:

I. The crucial problem of all theology is the connection between the original revelation and its realization *hic et nunc*. How to preserve the specificity both of Scripture and of the preaching that communicates it while never simply repeating the sacred text? What is the importance and above all the justification of preaching, theology and doctrine, compared with Scripture? The pure historicism of

---

[5] The confession of the depth of the Father; the 'sanctification of the Name' (for the Jews this was an inner act of martyrdom); the coming of the Kingdom-Holy Spirit; the final harmony of the wills which ends history; the ultimate supersubstantial bread, the last meal, without which the last time would be intolerable; the testing in the time of the Antichrist; the Trinitarian doxology of the Kingdom.

liberal theology on the one hand and the realistic monism of 'dialectical' theology on the other appear to be dead ends, perhaps because they lack the true dialectic of theandrism, the dialectic contained in the doctrine of Chalcedon, between what is 'given' and what is 'done'. As Luther asks, 'So Christ has two natures. How does that affect me?'[6] 'For Luther, the mystery of the Incarnation is not so much that God has taken human nature, but that he has taken it through human sin.'[7] Karl Barth considers that Luther's Christology, taken to its conclusion, tends towards Monophysitism, while that of Calvin tends rather towards Nestorianism.[8] Reformed Christianity does not seem to attach sufficient importance to Trinitarian balance, and this is where the theology of the Holy Spirit is particularly illuminating. The Holy Spirit appears in the unique epiphany of the Word and announces it, *actualizes* it unceasingly. This unity of source unites the act and the actualization, the *traditum* and the *actus tradendi*, what was originally given and its actual communication from day to day. God has spoken in Christ, and in the Spirit has continued to interpret his own Word, to make it present in every age through the Tradition. The Church's preaching has made of history a continuous tradition, illuminated at every moment by the Holy Spirit. The sacraments take the place of the gospel 'miracles' and continue the *historical visibility* of Christ, which lives on in the liturgical memorial, and is announced by the word. These together perpetuate his real presence through the time of the Church, which is that of the Tradition. The inner identity of all these elements is the very essence and fact of the catholicity of the Church. The Council of Ephesus (431) says on the subject of the Council of Nicaea that 'the Fathers were assembled there with the Holy Spirit.'[9] St Cyril of Alexandria declares that Christ presides invisibly and enlightens the councils.[10]

II. Karl Barth draws attention to a great ambiguity in the use of the term 'word' which means variously: the second person of the Trinity, the transcendent act of God addressed to humanity, Scripture, or preaching and interpretation.

The inner witness of the Holy Spirit testifies to the inspired nature of the Bible, and should never be confused with *interpretation*. The latter requires the epiclesis and the action of the divine Spirit-Interpreter at the heart of the constituted Body, the Church. The Spirit of Truth thus inaugurates its own word, or to be more precise, the 'Spirit of the Word'. It neither adds anything new to the Word of the Saviour, nor duplicates it, but *interprets* it; through the letter it brings us the spirit. That is why the Apostolic Council of Jerusalem used the formula 'it seemed good

---

6 *Works*, Ed. Erlangen, 35, 207.
7 Maurer, *Von der Freiheit eines Christenmenschen*, Göttingen 1949, p. 39.
8 *Kirchl. Dogm.*, 1, 2, p. 27.
9 Denzinger, 125.
10 *Ep. 55 de Symb.*, P.G. 77, 293.

to the Holy Spirit and to us'. Guided by the Spirit, the Apostles inaugurated the 'Apostolic Tradition' and thus brought into being the *principle of transmission*. So what is the *bond* between the Apostolic Tradition and the Tradition of the Church, and where exactly does the Reformers' own tradition fit in? What universal criterion is there that every church can use to measure its conformity to the Apostolic Tradition, and who is to do the measuring? At the Council of Jerusalem we see the Apostolic college exercising its power to take decisions – for example accrediting St Paul as an 'Apostle by theft' – and their decisions are decisions of the Church. How is the college constituted? The Reformed Churches submit their 'confessions of faith' to the criticism of Scripture, and the people in charge of this process are the theologians. These identify, for example, the essence of the Scriptures with justification by faith (a concept unknown in such terms to Patristic Tradition, for which the essential point is the recapitulation of all in Christ) and using that criterion, they 'reform' the Apostolic and Patristic inheritance – but by whose authority? Justification, sanctification, *sola fide* and *sola scriptura, semper justus et peccator*, sin and grace, all these doctrinal notions are the fruit of human work on the sacred text; the objective truth of the text assumes an objective criterion decided by the Church. The rule of faith, the Apostles' Creed, is normative for all, but it does not go back to the Apostles. What value can Acts of the Spirit have for the post-Apostolic Church?

III. 'The Church is judged by the Word.' This can be taken in two ways: do the theologians judge the bishops, or does the Holy Spirit judge the Church by the Church, i.e., by means of the Spirit of the Word. By elevating the Bible *above* the Church, we are in danger of no longer reading it *in* the Church, in the context of liturgical prayer and worship, where the '*Spirit* intercedes with sighs too deep for words' (Rom. 8.26).

IV. *Sola fide – sola Scriptura*, the two signify *grace*, the gift of God which is offered to humanity. Human beings put all their confidence in the Word, receive it, incorporate it into their being, and are themselves incorporated into the Word. But can such absolute abundance be received *passively*? To the action of God there is a corresponding human reaction. To reduce the whole of the Mystery to the sole act of God, who speaks, and in humankind hears and answers himself, runs the risk of suppressing the human, suppressing the dialogue; whereas God calls Man 'thou'.

V. Can the presence of God be reduced to the form of the Word alone? Are the sacraments *added* to the Word to confirm it more fully (*Confession de La Rochelle*, art. 34)? Now, the liturgy, in its most ancient Apostolic form, strongly emphasizes the consummation of the Word in the Eucharist. At Emmaus the Lord interprets the Scriptures to the disciples, but it is at the moment of the breaking of the bread that their eyes are opened. The Eucharist interprets Christ as putting himself at the heart of the New Testament message: Christ does not only preach, he is sacrificed, and the great silence of the Sabbath introduces the age of the Resurrection. Does not the *Communio Sanctorum* come *essentially* from the *Communio sacramentorum*? Do not the sacraments actualize the work of Christ, just as the Tradition actualizes the revelation, its appropriation by the historical Body of the Church?

VI. 'All comes from God', but since the Incarnation there has been that which comes from God and that which comes from the Humanity of Christ and which is 'ours' (consubstantial). The question of the two natures in Christ may have been of no interest to Luther, but there has been a great deal of progress in theology since his day and the principle of 'theandrism', spelt out at the Council of Chalcedon, has returned in our own time to claim our full attention.

VII. It is not a waste of time, in ecumenical discussion, to draw attention to subtle differences of meaning in the same terms according to how they are used in East and West. Thus, 'grace' in Latin conveys the notion of pardon and something free of charge, and in Greek (especially New Testament Greek) means a gift and its reception. The 'Truth', of ethico-juridical origin, is for us something that we know for certain, but for the Greeks it is an immutable principle in itself. 'Sacrament', in the West, refers to the sacred and sacerdotal, whereas the equivalent, 'mystery', in the East, is something from above and from the Holy Spirit. The word *Sobornost*, in Russian ecclesiology, comes from conciliar, or council, but indicates, more profoundly than any idea of 'power', the principle of communion that brings about 'oneness' in Christ. The same terms may be given *juridical* or *ontological* emphasis, which is why terms such as imputative, declarative, forensic on the one hand, and satisfaction and merit on the other, are utterly foreign to the Orthodox, for whom, by contrast, more biblical terms, such as participation and likeness, are central.

VIII. Is it not symptomatic of Orthodoxy that the height of its spirituality should be *hesychia*, silence of the spirit, which brings us into the burning proximity of God, and that the 'Jesus prayer' should teach a single word, the Name, and in that, the divine Presence? After words and speeches, apophasis invites us to honour the Word without words and to progress to another way of knowing, enlightenment through communion.

5. THE CHARISMATIC DIMENSION OF THE CHURCH

According to the teaching of St Cyprian, the sacraments are valid and effective only *in* the Church: outside the Church, no sacrament. This has never been accepted as official doctrine by the Church, and in practice the Baptism at least of non-Orthodox is accepted; in the case of schism, Unction and Holy Order are still recognized. So the sacraments exist in a charismatic halfway house outside the Church; the action of the Holy Spirit is not restricted within canonical limits. When we say that the sacraments are valid or effective only *in* the Church, then the meaning of *in* becomes very mysterious, because it transcends the visible frontier defined by the canons. No act that is not an act of the Church can be treated as a sacrament on grounds of pastoral economy; the Church gives or withholds recognition to something according to whether it truly exists, but it cannot change the nature of the act. Similarly, it is clearly impossible for the rite of reception of a non-Orthodox into the Church to bestow retrospective validity upon acts done in the past.

St Augustine judges that, in the case of schism, the sacraments are valid because there is still unity of the Spirit, but ineffective because there has been a breach of peace (the Church being 'the unity of the Spirit in the bond of peace' Eph. 4.3) which implies the notion of *ex opere operato*. Fortunately no Church has ever pressed this argument to its logical conclusion, which would be the reciprocal negation of all sanctifying grace, the negation of Christianity.

Non-Orthodox are, by definition and by choice, not in the Orthodox Church, but the Church is greater than human divisions; wherever there is faith and the desire for salvation the Church is present and at work. We know where the Church is, but we should not presume to say where the Church is not.

6. THE ORTHODOX PRESENCE

In the absence of the Roman Church, Orthodoxy alone can preserve true ecumenism, keep it from sliding towards pan-Protestantism. The central declaration of Toronto – 'Membership in the World Council of Churches does not imply that a church treats its own conception of the Church as merely relative' – puts Orthodoxy at its ease. While being impeccable as to its divinity, and infallible in the purity of its faith and of its ecclesiology, it considers every heterodoxy as a phenomenon of its own life, occurring within its own historical existence. Every baptized Christian who professes the Trinitarian faith is a member, more or less loosely attached, of Orthodoxy, more or less removed from its eucharistic heart. In accordance with its charity any zealous proselytism of individuals is ruled out; it will not deny part of its own faith, but by tradition rejects certain methods of witness: totalitarian conformity, hasty unity, unthinking conservatism.[11]

The ecumenical effort directed towards Tradition would be more effective if the Reformed Churches would only attend more closely to the fundamental value

---

[11] St Irenaeus gives a strong warning against the doctrinaire extremism that, from false prudence, excludes the gift of prophecy from the Church (*Adv. haeres.*, III, 11, 9).

of the priesthood established by the divine act as an active witness chiefly in the celebration of the Eucharist and the rule of faith; and if the Roman Catholic Church attended to the supreme importance of the life of the Church in the period before the separation, when the Councils were the acknowledged authority and the Body was in full communion. If these conditions were restored the infallibility of the Pope could become a local tradition. There is still too much ignorance about the Fathers. It is essential that they should be rediscovered and their power be allowed to enrich the Church in the creative continuation of the Tradition. But even before that, we must jointly return to the sources – the Scriptures and the Patristic tradition of the Councils, towards a reinvigorated spirituality re-centred and reorientated on the essential Paschal and Parousial mystery, where we shall all meet in the common life which is our most precious possession; such a return to sources is the only possible way to achieve the great goal of Christian unity.

We have laid great stress on the advantages enjoyed by Orthodoxy. Controversy between Protestant and Catholic theologians is often inconclusive because they are using the same categories of thought. Orthodoxy offers a different, Patristic ground for debate, where the same problems can be discussed in different terms and solutions found that would otherwise be unachievable. Such would be the problems of faith and works, of liberty and grace, of authority and prophecy, of celibacy and marriage. Finally, Orthodoxy requires no obedience to a historical institution, but invites all to embrace the truth (for example the Nicene Creed and the definitions of the seven Councils). It is not a matter of theologians presenting their demands, but of the truth receiving and leading others into communion with Orthodoxy. And in all this Orthodoxy never endangers its own historical culture or the traditions of the Fathers.

7. HOLINESS

According to the Scriptures, in the last days, the Holy Spirit will be manifestly at work in a very particular way, after an intense preparation of prayer and invocation, 'the ecumenical epiclesis' which is the appeal to the Father to send his Spirit on scattered Christianity. More than ever we come face to face with his mystery: 'Thy Name so greatly desired and constantly proclaimed, no one is able to say what it is.' Orthodox, Catholics, Protestants, it is not for us to relativize the doctrinal truths. Only the Spirit can transcend the barriers, not relativizing anything, but completing and integrating all the aspects of the Christian faith in their infinitely subtle fullness.

On the day of the Epiphany, the descent of the Dove traces the movement that carries the Father towards his Son. The Dove continues its flight, in the movement that carries us towards the Word; for, as the Epistle to the Hebrews (12.14) says, 'Pursue peace with everyone, and the holiness without which no one will see the Lord.' 'The creature possesses no gift which does not come from the Spirit; he is the sanctificator uniting us to God,' says St Basil, and St Gregory of Nyssa and Evagrius constantly remind us, 'The theologian is the person who knows how to pray.' Perhaps ecumenism suffers from too much theological discussion and not enough liturgy; talk inevitably takes precedence over prayer. But Scripture repeats urgently, 'The end of all things is at hand', 'I come quickly', 'It is the last time.' More than ever before, the immediate spiritual necessity is holiness; it is in the Saints that the Church speaks and preaches the best and finds adequate expression. 'You have been anointed by the Holy One, and all of you have knowledge' (1 John 2.20). Unction, the χρίσμα of the Kingdom marks out the saints of the last times. The acquisition of the Holy Spirit and his gifts, the penetration of the whole of his being through the charisms 'so that Christ will be formed in us', becomes more than ever the essential feature of the Christian life. 'What sort of people ought you to be in leading lives of holiness and godliness, waiting for and hastening the coming of the day of God?' (2 Pet. 3.11-12) Here and now, in the realm of history, the life of the ecumenical congregation can be intensified till it becomes the practice of radiant charity, 'the unity of the Spirit in the bond of peace,' a powerful prophecy of the Kingdom. And now the standard will be set by monasticism, in its eschatological maximalism, in its impatience for the Parousia; that state of the spirit – the seal of the unction being given to all – can spring up in every Christian tradition, uniting all more deeply in the liturgy of expectation and active preparation, in the ardent invocation of the final epiclesis. In the magnificent words of St Gregory of Nyssa, who was called by the second Council 'Father of the Fathers',[12] '*The Divine power can find hope where there is no longer any hope, and a way through the impenetrable.*'[13] Any limit contains in its essence what is beyond it, what transcends it.[14] 'There is only one way of knowing... to reach out untiringly beyond the known.'[15]

We must not forget the solemn warning of St Maximus the Confessor, that we deserve punishment 'not only for the evil we have done, but just as much for the good we have not done, and for not loving our neighbour.'[16]

A picture will perhaps explain this better than words. Inside an Orthodox church is the iconostasis, the wall that separates the sanctuary from the central nave, the Kingdom from the world. At first, this was a simple barrier to keep the people from the altar and preserve order during services. As time went on, under the guidance of liturgical inspiration, this dividing line was embellished with icons arranged in order and covering the surface of the iconostasis. The whole

---

12 Mansi, 13, 293.
13 *De hom. op.*; *P.G.* 44, 128 B.
14 *Vita Moys.*, *P.G.* 44, 401 B.
15 *In Cant.*, hom. 12; *P.G.* 44, 1024 BC.
16 *Lib. asc.*; *P.G.* 90, 932 C.

design is centred on the Christ of the *Deesis*, seated in majesty, while the saints stand around, reflecting the light that radiates from him. At a glance it conveys the marvellous metamorphosis: what was once a dividing wall has become a bridge, *totus Christus* made up of his saints, the passing – Pasch – of all and every one of us towards the Kingdom.

We are all thus invited to penetrate more deeply into the dazzling presence of Christ, his birth-Parousia by the breath of the Spirit; this miraculous spirit-filled Nativity – which is already the Kingdom – can turn our separation into a bond, into unity. Orthodox, Catholics, Protestants travelling the path of sanctity to the end, which is Christ, can become living icons united in the iconostasis of the Temple of God, its Royal Doors opening into the abyss of the Father.

INDEX

U

universe 26, 47, 74, 77, 103, 111, 132,
144, 154, 159, 165, 209, 217,
220, 236, 241, 245, 266, 339
upper room 63, 168, 213-4, 220, 225,
241, 260
utopia 19, 43, 310, 314, 317, 321

V

Vatican Council 10, 32, 37, 140
Velichkovsky, Paissy 43-4, 55
Vespers 160, 245, 247, 249
vine 127, 209, 230, 243
virgin 51, 67, 73-4, 82-3, 107, 110, 125,
147, 150, 153-62, 201, 230,
249, 259, 273, 288, 292
virginity 67, 107, 156-61, 197, 299, 300,
303, 313
virtue 20, 27, 60, 65, 78, 91, 108-10,
120, 145, 149, 231, 240, 269,
279, 285-90, 318
vision 13, 24-7, 31, 37-8, 56-62, 66, 93,
99-103, 108, 117-21, 124, 132,
181, 208, 216-8, 222, 227-8,
232-45, 250, 260-1, 328
vocation 11, 28, 31, 51, 80, 89, 104, 151,
239, 245, 299, 303, 310-1, 345
vows 29, 270, 288
Vycheslavtsev, B. 74-5

W

water 23, 83, 107, 114-6, 127, 153, 161,
209-15, 218-9, 229-30, 235,
250-1, 255, 260, 270, 279-82,
286, 293, 299-301, 306, 314,
332, 344
Wensinck, A. J. 67, 110, 127, 214, 217,
337

West 10, 13, 18-9, 26-9, 33, 36-40, 51,
55, 61, 96, 109, 124, 144-6,
168, 179, 183, 189-91, 225,
231, 251, 255, 269, 282, 324,
333, 341-3, 349
western churches 10, 47, 227, 343
wheat 162, 209, 238, 245, 320, 326, 335
will, human 18, 68, 81, 189, 274, 345
will, the 18, 33, 68, 79-84, 93, 99-101,
108-14, 124, 149, 152, 157-9,
168, 173, 189, 194-6, 270, 274,
277, 294, 319, 323, 330, 339, 345
wine 83, 102, 107, 127, 153, 156-8, 161,
210, 230, 245, 251-60, 293,
300-1
wisdom 22, 25-6, 35, 45-7, 50, 56, 68-
70, 77, 81-2, 87, 93-4, 110-1,
117, 126, 133, 156, 161, 168,
173, 180-3, 199, 249, 262-4,
268, 278, 301, 309, 312, 327-
30, 337
works 33, 42, 55-7, 68, 100, 110, 116-7,
180, 185, 192, 200, 235, 242,
273, 278, 295, 325, 329, 335,
347, 351
World Council of Churches 341, 350
worship 18, 33, 38, 51, 89, 101-5, 151,
164, 168, 171, 180, 192, 202-4,
216, 221-3, 229, 245, 257-65,
277, 293, 311-2, 320, 327, 348

Y

YHWH 100, 257, 324, 345

Z

Zwingli 251